THE PLEASURES OF
PHILOSOPHY

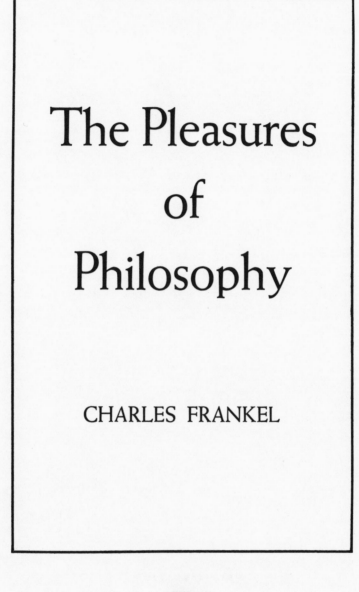

The Pleasures
of
Philosophy

CHARLES FRANKEL

W · W · NORTON &  COMPANY · INC ·
NEW YORK

FIRST EDITION

Copyright © 1972 by W. W. Norton & Company, Inc. All rights
reserved. Published simultaneously in Canada by George J. McLeod,
Limited, Toronto. Printed in the United States of America.

Library of Congress Catalog Card No. 76-158085

SBN 393 01089 9

1 2 3 4 5 6 7 8 9 0

For S.F.H. and H.O.H.

Contents

5. The Significance of Philosophy   245

Acknowledgments

"The Christian Epic" is reprinted by permission of Charles Scribner's Sons from *Reason in Religion* by George Santayana. Copyright 1905 Charles Scribner's Sons; renewal copyright 1933 George Santayana. Also reprinted by permission of Constable & Company Limited.

The selections from Plato's *Republic* and the *Symposium*, translated by W. H. D. Rouse, are reprinted by permission of The New American Library, Inc., from *Great Dialogues of Plato*, revised edition, translated by W. H. D. Rouse, edited by Eric H. Warmington and Philip G. Rouse. Copyright © 1956, 1961 John Clive Graves Rouse.

The selection from *The Confessions of St. Augustine*, translated by John K. Ryan, is reprinted by permission of Doubleday and Company, Inc. Copyright © 1960 by Doubleday and Company, Inc.

The selection from Dostoyevsky's *Letters from the Underworld* is from the book *Letters from the Underworld and Other Tales* by Fyodor Dostoyevsky. Translated by C. J. Hogarth. Everyman's Library Edition. Published by E. P. Dutton and Co., Inc., and reprinted with their permission.

The selection from Friedrich Nietzsche's *Twilight of the Idols* is reprinted by permission of The Viking Press, Inc., from *The Portable Nietzsche*, translated by Walter Kaufmann. Copyright 1954 by The Viking Press, Inc.

The selection from Bergson's *An Introduction to Metaphysics* is reprinted by permission of G. P. Putnam's Sons, from *An Introduction to Metaphysics* by Henri Bergson, translated by T. E. Hulme. Copyright 1912 by G. P. Putnam's Sons.

Bertrand Russell's "Obituary" is from the book *Unpopular Essays* by Bertrand Russell. Copyright 1950 by Bertrand Russell. It is reprinted by permission of the publisher, Simon and Schuster.

The selection from "Mysticism and Logic" is an abridgment from the essay of that name appearing in *Mysticism and Logic and Other Essays* by Bertrand Russell, published by George Allen and Unwin Ltd., and is reprinted here with the permission of the publisher.

The essay by Friedrich Waismann, "How I See Philosophy," first appeared in *Contemporary British Philosophy*, third series, edited by H. D. Lewis (1956). It is reprinted here in abridged form with the permission of the publisher, George Allen and Unwin Ltd.

The passage from Plato's *Seventh Epistle* appears in the translation by F. M. Cornford, and is quoted from the Introduction to Mr. Cornford's edition of Plato's *Republic*, published by Oxford University Press, 1945. It is used here with the permission of the publisher.

THE PLEASURES OF
PHILOSOPHY

Foreword

Philosophy has given me many pleasures, various and intense. In this book I have brought together some of the writings by philosophers that I have most enjoyed, in the hope of passing my pleasure on. This may seem a light-hearted approach to a serious subject, but it is, I think, the best way to understand the lure and durability of philosophy. In any case, it is the approach that those who have studied it most seriously and made the most significant contributions to it have usually taken. They have been surprised by the subject, have puzzled over it, damned it, complained that they would never understand it, and have happily kept coming back for more.

The questions that philosophy asks have fascinated men for millennia. The answers that philosophers have given to these questions have had an immense influence on our ideas about the world, on our social institutions and moral attitudes, and on our religious beliefs and unbeliefs. Yet philosophy begins again in each generation, because no thoughtful man can take these answers as they are given; he must go over them for himself. And there is no knowing what may lead a man to philosophy. In trying to determine where he stands in a time of political turmoil, or in attempting to adapt the familiar ideas with which he grew up to new scientific theory, or simply in asking whether, in going about his daily business, he is doing the world or himself any good, he may enter philosophy's territory inadvertently. If he does so, he had better be careful. For those who have gone into philosophy deeply have usually responded to it as to something overmastering. It has taken them over, perhaps taken them in, but they have gladly succumbed to it.

How does philosophy exercise this suasion? It has immediate rewards. The subject, simply on its surface, can please and dazzle. No writer has been a more sympathetic and yet more ironical portraitist of human beings and their ideals than Plato. The pages of David Hume's works are filled with lucid, compact arguments, at once elegant and unpretentious, that let the air out of clichés and give us the feeling of having won a victory, at least for a moment, over cant and hypocrisy. To go along with René Descartes as he puts on his mask of innocence and asks us to examine our beliefs without prejudice is to find a pleasure not unlike that of reading Voltaire's Candide: we know that we are in the grip of a shrewd and worldly man who has an axe to grind and that he is playing a trick on us, but we are arrested by the trick, held in midpassage by it, and released at the end both amused and bemused.

Philosophers are commonly celebrated for the loftiness of their themes, for their erudition, for their intellectual acuteness and vision. But a considerable number of them have been masters of prose as well as of logic, of the drama of argument as well as of its formal structure. Charles Peirce's no-nonsense approach to a problem, George Santayana's powers of metaphor and emotional comprehension, Bertrand Russell's cool assurance and sudden bursts of puckishness, are pleasing in themselves. They give the same excitement that seeing someone hit a tennis ball well does. They are difficult achievements made to look easy—instances of great energies under control, of effort disciplined to accomplish a purpose economically. Many philosophers who have made no apparent attempt, indeed, to present their ideas in an attractive form have nevertheless communicated much more than an abstract argument. The emotion that runs through Spinoza's philosophy, its consuming passion for dispassion, is all the more evident because he puts his case as though it were a demonstration in geometry.

A well-constructed philosophy has straightforward literary values. It has a beat, a rhythmic movement from the statement of a problem to its resolution, and from the complicating of the problem to its more complete resolution. There can be twists and turns in its argument like the twists and turns of an ingeniously told story. And there are recognition scenes, like the climactic episodes in novels and plays in which people come finally to realize what they have done or suffered, or what their fate really is. In a paragraph, or even in a sentence, a first-rate philosopher can turn an argument on its head, expose a truth that has eluded us, and suddenly provide insight or explanation where before there was only confusion.

In chaste textbook summaries a philosophy is a static thing, an announcement of a man's cold conclusions. Encountered at first hand, it is an exploration, an experience that moves and mounts and has a beginning, a middle, and an end. That is one reason why I have let philosophers speak for themselves in this book, and why, in my comments on what they say, I have tried to speak as they do, personally and directly, and without regard to the encrusted conventions, the jargon and the isms, that have come to surround so much philosophic discussion. A philosophy is a living thing, a personal testament, and it should be seen in that way before it is labeled and assigned its place on the library shelves.

But the immediately pleasurable surface aspects of philosophy are far from being its only pleasures. Students of poetry, the novel, and the plastic arts speak of "the shock of recognition" which these arts afford us. Philosophy gives the same shock, the same delight. It makes us freshly aware of what is in front of us, provokes us into seeing it differently, brings its larger background forward into our consciousness.

A philosopher catches us because he releases us from our ordinary tongue-tied and wooden-headed condition. When we read William James on the difference between a "tough-minded" and a "tender-minded" attitude toward life, the concepts may really be new, and yet we feel that he is putting into words our own thoughts. At any rate, he makes us believe he is doing so. And a philosopher may show us that what we think—and sometimes what we have regarded as so banal or commonplace as not to require any thinking—is in fact odd and singular. "What, then, is time?" asks St. Augustine. "If no one asks me, I know; if I want to explain it to someone who does ask me, I do not know." The experience of time, one of the most ordinary experiences in the world, turns out, as Augustine reflects on it, to have levels and levels of puzzle and ambiguity, and to require us, before we are through, to think about the stillness of eternity.

And a philosopher may also show us that the things we take to be odd and singular are not really so strange as they seem. When they are viewed as incidents in a recurrent pattern, we recognize that they are only to be expected. If a man sees himself as a natural being caught in a web of universal cause and effect, Spinoza suggests, if he sees himself *sub specie aeternitatis*, he will not be surprised that he is the fool that he is. And recognizing this, he will be less a fool.

There is a dialogue of Plato's, the *Meno*, in which Socrates, merely by asking questions, leads an untutored slave boy to discover for himself basic truths of geometry. Plato believed, and meant in this dialogue to show, that knowledge is a form of remembering: we have knowledge when we work our way back to ideas that have all along been in our minds, when we recognize truths that we have somehow forgotten. Whether or not a person accepts Plato's view of knowledge, it is the kind of view to which he will be tempted to come if he reflects on one of the repeated pleasures that reading or discussing philosophy gives. Again and again a gifted philosopher will seem only to be saying what we have been wanting to say and have not had the words for. He doesn't seem to be telling us what we didn't know; he seems only to be pulling our own thoughts together, to be putting us in tune with ourselves.

Perhaps this is why an individual who has been caught in philosophy's trap is so often likely to feel, even though philosophy lives on debate and a philosopher must love to argue, that there is a kind of impertinence or small-mindedness in attempting to pick fault with a philosopher. In the end, one may disagree with Bertrand Russell's criticisms of mysticism, or, at the other extreme, with Augustine's attacks on the powers of human reason, but in the moments when one is thinking along with either of these men one is apt to have a sensation like that of remembering a hitherto elusive name, or of finding one's mind unexpectedly flooded with the image and feel of a landscape, immediate and sensuous, that was once seen but has long since been forgotten. An impression that we often get from reading a philosopher is that what he is saying is inevitable, that we ourselves are speaking as much as he. Indeed, we may feel that what speaks is neither we nor he, but an impersonal truth.

"Socrates, I really could not contradict you," sighs young Agathon in Plato's *Symposium;* "let it be as you say." "Contradict the truth, you should say, beloved Agathon," replies Socrates, who has encircled Agathon in his dialectic; "you can't do that, but to contradict Socrates is easy enough." Socrates' modesty is winning; it is also disingenuous. One of the dangers of philosophy is that the philosopher not only can help you to recognize what you think but can lure you into the belief that there is no alternative to thinking that way. Needless to say, this is an agreeable experience. In philosophy one speaks of argument by deduction and of argument by induction, but much philosophy is argument by seduction.

But if philosophy can be an intoxicant, it can also give us the pleasure of a draft of cold water the morning after. For it does more than help us to recognize the thoughts that are in our minds. It helps us to re-cognize them, to see them, and the world beyond them, in a strange new light. A philosopher may seem to be merely a midwife, as Socrates described himself, not telling us what to think but bringing our own thoughts into the open. And yet he detaches us from these ideas. They come to seem not normal but doubtful, not ordinary but extraordinary.

For example, the eighteenth-century Anglo-Irish philosopher Bishop Berkeley left Samuel Johnson almost speechless with stupefaction because he denied what anyone would think was the most elementary of truths—namely, that matter exists. The Bishop needed merely to kick a stone, said Dr. Johnson, and he would discover how wrong he was. But that, of course, was Berkeley's precise argument, and he thought it proved the opposite point: when you kick a stone you feel a pain in your foot, but if you didn't have senses, and a consciousness in which sense impressions registered, you wouldn't feel that pain; so the stone, as far as you are concerned, is a mental event. And if the stone exists when no mortal creature senses it, as of course any man who isn't mad has to believe, then this must be because it is present in the eternal and unwavering mind of God. To be is to be perceived, and Mind is the substratum of the universe, not matter. To believe in matter abstracted from Mind is just like accepting the existence of ghosts: it is to believe in the existence of something separated from the conditions necessary for its existence.

What is it that makes such an argument arresting? No doubt there are those who find Berkeley's philosophy reassuring because it suggests that religion is closer to the truth than science. And there are no doubt others who simply find in it further evidence for their belief that bishops will go to any length to defend the faith. None of this explains, however, why believers and atheists and all sorts of people in between have kept returning to Berkeley, and have felt uncomfortable, and yet somehow exhilarated, in the presence of his philosophy. What is arresting about that philosophy is precisely the irritation that it provoked in Dr. Johnson. It is the irritation of a challenge to what we take to be common sense; it is the double irritation of realizing that Berkeley has challenged common sense on utterly commonsensical grounds. Why do we believe that a thing exists? Common sense tells us that we do so because we can see or hear or touch it. Then the existence of anything lies in the perception of it, and everything is mental, something in the mind.

Whether we agree with Berkeley or not, he has stopped us in midpassage. We have to review our habitual reactions. We see that there is something unexpected and incoherent in our ordinary thinking. The effect is intellectual: the philosopher has shaken us up, loosened our assumptions, made it easier for us to hold them at arm's length and consider their merits. And the effect is also esthetic: a philosopher has asked us to imagine the world as though it were the landscape of God's mind. Seen in this perspective, the world is more vibrant; its material aspects recede to the shadows, and its spiritual and moral qualities come to the foreground. A shift of perspective has taken place in our minds which is like the shift in our visual perspective when we look at a Van Gogh or a Picasso.

Plato repeatedly describes how philosophers, having glimpsed the truths of a more perfect world, come back to the ordinary scene and are not quite able to believe in it. It seems a tissue of insubstantial illusions to them. And they, in turn, appear to those untouched by philosophy to be curiously naïve, oddly disengaged from the opinions that rule the world. The truth to which Plato points is that philosophy can shock us into seeing that there are alternatives to our routine ways of reacting to our experience. Using its own distinctive tools, it offers what literature or painting also offers—the arrest of attention, the liberation from half-consciousness, a freshened, more zestful appreciation of the singularity of things. Under the spell of an ingenious argument in philosophy, we find that what is immediately in front of us can take on an edge, a sharpness, as though we had never seen it before. We are surprised that things are as they are; for the moment we are innocent again, and wonder, as children wonder, why they aren't different. Philosophy is a sophisticated man's way of recovering his naïveté. Though it deals in words and abstractions, it is a way of releasing the imagination and invigorating and deepening the life of the senses.

But philosophy reminds us, too, that what surprises us should not do so: the problems that we take to be special to us, the situations we have imagined to be peculiarly our own, turn out to be illustrations of recurrent themes in human experience. And yet, even though philosophy takes us out of ourselves and our own time and provides us with another perspective from which to view the present, it doesn't make the present recede; it allows us to see it in sharper focus. If it brings mellowness, it does so not by fuzzing the issues but by sharpening them.

Some of the questions that seem most pervasive at this moment have to do with the validity of logic. Is it a snare? Is argument, with its appeal to impersonal evidence, just a way of hiding the fact that one is trying to impose one's will on others? This is the question we will find Nietzsche asking. To read his attack on Socrates as a man who substituted debate for more honest forms of combat is to be plunged into the middle of current controversies about the role of reason. It is to hear an everyday insinuation turned into an open assertion: logic is sophistry, the frightened man's way of denying another man the right to his personal vision, the cold man's way of denying the reality of passion and the truth to be found in suffering and ecstasy. But it is to come face to face with this position in its best form, to see it in more of its implications and as part of an ancient contest.

Does the whole process of education rest simply on the exercise of authority? Is it an effort simply to fill students' minds with what the established society thinks they should believe? Is another education possible, one that would allow each individual to use his own mind and find the truth for himself? These are questions that Descartes asks, and his answer rehearses one possible response. Thus we meet philosophers as contemporaries. Their problems are our problems, but our problems molded into shape. They are not men out of the past. They are men who show us that the past is our present, who help us to see this present as part of the constant present in which reflective men have usually lived. By penetrating deeply enough into the problems that were theirs, and that are ours, they disentangle the enduring and central features of these problems, and give us an ampler, more poignant, better focused sense of what is at issue here and now. Their ideas are not simply as "relevant" as the ideas in today's editorial. Because they go to the heart of the matter and because they bring out aspects of it that we are likely to forget amid the pressures and prejudices of the moment, they offer more than easy "relevance."

Plato, in a quite different time and culture, showed that democracy, in its fear of social distinctions, can generate a muddleheadedness that denies the differences between man and woman or old and young. "Teacher fears pupil in such a state of things, and plays the toady; pupils despise their teachers and tutors, and in general, the young imitate their elders and stand up to them in word and deed. Old men give way to the young; they are all complaisance and wriggling, and behave like young men themselves so as not to be thought disagreeable or dictatorial. . . . Ah, I almost forgot to tell how great equality and liberty there is between women and men, between men and women." And David Hume, when he argues in a modest and humorous manner that reason doesn't give us certainty, puts to shame the latest author who announces the same truth with an air of discovery and in a vocabulary of fashionably new polysyllables.

To see our problems on such a lengthened time scale is not, of course, to find their solution. But it is at least to view our problems and ourselves in a light less fitful and provincial than the light that comes from our own corner of space and time. We see the dilemmas we face, the mistakes we make, and the hopes to which, despite our dilemmas and mistakes, we keep returning, as part of a continuing human experience, and are helped to recover perspective and a sense of proportion. Our anxieties become more tolerable and our certainties less arrogant. We are reminded that other men have been foolishly certain before us, and we are reminded, too, that our aspirations are not ours alone.

This is one reason why, with an exception or two, I have chosen selections from philosophers of periods other than our own. Philosophy in the present century, and particularly in the last twenty-five to fifty years, has become more professional—or perhaps the word is professorial. Philosophers have been trying to "keep up," to respond to the latest articles in the learned journals, to act like physicists or psychologists, writing in rapidly changing fields. There have been good results. There is a precision and care in contemporary philosophy, a willingness to give small problems attention and not slide by them, a level of sophisticated technique, which has led to the tightening of arguments and the clarification of many old issues. But these gains have come at a certain cost. To read most contemporary philosophers, one must be aware of the immediate background of what one is reading, of minor ripples in the history of thought, and of fashions that have made their little flurry and then died away. In a word, much contemporary philosophy is dated. Contemporary philosophers have "kept up," but they have kept up with what has very often turned out to be evanescent. The philosophers for whom the larger, perennial issues of philosophy are central have turned out to abide in a steadier stream of thought. The concerns that move them have kept up with the world because the world has never, for very long, been able to depart from their concerns. And so it is, I think, that the impulse that keeps philosophy going —the impulse that keeps even contemporary philosophy going, though it is now more hidden—is communicated best, at the beginning, by the classic philosophers. Strangely, they need less translation. To read them is an indispensable introduction to contemporary philosophy, and it is the best way to have one's first experience of philosophy's "shock of recognition."

But what is the impulse that keeps philosophy going? To begin to discover its source, we must go back to the human constitution. Philosophy is a unique combination of reason and passion. Philosophers try to be very explicit, to argue everything out, to appeal to logic and evidence. All this activity is indispensable, and offers rousing entertainment; but the original raw materials of philosophy are human hopes and fears, human emotions and aspirations, human habits of thought—blocked and trying to get free.

For philosophy begins in the imperious need to know what one thinks when one is in pain from not knowing. It is what happens to a man when his thoughts are confused and his feelings are mixed, when none of the prevailing conventions or accepted authorities will help him, and when he tries to think his way out of this condition instead of falling into madness or apathy. Aristotle suggests this when he remarks that philosophy begins in wonder. It grows out of perplexity, out of the consciousness of discordance in the world. It is an effort to defeat this discordance either by finding a deeper order in the world or by achieving greater clarity and surer grounds for conviction in one's own thinking. There are many ways of reacting to the ubiquitous human experiences of surprise, disappointment, confusion, and insecurity. Philosophers react by trying to find beliefs and ideals that can endure beyond surprise and disappointment.

Those who become philosophers are perhaps particularly aware of the discordance in the world, for if one considers a wide-ranging list of philosophers one finds that they seem to be strong-minded men who happen to be strongly of two minds: Marcus Aurelius, a Roman emperor who felt enslaved by the duties of his office; G. E. Moore, a Cambridge don monastically devoted to philosophy because he wanted to defend common sense against the astonishing things that philosophers said; Sören Kierkegaard, a defender of Christian faith on the ground that it could not be rationally defended; Aristotle, the unfailing spokesman for prudence and sobriety, who had a sense of the danger of general ideas and a passion for generalization; Karl Marx, a revolutionary who hated utopianism and a prophet who scorned moralists; George Santayana, an atheist and a Catholic all at once. At first glance, these men seem more than merely different. Each comes forward, through his philosophy, so sharply etched and so idiosyncratically himself that he seems to bring a whole special world with him. And yet there is something that unites them and makes them members of a single tribe.

In each of them there is the evidence of an inner tension that has somehow been faced, controlled, and used. Each has struggled against a split inside himself between one set of beliefs and another, between what he thought was true and what he wished were true, between his sympathy for one ideal or his desire for one style of life and his sympathy or desire for others. And each has struck a kind of balance; each has reached a precarious equipoise in which doubt and affirmation, acceptance of his condition and renunciation of it, are blended.

Sometimes philosophers come down strongly on one side. But the very fact that they continue to argue shows that they are aware of the other side and cannot get it out of their minds. And those who remain most acutely sensitive to both sides, who retain a kind of nostalgia for the position they have rejected, are usually the philosophers who have made the greatest contributions to philosophy and have spoken most movingly to their fellows. Plato, St. Augustine, Spinoza, John Stuart Mill, and William James are cases in point. Even philosophers like Immanuel Kant and Ludwig Wittgenstein, who have written in a manner that restricts their audience mainly to other professional philosophers, owe their influence as much to this fact as to the brilliance of their arguments. They were men at odds with themselves, and the stakes for which they engaged in philosophy were emotional as well as intellectual. This emotional involvement is what gives substance to what they say and makes them something other than mere virtuosos. Their magnetism is more than purely cerebral.

John Dewey railed throughout his life against what he called "dualism" in philosophy—the tendency of philosophers to divide the world into two parts, and to put what they thought was real and valuable in one insulated compartment while consigning what they thought was less important to a separate compartment, which could be neglected. By succumbing to this tendency, Dewey thought, philosophers had performed a disservice to the world. They had separated morals from a concern with facts, and they had separated the controls of logic from human practice. But Dewey himself was torn between moral idealism and moral realism, between a positivistic reliance on the limited methods of the sciences and a metaphysical desire to grasp the system of things entire. "Dualism" may be the wrong conclusion to reach in philosophy, but it is philosophy's starting point. For a philosophy is a man's attempt to find or recover single-mindedness while paying attention to the facts or hunches, the feelings or hopes or fears, that disturb this single-mindedness.

This is why Plato, whose philosophical dualism, half ironical, half all-too-serious, has haunted the Western mind for more than two millennia, is not only philosophy's progenitor but also its greatest teacher. Dialogue—Plato's chosen form—is a form to which philosophy naturally lends itself. Most philosophers do not employ it explicitly, but they do so implicitly, for their arguments are generally intelligible only as debate with others. But in the end, philosophy is probably best seen as the philosopher's debate with himself. The internal dialogue of the philosopher, the inner struggle and the inner movement of his mind from confusion and ambivalence to clarity and commitment, is what gives philosophy its force and its contagion.

The usual introductions to philosophy present the subject as though it were a procession of abstract doctrines marching down from some Olympus, or as though it were a collection of curious problems to which philosophers, standing in an orderly line, give their answers as they might answer questions about the customs of the Arunta or the flora and fauna of the Amazon. The result is that philosophers are made to look not like themselves, but like busts of themselves. But the matter of philosophy is not so distant, and philosophy is not the creation of men who were born knowing it all. It is the product of uncertain men struggling amid contradictory ideas and inclinations to strike a balance and attain some breadth of view. It is because the subject carries this heavy emotional investment that technique is important in it. Logic, precision, orderliness, detachment, and care are indispensable because they are instruments for protecting us in dangerous waters. In philosophy the desire for intellectual and emotional integration can be so strong that we may be only too eager to deny logic and the facts in order to appease it. Hence technique in philosophy is admirable: it is a triumph against considerable odds. But philosophy's achievements have poignancy because the subject is a mirror of the human situation, of human inconsistency and irresolution, but of inconsistency and irresolution honestly faced and—with difficulty—sometimes overcome. Philosophy speaks not for God, but for the muddled human race.

Philosophy has its sources in broad social and intellectual dislocations, and not only in the dislocations of individual minds. The existence of vigorous philosophical debate in a society is a sign that it has radical problems. Philosophy, accordingly, is often unwelcome: it calls attention to matters that people would rather sweep under the rug.

There is no single social or intellectual problem that can be said to constitute the essence of philosophy. Men have become philosophers because they have been worried about the conflict between religion and science, or about the clash between old and new moral standards, or about the meaning of new theories in physics which seem to challenge accepted notions about the nature of causal laws. But when an era or a culture breaks out in a philosophical rash, we can be sure of one thing: it lacks an unchallenged orthodoxy or an easy, genial consensus on important matters. Philosophy is the product of collisions between different points of view— collisions that are massive and repeated, and that involve not just particular ideas about particular matters but entire systems of thought.

The philosophy of St. Thomas Aquinas, for example, was the great intellectual achievement of the high Middle Ages. It is looked upon now, in many quarters, as the very symbol of orthodoxy. But in its own time it was something rather different. It represented St. Thomas' response to the pagan wisdom of Aristotle, which had recently been rediscovered. It was his effort to be receptive to ideas and values fundamentally different from those of Augustinian Christianity, and to weave them together with the older doctrines in a harmonious pattern. Similarly, the philosophy of Descartes grew out of his effort to show that the new mathematical sciences of his day should be accepted even though they were in apparent conflict with the scholastic philosophy descended from St. Thomas. Or, to shift to our own century, a major movement in the philosophy of law began when Oliver Wendell Holmes, Louis Brandeis, and others proposed to interpret words like "freedom," "property," and "due process of law" in terms of the new conditions of industrial society. Major practices in American life have gradually been changed in consequence—among them practices concerning employers' liability, the minimum wage, unions and collective bargaining, the relations between the races.

The causes of such geological shifts in the social or intellectual terrain are various. Major technological changes are one cause; the influx of new ideas from another culture, the emergence of upsetting scientific theories like those of Darwin and Einstein, the rise of hitherto submerged social classes, the development to the breaking point of social tendencies like urbanization, are others. Philosophy, which is stimulated to life by such developments, has the function of interpreting them, of fitting them into a new framework of assumptions and values, and of clarifying the choices they pose.

Accordingly, the issues with which philosophy is concerned are not fixed. Aristotle may have commented wisely on the science of his day, but a twentieth-century philosopher, dealing with quantum mechanics or the significance of the theory of games for human decision making, has problems different from Aristotle's. Spinoza's *Ethics* speaks to men in any age, but a man who has caught Spinoza's vision, if he lives in a busier and more democratic era, must speak for himself and translate that vision into terms that are pertinent to his condition and to that of his contemporaries. The problems that provoke philosophical reflection differ from age to age, and have specific characteristics which have to be dealt with in their own terms. It is probably a mistake, therefore, to think of philosophy as a subject with an eternal collection of unchanging problems to which it seeks some finally true answer.

But there is, nevertheless, a kind of continuity, a unifying thread, that joins together philosophers in different circumstances. Massive intellectual and social conflicts of the sort that have characteristically produced philosophy have a common feature: they involve the clash of basic premises and standards; the rules by which men might work their way through to a solution are themselves in doubt. In consequence, old definitions have to be remade, and the postulates formerly accepted as the starting points for discussion have to be uprooted and supplanted. Caught in a quarrel between democratic and antidemocratic theories of government, a philosopher has to argue not simply about the merits of democracy in comparison with its rivals, but about the purposes or principles by which any system of government should be judged. He has to argue, indeed, about how an argument involving basic political disagreements should even be conducted. Similarly, if some people maintain that the only reliable path to truth is science, and others assert that, in its concern with observable fact, science leaves out the whole domain of moral and spiritual truth, a philosopher must ask what can possibly be meant by "truth." The philosophical effort thus forces men, in age after age, to reflect on the nature of truth and goodness, the foundations of logic, the authority of experience. And so philosophy takes off on its own. In the course of time it develops special techniques for dealing with these problems, and paradigmatic positions with regard to them. Philosophers in different climates have something to say to one another, and learn to speak beyond their own situation to the situation of others. The thought even arises that there can be progress in philosophy.

But that is a question that the reader will be in a better position to consider after he has finished this book. Certainly philosophers have had their doubts about progress in philosophy, despite every effort they have made to uncover the ultimate philosophical truth, and to persuade their colleagues that they have done so. Bertrand Russell once defined philosophy as an unusually ingenious attempt to think fallaciously. Immanuel Kant said that much philosophy reminded him of one man trying to milk a he-goat while another man held a sieve. Socrates repeatedly compared philosophers to madmen, poets, and people who had lost their heads in love.

And yet, whether philosophy progresses or not, these remarks represent the amused self-mockery of men who have been enslaved by the subject and who have known that they would remain its slaves whether or not they found in it the answers they were seeking. There is, in fact, something a bit deceptive about philosophy. People often come to it with the hope that they will find an answer to some problem—say, the existence of God, or the nature of justice. They want, in effect, not to be troubled by the problem any longer, and they think of philosophy as the pharmacy where they will find the medicine to stop the pain. And sometimes philosophy performs this function. Sometimes, too, philosophers give the impression that this is all that they are trying to do: they are in the business of supplying solutions to problems in the way that a druggist fills prescriptions. But the impression is in good part an illusion. What philosophy offers, in the main—its contribution to human advancement—is not answers, and certainly not simple and final answers, but emancipation from the expectation that there are such answers. It is instruction in the art and pleasure of asking questions.

"One cannot learn philosophy," Immanuel Kant said. "One can only learn to philosophize." Few philosophers, if any, have solved problems to the satisfaction of all other philosophers; many famed philosophers have not even solved them to their own satisfaction. They have started arguments, not ended them. Yet they have stayed with the subject, as have countless laymen who have come to philosophy hoping for answers and have remained in its presence, enthralled by its questions. For philosophy, though it sets out to solve problems, and perhaps occasionally does solve them, has a more important by-product. It gives a kind of pleasure that is like the pleasure of acquiring knowledge or unscrambling a puzzle, and yet is not quite either of these. It is the pleasure of self-recognition, of imagining new possibilities, of feeling one's ideas and emotions reintegrated and connected to a larger scheme.

Philosophy, in short, has a life of its own. It is not to be judged by the standards by which other subjects are judged. If it gives knowledge, the knowledge is of a special sort. If it brings vision or serenity, this is not the vision or serenity that puts the mind at rest; rather, it sets the mind in motion. And though philosophy is important for its myriad contributions to human civilization, it hasn't survived because it is important. It is important because it has survived—because whether it is useful or not, whether it makes "progress" or not, men have returned to it and have put their ardent efforts into it. The survival of philosophy tells us something about the human animal. It suggests that there is something impish and untamed even in what we take to be the more peaceful and civilized aspect of human nature—an irreverence and mischievousness, a refusal to leave well enough alone, a sheer joy in upsetting applecarts.

Philosophy has met political repression, religious persecution, the animosity of practical men who have ridiculed it for asking foolish questions, the indignation of other men, practical and impractical, who have resented the fact that it so rarely reassures them that the beliefs they hold are true. And today it is meeting other challenges as well. Like other agreeable activities, like music, the theater, and even the relations between the sexes, it is treated as a battleground for warring schools, or as a temple from which messages of redemption come, or simply as an occasion for interesting new technical experiments. In the process it is turned into a cult or a mystery or something exclusively for adepts. Its intrinsic excitements are hidden, and the fact that it springs from a human impulse as natural as the impulse to sing or mimic is forgotten.

And yet the subject keeps bouncing back to make trouble. Philosophy testifies to man's capacity to take pleasure in the free play of intelligence. It is, in fact, man's supreme effort to think about his condition, to reflect on the powers and uses of his intelligence and on its qualifications to serve as a guide to truth and right conduct. Albert Camus said that an intellectual is a man who watches himself as he works. Philosophy is this way of living and working turned into a systematic discipline and a deliberately cultivated source of delight.

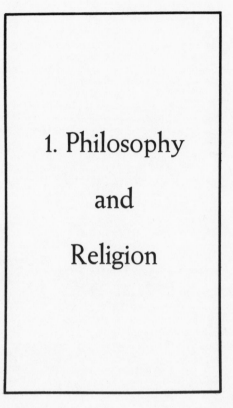

1. Philosophy

and

Religion

*R*eflection on religion has been a principal route leading men into philosophy. For religion is a two-sided phenomenon. In its orthodox forms it asks men to believe in miracles, imposes on them commands which run counter to their instincts, and is in many ways a record of intolerance and fanaticism. Yet some of the profoundest minds have been sustained by religion, and it has nurtured some of the most penetrating visions of the human condition and some of the most appealing models of human personality. Is there some balance that can be struck between these two sides of religion? What rational purpose does religion serve in the world? In what way, if at all, do religious beliefs make sense? To explore these questions seriously is to be launched into philosophy.

Here are three philosophers who have tried to think these problems through. One is an eighteenth-century French freethinker, Denis Diderot; the second an Anglo-Irish bishop, George Berkeley; the third the early twentieth-century philosopher George Santayana, born in Spain and brought up in America, who believed that there is no God but that Mary is His mother.

Denis Diderot

One of the reasons most frequently given for the assertion that religion is essential in human life is that it is necessary for morality. If there is no God, why isn't any kind of conduct permissible? In the impish conversation that follows, Denis Diderot asks, What motive can an unbeliever have for doing good? But by the time the dialogue has ended, Diderot has turned this question around. He leaves us wondering whether an unbeliever doesn't have a sounder basis for morality than a believer.

Diderot was born in 1713 and died in 1784. He was the editor of the famous eighteenth-century *Encyclopédie*, which summed up the scientific thought and enlightened opinion of the age. With Voltaire and Rousseau, he was the central figure in the French Enlightenment. Alexis de Tocqueville, looking back on the French Revolution, said that it was a unique event in history because it was the first revolution which had been caused so largely by men of letters. As editor of the *Encyclopédie*, Diderot was in effect the corresponding secretary for the intellectual leadership that prepared the way for the Revolution. Almost certainly he never envisaged an upheaval of the dimensions of the Revolution, and almost certainly he would not have approved either the Terror or its Napoleonic aftermath. But he sensed that he was the spokesman for a major upheaval in ideas that was bound to bring greater freedom and equality for mankind, and his view of the intellectual life was the view of an activist who wanted ideas to make a practical difference and who thought that they could. He journeyed to the Russian court, and attempted to teach Catherine the Great the principles of the new, liberal philosophy, thumping her knees, it is reported, in his enthusiasm for his work.

Yet he was anything but a slavish expositor of fashionable ideas. A critic of conservative and orthodox opinion, he was also a critic of the orthodoxies current among intellectuals. His greatest work, *Rameau's Nephew*, reads as though Dostoyevsky might have written it after having gone to school with Voltaire. Diderot's large-mindedness was matched by his personal generosity. He was gregarious and charming, lavish with his energy and friendship, and capable of devoting as much time to helping others with their ideas as he spent working on his own. The story is told that when a man once came to Diderot's door carrying a document libeling him and demanding money not to make it public, Diderot set to work improving the document's literary style.

By all accounts, Diderot was also one of the great nonstop talkers of his period. Intellectual life in eighteenth-century France was to a large extent lived in public. Its center was the *salon*, where writers, artists, philosophers, and scientists conversed with fashionable ladies and gentlemen, and, as it were, wrote their books aloud. Diderot's work shows the stamp of this special intellectual culture, which fitted his talents. As the present dialogue shows, his métier was conversation. The Maréchale who figures in it is said to have been the Maréchale de Broglie, and Diderot is supposed to have had an actual conversation with her on the subject of morality and religion. It is certain that he had a good many such conversations and that what we read here is their distillation. The dialogue was published in 1777. The translation, here given in its entirety, is by Francis Birrell.

Conversation of a Philosopher with the Maréchale de ———

I had some business or other with Maréchal de ———. I went to his house one morning. He was out. I was shown in to Madame la Maréchale. She is a charming woman, beautiful and pious as an angel: and she has a tone of voice and naïveté of speech which entirely suit her face. She was dressing. A chair is drawn up. I sit down and we talk. As a result of some observations on my part which edified and surprised her (for she holds that the man who denies the Blessed Trinity is a ruffian who will end on the gallows), she said to me:

Are you not M. Crudeli?

CRUDELI. Yes.

MARÉCHALE. The man who believes in nothing?

CRUDELI. I am.

MARÉCHALE. But your morals are the same as a believer's.

CRUDELI. Why not, if that believer is an honest man?

MARÉCHALE. And you put that morality into practice?

CRUDELI. As well as I can.

MARÉCHALE. What! you do not steal, or kill, or pillage?

CRUDELI. Very rarely.

MARÉCHALE. Then what do you get out of not believing?

CRUDELI. Nothing; but does one believe in order to get something out of it?

MARÉCHALE. I do not know. But a little self-interest comes in useful both for this world and the next.

CRUDELI. I am a little sorry for our poor human race, to be no better than that.

MARÉCHALE. So you do not steal at all?

CRUDELI. I promise you, not.

MARÉCHALE. But if you are neither a thief nor an assassin, you must admit you are hardly consistent.

CRUDELI. Why so?

MARÉCHALE. Because I think if I had nothing to fear or to hope, after death, I should allow myself a good many little pleasures here below. I admit I lend to God at a stiff rate of interest.

CRUDELI. So you think, perhaps.

MARÉCHALE. It is not a matter of thinking. It is a fact.

CRUDELI. But might one ask, What are those things you would allow yourself, if you did not believe?

MARÉCHALE. One might not. They are only for my confessor's ears.

CRUDELI. For my part, I never expect any return on my money.

MARÉCHALE. All beggars are in that situation.

CRUDELI. You would rather I were a usurer?

MARÉCHALE. Why, yes. One can be as usurious with God as one pleases. He cannot be ruined. It is hardly delicate, I know. But what does that matter? As the essential thing is to get into Heaven either by cunning or by force, we must use every means, and neglect no source of profit. Alas! whatever we do, we shall get but scanty recognition compared with what we had looked for. And you, you look for nothing?

CRUDELI. Nothing.

MARÉCHALE. But that is very sad. Agree then—you are either a rogue or a madman.

CRUDELI. But I cannot.

MARÉCHALE. But what motive can an unbeliever have for being good, unless he be mad?

CRUDELI. I shall tell you.

MARÉCHALE. I shall be most grateful.

CRUDELI. Do you not think a man can be born with such a happy disposition as to find real pleasure in doing good?

MARÉCHALE. I do.

CRUDELI. And that he may have received an excellent education, which will strengthen his natural leaning towards benevolence.

MARÉCHALE. Certainly.

CRUDELI. And that, in later life, experience may have convinced us that on the whole it is better for one's happiness in this world to be an honest man than a rogue.

MARÉCHALE. Why, yes. But how can he be an honest man, when evil principles united with the passions involve us in evil?

CRUDELI. By inconsistency. And is there anything commoner than inconsistency?

MARÉCHALE. Alas! Unfortunately not. We believe, yet every day we behave as though we did not.

CRUDELI. And without believing, one behaves very much as if one did.

MARÉCHALE. If you like. But what can be the harm in having one reason the more, religion, for doing good, and one reason the less, unbelief, for doing wrong?

CRUDELI. None, if religion were a motive for doing good and unbelief for doing wrong.

MARÉCHALE. But can there be any doubt about it? What is the essence of religion but to check our vile corrupted nature, and that of unbelief but to abandon it to its own wickedness by relieving it of fear?

CRUDELI. That is going to involve us in a long discussion.

MARÉCHALE. What of that? The Maréchal will not be back for a bit. And we are better employed in rational discussion than in slandering our neighbours.

CRUDELI. Then I must go back a little.

MARÉCHALE. As far as you like, provided you make yourself understood.

CRUDELI. If I do not, it will be entirely my fault.

MARÉCHALE. That is very polite of you. But you must know I have hardly read anything but my Prayer Book, and I do almost nothing but study the Gospels and breed children.

CRUDELI. Two duties you have admirably fulfilled.

MARÉCHALE. As regards the children, yes. Here are six round me and in a few days you will be able to see a seventh on my knee. But begin.

CRUDELI. Well. Is there any good in this world which has not got its drawbacks?

MARÉCHALE. None.

CRUDELI. And any evil which has not got its advantages?

MARÉCHALE. None.

CRUDELI. What then do you call a good or an evil?

MARÉCHALE. An evil is that which has more drawbacks than advantages, and a good that which has more advantages than drawbacks.

CRUDELI. I hope you will be good enough to remember your definition of good and evil?

MARÉCHALE. I will. But do you call that a definition?

CRUDELI. Yes.

MARÉCHALE. Then it is philosophy?

CRUDELI. And very good philosophy, too.

MARÉCHALE. So I have made philosophy!

CRUDELI. So you are convinced that religion has more advantages than drawbacks. Hence you call it a good?

MARÉCHALE. Yes.

CRUDELI. And for my part, I have no doubt your bailiff robs you a little less just before Easter than he does a few days afterwards, and that from time to time religion prevents a number of small evils and produces a number of small goods.

MARÉCHALE. Little by little, that tots up.

CRUDELI. But do you think that these poky little advantages make up adequately for the terrible ravages religion has caused in the past and will cause in the future? Remember it has created and now perpetuates the most violent national hatreds. No Mussulman but believes he is doing an action agreeable to God and the holy prophet in exterminating every Christian. And the Christians on their side are scarcely more tolerant. Think how it has created and still perpetuates in the same country divisions rarely suppressed without the shedding of blood. Our own history offers us examples all too recent and too tragic. Think how it has created and still perpetuates, in society between citizens, and in the family between relatives, the most violent and most lasting of hatreds. Christ said he had come to separate husband from wife, mother from children, brother from sister, friend from friend. And his prediction has been all too faithfully fulfilled.

MARÉCHALE. These are abuses, not the essentials, of the thing.

CRUDELI. It is, if abuses and essentials are inseparable.

MARÉCHALE. And how can you demonstrate that religion and its abuses are inseparable?

CRUDELI. Very easily. Suppose a misanthrope had set out to harm the human race, what could he have invented better than belief in an incomprehensible being about whom men should never agree and to whom they should attach more importance than to their own lives. Now is it possible to separate from the notion of a Divinity the most profound incomprehensibility and the greatest importance?

MARÉCHALE. No.

CRUDELI. Your conclusion, then?

MARÉCHALE. My conclusion is that it is an idea which might well be disastrous, if lunatics got hold of it.

CRUDELI. And you may add that lunatics always have been and always will be in the vast majority; and that the most dangerous lunatics are those made so by religion, and that the disturbers of society know how to make good use of them when occasion arises.

MARÉCHALE. But we must have something with which to frighten men off those actions, which escape the severity of the laws. Destroy religion, and what will you put in its place?

CRUDELI. And suppose I had nothing to put in its place, there would always be one terrible prejudice the less. Besides, in no century and with no nation have religious opinions been the basis of national morals. The gods adored by the ancient Greeks and Romans, the most virtuous of people, were the merest scum: a Jupiter who should have been burnt alive: a Venus fit for a reformatory: a Mercury who ought to be in a jail.

MARÉCHALE. So you think it does not matter at all whether we be Christians or pagans; that we should be none the worse for being pagans and are none the better for being Christians?

CRUDELI. Honestly, I am certain of it, unless we should be slightly merrier for being pagans.

MARÉCHALE. That cannot be.

CRUDELI. But are there any Christians? I have never seen one.

MARÉCHALE. And you say that to me?

CRUDELI. No, not to you, but to one of my neighbours, who is as honest and pious as you: who thinks herself a Christian in all sincerity just as you do.

MARÉCHALE. And you made her admit she was wrong?

CRUDELI. In a moment.

MARÉCHALE. And how?

CRUDELI. I opened a New Testament, which she had used a great deal, for it was very worn. I read her the Sermon on the Mount, and after each article I asked her—Do you do that? Or that? Or even that? I went one further. She is very beautiful, and although most good and pious, she is well aware of the fact. She has a very white skin, and although she does not attach any great importance to this slender merit, she does not mind it being praised. Her throat is as handsome as throat can be: and although she is very modest, she thinks it as well that this should be noticed.

MARÉCHALE. But if only herself and her husband know it?

CRUDELI. Certainly, I think her husband knows it better than anyone else. But for a woman who prides herself on being such a tremendous Christian this is not enough. I said to her: "Is it not written in the Gospel that he who lusts after his neighbour's wife has committed adultery in his heart?"

MARÉCHALE. And she answered Yes.

CRUDELI. And I said: And is not adultery committed in the heart as surely damned as adultery of the most thoroughgoing kind?

MARÉCHALE. And she answered Yes.

CRUDELI. And I said: And if the man is damned for the adultery he has committed in his heart, what will be the fate of the woman who invites all those who come near her to commit this crime? This last question embarrassed her.

MARÉCHALE. I understand; for she did not, very carefully, cover up this throat of hers, which is handsome as throat can be.

CRUDELI. That is so. She replied it was a convention, as if anything were more conventional than to call oneself a Christian and not be one. And also that one must not dress absurdly, as if there could be any comparison between a trifling little absurdity and one's eternal damnation, as well as the damnation of one's neighbour. And also that she was in the hands of her dressmaker, as if it were not better to change one's dressmaker than to throw over one's religion. And that it was the whim of her husband, as if a husband were sufficiently insensate to demand from his wife the forgetfulness of decency and duty, and as if a true Christian should push obedience to a preposterous husband to the point of sacrificing the will of God and despising the threats of her Redeemer.

MARÉCHALE. I knew all those childish answers before you mentioned them. And perhaps I should have employed them like your neighbour. And we should both have been insincere. But what line did she take after your protest?

CRUDELI. The day after our conversation (it was a festival of the Church), as I was going up to my room, my beautiful and pious neighbour was coming down, on the way to Mass.

MARÉCHALE. Dressed as usual.

CRUDELI. Dressed as usual. I smiled. She smiled. We passed each other without speaking. And she, an honest woman! a Christian! a pious woman! And after this sample, and one hundred thousand others exactly like it, what real influence can I allow religion to have on morals? Practically none, and so much the better.

MARÉCHALE. What! so much the better?

CRUDELI. Yes. If twenty thousand Parisians took it into their heads to base their conduct strictly on the Sermon on the Mount . . .

MARÉCHALE. Well, there would be a few handsome throats better covered.

CRUDELI. And so many lunatics that the commissioner of police would not know what to do with them: for our asylums would never hold them. There are two moralities in Inspired Books. One general and common to all nations and all religions, which is more or less observed: the other, peculiar to each nation and each religion in which people believe, which they preach in church and praise up at home, but which is not observed at all.

MARÉCHALE. And to what is this preposterous state of affairs due?

CRUDELI. To the impossibility of subjecting a nation to a rule which suits only a few melancholiacs, who have imposed it on their characters. It is with religious as with monastic institutions; they relax with time. They are lunacies which cannot hold out against the constant impulse of nature, which brings us back under her law. See to it that private good be so closely united to public good that a citizen can hardly harm society without harming himself. Promise virtue its reward, as you have promised wickedness its punishment. Let virtue lead to high offices of state, without distinction of faith, wherever virtue is to be found. Then you need only count on a small number of wicked men, who are involved in vice by a perversity of nature which nothing can correct. No. Temptation is too near: hell too far off. Look for nothing worth the attention of a wise law-giver from a system of fantastic opinions, which imposes only on children: which encourages crime by its convenient system of penances: which sends the guilty man to ask pardon of God for harm done to man, and which degrades the order of natural and moral duties by subordinating it to an order of imaginary duties.

MARÉCHALE. I do not follow.

CRUDELI. Let me explain. But I think I hear the Maréchal's carriage coming back just in time to prevent my saying something silly.

MARÉCHALE. Say it. I shall not understand you. I am an adept at understanding only what gives me pleasure.

CRUDELI. I went up to her and said quite low in her ear: "Ask the vicar of your parish, which of the two crimes is, in his opinion, the more heinous —to piss into a sacred vessel or to blacken the reputation of an honest woman. He will shudder with horror at the first, and the civil law, which scarcely notices calumny while punishing sacrilege with fire, will complete the confusion of ideas and the corruption of the intelligence."

MARÉCHALE. I know more than one woman who would never eat meat on a Friday and who . . . I was going to make my silly contribution. Go on.

CRUDELI. But I simply must speak to the Maréchal.

MARÉCHALE. One moment more, and then we will go and see him together. I do not quite see how to answer you, but you have not made me change my opinion.

CRUDELI. I did not set out to change it. It is with religion as with marriage. Marriage, which has wrecked so many lives, has made for your happiness and for that of the Maréchal. You have both of you done well to marry. Religion, which has made, does make, and will make so many men wicked, has made you better still: you do well to keep it. It is sweet to you to imagine beside you, and above your head, a great and powerful being who sees you walk upon the earth, and this idea strengthens your steps. Continue to be happy in this august guarantor of your thoughts, in this spectator, in this sublime model for your actions.

MARÉCHALE. I see you have not got the proselytizing mania.

CRUDELI. Not in the least.

MARÉCHALE. I think the better of you for it.

CRUDELI. I allow everyone to think as he pleases, provided I am allowed to think as I please. And then those who exist in order to free themselves from these prejudices are scarcely in need of being catechized.

MARÉCHALE. Do you think man can get along without superstition?

CRUDELI. Not as long as he remains ignorant and timid.

MARÉCHALE. Well then, superstition for superstition, ours is as good as another.

CRUDELI. I do not think so.

MARÉCHALE. Now tell me sincerely. Does the idea of being nothing after death not distress you?

CRUDELI. I would rather exist, though I do not know why a Being who has been once capable of making me wretched for no reason should not enjoy doing so twice.

MARÉCHALE. But if, despite this drawback, the hope of a life to come appear to you consoling and sweet, why tear it from us?

CRUDELI. I do not entertain this hope because desire for it has not

blinded me to its hollowness; but I take it away from no one else. If anyone can believe they will see without eyes, hear without ears, think without
a head, love without a heart, feel without senses, exist without being anywhere, and be something without place or size, very well.

MARÉCHALE. But who made this world?

CRUDELI. I ask you.

MARÉCHALE. God.

CRUDELI. And what is God?

MARÉCHALE. A spirit.

CRUDELI. And if a spirit makes matter, why should not matter make a
spirit!

MARÉCHALE. And why should it?

CRUDELI. Because I see it do so every day. Do you believe animals have
souls?

MARÉCHALE. Certainly I do.

CRUDELI. Could you tell me, for example, what happens to the soul of
the Peruvian serpent, hung on the chimney and exposed to the smoke for
two years together while it is drying?

MARÉCHALE. How can it matter to me what happens to it?

CRUDELI. So you do not know that this serpent, after being dried and
smoked, is resuscitated and reborn?

MARÉCHALE. I do not believe it for a moment.

CRUDELI. Yet a very clever man, Bouguer,[1] asserts it.

MARÉCHALE. Your clever man is a liar.

CRUDELI. But suppose he were telling the truth?

MARÉCHALE. I should get off with believing that animals are machines.

CRUDELI. And man, who is only a machine a little more perfected than
any other. . . . But the Maréchal.

MARÉCHALE. One more question and it is the last. Does your unbelief
leave you calm?

CRUDELI. As calm as it is possible to be.

MARÉCHALE. But suppose you were mistaken?

CRUDELI. Suppose I were?

MARÉCHALE. Suppose everything you believe false were true and you
were damned. Monsieur Crudeli, it is a terrible thing to be damned. To
burn through eternity. It is a long time.

CRUDELI. La Fontaine thought we should be as comfortable as fishes in
water.

MARÉCHALE. Yes, yes, but your La Fontaine became very serious at the
end, and I expect the same of you.

CRUDELI. I can answer for nothing when my brain has softened. But if
I end with one of those illnesses which leave the dying man in possession

1. Inventor of the Heliometer.—*Translator.*

of his powers, I shall be no more distressed at the expected moment than I am now.

MARÉCHALE. Your fearlessness amazes me.

CRUDELI. I am much more amazed at the fearlessness of the dying man who believes in a severe judge, in one who weighs our most secret thoughts, and in whose balance the justest man would be lost through vanity if he did not tremble to find himself too light. If this dying man could choose between being wiped out and going before this tribunal, I should be much more amazed by his fearlessness if he hesitated to choose the first: unless, indeed, he were more insensate than the companion of Saint Bruno or more intoxicated with his own merits than Bohola.

MARÉCHALE. I have read the account of the associate of Saint Bruno, but I have never heard of your Bohola.

CRUDELI. He was a Jesuit of the College at Pinsk in Lithuania, who left at his death a casket full of money with a note written and signed in his own hand.

MARÉCHALE. And the note?

CRUDELI. . . . was as follows: "I want my dear colleague, to whom I hand over this casket, to open it when I have performed miracles. The money inside will go to the expenses in connection with my beatification. I have added some authentic memoirs in confirmation of my virtues which will be useful to those engaged on writing my life."

MARÉCHALE. But it is a roaring farce.

CRUDELI. To me, yes; but not to you: your God has got no sense of humour.

MARÉCHALE. That is so.

CRUDELI. It is very easy to sin grievously against your law.

MARÉCHALE. I agree. It is.

CRUDELI. The justice that will decide your fate is very stern.

MARÉCHALE. True.

CRUDELI. And if you believe in the oracles of your creed, the number of the saved is small.

MARÉCHALE. Oh, I am no Jansenist: [2] I look only at the bright side of the medal. In my eyes the blood of Jesus Christ has flowed far. I should think it very odd if the Devil, who never sacrificed his son, nevertheless got the lion's share.

CRUDELI. Do you damn Socrates, Phocion, Aristides, Cato, Trajan, Marcus Aurelius? [3]

MARÉCHALE. Gracious me, no! Only wild beasts can believe that. Saint Paul said everyone will be judged by his own law and Saint Paul is right.

CRUDELI. And by what law will the unbeliever be judged?

2. Member of a Catholic sect that stressed man's fallen condition.—*Editor.*
3. All noble pagans.—*Editor.*

MARÉCHALE. Your case is rather different. You are one of those cursed inhabitants of Corozaïn and Betzaïda who shut their eyes to the light that shone on them, and put wax in their ears so as not to hear the voice of reason which spoke to them.

CRUDELI. But these Corozaïnians and Betzaïdans were unique if they were free to believe or not to believe.

MARÉCHALE. They saw prodigies enough to have raised the price of sackcloth and ashes in Tyre and Sidon.

CRUDELI. These inhabitants of Tyre and Sidon were intelligent, the Corozaïnian and Betzaïdan mere fools. But is it for him who made them fools to punish them for their folly? Just now I related to you an actual occurrence. Now I want to tell you a story: A young Mexican . . . But the Maréchal?

MARÉCHALE. I will send to find out if we can see him. Well then, your young Mexican?

CRUDELI. Tired of his work, walked one day upon the seashore. He saw a plank with one end in the water and the other on the beach. He takes his seat on the plank; and turning his gaze on the huge space stretched out before him, said. "It is certain my grandmother is talking nonsense when she romances about some inhabitants or other who, God knows when, came here heaven knows where from, but from some country beyond the seas. Why, there is no commonsense in it. Cannot I see the sea merging in the sky? And can I believe, against the evidence of my senses, an old story of unknown date, which everyone rearranges to suit himself, which is a mere farrago of preposterous incidents over which men eat their hearts out, and tear out the whites of their eyes." As he reasoned thus, the undulating waters rocked him on his plank and he fell asleep. As he sleeps, the wind gets up, the waves carry the barque away, and behold our young reasoner started on his voyage.

MARÉCHALE. Alas! that is just like us. We are each on his plank: the wind blows and the waves carry us away.

CRUDELI. He was already far from the mainland when he awoke. And who was mighty surprised to find himself on the open sea? Why, our young Mexican. And who was more surprised still? He again, when the sea seemed to merge in the sky on every side, now that he had lost sight of the beach where he had been walking only a moment before. Then he began to suspect that he might have been mistaken, and that if the wind continued in the same quarter he might be carried on shore, amongst those inhabitants of whom his mother had talked to him so often.

MARÉCHALE. But you say nothing about his agitation.

CRUDELI. He felt none. He said to himself: "What does that matter to me, as long as I get on shore? I have argued like a fool, certainly. But I was sincere with myself, and that is all that can be expected of me. If it be not a virtue to be intelligent, it is not a crime to be a fool." Meanwhile, the wind went on blowing, the man and the plank drifted along, and the unknown shore began to appear. He touches land, and there he is!

MARÉCHALE. We shall meet again there one day, M. Crudeli.

CRUDELI. I sincerely hope so. Wherever it may be, I shall always be flattered to pay you my addresses. Scarcely had he left his plank and set foot on the sand when he perceived a venerable old man standing by his side. The Mexican asked him where he was and whom he had the honour of addressing. "I am the sovereign of the country," answered the old man. At once the young man prostrated himself. "Get up," said the old man; "you have denied my existence?" "I have." "And the existence of my empire?" "I have." "I forgive you that because you acted in good faith. But the rest of your thoughts and actions have not been equally innocent." Then the old man, who held him by the ear, recalled to him all the errors of his life. And at each article the young Mexican bowed his head and beat his breast and prayed for pardon. . . . There now. Put yourself a moment in the place of the old man and tell me what you would have done. Would you have taken this insensate young man by the hair and joyfully dragged him along the beach for ever?

MARÉCHALE. To tell you the truth, no.

CRUDELI. And if one of your six pretty children, after escaping from the paternal roof, and committing every conceivable sort of folly, came home repentant?

MARÉCHALE. I should run to meet him. I should clasp him in my arms and bathe him with my tears. But his father the Maréchal would not take the thing so lightly.

CRUDELI. The Maréchal is not a tiger.

MARÉCHALE. Far from it.

CRUDELI. He would make rather a scene about it. But he would forgive in the end.

MARÉCHALE. Certainly.

CRUDELI. Especially if he came to reflect that, before becoming the father of the child, he had known all that was going to happen to it, and that punishing him for his faults would be of no use to himself, the guilty one, or his brothers.

MARÉCHALE. The Maréchal and the old man are two different people.

CRUDELI. You mean to say that the Maréchal is better than the old man?

MARÉCHALE. Heaven forbid! I mean to say that if my notion of justice is not the same as the Maréchal's perhaps the notion of the Maréchal will not be the same as the old man's.

CRUDELI. But you cannot have realized the consequences of that answer. Either the general definition applies equally to you, to the Maréchal, to me, to the young Mexican and the old man, or I can no longer say what is what, or how one pleases or displeases the old man.

We had reached this point when we were told that the Maréchal expected us. As I gave his wife my hand, she said: It is enough to make one's head go round, is it not?

CRUDELI. Why, if one's head is a good one?

MARÉCHALE. After all, the simplest course is to act on the assumption that the old man exists.

CRUDELI. Even when one does not believe it?

MARÉCHALE. And when one does believe it, not to rely too much on his good nature.

CRUDELI. That is the safest way, if not the politest.

MARÉCHALE. By the way, if you had to state your principles to the magistrates, would you make a clean breast of them?

CRUDELI. I should do my best to hinder the magistrates performing a brutal act.

MARÉCHALE. Oh, you coward! And if you were at the point of death, would you submit to the ceremonies of the Church?

CRUDELI. I should not fail to do so.

MARÉCHALE. Oh, you wretched hypocrite!

George Berkeley

Do Diderot's arguments leave something out? Has he missed the point of religion? Men who have been perfectly aware of arguments like his have nevertheless been convinced that religion expresses a truth about the world which cannot be expressed in any other way. What is this truth that believers find in religion? And is it in fact a truth?

What religion teaches, says George Berkeley, an eloquent Anglican bishop in eighteenth-century Ireland, is what every man really knows—that there is a God and that the world in which we live and move and have our being is God's way of speaking to us. Of course, not every man knows that he knows this truth. But Berkeley thinks that if his readers will only examine the everyday assumptions by which they live, they will discover—with a little assistance from him—that no truth could be more evident.

But if religion only celebrates what every man knows, why does anyone ever have doubts about its truth? Berkeley's answer is that men forget their common sense. They are seduced out of it by splashy ideas, put forward, usually, in the name of "science." They think that science demonstrates that the world is composed of matter and of matter alone, and so they conclude that there is no room in it for spiritual entities like God or the soul. But this view is all wrong, says Berkeley. Merely consider: the evidence leading us to say that a thing exists—the evidence on which science itself relies—is that this thing is perceived by the senses, or can be inferred from what is perceived. Therefore, things that exist have to be the objects of some perceiving mind. Two conclusions follow. First, everything that exists is mental—a presence in a mind—not material. Second, there has to be a God. For since, as we cannot help believe, things do exist which no mortal creature perceives, there must be a God who perceives them.

To understand Berkeley's argument, one must recognize that when he denies the existence of "matter" he isn't denying "matter" in its ordinary sense. He believes quite firmly that things like mud, dirt, and stones exist, and are sticky, dusty, or solid, just as they seem to be. This, in fact, is precisely the position he wants to defend. But he denies the existence of the "matter" in which misguided people who draw the wrong conclusions from abstract sciences like physics or chemistry believe. They say that behind or beneath the mud, dirt, and stones of our everyday experience there is something else—some unperceivable combination of atoms, some realm of invisible material events—which is more real than the world of our ordinary common sense. It is this belief in "matter," Berkeley thinks, which leads people to say that spiritual things are all illusory, and it is this belief that he wishes to refute.

Similarly, the reader should be aware that Berkeley uses the word "idea" in a special way. Ordinarily, the word stands for a notion or picture or plan in one's mind, as distinguished from a genuine event that actually takes place in the world. After hearing a disease described to us, for example, we speak of having an "idea" of it, something quite different from having the disease itself. For Berkeley, however, an "idea" is anything that enters our consciousness, whether it really exists or is a figment of the imagination. This way of using the word may seem odd, but it is deliberate. He wants to show that everything that exists is a mental or spiritual, not a material, thing.

Is Berkeley's argument valid? To dissect a magician's performance in advance is unforgivable; I shall save my answer for a later page. Suffice it to say that the reader is about to witness a philosopher's trick of prestidigitation. The reader has already seen one example of this kind of trick, in the preceding dialogue by Diderot. Diderot starts by asking the usual question the religious believer asks: If a man doesn't believe in God, how can he be moral? But he turns matters around so that it seems at least as sensible to ask: If a man believes in God, how can he be moral? Berkeley's sleight of hand is even more stunning. Skeptics and atheists who attack religion are in the habit of saying that the belief in God is a belief in something occult, undefinable, or impossible. Berkeley turns this accusation back on the accusers: the man who believes in "matter," he says, believes in something even more occult than God, and something which, if it existed, would be the greatest miracle of all.

Berkeley was born in 1685 and died in 1753. He wrote on economic and social issues as well as on philosophy, and was an active participant in the life of his time. He once hoped to establish a college in the Bermudas, and spent three years in Rhode Island waiting unsuccessfully for funds, which had been promised him by the British government, to support this project. But he also had some good luck with regard to money. He was an acquaintance of Jonathan Swift's, and when he was thirty-eight Esther Vanhomrigh, the lady whom Swift called "Vanessa," left him half her fortune. It appears that Berkeley had met her only once, at dinner. Diderot, who had a fearful struggle keeping the *Encyclopédie* going, never had this kind of luck. This suggests that religious faith has rewards that agnosticism does not, but this is an unphilosophical reflection.

Berkeley wrote the book in which he first stated his philosophy—*A Treatise concerning the Principles of Human Knowledge*—when he was still in his twenties. Though it is now regarded as a classic, it was a resounding failure when it appeared, and there were critics who called him mad. Subsequently, he wrote the *Three Dialogues between Hylas and*

Philonous in an effort to state his views in a clearer and more entertaining form. These dialogues are among the supreme examples of the philosophical dialogue in the English language. The selection that follows includes key passages from each of them. Philonous, of course, speaks for Berkeley. Hylas is the straight man.

Three Dialogues between Hylas and Philonous, in Opposition to Skeptics and Atheists

THE PREFACE

. . . If the principles which I here endeavor to propagate are admitted for true, the consequences which, I think, evidently flow from thence are that atheism and skepticism will be utterly destroyed, many intricate points made plain, great difficulties solved, several useless parts of science retrenched, speculation referred to practice, and men reduced from paradoxes to common sense.

And, although it may, perhaps, seem an uneasy reflection to some that, when they have taken a circuit through so many refined and unvulgar notions, they should at last come to think like other men, yet, methinks, this return to the simple dictates of nature, after having wandered through the wild mazes of philosophy, is not unpleasant. It is like coming home from a long voyage: a man reflects with pleasure on the many difficulties and perplexities he has passed through, sets his heart at ease, and enjoys himself with more satisfaction for the future.

As it was my intention to convince skeptics and infidels by reason, so it has been my endeavor strictly to observe the most rigid laws of reasoning. And to an impartial reader I hope it will be manifest that the sublime notion of a God and the comfortable expectation of immortality do naturally arise from a close and methodical application of thought—whatever may be the result of that loose, rambling way, not altogether improperly termed Free-thinking, by certain libertines in thought who can no more endure the restraints of logic than those of religion or government. . . .

THE FIRST DIALOGUE

PHILONOUS. Good morrow, Hylas. I did not expect to find you abroad so early.

HYLAS. It is indeed something unusual; but my thoughts were so taken up with a subject I was discoursing of last night that, finding I could not sleep, I resolved to rise and take a turn in the garden.

PHILONOUS. It happened well, to let you see what innocent and agreeable pleasures you lose every morning. Can there be a pleasanter time of the day or a more delightful season of the year? That purple sky, these wild but sweet notes of birds, the fragrant bloom upon the trees and flowers, the gentle influence of the rising sun—these and a thousand nameless beauties of nature inspire the soul with secret transports; its faculties, too, being at this time fresh and lively, are fit for those meditations which the solitude of a garden and tranquility of the morning naturally dispose us to. But I am afraid I interrupt your thoughts, for you seemed very intent on something.

HYLAS. It is true, I was, and shall be obliged to you if you will permit me to go on in the same vein; not that I would by any means deprive myself of your company, for my thoughts always flow more easily in conversation with a friend than when I am alone; but my request is that you would suffer me to impart my reflections to you.

PHILONOUS. With all my heart, it is what I should have requested myself if you had not prevented me.

HYLAS. I was considering the odd fate of those men who have in all ages, through an affectation of being distinguished from the vulgar, or some unaccountable turn of thought, pretended either to believe nothing at all or to believe the most extravagant things in the world. This, however, might be borne if their paradoxes and skepticism did not draw after them some consequences of general disadvantage to mankind. But the mischief lies here: that when men of less leisure see them who are supposed to have spent their whole time in the pursuits of knowledge professing an entire ignorance of all things or advancing such notions as are repugnant to plain and commonly received principles, they will be tempted to entertain suspicions concerning the most important truths, which they had hitherto held sacred and unquestionable.

PHILONOUS. I entirely agree with you as to the ill tendency of the affected doubts of some philosophers and fantastical conceits of others. I am even so far gone of late in this way of thinking that I have quitted several of the sublime notions I had got in their schools for vulgar opinions. And I give it you on my word, since this revolt from metaphysical notions to the plain dictates of nature and common sense, I find my understanding strangely enlightened, so that I can now easily comprehend a great many things which before were all mystery and riddle.

HYLAS. I am glad to find there was nothing in the accounts I heard of you.

PHILONOUS. Pray, what were those?

HYLAS. You were represented in last night's conversation as one who maintained the most extravagant opinion that ever entered into the mind of man, to wit, that there is no such thing as "material substance" in the world.

PHILONOUS. That there is no such thing as what philosophers call "material substance," I am seriously persuaded; but if I were made to see anything absurd or skeptical in this, I should then have the same reason to renounce this that I imagine I have now to reject the contrary opinion.

HYLAS. What! Can anything be more fantastical, more repugnant to common sense or a more manifest piece of skepticism than to believe there is no such thing as matter?

PHILONOUS. Softly, good Hylas. What if it should prove that you, who hold there is, are, by virtue of that opinion, a greater skeptic and maintain more paradoxes and repugnances to common sense than I who believe no such thing?

HYLAS. You may as soon persuade me the part is greater than the whole, as that, in order to avoid absurdity and skepticism, I should ever be obliged to give up my opinion in this point.

PHILONOUS. Well then, are you content to admit that opinion for true which, upon examination, shall appear most agreeable to common sense and remote from skepticism?

HYLAS. With all my heart. Since you are for raising disputes about the plainest things in nature, I am content for once to hear what you have to say. . . .

PHILONOUS. Shall we therefore examine which of us it is that denies the reality of sensible things or professes the greatest ignorance of them, since, if I take you rightly, he is to be esteemed the greatest skeptic?

HYLAS. That is what I desire.

PHILONOUS. What mean you by "sensible things?"

HYLAS. Those things which are perceived by the senses. Can you imagine that I mean anything else?

PHILONOUS. Pardon me, Hylas, if I am desirous clearly to apprehend your notions, since this may much shorten our inquiry. Suffer me then to ask you this further question. Are those things only perceived by the senses which are perceived immediately? Or may those things properly be said to be said to be "sensible" which are perceived mediately, or not without the intervention of others?

HYLAS. I do not sufficiently understand you.

PHILONOUS. In reading a book, what I immediately perceive are the letters, but mediately, or by means of these, are suggested to my mind the notions of God, virtue, truth, etc. Now, that the letters are truly sensible things, or perceived by sense, there is no doubt; but I would know whether you take the things suggested by them to be so too.

HYLAS. No, certainly; it were absurd to think God or virtue sensible things, though they may be signified and suggested to the mind by sensible marks with which they have an arbitrary connection.

PHILONOUS. It seems, then, that by "sensible things" you mean those only which can be perceived immediately by sense.

HYLAS. Right.

PHILONOUS. Does it not follow from this that, though I see one part of the sky red, and another blue, and that my reason does thence evidently conclude there must be some cause of that diversity of colors, yet that cause cannot be said to be a sensible thing or perceived by the sense of seeing?

HYLAS. It does.

PHILONOUS. In like manner, though I hear variety of sounds, yet I cannot be said to hear the causes of those sounds.

HYLAS. You cannot.

PHILONOUS. And when by my touch I perceive a thing to be hot and heavy, I cannot say, with any truth or propriety, that I feel the cause of its heat or weight.

HYLAS. To prevent any more questions of this kind, I tell you once for all that by "sensible things" I mean those only which are perceived by sense, and that in truth the senses perceive nothing which they do not perceive immediately, for they make no inferences. The deducing therefore of causes or occasions from effects and appearances, which alone are perceived by sense, entirely relates to reason.

PHILONOUS. This point then is agreed between us—that *sensible things are those only which are immediately perceived by sense.* You will further inform me whether we immediately perceive by sight anything besides light and colors and figures; or by hearing, anything but sounds; by the palate, anything beside tastes; by the smell, besides odors; or by the touch, more than tangible qualities.

HYLAS. We do not.

PHILONOUS. It seems, therefore, that if you take away all sensible qualities, there remains nothing sensible?

HYLAS. I grant it.

PHILONOUS. Sensible things therefore are nothing else but so many sensible qualities or combinations of sensible qualities? . . .

[The dialogue proceeds with Philonous showing, by a series of arguments, that the idea of a "material substance" is an idea without content, for we never perceive such a substance, nor do we have grounds, in what we do perceive, to infer its existence. Hylas twists and turns in his effort to escape the force of Philonous' analysis, but to no avail. However, as the discussion proceeds, he gradually becomes more careful and somewhat more sophisticated, and finally comes up with the argument that "ideas," which exist within the mind, are not, after all, the only objects that exist. There are also "real things or external objects." Accordingly, Philonous' demonstrations that "matter" is not an "idea" don't prove that "matter" doesn't exist. The dialogue proceeds.]

HYLAS. To speak the truth, Philonous, I think there are two kinds of objects: the one perceived immediately, which are likewise called "ideas"; the other are real things or external objects, perceived by the mediation of ideas which are their images and representations. Now I own ideas do not exist without the mind, but the latter sort of objects do. I am sorry I did not think of this distinction sooner; it would probably have cut short your discourse.

PHILONOUS. Are those external objects perceived by sense or by some other faculty?

HYLAS. They are perceived by sense.

PHILONOUS. How! is there anything perceived by sense which is not immediately perceived?

HYLAS. Yes, Philonous, in some sort there is. For example, when I look on a picture or statue of Julius Caesar, I may be said, after a manner, to perceive him (though not immediately) by my senses.

PHILONOUS. It seems then you will have our ideas, which alone are immediately perceived, to be pictures of external things: and that these also are perceived by sense inasmuch as they have a conformity or resemblance to our ideas?

HYLAS. That is my meaning.

PHILONOUS. And in the same way that Julius Caesar, in himself invisible, is nevertheless perceived by sight, real things, in themselves imperceptible, are perceived by sense.

HYLAS. In the very same.

PHILONOUS. Tell me, Hylas, when you behold the picture of Julius Caesar, do you see with your eyes any more than some colors and figures, with a certain symmetry and composition of the whole?

HYLAS. Nothing else.

PHILONOUS. And would not a man who had never known anything of Julius Caesar see as much?

HYLAS. He would.

PHILONOUS. Consequently, he has his sight and the use of it in as perfect a degree as you?

HYLAS. I agree with you.

PHILONOUS. Whence comes it then that your thoughts are directed to the Roman emperor, and his are not? This cannot proceed from the sensations or ideas of sense by you then perceived, since you acknowledge you have no advantage over him in that respect. It should seem therefore to proceed from reason and memory, should it not?

HYLAS. It should.

PHILONOUS. Consequently, it will not follow from that instance that anything is perceived by sense which is not immediately perceived. Though I grant we may, in one acceptation, be said to perceive sensible things mediately by sense—that is, when, from a frequently perceived connection, the immediate perception of ideas by one sense suggest to the mind others, perhaps belonging to another sense, which are wont to be connected with them. For instance, when I hear a coach drive along the streets, immediately

I perceive only the sound; but from the experience I have had that such a sound is connected with a coach, I am said to hear the coach. It is nevertheless evident that, in truth and strictness, nothing can be *heard* but *sound;* and the coach is not then properly perceived by sense, but suggested from experience. . . .

Whatever we perceive is perceived either immediately or mediately— by sense, or by reason and reflection. But, as you have excluded sense, pray show me what reason you have to believe their [material things] existence, or what *medium* you can possibly make use of to prove it, either to mine or your own understanding.

HYLAS. To deal ingenuously, Philonous, now I consider the point, I do not find I can give you any good reason for it. But this much seems pretty plain, that it is at least possible such things may really exist. And as long as there is no absurdity in supposing them, I am resolved to believe as I did, till you bring good reasons to the contrary.

PHILONOUS. What! is it come to this, that you only believe the existence of material objects, and that your belief is founded barely on the possibility of its being true? Then you will have me bring reasons against it, though another would think it reasonable the proof should lie on him who holds the affirmative. And, after all, this very point which you are now resolved to maintain, without any reason, is in effect what you have more than once during this discourse seen good reason to give up. But to pass over all this— if I understand you rightly, you say our ideas do not exist without the mind, but that they are copies, images, or representations of certain originals that do?

HYLAS. You take me right.

PHILONOUS. They are then like external things?

HYLE. They are.

PHILONOUS. Have those things a stable and permanent nature, independent of our senses, or are they in a perpetual change, upon our producing any motions in our bodies, suspending, exerting, or altering our faculties or organs of sense?

HYLAS. Real things, it is plain, have a fixed and real nature, which remains the same notwithstanding any change in our senses or in the posture and motion of our bodies; which indeed may affect the ideas in our minds, but it were absurd to think they had the same affect on things existing without the mind.

PHILONOUS. How then is it possible that things perpetually fleeting and variable as our ideas should be copies or images of anything fixed and constant? Or, in other words, since all sensible qualities, as size, figure, color, etc., that is, our ideas, are continually changing upon every alteration in the distance, medium, or instruments of sensation—how can any determinate material objects be properly represented or painted forth by several distinct things each of which is so different from and unlike the rest? Or, if you say it resembles some one only of our ideas, how shall we be able to distinguish the true copy from all the false ones?

HYLAS. I profess, Philonous, I am at a loss. I know not what to say to this.

PHILONOUS. But neither is this all. Which are material objects in themselves—perceptible or imperceptible?

HYLAS. Properly and immediately nothing can be perceived but ideas. All material things, therefore, are in themselves insensible and to be perceived only by their ideas.

PHILONOUS. Ideas then are sensible, and their archetypes or originals insensible?

HYLAS. Right.

PHILONOUS. But how can that which is sensible be like that which is insensible? Can a real thing, in itself *invisible*, be like a *color*, or a real thing which is not *audible* be like a *sound?* In a word, can anything be like a sensation or idea, but another sensation or idea?

HYLAS. I must own, I think not.

PHILONOUS. Is it possible there should be any doubt on the point? Do you not perfectly know your own ideas?

HYLAS. I know them perfectly, since what I do not perceive or know can be no part of my idea.

PHILONOUS. Consider, therefore, and examine them, and then tell me if there be anything in them which can exist without the mind, or if you can conceive anything like them existing without the mind?

HYLAS. Upon inquiry I find it is impossible for me to conceive or understand how anything but an idea can be like an idea. And it is most evident that *no idea can exist without the mind.*

PHILONOUS. You are, therefore, by your principles forced to deny the reality of sensible things, since you made it to consist in an absolute existence exterior to the mind. That is to say, you are a downright skeptic. So I have gained my point, which was to show your principles led to skepticism.

HYLAS. For the present I am, if not entirely convinced, at least silenced.

PHILONOUS. I would fain know what more you would require in order to reach a perfect conviction. Have you not had the liberty of explaining yourself all manner of ways? Were any little slips in discourse laid hold and insisted on? Or were you not allowed to retract or reinforce anything you had offered, as best served your purpose? Has not everything you could say been heard and examined with all the fairness imaginable? In a word, have you not in every point been convinced out of your own mouth? And, if you can at present discover any flaw in any of your former concessions, or think of any remaining subterfuge, any new distinction, color, or comment whatsoever, why do you not produce it?

HYLAS. A little patience, Philonous. I am at present so amazed to see myself ensnared, and as it were imprisoned in the labyrinths you have drawn me into, that on the sudden it cannot be expected I should find my way out. You must give me time to look about me and recollect myself.

PHILONOUS. Hark; is not this the college bell?

HYLAS. It rings for prayers.

PHILONOUS. We will go in then, if you please, and meet here again tomorrow morning. In the meantime, you may employ your thoughts on this morning's discourse and try if you can find any fallacy in it, or invent any new means to extricate yourself.

HYLAS. Agreed.

THE SECOND DIALOGUE

HYLAS. I beg your pardon, Philonous, for not meeting you sooner. All this morning my head was so filled with our late conversation that I had not leisure to think of the time of the day, or indeed of anything else.

PHILONOUS. I am glad you were so intent upon it, in hopes if there were any mistakes in your concessions, or fallacies in my reasonings from them, you will now discover them to me.

HYLAS. I assure you I have done nothing ever since I saw you but search after mistakes and fallacies, and, with that view, have minutely examined the whole series of yesterday's discourse; but all in vain, for the notions it led me into, upon review, appear still more clear and evident; and the more I consider them, the more irresistibly do they force my assent.

PHILONOUS. And is not this, think you, a sign that they are genuine, that they proceed from nature and are conformable to right reason? Truth and beauty are in this alike, that the strictest survey sets them both off to advantage, while the false luster of error and disguise cannot endure being reviewed or too nearly inspected.

HYLAS. I own there is a great deal in what you say. Nor can anyone be more entirely satisfied of the truth of those odd consequences so long as I have in view the reasonings that lead to them. But when these are out of my thoughts, there seems, on the other hand, something so satisfactory, so natural and intelligible in the modern way of explaining things that I profess I know not how to reject it.

PHILONOUS. I know not what you mean.

HYLAS. I mean the way of accounting for our sensations or ideas.

PHILONOUS. How is that?

HYLAS. It is supposed the soul makes her residence in some part of the brain, from which the nerves take their rise, and are thence extended to all parts of the body; and that outward objects, by the different impressions they make on the organs of sense, communicate certain vibrative motions to the nerves, and these, being filled with spirits, propagate them to the brain or seat of the soul, which, according to the various impressions or traces thereby made in the brain, is variously affected with ideas.

PHILONOUS. And call you this an explication of the manner whereby we are affected with ideas?

HYLAS. Why not, Philonous; have you anything to object against it?

PHILONOUS. I would first know whether I rightly understand your hypothesis. You make certain traces in the brain to be the causes or occasions of our ideas. Pray tell me whether by the "brain" you mean any sensible thing.

HYLAS. What else think you I could mean?

PHILONOUS. Sensible things are all immediately perceivable; and those things which are immediately perceivable are ideas, and these exist only in the mind. This much you have, if I mistake not, long since agreed to.

HYLAS. I do not deny it.

PHILONOUS. The brain therefore you speak of, being a sensible thing, exists only in the mind. Now I would fain know whether you think it reasonable to suppose that one idea or thing existing in the mind occasions all other ideas. And if you think so, pray how do you account for the origin of that primary idea or brain itself?

HYLAS. I do not explain the origin of our ideas by that brain which is perceivable to sense, this being itself only a combination of sensible ideas, but by another which I imagine.

PHILONOUS. But are not things imagined as truly *in the mind* as things perceived?

HYLAS. I must confess they are.

PHILONOUS. It comes, therefore, to the same thing; and you have been all this while accounting for ideas by certain motions or impressions of the brain, that is, by some alterations in an idea, whether sensible or imaginable it matters not.

HYLAS. I begin to suspect my hypothesis.

PHILONOUS. Besides spirits, all that we know or conceive are our own ideas. When, therefore, you say all ideas are occasioned by impressions in the brain, do you conceive this brain or no? If you do, then you talk of ideas imprinted in an idea causing that same idea, which is absurd. If you do not conceive it, you talk unintelligibly, instead of forming a reasonable hypothesis.

HYLAS. I now clearly see it was a mere dream. There is nothing in it.

PHILONOUS. You need not be much concerned at it, for, after all, this way of explaining things, as you called it, could never have satisfied any reasonable man. What connection is there between a motion in the nerves and the sensations of sound or color in the mind? Or how is it possible these should be the effect of that?

HYLAS. But I could never think it had so little in it as now it seem to have.

PHILONOUS. Well then, are you at length satisfied that no sensible things have a real existence, and that you are in truth an arrant *skeptic?*

HYLAS. It is too plain to be denied.

PHILONOUS. Look! are not the fields covered with a delightful verdure? Is there not something in the woods and groves, in the rivers and clear springs, that soothes, that delights, that transports the soul? At the prospect of the wide and deep ocean, or some huge mountain whose top is lost in the clouds, or of an old gloomy forest, are not our minds filled with a pleasing horror? Even in rocks and deserts is there not an agreeable wildness? How sincere a pleasure is it to behold the natural beauties of the earth! To preserve and renew our relish for them, is not the veil of night alternately drawn over her face, and does she not change her dress with the seasons? How aptly are the elements disposed! What variety and use in the meanest productions of nature! What delicacy, what beauty, what contrivance in animal and vegetable bodies! How exquisitely are all things suited, as well to their particular ends as to constitute apposite parts of the whole! And while they mutually aid and support, do they not also set off and illustrate each other? Raise now your thoughts from this ball of earth to all those glorious luminaries that adorn the high arch of heaven. The motion and situation of the planets, are they not admirable for use and order? Were those (miscalled "erratic") globes ever known to stray in their repeated journeys through the pathless void? Do they not measure areas round the sun ever proportioned to the times? So fixed, so immutable are the laws by which the unseen Author of nature actuates the universe. How vivid and radiant is the luster of the fixed stars! How magnificent and rich that negligent profusion with which they appear to be scattered throughout the whole azure vault! Yet, if you take the telescope, it brings into your sight a new host of stars that escape the naked eye. Here they seem contiguous and minute, but to a nearer view, immense orbs of light at various distances, far sunk in the abyss of space. Now you must call imagination to your aid. The feeble narrow sense cannot descry innumerable worlds revolving round the central fires, and in those worlds the energy of an all-perfect Mind displayed in endless forms. But neither sense nor imagination are big enough to comprehend the boundless extent with all its glittering furniture. Though the laboring mind exert and strain each power to its utmost reach, there still stands out ungrasped a surplusage immeasurable. Yet all the vast bodies that compose this mighty frame, how distant and remote soever, are by some secret mechanism, some divine art and force linked in a mutual dependence and intercourse with each other, even with this earth, which was almost slipt from my thoughts and lost in the crowd of worlds. Is not the whole system immense, beautiful, glorious beyond expression and beyond thought! What treatment, then, do those philosophers deserve who deprive these noble and delightful scenes of all reality? How should those principles be entertained that lead us to think all the visible beauty of the creation a false imaginary glare? To be plain, can you expect this skepticism of yours will not be thought extravagantly absurd by all men of sense?

HYLAS. Other men may think as they please, but for your part you have nothing to reproach me with. My comfort is you are as much a skeptic as I am.

PHILONOUS. There, Hylas, I must beg leave to differ from you.

HYLAS. What! have you all along agreed to the premises, and do you now deny the conclusion and leave me to maintain those paradoxes by myself which you led me into? This surely is not fair.

PHILONOUS. I deny that I agreed with you in those notions that led to skepticism. You indeed said the *reality* of sensible things consisted in an *absolute existence* out of the minds of spirits, or distinct from their being perceived. And, pursuant to this notion of reality, you are obliged to deny sensible things any real existence; that is, according to your own definition, you profess yourself a skeptic. But I neither said nor thought the reality of sensible things was to be defined after that manner. To me it is evident, for the reasons you allow of, that sensible things cannot exist otherwise than in a mind or spirit. Whence I conclude, not that they have no real existence, but that, seeing they depend not on my thought and have an existence distinct from being perceived by me, *there must be some other mind wherein they exist.* As sure, therefore, as the sensible world really exists, so sure is there an infinite omnipresent Spirit, who contains and supports it.

HYLAS. What! this is no more than I and all Christians hold; nay, and all others, too, who believe there is a God and that He knows and comprehends all things.

PHILONOUS. Aye, but here lies the difference. Men commonly believe that all things are known or perceived by God, because they believe the being of a God; whereas I, on the other side, immediately and necessarily conclude the being of a God, because all sensible things must be perceived by him.

HYLAS. But so long as we all believe the same thing, what matter is it how we come by that belief?

PHILONOUS. But neither do we agree in the same opinion. For philosophers, though they acknowledge all corporeal beings to be perceived by God, yet they attribute to them an absolute subsistence distinct from their being perceived by any mind whatever, which I do not. Besides, is there no difference between saying, *there is a God, therefore He perceives all things,* and saying, *sensible things do really exist; and if they really exist, they are necessarily perceived by an infinite mind: therefore there is an infinite mind, or God?* This furnishes you with a direct and immediate demonstration, from a most evident principle, of the *being of a God.* Divines and philosophers had proved beyond all controversy, from the beauty and usefulness of the several parts of the creation, that it was the workmanship of God. But that—setting aside all help of astronomy and natural philosophy, all contemplation of the contrivance, order and adjustment of things—an infinite mind should be necessarily inferred from the bare *existence* of the sensible world is an advantage peculiar to them only who have made this easy reflection, that the sensible world is that which we perceive by our several senses; and that nothing is perceived by the senses besides ideas; and that no idea or archetype of an idea can exist otherwise than in a mind. You may now, without any laborious search into the sciences, without any subtlety of reason or tedious length of discourse, oppose and baffle the most strenuous advocate for atheism, those miserable refuges, whether in an eternal succession of unthinking causes and effects or in a fortuitous concourse of atoms; those wild imaginations of Vanini, Hobbes, and Spinoza: in a word, the whole system of atheism, is it not entirely overthrown by this single reflection on the repugnancy included in supposing the whole or any part, even the most rude and shapeless, of the visible world to exist without a mind? Let any one of those abettors of impiety but look into his own thoughts, and there try if he can conceive how so much as a rock, a desert, a chaos, or confused jumble of atoms, how anything at all, either sensible or imaginable, can exist independent of a mind, and he need go no further to be convinced of his folly. Can anything be fairer than to put a dispute on such an issue and leave it to a man himself to see if he can conceive, even in thought, what he holds to be true in fact, and from a notional to allow it a real existence?

HYLAS. It cannot be denied there is something highly serviceable to religion in what you advance. . . .

THE THIRD DIALOGUE

PHILONOUS. Tell me, Hylas, what are the fruits of yesterday's meditation? Has it confirmed you in the same mind you were in at parting, or have you since see cause to change your opinion?

HYLAS. Truly my opinion is that all our opinions are alike vain and uncertain. What we approve today, we condemn tomorrow. We keep a stir about knowledge and spend our lives in the pursuit of it, when, alas! we know nothing all the while; nor do I think it possible for us ever to know anything in this life. Our faculties are too narrow and too few. Nature certainly never intended us for speculation.

PHILONOUS. What! say you we can know nothing, Hylas?

HYLAS. There is not that single thing in the world whereof we can know the real nature, or what it is in itself. . . .

PHILONOUS. You amaze me. Was ever anything more wild and extravagant than the notions you now maintain? And is it not evident you are led into all these extravagances by the belief of *material substance?* This makes you dream of those unknown natures in everything. It is this [which] occasions your distinguishing between the reality and sensible appearances of things. It is to this you are indebted for being ignorant of what everybody else knows perfectly well. Nor is this all: you are not only ignorant of the true nature of everything, but you know not whether any thing really exists or whether there are any true natures at all, forasmuch as you attribute to your material beings an absolute or external existence wherein you suppose their reality consists. And as you are forced in the end to acknowledge such an existence means either a direct repugnancy or nothing at all, it follows that you are obliged to pull down your own hypothesis of material substance and positively to deny the real existence of any part of the universe. And so you are plunged into the deepest and most deplorable skepticism that ever man was. Tell me, Hylas, is it not as I say?

HYLAS. I agree with you. "Material substance" was no more than a hypothesis, and a false and groundless one, too. I will no longer spend my breath in defense of it. But whatever hypothesis you advance or whatsoever scheme of things you introduce in its stead, I doubt not it will appear every whit as false; let me but be allowed to question you upon it. That is, suffer me to serve you in your own kind, and I warrant it shall conduct you through as many perplexities and contradictions to the very same state of skepticism that I myself am in at present.

PHILONOUS. I assure you, Hylas, I do not pretend to frame any hypothesis at all. I am of a vulgar cast, simple enough to believe my senses and leave things as I find them. To be plain, it is my opinion that the real things are those very things I see and feel, and perceive by my senses. These I know and, finding they answer all the necessities and purposes of life, have no reason to be solicitous about any other unknown beings. A piece of sensible bread, for instance, would stay my stomach better than ten thousand times as much of that insensible, unintelligible real bread you speak of. It is likewise my opinion that colors and other sensible qualities are on the objects. I cannot for my life help thinking that snow is white, and fire hot. You, indeed, who by "snow" and "fire" mean certain external, unperceived, unperceiving substances are in the right to deny whiteness or heat to be affections inherent in them. But I who understand by those words the things I see and feel am obliged to think like other folks. And as I am no skeptic with regard to the nature of things, so neither am I as to their existence. That a thing should be really perceived by my senses and at the same time not really exist is to me a plain contradiction, since I cannot prescind or abstract, even in thought, the existence of a sensible thing from its being perceived. Wood, stones, fire, water, flesh, iron, and the like things which I name and discourse of are things that I know. And I should not have known them but that I perceived them by my senses; and things perceived by the senses are immediately perceived; and things immediately perceived are ideas; and ideas cannot exist without the mind; their existence therefore consists in being perceived; when, therefore, they are actually perceived, there can be no doubt of their existence. Away then with all that skepticism, all those ridiculous philosophical doubts. What a jest is it for a philosopher to question the existence of sensible things till he has it proved to him from the veracity of God, or to pretend our knowledge in this point falls short of intuition or demonstration! I might as well doubt of my own being as of the being of those things I actually see and feel.

HYLAS. Not so fast, Philonous: You say you cannot conceive how sensible things should exist without the mind. Do you not?

PHILONOUS. I do.

HYLAS. Supposing you were annihilated, cannot you conceive it possible that things perceivable by sense may still exist?

PHILONOUS. I can, but then it must be in another mind. When I deny sensible things an existence out of the mind, I do not mean my mind in particular, but all minds. Now it is plain they have an existence exterior to my mind, since I find them by experience to be independent of it. There is therefore some other mind wherein they exist during the intervals between the times of my perceiving them, as likewise they did before my birth, and would do after my supposed annihilation. And as the same is true with regard to all other finite created spirits, it necessarily follows there is an *omnipresent eternal Mind* which knows and comprehends all things, and exhibits them to our view in such a manner and according to such rules as He Himself has ordained and are by us termed the "laws of nature."

HYLAS. Answer me, Philonous. Are all our ideas perfectly inert beings? Or have they any agency included in them?

PHILONOUS. They are altogether passive and inert.

HYLAS. And is not God an agent, a being purely active?

PHILONOUS. I acknowledge it.

HYLAS. No idea, therefore, can be like unto or represent the nature of God.

PHILONOUS. It cannot.

HYLAS. Since, therefore, you have no idea of the mind of God, how can you conceive it possible that things should exist in His mind? Or, if you can conceive the mind of God without having an idea of it, why may not I be allowed to conceive the existence of matter, nothwithstanding I have no idea of it?

PHILONOUS. As to your first question: I own I have properly no *idea* either of God or any other spirit; for these, being active, cannot be represented by things perfectly inert as our ideas are. I do nevertheless know that I, who am a spirit or thinking substance, exist as certainly as I know my ideas exist. Further, I know what I mean by the terms "I" and "myself"; and I know this immediately or intuitively, though I do not perceive it as I perceive a triangle, a color, or a sound. The mind, spirit, or soul is that indivisible unextended thing which thinks, acts, and perceives. I say "indivisible," because unextended; and "unextended," because extended, figured, movable things are ideas; and that which perceives ideas, which thinks and wills, is plainly itself no idea, nor like an idea. Ideas are things inactive and perceived. And spirits a sort of beings altogether different from them. I do not therefore say my soul is an idea, or like an idea. However, taking the word "idea" in a large sense, my soul may be said to furnish me with an idea, that is, an image or likeness of God, though indeed extremely inadequate. For all the notion I have of God is obtained by reflecting on my own soul, heightening its powers, and removing its imperfections. I have, therefore, though not an inactive idea, yet in *myself* some sort of an active thinking image of the Deity. And though I perceive Him not by sense, yet I have a notion of Him, or know Him by reflection and reasoning. My own mind and my own ideas I have an immediate knowledge of; and, by the help of these, do mediately apprehend the possibility of the existence of other spirits and ideas. Further, from my own being, and from the dependency I find in myself and my ideas, I do, by an act of reason, necessarily infer the existence of a God and of all created things in the mind of God. So much for your first question. For the second: I suppose by this time you can answer it yourself. For you neither perceive matter objectively, as you do an inactive being or idea, nor know it, as you do yourself by a reflex act; neither do you mediately apprehend it by similitude of the one or the other, nor yet collect it by reasoning from that which you know immediately. All which makes the case of *matter* widely different from that of the *Deity*. . . .

HYLAS. And now I warrant you think you have made the point very clear, little suspecting that what you advance leads directly to a contradiction. Is it not an absurdity to imagine any imperfection in God?

PHILONOUS. Without a doubt.

HYLAS. To suffer pain is an imperfection?

PHILONOUS. It is.

HYLAS. Are we not sometimes affected with pain and uneasiness by some other being?

PHILONOUS. We are.

HYLAS. And have you not said that being is a spirit, and is not that spirit God?

PHILONOUS. I grant it.

HYLAS. But you have asserted that whatever ideas we perceive from without are in the mind which affects us. The ideas, therefore, of pain and uneasiness are in God, or, in other words, God suffers pain; that is to say, there is an imperfection in the divine nature, which, you acknowledge, was absurd. So you are caught in a plain contradiction.

PHILONOUS. That God knows or understands all things, and that He knows, among other things, what pain is, even every sort of painful sensation, and what it is for His creatures to suffer pain, I make no question. But that God, though He knows and sometimes causes painful sensations in us, can Himself suffer pain I positively deny. We, who are limited and dependent spirits, are liable to impressions of sense, the effects of an external agent, which, being produced against our wills, are sometimes painful and uneasy. But God, whom no external being can affect, who perceives nothing by sense as we do, whose will is absolute and independent, causing all things, and liable to be thwarted or resisted by nothing, it is evident such a Being as this can suffer nothing, nor be affected with any painful sensation or, indeed, any sensation at all. We are chained to a body; that is to say, our perceptions are connected with corporeal motions. By the law of our nature we are affected upon every alteration in the nervous parts of our sensible body; which sensible body, rightly considered, is nothing but a complexion of such qualities or ideas as have no existence distinct from being perceived by a mind; so that this connection of sensations with corporeal motions means no more than a correspondence in the order of nature between two sets of ideas, or things immediately perceivable. But God is a pure spirit, disengaged from all such sympathy or natural ties. No corporeal motions are attended with the sensations of pain or pleasure in His mind. To know everything knowable is certainly a perfection, but to endure or suffer or feel anything by sense is an imperfection. The former, I say, agrees to God, but not the latter. God knows or has ideas, but His ideas are not conveyed to Him by sense, as ours are. Your not distinguishing where there is so manifest a difference makes you fancy you see an absurdity where there is none. . . .

HYLAS. After all, can it be supposed God would deceive all mankind? Do you imagine He would have induced the whole world to believe the being of matter if there was no such thing?

PHILONOUS. That every epidemical opinion arising from prejudice, or passion, or thoughtlessness may be imputed to God, as the Author of it, I believe you will not affirm. Whatsoever opinion we father on Him, it must be either because He has discovered it to us by supernatural revelation or because it is so evident to our natural faculties, which were framed and given us by God, that it is impossible we should withhold our assent from it. But where is the revelation? Or where is the evidence that extorts the belief of matter? Nay, how does it appear that matter, taken for something distinct from what we perceive by our senses, is thought to exist by all mankind, or, indeed, by any except a few philosophers who do not know what they would be at? Your question supposes these points are clear; and, when you have cleared them, I shall think myself obliged to give you another answer. In the meantime let it suffice that I tell you I do not suppose God has deceived mankind at all.

HYLAS. But the novelty, Philonous, the novelty! There lies the danger. New notions should always be discountenanced; they unsettle men's minds, and nobody knows where they will end.

PHILONOUS. Why the rejecting a notion that has no foundation, either in sense or in reason or in Divine authority, should be thought to unsettle the belief of such opinions as are grounded on all or any of these, I cannot imagine. That innovations in government and religion are dangerous and ought to be discountenanced, I freely own. But is there the like reason why they should be discouraged in philosophy? The making anything known which was unknown before is an innovation in knowledge; and if all such innovations had been forbidden, men would not have made a notable progress in the arts and sciences. But it is none of my business to plead for novelties and paradoxes. That the qualities we perceive are not on the objects, that we must not believe our senses, that we know nothing of the real nature of things and can never be assured even of their existence, that real colors and sounds are nothing but certain unknown figures and motions, that motions are in themselves neither swift nor slow, that there are in bodies absolute extensions without any particular magnitude or figure, that a thing stupid, thoughtless, and inactive operates on a spirit, that the least particle of a body contains innumerable extended parts—these are the novelties, these are the strange notions which shock the genuine un-corrupted judgment of all mankind, and, being once admitted, embarrass the mind with endless doubts and difficulties. And it is against these and the like innovations I endeavor to vindicate Common Sense. It is true, in doing this I may, perhaps, be obliged to use some ambages and ways of speech not common. But if my notions are once thoroughly understood, that which is most singular in them will, in effect, be found to amount to no more than this—that it is absolutely impossible and a plain contradiction to suppose any unthinking being should exist without being perceived by a mind. And if this notion be singular, it is a shame it should be so at this time of day and in a Christian country. . . .

HYLAS. I must needs own, Philonous, nothing seems to have kept me from agreeing with you more than . . . *mistaking the question*. In denying matter, at first glimpse I am tempted to imagine you deny the things we see and feel, but, upon reflection, find there is no ground for it. What think you, therefore, of retaining the name "matter" and applying it to *sensible things?* This may be done without any change in your sentiments; and believe me, it would be a means of reconciling them to some persons who may be more shocked at an innovation in words than in opinion.

PHILONOUS. With all my heart; retain the word "matter" and apply it to the objects of sense, if you please, provided you do not attribute to them any subsistence distinct from their being perceived. I shall never quarrel with you for an expression. "Matter" or "material substance" are terms introduced by philosophers, and, as used by them, imply a sort of independence, or a subsistence distinct from being perceived by a mind; but are never used by common people, or, if ever, it is to signify the immediate objects of sense. One would think, therefore, so long as the names of all particular things with the terms "sensible," "substance," "body," "stuff," and like, are retained, the word "matter" should be never missed in common talk. And in philosophical discourses it seems the best way to leave it quite out, since there is not, perhaps, any one thing that has more favored and strengthened the depraved bent of the mind toward atheism than the use of that general confused term.

HYLAS. Well, but, Philonous, since I am content to give up the notion of an unthinking substance exterior to the mind, I think you ought not to deny me the privilege of using the word "matter" as I please, and annexing it to a collection of sensible qualities subsisting only in the mind. I freely own there is no other substance, in a strict sense, than spirit. But I have been so long accustomed to the term "matter" that I know not how to part with it. To say there is no matter in the world is still shocking to me. Whereas to say there is no matter if by that term be meant an unthinking substance existing without the mind, but if by matter is meant some sensible thing whose existence consists in being perceived, then there is matter—this distinction gives it quite another turn; and men will come into your notions with small difficulty when they are proposed in that manner. For, after all, the controversy about matter in the strict acceptation of it lies altogether between you and the philosophers, whose principles, I acknowledge, are not near so natural or so agreeable to the common sense of mankind and Holy Scripture as yours. There is nothing we either desire or shun but as it makes, or is apprehended to make, some part of our happiness or misery. But what has happiness or misery, joy or grief, pleasure or pain to do with absolute existence or with unknown entities abstracted from all relation to us? It is evident things regard us only as they are pleasing or displeasing; and they can please or displease only so far forth as they are perceived. Further, therefore, we are not concerned; and thus far you leave things as you found them. Yet still there is something new in this doctrine. It is plain, I do not now think with the philosophers, nor yet altogether with the vulgar. I would know how the case stands in that respect, precisely you have added to or altered in my former notions.

PHILONOUS. I do not pretend to be a setter-up of new notions. My endeavors tend only to unite and place in a clearer light that truth which was before shared between the vulgar and the philosophers, the former being of opinion that *those things they immediately perceive are the real things*, and the latter, that *the things immediately perceived are ideas which exist only in the mind*. Which two notions put together do, in effect, constitute the substance of what I advance.

HYLAS. I have been a long time distrusting my senses; methought I saw things by a dim light and through false glasses. Now the glasses are removed and a new light breaks in upon my understanding. I am clearly convinced that I see things in their native forms and am no longer in pain about their *unknown natures* or *absolute existence*. This is the state I find myself in at present, though, indeed, the course that brought me to it I do not yet thoroughly comprehend. You set out upon the same principles that Academics, Cartesians, and the like sects usually do, and for a long time it looked as if you were advancing their philosophical skepticism; but, in the end, your conclusions are directly opposite to theirs.

PHILONOUS. You see, Hylas, the water of yonder fountain, how it is forced upwards, in a round column, to a certain height, at which it breaks and falls back into the basin from whence it rose, its ascent as well as descent proceeding from the same uniform law or principle of gravitation. Just so, the same principles which, at first view, lead to skepticism, pursued to a certain point, bring men back to common sense.

George Santayana

There are philosophers, like Berkeley, who think the universe unintelligible unless God exists. There are others, like Diderot, who regard the existence of God as a hypothesis that men can live without. But there is a third position: this is the view that such arguments about the truth or practical utility of religion miss the point, that the function of religion is to fill out the world by adding to it an imaginative dimension. Though literally false, religion is to be considered true in the way that all great myths are true—metaphorically or dramatically; it is an expression, in story, prayer, and ritual, of basic human experiences and aspirations. This is the position of George Santayana. "Religions," he writes, "are the great fairy tales of the conscience." He means these words as praise, not condemnation.

Santayana was born in Spain in 1863, of Spanish parents, but after the age of nine was brought up in Boston, by his mother. He went to Harvard, and subsequently taught there for more than twenty years. But his attitude toward Harvard, and toward Boston and the United States, was rather like his attitude toward religion: he appreciated them and could look on them with sympathy, but he could not enroll as a believer in the cause. And he found less to satisfy his imagination in America than in Europe. What he called "the Protestant combination of earnestness and waywardness," of excessive moralism and flights of introspective fancy, repelled him, as did American society's commercialism and its busybody pressure on the individual. Accordingly, Santayana left America while he was still in his forties, and spent the remaining years of his life in Europe.

Santayana, however, continued to write principally for an American audience. Though Spanish was his first language, he is one of the great masters of English prose. As he said of himself, "In renouncing everything else for the sake of English letters I might be said to have been guilty, quite unintentionally, of a little stratagem, as if I had set out to say plausibly in English as many un-English things as possible." [1] Santayana's death was like his life in its paradoxes. He died in 1952 in Rome, in an Anglican nursing home, a man who identified himself as an American writer though he held a Spanish passport, and who was willing to be called a Catholic although he refused the vows of the faith.

1. "A General Confession," in Paul Arthur Schilpp, ed., *The Philosophy of George Santayana* (Evanston and Chicago, Northwestern University, 1940), p. 7.

Santayana gave a brief description of his approach to religion in an autobiographical statement he wrote in 1930:

"My mother, like her father before her, was a Deist: she was sure there was a God, for who else could have made the world? But God was too great to take special thought for man: sacrifices, prayers, churches, and tales of immortality were invented by rascally priests in order to dominate the foolish. My father, except for the Deism, was emphatically of the same opinion. Thus, although I learned my prayers and catechism by rote, as was then inevitable in Spain, I knew that my parents regarded all religion as a work of human imagination: and I agreed, and still agree, with them there. But this carried an implication in their minds against which every instinct in me rebelled, namely that the works of human imagination are bad. No, said I to myself even as a boy: they are good, they alone are good; and the rest—the whole real world—is ashes in the mouth.[2]

The following selection is Chapter VI of Santayana's *Reason in Religion*, published in 1905, one of the five volumes comprising *The Life of Reason*. *The Life of Reason* was described by the late Professor Morris Raphael Cohen, a critic not overly prone to enthusiasm, as the finest work in philosophy ever produced in America.

The Christian Epic

Revolutions are ambiguous things. Their success is generally proportionate to their power of adaptation and to the reabsorption within them of what they rebelled against. A thousand reforms have left the world as corrupt as ever, for each successful reform has founded a new institution, and this institution has bred its new and congenial abuses. What is capable of truly purifying the world is not the mere agitation of its elements, but their organisation into a natural body that shall exude what redounds and absorb or generate what is lacking to the perfect expression of its soul.

Whence fetch this seminal force and creative ideal? It must evidently lie already in the matter it is to organise; otherwise it would have no affinity to that matter, no power over it, and no ideality or value in respect to the existences whose standard and goal it was to be. There can be no goods antecedent to the natures they benefit, no ideals prior to the wills they define. A revolution must find its strength and legitimacy not in the reformer's conscience and dream but in the temper of that society which he would transform; for no transformation is either permanent or desirable which does not forward the spontaneous life of the world, advancing those issues toward which it is already inwardly directed. How should a gospel bring glad tidings, save by announcing what was from the beginning native to the heart?

No judgment could well be shallower, therefore, than that which

2. *Ibid.*

condemns a great religion for not being faithful to that local and partial impulse which may first have launched it into the world. A great religion has something better to consider: the conscience and imagination of those it ministers to. The prophet who announced it first was a prophet only because he had a keener sense and clearer premonition than other men of their common necessities; and he loses his function and is a prophet no longer when the public need begins to outrun his intuitions. Could Hebraism spread over the Roman Empire and take the name of Christianity without adding anything to its native inspiration? Is it to be lamented that we are not all Jews? Yet what makes the difference is not the teaching of Jesus—which is pure Hebraism reduced to its spiritual essence—but the worship of Christ—something perfectly Greek. Christianity would have remained a Jewish sect had it not been made at once speculative, universal, and ideal by the infusion of Greek thought, and at the same time plastic and devotional by the adoption of pagan habits. The incarnation of God in man, and the divinisation of man in God are pagan conceptions, expressions of pagan religious sentiment and philosophy. Yet what would Christianity be without them? It would have lost not only its theology, which might be spared, but its spiritual aspiration, its artistic affinities, and the secret of its metaphysical charity and joy. It would have remained unconscious, as the Gospel is, that the hand or the mind of man can ever construct anything. Among the Jews there were no liberal interests for the ideal to express. They had only elementary human experience—the perpetual Oriental round of piety and servitude in the bosom of a scorched, exhausted country. A disillusioned eye, surveying such a world, could find nothing there to detain it; religion, when wholly spiritual, could do nothing but succour the afflicted, understand and forgive the sinful, and pass through the sad pageant of life unspotted and resigned. Its pity for human ills would go hand in hand with a mystic plebeian insensibility to natural excellence. It would breathe what Tacitus, thinking of the liberal life, could call *odium generis humani;* it would be inimical to human genius.

There were, we may say, two things in Apostolic teaching which rendered it capable of converting the world. One was the later Jewish morality and mysticism, beautifully expressed in Christ's parables and maxims, and illustrated by his miracles, those cures and absolutions which he was ready to dispense, whatever their sins, to such as called upon his name. This democratic and untrammelled charity could powerfully appeal to an age disenchanted with the world, and especially to those lower classes which pagan polity had covered with scorn and condemned to hopeless misery. The other point of contact which early Christianity had with the public need was the theme it offered to contemplation, the philosophy of history which it introduced into the western world, and the delicious unfathomable mysteries into which it launched the fancy. Here, too, the figure of Christ was the centre for all eyes. Its lowliness, its simplicity, its humanity were indeed, for a while, obstacles to its acceptance; they did not really lend themselves to the metaphysical interpretation which was required. Yet even Greek fable was not without its Apollo tending flocks and its Demeter mourning for her lost child and serving in meek disguise the child of another. Feeling was ripe for a mythology loaded with pathos. The humble life, the homilies, the sufferings of Jesus could be felt in all their incomparable beauty all the more when the tenderness and tragedy of them, otherwise too poignant, were relieved by the story of his miraculous birth, his glorious resurrection, and his restored divinity.

The gospel, thus grown acceptable to the pagan mind, was, however, but a grain of mustard-seed destined to branch and flower in its new soil in a miraculous manner. Not only was the Greek and Roman to refresh himself under its shade, but birds of other climates were to build their nests, at least for a season, in its branches. Hebraism, when thus expanded and paganised, showed many new characteristics native to the minds which had now adopted and transformed it. The Jews, for instance, like other Orientals, had a figurative way of speaking and thinking; their poetry and religion were full of the most violent metaphors. Now to the classic mind violent and improper metaphors were abhorrent. Uniting, as it did, clear reason with lively fancy, it could not conceive one thing to *be* another, nor relish the figure of speech that so described it, hoping by that unthinkable phrase to suggest its affinities. But the classic mind could well conceive transformation, of which indeed nature is full; and in Greek fables anything might change its form, become something else, and display its plasticity, not by imperfectly being many things at once, but by being the perfection of many things in succession. While metaphor was thus unintelligible and confusing to the Greek, metamorphosis was perfectly familiar to him. Wherever Hebrew tradition, accordingly, used violent metaphors, puzzling to the Greek Christian, he rationalised them by imagining a metamorphosis instead; thus, for instance, the metaphors of the Last Supper, so harmless and vaguely satisfying to an Oriental audience, became the doctrine of transubstantiation —a doctrine where images are indeed lacking to illustrate the concepts, but where the concepts themselves are not confused. For that bread should *become* flesh and wine blood is not impossible, seeing that the change occurs daily in digestion; what the assertion in this case contradicts is merely the evidence of sense.

Thus at many a turn in Christian tradition a metaphysical mystery takes the place of a poetic figure; the former now expressing by a little miraculous drama the emotion which the latter expressed by a tentative phrase. And the emotion is thereby immensely clarified and strengthened; it is, in fact, for the first time really expressed. For the idea that Christ stands upon the altar and mingles still with our human flesh is an explicit assertion that his influence and love are perpetual; whereas the original parable revealed at most the wish and aspiration, contrary to fact, that they might have been so.

By substituting embodiment for allegory, the Greek mind thus achieved something very congenial to its habits: it imagined the full and adequate expression, not in words but in existences, of the emotion to be conveyed. The Eucharist is to the Last Supper what a centaur is to a horseman or a tragedy to a song. Similarly a Dantesque conception of hell and paradise embodies in living detail the innocent apologue in the gospel about a separation of the sheep from the goats. The result is a chimerical metaphysics, containing much which, in reference to existing facts, is absurd; but that metaphysics, when taken for what it truly is, a new mythology, utters the subtler secrets of the new religion not less ingeniously and poetically than pagan mythology reflected the daily shifts in nature and in human life.

Metaphysics became not only a substitute for allegory but at the same time a background for history. Neo-Platonism had enlarged, in a way suited to the speculative demands of the time, the cosmos conceived by Greek science. In an intelligible region, unknown to cosmography and peopled at first by the Platonic ideas and afterward by Aristotle's solitary God, there was now the Absolute One, too exalted for any predicates, but manifesting its essence in the first place in a supreme Intelligence, the second hypostasis of a Trinity; and in the second place in the Soul of the World, the third hypostasis, already relative to natural existence. Now the Platonists conceived these entities to be permanent and immutable; the physical world itself had a meaning and an expressive value, like a statue; but no significant history. When the Jewish notion of creation and divine government of the world presented itself to the Greeks, they hastened to assimilate it to their familiar notions of imitation, expression, finality, and significance. And when the Christian spoke of Christ as the Son of God, who now sat at his right hand in the heavens, their Platonic disciples immediately thought of the Nous or Logos, the divine Intelligence, incarnate as they had always believed in the whole world, and yet truly the substance and essence of divinity. To say that this incarnation had taken place pre-eminently, or even exclusively, in Christ was not an impossible concession to make to pious enthusiasm, at least if the philosophy involved in the old conception could be retained and embodied in the new orthodoxy. Sacred history could thus be interpreted as a temporal execution of eternal decrees, and the plan of salvation as an ideal necessity. Cosmic scope and metaphysical meaning were given to Hebrew tenets, so unspeculative in their original intention, and it became possible even for a Platonic philosopher to declare himself a Christian.

The eclectic Christian philosophy thus engendered constitutes one of the most complete, elaborate, and impressive products of the human mind. The ruins of more than one civilisation and of more than one philosophy were ransacked to furnish materials for this heavenly Byzantium. It was a myth circumstantial and sober enough in tone to pass for an account of facts, and yet loaded with enough miracle, poetry, and submerged wisdom to take the place of a moral philosophy and present what seemed at the time an adequate ideal to the heart. Many a mortal, in all subsequent ages, perplexed and abandoned in this ungovernable world, has set sail resolutely for that enchanted island and found there a semblance of happiness, its narrow limits give so much room for the soul and its penitential soil breeds so many consolations. True, the brief time and narrow argument into which Christian imagination squeezes the world must seem to a speculative pantheist childish and poor, involving, as it does, a fatuous perversion of nature and history and a ridiculous emphasis laid on local events and partial interests. Yet just this violent reduction of things to a human stature, this half-innocent, half-arrogant assumption that what is important for a man must control the whole universe, is what made Christian philosophy originally appealing and what still arouses, in certain quarters, enthusiastic belief in its beneficence and finality.

Nor should we wonder at this enduring illusion. Man is still in his childhood; for he cannot respect an ideal which is not imposed on him against his will, nor can he find satisfaction in a good created by his own action. He is afraid of a universe that leaves him alone. Freedom appals him; he can apprehend in it nothing but tedium and desolation, so immature is he and so barren does he think himself to be. He has to imagine what the angels would say, so that his own good impulses (which create those angels) may gain in authority, and none of the dangers that surround his poor life make the least impression upon him until he hears that there are hobgoblins hiding in the wood. His moral life, to take shape at all, must appear to him in fantastic symbols. The history of these symbols is therefore the history of his soul.

There was in the beginning, so runs the Christian story, a great celestial King, wise and good, surrounded by a court of winged musicians and messengers. He had existed from all eternity, but had always intended, when the right moment should come, to create temporal beings, imperfect copies of himself in various degrees. These, of which man was the chief, began their career in the year 4004 B.C., and they would live on an indefinite time, possibly, that chronological symmetry might not be violated, until A.D. 4004. The opening and close of this drama were marked by two magnificent tableaux. In the first, in obedience to the word of God, sun, moon, and stars, and earth with all her plants and animals, assumed their appropriate places, and nature sprang into being with all her laws. The first man was made out of clay, by a special act of God, and the first woman was fashioned from one of his ribs, extracted while he lay in a deep sleep. They were placed in an orchard where they often could see God, its owner, walking in the cool of the evening. He suffered them to range at will and eat of all the fruits he had planted save that of one tree only. But they, incited by a devil, transgressed this single prohibition, and were banished from that paradise with a curse upon their head, the man to live by the sweat of his brow and the woman to bear children in labour. These children possessed from the moment of conception the inordinate natures which their parents had acquired. They were born to sin and to find disorder and death everywhere within and without them.

At the same time God, lest the work of his hands should wholly perish, promised to redeem in his good season some of Adam's children and restore them to a natural life. This redemption was to come ultimately through a descendant of Eve, whose foot should bruise the head of the serpent. But it was to be prefigured by many partial and special redemptions. Thus, Noah was to be saved from the deluge, Lot from Sodom, Isaac from the sacrifice, Moses from Egypt, the captive Jews from Babylon, and all faithful souls from heathen forgetfulness and idolatry. For a certain tribe had been set apart from the beginning to keep alive the memory of God's judgments and promises, while the rest of mankind, abandoned to its natural depravity, sank deeper and deeper into crimes and vanities. The deluge that came to punish these evils did not avail to cure them. "The world was renewed [1] and the earth rose again above the bosom of the waters, but in this renovation there remained eternally some trace of divine vengeance. Until the deluge all nature had been exceedingly hardy and vigorous, but by that vast flood of water which God had spread out over the earth, and by its long abiding there, all saps were diluted; the air, charged with too dense and heavy a moisture, bred ranker principles of corruption. The early constitution of the universe was weakened, and human life, from stretching as it had formerly done to near a thousand years, grew gradually briefer. Herbs and roots lost their primitive potency and stronger food had to be furnished to man by the flesh of other animals. . . . Death gained upon life and men felt themselves overtaken by a speedier chastisement. As day by day they sank deeper in their wickedness, it was but right they should daily, as it were, stick faster in their woe. The very change in nourishment made manifest their decline and degradation, since as they became feebler they became also more voracious and blood-thirsty."

Henceforth there were two spirits, two parties, or, as Saint Augustine called them, two cities in the world. The City of Satan, whatever its artifices in art, war, or philosophy, was essentially corrupt and impious. Its joy was but a comic mask and its beauty the whitening of a sepulchre. It stood condemned before God and before man's better conscience by its vanity, cruelty, and secret misery, by its ignorance of all that it truly behoved a man to know who was destined to immortality. Lost, as it seemed, within this Babylon, or visible only in its obscure and forgotten purlieus, lived on at the same time the City of God, the society of all the souls God predestined to salvation; a city which, however humble and inconspicuous it might seem on earth, counted its myriad transfigured citizens in heaven, and had

1. Bossuet: Discours sur l'histoire universelle, Part II, Chap. I.—*Author.*

its destinies, like its foundations, in eternity. To this City of God belonged, in the first place, the patriarchs and the prophets who, throughout their plaintive and ardent lives, were faithful to what echoes still remained of a primeval revelation, and waited patiently for the greater revelation to come. To the same city belonged the magi who followed a star till it halted over the stable in Bethlehem; Simeon, who divined the present salvation of Israel; John the Baptist, who bore witness to the same and made straight its path; and Peter, to whom not flesh and blood, but the spirit of the Father in heaven, revealed the Lord's divinity. For salvation had indeed come with the fulness of time, not, as the carnal Jews had imagined it, in the form of an earthly restoration, but through the incarnation of the Son of God in the Virgin Mary, his death upon a cross, his descent into hell, and his resurrection at the third day according to the Scriptures. To the same city belonged finally all those who believing in the reality and efficacy of Christ's mission, relied on his merits and followed his commandment of unearthly love.

All history was henceforth essentially nothing but the conflict between these two cities; two moralities, one natural, the other supernatural; two philosophies, one rational, the other revealed; two beauties, one corporeal, the other spiritual; two glories, one temporal, the other eternal; two institutions, one the world, the other the Church. These, whatever their monentary alliances or compromises, were radically opposed and fundamentally alien to one another. Their conflict was to fill the ages until, when wheat and tares had long flourished together and exhausted between them the earth for whose substance they struggled, the harvest should come; the terrible day of reckoning when those who had believed the things of religion to be imaginary would behold with dismay the Lord visibly coming down through the clouds of heaven, the angels blowing their alarming trumpets, all generations of the dead rising from their graves, and judgment without appeal passed on every man, to the edification of the universal company and his own unspeakable joy or confusion. Whereupon the blessed would enter eternal bliss with God their master and the wicked everlasting torments with the devil whom they served.

The drama of history was thus to close upon a second tableau: long-robed and beatified cohorts passing above, amid various psalmodies, into an infinite luminous space, while below the damned, howling, writhing, and half transformed into loathsome beasts, should be engulfed in a fiery furnace. The two cities, always opposite in essence, should thus be finally divided in existence, each bearing its natural fruits and manifesting its true nature.

Let the reader fill out this outline for himself with its thousand details; let him remember the endless mysteries, arguments, martyrdoms, consecrations that carried out the sense and made vital the beauty of the whole. Let him pause before the phenomenon; he can still afford, if he wishes to understand history or the human mind, to let the apparition float by unchallenged without delivering up its secret. What shall we say of this Christian dream?

Those who are still troubled by the fact that this dream is by many taken for a reality, and who are consequently obliged to defend themselves against it, as against some dangerous error in science or in philosophy, may be allowed to marshal arguments in its disproof. Such, however, is not my intention. Do we marshal arguments against the miraculous birth of Buddha, or the story of Cronos devouring his children? We seek rather to honour the piety and to understand the poetry embodied in those fables. If it be said that those fables are believed by no one, I reply that those fables are or have been believed just as unhesitatingly as the Christian theology, and by men no less reasonable or learned than the unhappy apologist of our own ancestral creeds. Matters of religion should never be matters of controversy. We neither argue with a lover about his taste, nor condemn him, if we are just, for knowing so human a passion. That he harbours it is no indication of a want of sanity on his part in other matters. But while we acquiesce in his experience, and are glad he has it, we need no arguments to dissuade us from sharing it. Each man may have his own loves, but the object in each case is different. And so it is, or should be, in religion. Before the rise of those strange and fraudulent Hebraic pretensions there was no question among men about the national, personal, and poetic character of religious allegiance. It could never have been a duty to adopt a religion not one's own any more than a language, a coinage, or a costume not current in one's own country. The idea that religion contains a literal, not a symbolic, representation of truth and life is simply an impossible idea. Whoever entertains it has not come within the region of profitable philosophising on that subject. His science is not wide enough to cover all existence. He has not discovered that there can be no moral allegiance except to the ideal. His certitude and his arguments are no more pertinent to the religious question than would be the insults, blows, and murders to which, if he could, he would appeal in the next instance. Philosophy may describe unreason, as it may describe force; it cannot hope to refute them.

Afterword

The philosophers we have just read are all masters of exposition, and scarcely need an interpreter to say for them what they say so well for themselves. It is often interesting and useful, however, to test one's own reaction to what one has read by setting it against the reaction of someone else. The purpose of this afterword, and of those that follow the sections to come, is to give the reader this opportunity.

A little philosophy, Francis Bacon once said, takes a man away from God; more philosophy leads him back. Perhaps so. But a less debatable proposition is that a little philosophy, addressed to the problems of religion, generates still more philosophy, addressed to questions that go beyond religion. The pages we have been reading exemplify this point. What, for example, lifts Diderot's dialogue above the level of just another tract against religion? It is the absence of the missionary zeal, the angry militance, which turns so many atheist and agnostic tracts into mirror images of the evils in religion that they denounce. For all its urbanity and lightheartedness—indeed, by means of its urbanity and lightheartedness, its spirit of play—the dialogue deals with a serious subject seriously. It explores alternatives, it entertains arguments, just to see where they lead. And so it raises questions which go beyond religion and are central to philosophy in general.

For Diderot, religious belief is a gamble. Speaking for himself, he doesn't think it's a very good one. Still, if a man wants to bet on religion, and is capable of living decently and allowing his fellows to hold their own different views, that is all that Diderot cares about as a practical matter. His purpose is not so much to refute religion as to deny that the world will collapse if people are permitted to think about religion as they please. The sauciness of the dialogue, its sallies and flirtatious byplay, aren't mere ornaments to his argument. They are intrinsic to it. They show that people can talk about religion without putting on long faces, and that they can disagree about it and the heavens won't fall.

And yet Diderot's critique of religion is devastating. It contains most of the central points in the atheist and agnostic indictments of religion. Intellectually, religion is presented as a standing contradiction. It asks us to worship a God who has made life on earth a misery for most human beings, and it portrays this God as a judge who cares more about our unquestioning acceptance of a creed than about the way we actually behave. And morally, religion is an outrage against human nature. It imposes the killjoy ideas of a few melancholiacs on the whole human species. It fills men with unreasoning fears, so that even the act of dying is poisoned by unnecessary anxieties. And it corrupts men's consciences by teaching that morality rests on a calculation of rewards and punishments.

Yet it isn't these straightforward criticisms of religion that constitute the most telling element in Diderot's position. It is his very willingness to be tolerant, along with the argument which underlies that willingness. For his argument cuts out the underpinnings from a common rejoinder to the kind of position he takes. Let it be admitted, this rejoinder goes, that there is some truth in the freethinker's idea that men can live morally even though they have no belief in the supernatural. No doubt some exceptional people have lived decent lives without such a belief. But the case for the mass of men is different. They will conclude that anything is permissible if there is no God. Diderot's response cuts to the heart of this contention. If men draw such a conclusion, he suggests, the blame lies with the teachings of religion. For it is religion that has taught men to assume that only God's command can make moral behavior obligatory; it is religion that has turned men aside from the spontaneous feelings for others which, by themselves, can spark moral conduct and which are indispensable to it. And so, if men become immoral when they renounce religion, it is religion that must bear the responsibility. It purchases adherence to its doctrines by spreading the self-fulfilling prophecy that if religion goes, morality goes. But men need not believe this, and should in fact be educated to think differently. The love of man, the desire to improve the human lot, is a quite sufficient warrant and motive for moral behavior. So far as men's actual behavior is concerned, it doesn't matter whether they are religious or not. What matters is their attitude toward their fellows.

But is the love of man, by itself, an adequate general motive for human morality? Can we count on it? Must we not assume a fundamental decency in human nature if we are to rely on this motive so heavily? And is the pure love of man, the impulse to philanthropy, perhaps too general and abstract to give sure guidance? Is it not possible, indeed, that philanthropy is a name for our unconscious moral imperialism, our desire to "help" others by making them over in our own image? These are questions that are left dangling in the dialogue we have read. Diderot was well aware of them. He explored them elsewhere, notably in *Rameau's Nephew;* but they are not questions to which a conversation with an elegant lady lends itself. And there is another question as well which his dialogue leaves dangling. What is the meaning to be attached to words like "good" and "bad," "right" and "wrong"? Do they refer to the satisfaction of human desires? Or do they refer to obedience to independent principles, to a higher plan, which human beings have not made for themselves but to which they are subject? Diderot's dialogue presupposes a secular, humanistic basis for morality, but it does not attempt to demonstrate the validity of this outlook.

Nor does it meet head on the argument that the major questions are begged when the validity of religion is discussed in secular terms. Isn't it it at least possible that when we speak of the "truth" of religion we do not mean by "truth" what we mean in science or in everyday affairs? Is there a single logic by which all questions should be discussed, no matter what they are? Or do certain kinds of belief—notably the beliefs of religion—require special kinds of argument and proof? These are questions central to philosophy, and we shall return to them later on. Diderot has taken us to the edge of them but no further in this dialogue.

Berkeley does discuss these matters, however, and, interestingly enough, he agrees with Diderot in one fundamental respect. He doesn't think that the discussion of religion requires a separate logic or any special, unique kind of argument. On the contrary, religion is just a matter of everyday common sense. It is people like Diderot, he says implicitly, who lose their common sense when they discuss religion. Indeed, in their idolizing of science they adopt arguments which they would be embarrassed to use in their ordinary affairs.

George Bernard Shaw once said that he took to writing comedies because he discovered that when he spoke the truth everybody laughed. Berkeley is in an old Irish tradition of argumentation: he insists that he is only saying what everybody really knows, and then he looks around in apparent surprise when everybody seems startled. His acquaintance Jonathan Swift did much the same thing in his essay *A Modest Proposal,* where he took the commonplace principles that were accepted in discussions of Ireland's economic condition, and, reasoning from them, concluded that the children of the Irish poor ought to be sold to the rich to be eaten. In this way the rich would have a new delicacy for their tables, the poor would have an additional source of income, and Ireland would solve its population problem. Berkeley plays the same trick on the scientific-minded men of his day. He shows that if they are right, then they are wrong: if they believe that all true knowledge depends on the evidence of the senses, then their "scientific" belief that the world is composed of matter is superstition.

But Berkeley isn't pulling anybody's leg. He expects to be believed. And this is his problem. There are a pair of well-known limericks indicating the kind of objections Berkeley's philosophy provokes, and the response he might make:

> There was a young man who said, "God
> Must think it exceedingly odd
>> If he finds that this tree
>> Continues to be
> When there's no one about in the Quad."

To which the reply goes:

> Dear Sir:
> Your astonishment's odd:

I am always about in the Quad.
And that's why the tree
Will continue to be,
Since observed by
            Yours faithfully,
                        God.

The greatest practical difficulty with Berkeley's philosophy, the largest single reason why it probably doesn't succeed in shoring up the faith of believers, is that it is so ingenious. "But the novelty, Philonous, the novelty!" complains poor, browbeaten Hylas. "There lies the danger. New notions should always be discountenanced; they unsettle men's minds, and nobody knows where they will end." The person who believes in God is usually not disposed to think that the demonstration of God's existence requires a debater's cleverness. Either he believes God's existence so obvious that it needs no elaborate support, or he thinks it a subject of such sublimity that the task of proof should be undertaken only by seers who have plumbed mysteries that lie far beyond ordinary human intelligence. And most probably he thinks, quite simply, that God's existence should be taken on faith. "Is not the whole system immense, beautiful, glorious beyond expression and beyond thought!" These are Berkeley's words, and they express the spontaneous attitude of a man of faith. Why doesn't he stop while he's ahead?

The answer is that the man is a philosopher, and that other philosophers have got under his skin. Proving the existence of God is only one of his objects; the other is to puncture the affectations of people who wrap themselves in "advanced" ideas and then go around talking nonsense. From the start, the one thing on which Philonous and Hylas agree is that there is nothing good to be said for "those men who have in all ages, through an affectation of being distinguished from the vulgar, or some unaccountable turn of thought, pretended either to believe nothing at all or to believe the most extravagant things in the world." Berkeley is a combatant in an age-old civil war in philosophy and intellectual life. He is a philosopher, an intellectual, who thinks that philosophers and intellectuals are too easily thrown off balance by big words and pretentious theories, and that they mislead their fellow men.

Berkeley, in short, is the plain man's philosopher. This is what gives his philosophy its passion and charm. And it is also what gives it, one must acknowledge, its slightly comic aspect. He wants to show that the plain man is right in what he normally thinks, and that people who have their heads turned by the latest intellectual fashions are wrong. But plain men are usually unaware that their views need elaborate defense, and Berkeley pays the same price that every other plain man's philosopher, from Socrates to Bertrand Russell's debating partner, G. E. Moore, has paid: the plain men end by thinking their defender the oddest philosopher of all.

Nevertheless, though plain men may think Berkeley mad, he *is* on their side. In his quarrel with other philosophers, he scores heavily. For example, reasoning from a "scientific" theory of perception which asserts that our visual sensations are produced by light rays which come from external objects, register on the retina of the eye, and are sent by nervous impulses to the brain, philosophers produce a puzzle: vision is an event inside our heads, and what we see is only in our minds. There is something "out there," something material which exists independently of us, which is the cause of our sensations but which we never directly observe. Thus, Bertrand Russell once said that when a brain surgeon looks at a patient's brain what he is really observing is a portion of his own brain! And from this way of thinking has come a mare's nest of problems: How do we prove the existence of a world outside our minds? And how do we explain the interaction between two such different entities as "matter" and "mind"?

Berkeley's reply to this way of thinking is at once neat and powerful. If all these learned theories are "scientific," he points out, then they must rest on observation. And if that is the case, then we should notice a simple fact: we do not *see* neurological movements in our brain. What we see, in the ordinary meaning of the word "see," is stars, the moon, a glove, a face, a landscape. To talk about the occurrence of physical events in the brain is, at best, to draw inferences from these observations. And since the evidence for the inferences cannot be stronger than the veracity of the original observations on which they rest, the theory that physical events occur in the brain cannot be used to cast wholesale doubt on the veracity of our observations. The same conclusion applies to scientific entities such as today's "atoms," "electrons," and the like. Whatever they prove, they don't prove that the world we commonly observe is an illusion. Common sense remains sovereign. I do not think that a successful retort to this central point of Berkeley's is possible.

However, his way of putting this point creates problems of its own. It is one thing to say that the evidence that a thing exists is that it is perceived, or can be validly inferred from what is perceived. It is quite another thing to say, "To be is to be perceived." What does this statement mean? That "to exist" *means* "to be perceived?" But we never use the word "exist" in this way. If a thing exists, it exists, quite independently of whether it is perceived or not. Or does Berkeley mean that, as a matter of fact, everything that exists happens also to be perceived? But Berkeley himself recognizes that of course this isn't true so far as human perception is concerned: there are a great many things in existence that human beings have never perceived. Only if we adopt the conclusion that God unwaveringly perceives all things can we save Berkeley's maxim. But in that case we have to use the conclusion of his argument also as one of its premises.

Berkeley gets into immaterialist waters which are, indeed, as muddy as the waters of materialism. He finds "matter" an indefensible concept because it refers to something unperceived and undefined—a something-I-know-not-what—but he leans heavily on the concept of "mind" or "spirit," which by his own admission is also unperceivable and undefinable. And there is a naïve, plain man's materialism to which Berkeley never replies. Our births don't take place at our command; our physical needs aren't subject, except within the narrowest limits, to our control; our deaths arrive no matter what we do. To assert the existence of "matter" and to say that it is primary in the world isn't to recognize a mysterious, unobserved entity; it is simply to believe that there is an executive order of nature which controls our birth, maturation, and death, and that it does so without regard to our desires or notions of justice and injustice. "Materialism" in this everyday sense is simply the conviction that the universe isn't our oyster and that no moral or spiritual design is apparent in the way it works. Perhaps this position is mistaken, but nothing Berkeley says refutes it.

Philonous, in fact, doesn't pay enough attention to some of Hylas' fumbling objections. If pain and uneasiness are real, Hylas suggests, then God must perceive them, and so he must be capable of pain and uneasiness. And is this not incompatible with the nature of a perfect Being? Philonous' response is that God "can suffer nothing, nor be affected with any painful sensation or, indeed, any sensation at all." So the mystery mounts: God "perceives" pain and uneasiness but he doesn't have a "sensation" of them. Berkeley's problem, in the end, turns out to be exactly the one that plagues most theological positions. How can God, who lacks the mortal human qualities of sensing and desiring, feel emotions like compassion or wrath? How does an eternal God come down into time? And how is the existence of evil compatible with His existence? Religion characteristically treats these questions as mysteries. Berkeley's effort to prove the existence of God underlines their mysteriousness.

Why, then, is he an important philosopher? It isn't because he does what he set out to do, disproving materialism and proving the existence of God. Rather, it is because, beyond his arguments, he suggests an arresting metaphor—the universe as God's mind—which allows us to experience the world as a message to us, as a scene in which a logic and harmony not of our own contriving are set forth for us to discover and adore. To see the world as Berkeley invites us to see it is to have each moment of our experience bathed in a supernal light. And Berkeley is important also because, by means of his arguments, he opens up many of the questions that have preoccupied philosophers since his time. How can mind and matter, which are so distinct one from the other, interact? Berkeley's suggestion is that, for consistency and clarity, we should get rid of these two substances and reduce the stuff of the universe to only one. His difficulties come mainly from the fact that he seeks to discard one term of the pair—"material substance" —while keeping the other—"spiritual substance." A better approach might have been to conceive of "matter" and "mind" not as separate "substances," but as alternative methods of categorizing aspects of our experience, as different ways of talking that are useful in different situations. This is an approach that a number of philosophers have taken—Aristotle and Spinoza before Berkeley, William James, John Dewey, and some of the followers of Ludwig Wittgenstein in our own day. Still, it is in part through the influence of Berkeley that many philosophers have moved in this direction. His arresting arguments have made men aware of the problems inherent in talking about "mind" as something separate from "matter." His contributions to the philosophy of religion are minor; his contributions to general philosophy are considerable.

Berkeley's treatment of religion, indeed, leaves out a crucial element. His approach is essentially cerebral, like Diderot's. The two men thing of religion as something to be attacked or defended, to be proved or disapproved. And the consequence is that in talking about religion they neglect one of its most obvious aspects—the fact that people turn to religion not because they are rationally persuaded that it is true, but because they are at a loss what to think. They give themselves to a faith not because they wish to do good, but because without that faith they aren't sure whether anything, good or bad, is worth doing at all. The most troubling question suggested by Diderot's dialogue is one he doesn't raise. "Do you not think a man can be born," he asks, "with such a happy disposition as to find real pleasure in doing good?" Of course this is possible. But what of the man who reacts to life as though it were a disease and finds no self-justifying good in it at all? Diderot conducts his conversation with a happy, well-protected, high-spirited woman with six pretty children around her and a seventh on the way. But what has he to say to those who are alone or who are broken in spirit and hope?

We must turn to Santayana. Like Diderot, Santayana is a materialist in natural philosophy; like Diderot, he also thinks that religion should be measured by its effects in this world. And yet, though he doesn't believe in a literal heaven, he believes in the worth of an idea of heaven. Religion, he agrees, is responsible for childish illusions; but it has also made mankind's imagination of human possibilities more spacious. In its relation to morality, its role, on one side, has been simply to frighten men into adherence to the conventions. But on the other side, its function has been to give men a broader and more charitable conception of morality than they would otherwise reach. Religion's morality, the morality of another world, exists to put human morality in its place. It teaches men not how to measure success in life, but how to take the measure of success and see its irony and ambiguity. It speaks not simply for civic virtue but for charity, not just for engagement in the world's affairs but for the value of a degree of disengagement. In a word, it does what a rational philosophy, in a different way, also does: it helps men to separate the ideal from the actual and to live in the light of the ideal.

From the point of view of a rational philosophy, then, what should be our attitude toward religion? Should we reject it for its superstitions and cruelties, or should we take it to our hearts for its portrayal of subline moral truths? The answer of Santayana is clear: a rational man will do both. Religion is valuable, but only for what is best in it. And a religion that achieved this best would be one that forswore all claims to being literally true. It would be frankly mythical and metaphorical, free from imperial ambitions, and content simply to add another dimension to life. But it would do what a rational philosophy cannot do, even though it would be wholly compatible with such a philosophy: it would be concrete and sensuous, and would offer a poetry and a collective life in which men could participate.

Can we read a practical proposal into Santayana's philosophy? Is he a kind of Unitarian? Is he suggesting that such a rational religion be organized and given an institutional form? Or does he suspect that the people whose need for religion is most urgent require a stronger potion? Nothing could be further from Santayana's spirit than to imagine that he could be the missionary for any religion, even a rational one. He thinks spirit inseparable from matter, except in the mind's eye. For him, it is the ideal possibility in religion that makes existing religions valuable; but that ideal is bound to be enveloped in the normal, mortal madness of the human species. And so, while we should take religion not for what it is but for the ideal in it, we must accept this ideal where we find it—preferably in our ancestral religion, if that religion will tolerate our adhering to it simply for the sake of the ideal it expresses. For a philosophy that undertook to make religion over in the name of pure ideality would be a mad philosophy. It would be like religion at its worst, sharing the impossible hope that spirit can exist apart from matter.

Is Santayana's position altogether different from that of the noblest spokesmen for religion? Usually, they are moved by religion perfected, religion as it speaks for God-made-man. From Santayana's point of view, to ask whether philosophy can give a defense of religion is like asking whether philosophy can give a defense of government and politics. One doesn't defend what inevitably exists; one tries to make the best of it. But making the best of what exists requires the ability to detect this best. Here philosophy can make its contribution. It alerts the mind to the ideal, and provides a critique of it. Inevitably, then, philosophic reason applied to religion will not fortify any orthodox faith. But neither will it destroy any faith if the men who hold this faith do not insist that it alone speaks the truth, or that it ever speaks the truth literally.

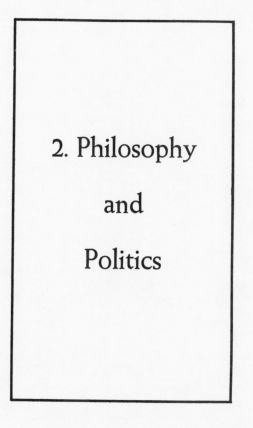

2. Philosophy

and

Politics

*P*olitics, like religion, has been one of the major catalysts of philosophical thought. The ancient Greeks' obsession with politics, more than anything else, led to their interest in philosophy. What can the philosopher bring to the understanding of politics? And what is it in politics that brings out the philosopher? In this section are reflections by Plato, Spinoza, and Santayana that will give a partial answer to these questions.

Plato

Plato, an Athenian who lived between 427 and 347 B.C., was the first system-atic philosopher in the Western tradition. He formulated most of the problems that have preoccupied philosophers ever since, and no single thinker has done more to shape the Western mind. The poetry of Dante and T. S. Eliot, the belief in mathematics as the avenue to the surest kind of knowledge, the theology of the Catholic Church, the political ideas of Lenin, all bear his imprint. And Plato was not only the first systematic philosopher but in many ways the most prototypical. His philosophy is the product of his extraordinary manysidedness, of his efforts to cope with the conflicting tendencies working within him. In Plato's character most of the tensions that make for philosophy were present: he was a social ideal-ist with a sense of political realities, an addict of logical argument with a deep strain of mysticism in him, a zealous searcher for a system of undeni-able truths who was endowed and troubled with a dramatist's sense of the fundamental discordances in the human scene and a dramatist's sympathy for all points of view. In one mind he brought together impulses that were conservative and radical, activist and contemplative, sensualist and ascetic.

The circumstances of his time which triggered his philosophical re-flections are also prototypical, and tell us a good deal about the way in which philosophy grows out of politics. Plato was born during the Pelopon-nesian War between Athens and Sparta, which lasted twenty-seven years. He grew up in a period when his native city, Athens, could still think of itself as the model of a free civilization, "the school of Hellas." But when he was twenty-three, Athens was disastrously defeated by Sparta, and he spent the rest of his life as the citizen of a city living mainly on its memo-ries. As the scion of an aristocratic family, Plato had been born into a tradition which took it for granted that participation in public life was man's noblest activity, and the special responsibility of those who were well-born and well-educated. He wrote for an era in which the social system that had nurtured this tradition had come apart, and the opportunity for public-spirited leadership seemed to have disappeared. The central pur-pose of his philosophy was to see whether Greek society could be remodeled so that it might again be governed by men of solid principle.

The particular events which seem to have affected Plato most deeply took place in the years 404-403. In 404, after Sparta defeated Athens, Spartan troops occupied the city, and a puppet regime, known as the

Tyranny of the Thirty, was installed. This oligarchic regime engaged in a reign of terror against partisans of Athenian democracy, and killed more Athenians, probably, than had been killed on the battlefields during the ten years preceding. In 403, however, supporters of democracy regained control of the city and concluded a peace treaty with the Spartans. Then, as is normal in this kind of affair, the new regime proceeded, in its turn, to pay its debts. It seized and tried those it held to be responsible for the Tyranny of the Thirty, and among those prosecuted was Plato's teacher, Socrates, who was accused of having demoralized the young and of having encouraged the treasonable acts of brilliant young leaders such as Alcibiades. Socrates denied the charges, but he was found guilty, and in 399, he was executed.

The following passage, from one of Plato's letters, expresses his reaction to these events:

When I was young, I had the same experience that comes to so many: I thought that, as soon as I should be my own master, I should enter public life. This intention was favored by certain circumstances in the political situation at Athens. The existing constitution was generally condemned, and a revolution took place.[1] . . . Some of the leaders were relatives and friends of mine, and they at once invited me to cooperate, as if this were the natural course for me to take. . . . It was not long before I saw these men make the former constitution seem like a paradise. In particular, they tried to send Socrates, my friend, then advanced in years—a man whom I should not hesitate to call the most righteous man then living—with other persons, to arrest one of the citizens by violence for execution. Their purpose, no doubt, was to implicate Socrates, with or without his will, in their proceedings. He refused, preferring to face any danger rather than be a party to their infamous deeds. Seeing all this and other things as bad, I was disgusted and drew back from the evils of the time.

Not long afterwards the Thirty fell and the whole constitution was changed. Once more I was attracted, though less eagerly, towards taking an active part in politics. In these unquiet times much was still going on that might move one to disgust, and it was no wonder that, during the revolutionary changes, some took savage vengeance upon their enemies; but on the whole the returning exiles showed great moderation. Unfortunately, however, some of the men in power brought my friend Socrates to trial on an abominable charge, the very last that could be made against Socrates—the charge of impiety. He was condemned and put to death—he who had refused to share the infamy of arresting one of the accusers' own friends when they themselves were in exile and misfortune.

When I considered these things and the men who were directing public affairs, and made a closer study, as I grew older, of law and custom, the harder it seemed to me to govern a state rightly. Without friends and trustworthy associates it was impossible to act; and these could not readily be found among my acquaintances, now that Athens was no longer ruled by the manners and institutions of our forefathers; and to make new associates was by no means easy. At the same time the whole fabric of law and custom was going from bad to worse at an alarming rate. The result was that I, who had at first been full of eagerness for a public career, when I saw all this happening and everything going to pieces, fell at last into bewilderment. I did not cease to think in what way this situation might be

1. This was the revolution of 404, leading to the Tyranny of the Thirty.

amended and in particular the whole organization of the state; but I was all the while waiting for the right opportunity for action.[2]

This is the background against which Plato wrote. His philosophizing may be said to have begun with a simple purpose—to vindicate his beloved teacher. But he came to realize that if he was to explain the life and death of Socrates adequately, he could not portray his execution simply as an accidental miscarriage of justice affecting a single individual. It had to be seen as the logical outcome of something that was seriously wrong in Athenian civilization. And if Socrates' life and death could be in any way redeemed, if his effort and sacrifice could be made worthwhile, the question had to be asked whether anything could be learned from the entire affair that could set Athens right again. Thus, Plato's effort to vindicate Socrates led him to a larger goal—to trace the reasons for the disintegration of Athens, and to propose a cure. And this, in turn, led him to ask what the purposes of politics are, how we can know what the good life is, and whether knowledge of the good can be taught. So Plato moved on to even more fundamental questions about the nature of human knowledge and the meaning of truth itself. The remodeling of Athens required, in short, an entire philosophy.

And at the center of this philosophy is a question that obsessed Plato throughout his life: What is the proper relation of a reflective and conscientious man to the life of action? Again and again in his work, implicitly or explicitly, Plato returns to the puzzle: Do principles and politics mix? Does a philosopher enter alien waters when he tries, in a practical way, to influence his country's affairs? When he was about forty, Plato was tempted by the chance to advise the ruler of Syracuse, Dionysius I, and journeyed to Sicily in the hope that he could turn this despot into a philosopher-king. To his embarrassment and despair, he became embroiled in the factional controversies and backbiting of the Syracusan court, and his friends had to arrange hastily for his departure. The experience seems to have confirmed Plato, at least for a while, in the view that a better way to influence politics over the long run is to teach philosophy to future statesmen.

This he did for most of the rest of his life at the Academy, the school which was founded for him by his friends at Athens. Yet he never quite gave up the hope that some more intimate connection could be established between philosophy and politics, between the search for the Good and the practicalities of the life of action. Only through such a connection, he was

2. Plato's *Seventh Epistle*. There is some argument among scholars concerning the authenticity of these letters, which tradition has attributed to him, but most agree that they probably state Plato's views accurately. A critical edition, discussing the case for and against their authenticity, has been prepared by Glenn R. Morrow (The Library of Liberal Arts, New York, 1962). The above translation is by F. M. Cornford, and is in the Introduction to his translation of *The Republic* (New York, Oxford University Press, 1969).

convinced, could the cities of man be made to cease from doing ill. His most influential book, *The Republic*, written during his forties or fifties, is the description of an ideal state in which properly trained statesmen would exercise absolute power. But Plato never gave up the hope that philosophy could do more than spin utopian dreams. In the final work of his old age, the *Laws*, he describes the constitution of a state that would be a compromise with the ideal but that might at least be attainable, Plato thus speaks with peculiar immediacy to our present situation. With one half of his mind, he asks how reason can be restored to the councils of men; with the other half, he wonders whether the world is capable of accepting the ministrations of reason, and if not, what a rational man should do and how he should live.

The selection that follows, from *The Republic*, states Plato's views on democracy. The most trenchant criticisms made of democracy throughout the centuries have leaned very heavily on it, and I know of no critique better calculated to make us think about democracy philosophically. Plato uses an especially effective device. He moves from the analysis of democracy as a political system to the description of a certain kind of man, whom he calls "the democratic man." This way of discussing the subject serves a number of purposes.

First, it focuses attention on democracy as a system of values, as a particular method of weighing the different goods of life and choosing among them. It reminds us that democracy isn't just a governmental mechanism, that it is also a moral outlook, and only one such outlook among many— one type of existence, which realizes certain possibilities of human life but rules out others.

Further, it reminds us that democracy, like any other political system, ought to be measured in terms of its most important product—the kind of human personality it fosters. Plato believes that for everything that exists there is an Idea, a perfect model of what that thing would be if it fulfilled its essential nature. We are enabled to recognize what democracy means when we are shown what type of character in man it ultimately favors. "Theory" and "theater" have a common root in the Greek word *thea*, which means "sight," "view." Plato's approach, which puts the typical "democratic man" on the stage for us, is a way of getting adherents of democracy to see themselves—to find out what they look like, to recognize what they are in essence, and to measure themselves against the standard of the Good.

Finally, by bringing together the analysis of a political system and the portrait of a particular kind of human character, Plato provides a way of understanding what happens to political systems. Most political systems that actually exist are, of course, mixtures—of "democratic," "oligarchic," "aristocratic," and "tyrannical" elements. But insofar as we abstract any one of these elements and trace out its fundamental logic or psychologic, we can explain why each type of political system tends to undergo the vicissitudes it does. Just as "character is destiny" in Greek tragedies, and the fate of a tragic hero—Oedipus, for example—is an inevitable consequence of his personality, so each type of political system carries within it the seeds of its own destiny. The destiny of democracy, Plato believes, the path down which it is fated to slide once it makes its great immoderate bets on liberty and equality for all, is to decline into tyranny.

The discussion that we shall read is taken from Book VIII of *The Republic.* I have supplied my own title for it. After Plato has drawn his picture of the perfect state, he asks whether such a state would be likely to survive indefinitely. His answer is that corruption and mortality are written into the very nature of political systems. In the perfect society the form of government is an "aristocracy"—rule by the best. But it will decline into "timocracy"—rule by men who love honor and position, whose wealth is in the land and whose prestige derives from their military prowess or traditions. (Plato's timocracy is what we commonly call "aristocracy.") Timocracy, in turn, is replaced by "oligarchy"—rule by the rich, based in cities, who have accumulated their wealth in commerce and industry and who measure all things by pecuniary standards. And oligarchy, in turn, gives way to "democracy"—rule by the many, and specifically by the poorer class of citizens. This is where the pages that follow take up the story.

The Republic, like all of Plato's works, is cast in dialogue form. The present translation is by W. H. D. Rouse. Socrates' interlocutors at this stage of the dialogue are two young men, brothers, Glaucon and Adeimantus.

Why Democracies Turn into Tyrannies

. . . "Democracy, then, as it seems, is the next thing to examine: how it arises, and what character it has. Then again we may observe the character of that kind of man and parade him for comparison."

"That, at least, would be our usual method of procedure," said he.

"Well then," said I, "the oligarchy changes into a democracy something in this way: through its insatiate desire for that which it sets before itself as a good and a duty—to become as rich as possible."

"How do you mean?"

"The rulers hold their position, I take it, because of their great possessions; and they will not make laws against undisciplined young men to prevent any who may turn up from running through their fortunes. They hope to lend money on the property of such men, and then buy it up, and so to become richer and more honourable than ever."

"Only too true!"

"Well, we have already clearly seen that to honour riches, and at the same time to acquire enough temperance, is a thing impossible for the citizens in a city; they must of necessity neglect one of the two."

"That is pretty clear," said he.

"So in the oligarchies by overlooking or even encouraging intemperance, they have sometimes compelled men not ignoble to become paupers."

"Very true indeed."

"And there they sit idle, I suppose, in the city, stings ready—that is, fully armed; some in debt, some disfranchised, some both, hating and plotting against those who have gotten their goods and everybody else, in love with revolution."

"This is true."

"And there are the moneymakers, stooping as they go and pretending not to see them; when any of the others submits, they wound him with a shot of money and carry off multiplicated interest, the offspring of the parent loan, and so they fill the city with drones and beggars."

"Yes indeed!" said he.

"Here is a fire of evil," said I, "blazing up, which they do not want to quench, although they could in two ways: one is what I suggested, by preventing a man from turning his property to any purpose he likes; the other is this—by doing away with such evils by a different law."

"And what is that other law?"

"The next best law, one that compels the citizens to care for virtue. For if it laid down that in most of the voluntary contracts a man must act on his own risk, people in the city would not be so shameless in their dealings, and not so many of those evils we have mentioned would come up at all."

"Far fewer," he said.

"But as things are," I said, "and for all such reasons, you see what a state the rulers have brought the ruled into; and as to themselves and their sons, are not the young people luxurious and lazy in matters concerning both body and soul? Are they not too soft to stand firm before both pleasures and pains, and idle?"

"Of course."

"And themselves—are they not careless of all else but making money, and do they not care no more for virtue than the poor do?"

"No more, indeed."

"So when, thus prepared, rulers and ruled are thrown together, on the march perhaps or in some other association, whether for festival or campaign, shipmates or tentmates, or even amidst the dangers of battle, then they can observe each other, and then the poor are not despised by the rich at all! Often enough a sinewy, sun-browned poor man may be posted in battle beside a rich man fostered in shady places, encumbered with alien fat, and sees him panting and helpless. Don't you suppose he reflects that his own cowardice has allowed such men to be rich? Will not one pass the word to another, when they meet together in private, 'We've got the fellows! There's nothing in them!' "

"I'm quite sure," said he, "that's what they do!"

"You know that an unhealthy body needs only to have a small push from without to make it fall ill, and sometimes even without that the body rebels against itself: just so a city which is in the same state as that body needs only a small excuse; if one party invites outside help from some oligarchic city, or another from a democratic city, it falls ill in the same way and fights against itself, or sometimes even without those outside develops internal strife."

"Only too true."

"So democracy, I suppose, comes into being when the poor conquer, and kill some of the other party and banish others, and share out the citizenship and government equally with the rest; and the offices in it are generally settled by lot." [1]

"Yes," he said, "that is how democracy is established, whether by force of arms, or by fear, as when the other party go out and escape."

"Well, then," I said, "how do these people live? And how does this constitution also work? For it is clear that such a man will prove to be the democratic."

"That is clear," said he.

"First of all, then, they are free men; the city is full of freedom and liberty of speech, and men in it may do what they like."

"So it is said, at least," he replied.

"Where there is liberty of action, it is clear that each man would arrange his own private life in it just as it pleased him."

"Yes, that is clear."

"Consequently, I suppose, all varieties of men would be produced under this system more than anywhere else."

"Of course."

"In fact," I said, "this is the most beautiful of constitutions. It is decked out with all sorts and conditions of manners, as a robe of many colours is embroidered with all the flowers of the field, and what could be more beautiful! Yes, perhaps," I went on, "many would judge it most beautiful, staring at it like a lot of women and children admiring a pretty frock!"

"Yes, indeed," said he.

"Yes indeed, bless you!" said I, "this is the city in which to look for a constitution."

"Why, if you please?"

"Because of this liberty! All sorts of contributions are there; and if anyone wants to fit up a city, as we have been doing, it is only necessary for him to go to a city governed by a democracy, and choose whatever fashion

1. As they were in Athens.—*Translator.*

of constitution pleases him, as if he had come to a bazaar of constitutions; then, having picked out his pattern, he can make his city accordingly."

"Perhaps at least," he said, "there would be plenty of patterns there."

"No necessity to be governor there," said I, "even if you are fit for it, no need to be ruled if you don't like it; you need not go to war if they fight, you need not keep the peace if the others keep it, unless you desire peace; if a law forbids you to be a magistrate or a judge, you may be magistrate and judge all the same if you take it into your head—what a lovely, heavenly life, while it lasts!"

"Yes, while it lasts," he said.

"And what a sweet temper there is in the convicts! Isn't it delightful? Haven't you seen in such a city, nothing less than men condemned to death or banishment calmly remaining and mixing in society; and how a man can go about like a hero returned from the dead, nobody noticing him or seeing him?"

"I've seen that often enough," he said.

"Toleration! No worrying in democracy about a trifle! What contempt of the solemn proclamations we made in founding our city, that no one could become a good man unless he had a superlative nature—unless from a boy he should play among beautiful things and study beautiful practices! How magnificently it tramples all this underfoot, and cares nothing what he practises before entering and living political life, but gives him honour if he only says he is loyal to the people!"

"What a noble constitution!" he exclaimed.

"These things, then," I said, "and other such like them are in democracy; a delightful constitution it would be, as it seems: no governor and plenty of colour; equality of a sort, distributed to equal and unequal alike."

"Oh yes, we know all that," said he.

"Now," said I, "look and see what kind of man corresponds in private character. Shall we begin as we did with the constitution, and ask how he is produced?"

"Yes," said he.

"Well, then, surely, in this way. The thrifty oligarchic man would have a son, I suppose, brought up under his father in his father's manners."

"Of course."

"But he, like his father, rules his own pleasures by force, those of them which are called unnecessary, those which cause spending and are not moneymaking."

"Clearly," said he.

"Now don't let us talk in the dark; suppose we first explain what we mean by desires necessary and not necessary."

"I am quite willing," said he.

"Then would it not be right to call those necessary which we cannot turn away, and those which benefit us when fulfilled? For it is plain necessity that we reach after both by our very nature. Don't you think so?"

"Certainly I do."

"Then we shall be right in giving these the title necessary."

"We shall."

"Very good. Those which a man could get rid of if he trained himself to do it from youth up, which also do no good by being in him—indeed some do harm—we should be right in saying that all these are unnecessary, shouldn't we?"

"Quite right."

"Suppose we take an example of each class to get a general notion."

"So we should."

"Then the desire of eating would be a necessary one, the desire for simple bread and meat, enough for health and vigour."

"So I think."

"The desire for bread is necessary on both counts, both because bread is beneficial and because a living man cannot suppress the desire for it."

"Yes."

"And the desire for meat, if it provides any help towards vigour."

"By all means."

"Very well. And we might fairly name any further desire unnecessary, a desire for other viands than those we have mentioned, one that can be corrected and trained from youth and can be got rid of by most people, which does harm to the body and harm to the soul as regards wisdom and temperance."

"Most rightly, indeed."

"And may we not call these desires spending desires, and the others moneymaking because they are useful in production?"

"Certainly."

"We will say the same of love-making and so forth."

"Just so."

"Well, didn't we name that fellow a drone just now, the one laden with such pleasures and desires and ruled by the unnecessary desires, and we called the one ruled by the necessary desires thrifty and oligarchic?"

"Sure enough we did."

"Now we just go back," said I, "and explain how the democratic man is produced. Here, it seems to me, is the usual way."

"What?"

"A young man brought up as we described, in parsimony and ignorance, gets a taste of the drones' honey, and finds himself among wild beasts fiery and dangerous, who are able to provide pleasures of every variety and complexity and condition; there you must see the beginning of his inward change from the oligarchic to the democratic."

"No doubt about that," said he.

"As the city then was changed by the alliance coming from without to assist one party within, like to assist like, so the young man changes by a crowd of desires from without coming to assist one of the parts within him, a crowd akin and alike."

"Undoubtedly."

"And if another alliance comes from somewhere to assist the oligarchic part in the man—from the father, perhaps, or others of the family, who warn and reproach him—then there is faction and anti-faction and a battle ensues within him against himself."

"To be sure."

"And sometimes, I suppose, the democratic part retreats before the oligarchic, some of the desires are destroyed, and some are banished; a little shame comes up in the young man's soul, and it is brought into order again."

"That does happen sometimes," he said.

"Then again, I take it, when the desires are banished others grow up unnoticed, through the father's lack of knowledge of right upbringing, and these become many and strong."

"Yes," he said, "at least that is what generally happens."

Then they draw him back to the same associations, and they spawn secretly and breed a multitudinous brood."

"Yes, to be sure."

"So in the end, I think, they storm the fortress of the young man's soul, and they find it empty of learning and beautiful practices and without words of truth, which are indeed the best sentinels and guardians in the minds of men whom the gods love."

"By far the best," said he.

"Now liars and impostors, I suppose, false words and opinions, charge up and occupy the place of the others in such a man."

"So they do," said he. "So then the young man comes back among these lotus-eaters and makes his home there openly; if any support comes from his family for the thrifty part of his soul, those bragging words bar up the gates of the royal castle in him, and will not let in even these allies, nor even receive any embassy of words from his older friends in private life. A battle follows, and they win; Shame they dub Silliness and cast it forth, a dishonoured outlaw; Temperance they dub Cowardice, trample it under foot and banish it; they persuade the man that moderation and decent spending are clownishness and vulgarity, and drive them out beyond the border by the help of a gang of unprofitable desires."

"Indeed they do!"

And so having purged and swept clean of such things the soul of this man, who is now in their power and being initiated into their grand Mysteries, they proceed at once to bring home again Violence and Anarchy and Licentiousness and Immodesty with a long train of attendants, resplendent with garlands about their heads; and they glorify them and call them by soft names—Violence is now Good Breeding, Anarchy is Liberty, Licentiousness is Magnificence, Immodesty is Courage. There," said I, "you see more or less how the young man who was being trained among necessary desires is led into the emancipation and release of unnecessary and unprofitable pleasures."

"And a very clear picture it is," he said.

"And so he lives, I think, after this, spending money and pains and study upon unnecessary pleasures no less than the necessary. But if he is fortunate and not too dissolute, if as he grows older the great riot abates a bit, he receives back again parts of the exiles, and does not yield himself wholly to the intruders; he carries on his pleasures, maintaining if you please a sort of equality among them; he gives over the rule of himself to any pleasure that comes along, as if it had gained that by lot—until he has had enough, then to another again, without disrespect for any, but cherishing all equally."

"Quite so."

"And not a word of truth," I said, "does he receive into the fortress of his soul, he will not even let it into the guardhouse. If anyone tells him that some pleasures belong to beautiful and good desires, others to those which are vile; some he should practise and respect, others he should chasten and enslave—at all such warnings, he nods his head up [2] and says, 'Not at all, they are all equal, and to be respected equally.'"

"Exactly," says he, "that's what he does in such a state of things."

"And so," said I, "he spends his life, every day indulging the desire that comes along; now he drinks deep and tootles on the pipes, then again he drinks water and goes in for slimming; at times it is bodily exercise, at times idleness and complete carelessness, sometimes he makes a show of studying philosophy. Often he appears in politics, and jumps up to say and do whatever comes into his head. Perhaps the fame of a military man makes him envious, and he tries that; or a lord of finance—there he is again. There is no discipline or necessity in his life; but he calls it delightful and free and full of blessings, and follows it all his days."

"Upon my word," said he, "that's a lifelike picture of the man who is all for equal laws."

"So you see," said I, "this, I think, is a variegated man, full of all sorts of conditions and manners, this is the beautiful, many-coloured man exactly like that city, one whose life many a man and many a woman would envy, having in himself patterns innumerable of constitutions and characters."

"That's the man!" said he.

"Very well. Let such a man be ranked beside our democracy as the democratic man rightly so called."

2. The ancient Greek gesture for No; modern Greeks and Turks still use it. —*Editor*.

"Yes, let him be ranked there!" said he.

"And now for the most beautiful constitution," said I, "and the most beautiful man—that's what is left for us to describe, tyranny and the tyrant."

"Exactly so," said he.

"Tell me then, my dear friend, how does tyranny come about? Of course democracy changes into this, so much is clear enough."

"Quite clear."

"Then does tyranny come out of democracy more or less in the same way as democracy comes out of oligarchy?"

"How?"

"What they set before them as their good," said I, "and through which oligarchy was established—that was riches, wasn't it?"

"Yes."

"So, then, oligarchy was destroyed by the insatiate desire of riches, and disregard of everything else for the sake of moneymaking."

"True," said he.

"Then is democracy also dissolved by insatiate desire for that which it defines as good?"

"What do you say it so defines?"

"Liberty," I said. "That, I suppose, you would always hear described as most beautiful in the democratic city, and therefore this is the only city where a man of free nature thinks life worth living."

"Oh yes," he said, "that word is on every tongue."

"Is it true then, as I was going to say, that the insatiate desire for this, and disregard of everything else, transforms the constitution here also and makes it want a tyranny?"

"How?" he asked.

"When a democratic city athirst for liberty gets worthless butlers presiding over its wine, and has drunk too deep of liberty's heady draught, then, I think, if the rulers are not very obliging and won't provide plenty of liberty, it calls them blackguards and oligarchs and chastises them."

"So they do," said he.

"Yes," I went on, "and any who obey the rulers they trample in the dust as willing slaves and not worth a jot; and rulers who are like subjects, and subjects who are like rulers, come in for the votes of thanks and the honours, public and private. In such a city must not your liberty go to all lengths?"

"Of course it must."

"And it must go creeping, my friend," said I, "into private houses too, and the end is, their anarchy even gets into the animals!"

"Why, how can that be?" he exclaimed.

"This is how," said I. "The father gets into the habit of behaving like the son and fears his own children, the son behaves like a father, and does not honour or fear his parents, 'must have liberty' he says. Settler is equal to citizen and citizen to settler, the foreigner is the same."

"Yes, that's what happens," he said.

"And there are these other trifles too," I said. "Teacher fears pupil in such a state of things, and plays the toady; pupils despise their teachers and tutors, and in general, the young imitate their elders and stand up to them in word and deed. Old men give way to the young; they are all complaisance and wriggling, and behave like young men themselves so as not to be thought disagreeable or dictatorial."

"Just so," said he.

"And behold the topmost pinnacle!" said I. "Mob liberty can go no further in such a city, when slaves bought with money, both men and women, are no less free than the buyers! Ah, I almost forgot to tell how great equality and liberty there is between women and men, between men and women!"

"Shall we say what now cometh to our lips," he rejoined, "as Aeschylus put it?"

"By all means," I said, "so I will. The domestic animals—how much more free-and-easy they are in a city like this than in others, no one would believe who had not seen it. There's really nothing to choose between missus and bitch, as the proverb goes.[3] Horses and asses, if you please, adopt the habit of marching along with the greatest freedom and haughtiness, bumping into everyone they meet who will not get out of the way; and all the other animals likewise are filled full of liberty."

"Oh, that's just my own dream come true!" said the other. "That often happens to me when I'm going out into the country."

"To sum up," said I, "observe what comes of all these things together: how touchy it makes the people! They fret at the least hint of servitude, and won't have it; for at last, you know, they care nothing for the laws written or unwritten, that no one may be their master in anything."

"Oh yes, I know that," said he.

"This then, my friend," said I, "is the beginning from which tyranny grows, such a beautiful, bright beginning!"

"Bright and gay indeed," he said, "but what comes after that?"

"The same as in the oligarchy," said I; "the same disease which destroyed that gets in here, stronger and more violent from this liberty, and enslaves democracy. And in fact that is what generally happens in the world. To do anything too much tends to take you to the opposite extreme, in weather and in plants and in living bodies, and so also in constitutions most of all."

"That is likely," said he.

3. Literally, "the bitches become just like their mistresses."—*Translator.*

"For too great liberty seems to change into nothing else than too great slavery, both in man and in city."

"Yes, that is likely."

"Then it is likely," said I, "that democracy is precisely the constitution out of which tyranny comes; from extreme liberty, it seems, comes a slavery most complete and most cruel."

"Yes," he said, "there is reason in that."

"But I think that is not what you asked about," I said; "you asked what kind of disease it was which grows up the same both in oligarchy and in democracy, and enslaves democracy."

"True," said he.

"Well, then," I said, "what I meant was that class of idle and extravagant men, of which the most manly part leads and the most unmanly part follows. You remember we likened them to drones, some with stings and some without."

"And quite right, too," said he.

"These two, then," said I, "make a mess of every constitution they get into, like hot phlegm and cold gall in the body; the good physician must beware of them both in good time, and so must the good lawgiver in the city, no less than the skilful beemaster. It is best not to let them get in at all; but if they do, cut them out, honeycombs and all."

"The very thing," said he, "the whole lot of them."

"Then let us take it in this way," said I, "so that we may see what we want more clearly."

"How, pray?"

"Let us assume that a democratic city is made up of three parts, as it really is. One, a class such as we have described, grows here because of democratic licence, no less than in the oligarchic city."

"That is true."

"And indeed much fiercer here than there."

"How so?"

"There they get no training and gather no strength, because they are excluded from the government as being held in no honour; but in democracy this is the dominant class, all but a few. The fiercest part of them talk and act while the others swarm round the platform and buzz; they never tolerate anyone who speaks on the other side, so that all business of state is managed by this class, with a few exceptions."

"Exactly," he said.

"Another class, besides, is always being separated from the mass."

"What class?"

"When all are busy in making money, the most orderly by nature, I suppose, generally become richest."

"That is likely."

"From them, I think, comes the most honey for the drones, and they are most easy to squeeze."

"Of course," he said; "how could one squeeze it out of those that have little?"

" 'The rich' is the name they go by, you see, drones' fodder."

"Pretty nearly," he said.

" 'People' will be the name of the third class; all who are handiworkers and outside politics, without much property of their own. This is the largest and most sovereign class in democracy, when it combines."

"So it is," he said, "but it does not often care to combine unless it can get a bit of the honey."

"Well, it does get a bit from time to time," I said, "depending on the ability of the president, in taking the property away from those who have it and distributing it among the people, to keep most of it themselves."

"Yes, it gets a share to that extent," he said.

"So those whom they plunder have to defend themselves, I suppose, by speaking before the people and taking action in what way they can."

"Of course."

"And so they are accused by the other party of plotting against the people, even if they have no wish to revolt, and they are said to be reactionary oligarchs."

"To be sure."

"In the end, when they see the people, ignorant and completely deceived by the false accusers, trying recklessly to do them wrong, then at last willy-nilly they become truly oligarchic, not willingly, but this evil thing also is put in them by that drone stinging them."

"Exactly so."

"Then come impeachments and sentences and lawsuits between them."

"Yes, indeed."

"So the common people will always put up for itself some special protector,[4] whom it supports and magnifies?"

"Yes, that's its way."

"One thing is clear then," I said, "that when a tyrant appears, he grows simply and solely from a protectorship as the root."

"That is quite clear."

"Then what is the beginning of this change from protector to tyrant? Isn't it when the protector begins to do like the man in the fable about the temple of Lycaian Zeus in Arcadia?"

"What fable?" he asked.

"That whoever tasted the one bit of human entrails minced up with all the sacrificial meat must be changed into a wolf. Haven't you heard the story?"

4. "Protector of the people" was a recognized title for the leading demagogue. Oliver Cromwell picked up this title in the seventeenth century.—*Editor.*

"I have."

"This is just the same. When the Protector of the People finds a very obedient mob; when he will not abstain from shedding tribal blood; when he drags someone into court by the usual unjust accusations, and incurs bloodguilt by destroying the life of a man; when, with unholy mouth and tongue, he tastes a kinsman's gore; when he banishes and executes, when he hints at abolition of debts and partition of estates—surely for such a one the necessity is ordained that he must either perish at the hands of his enemies, or become a tyrant, and be a wolf instead of a man?"

"Such must be his fate of necessity," said he.

"That is the man then," said I, "who comes to lead a party against those who possess property."

"That's the man," said he.

"He may be banished then, and return in despite of his enemies a tyrant finished and complete?"

"That is clear."

"And if they are unable to banish him, or to accomplish his death by setting the mind of the city against him, they may plot violent death for him in secret?"

"At least that often happens," he said.

"And to prevent this those who get so far always hit on the tyrant's notorious plea—they beg the people to give them a bodyguard, in order that the people's champion may be kept safe for themselves."

"They do indeed," said he.

"So the people grant the bodyguard; fearing for him, I suppose, but quite easy about themselves."

"Exactly."

"And when a man sees this who has money and with his money the repute of being a people-hater, then my friend, that man thinks of the oracle given to Crœsus; and

> Along the pebbly Hermos
> He flees, he does not wait, he has no shame
> To be a coward."

"Not he!" said the other. "He would have no second chance to be ashamed."

"And anyone caught," I said, "would be done to death."

"Naturally."

"Meanwhile your Protector himself does not lie low, grand in his grandeur, at all; no, he knocks down crowds of others and stands towering in the coach of state, Protector no longer but Tyrant finished and complete."

"That's a matter of course," he said.

"Now suppose we describe the happiness," said I, "happiness of man and city, in which such a creature would make his appearance."

"By all means," he said, "let us describe that."

"Well, then," I said, "at first, in the early days, he greets everyone he meets with a broad smile; says he is no tyrant, and promises all sorts of things in private and in public, frees them from their debts and parcels out the land to the people and to those about him, pretends to be gracious and friendly to all the world."

"He has to do it," said he.

"As to outside enemies, when he has made terms with some and destroyed others, I take it, and when all is quiet from that source, he is forever stirring up some war in order that the people may want a leader."

"That is likely."

"And, moreover, in order that they may become poor by having to pay taxes, and stick to their daily rounds, and be less likely to plot against him."

"That's clear."

"And if he suspects that any harbour a free spirit and will not endure his rule, he wants an excuse to destroy them by exposing them to the enemy. For all these reasons the tyrant must always be stirring up war."

"So he must."

"Then by doing this he becomes more and more detestable to the citizens."

"Of course."

"You may expect that some of those who helped to set him up, the bravest of them, being now in power themselves, will speak freely before him and among themselves, and reproach him with what is happening."

"Quite likely."

"So he must quietly get rid of all these if he is to rule, until not a single one is left, either friend or foe, who is of any use."

"That is clear."

"He must look sharp to see, then, who is brave, who is magnanimous, who is prudent, who rich; and so happy and fortunate he is that he is bound to be enemy to all these whether he likes it or not, and to scheme against them until he has purged the city."

"A fine purge that!" said he.

"Yes," I said, "the opposite of what doctors do for the body; they clear away the worst and leave the best; he does just the opposite."

"He can't help it, as it seems," said he, "if he is to remain ruler."

"And so a blessed necessity binds him," said I, "which commands him to have worthless creatures about him for the most part, and to be hated by them too, or else to live no longer."

"Blessed indeed," said he.

"Consequently, the more the citizens detest him for doing this, the more bodyguards he will need and the more trusty."

"Of course."

"Well, who are his trusty guards, and where will he find them?"

"They will come of themselves," he said, "plenty of them, on wings of the wind, if he pays their wages."

"Drone!" I said. "Drones, by the Dog! That is what you seem to mean again, mercenaries from anywhere."

"True," said he, "that's what I mean."

"What!" I asked, "no recruits from home? Won't he want—"

"Whom?"

"—the slaves; he will take them from the citizens, and set them free, and add them to the bodyguard about his person."

"Sure enough," he said, "those will be the most trusty of all."

"Oh, what a blessed thing is your tyrant!" I exclaimed. . . .

Baruch Spinoza

At the start of his *Political Treatise,* passages from which we are about
to read, Baruch Spinoza asks the same question that gnawed at Plato
throughout his life: Why do philosophers, the apostles of reason, have
so little influence on political affairs? The answer, Spinoza believes, is that
philosophers will not accept men as they are but prefer to damn mankind
for being what it cannot help but be. The result is to condemn philosophy
to futility so far as practical affairs are concerned.

The proper approach, according to Spinoza, is to base one's political
philosophy on the unavoidable necessities of the human scene. Men hold
different views, they tend to think that their own interests should triumph,
and when they argue that there are ultimate moral laws which God or
Nature prescribes for everybody, these laws are almost always simply
their own values disguised. Unreasonable though such conduct may be,
there it is. And politics is the effort to manage this competition, diversity,
and struggle. On the whole, Spinoza thinks that liberal democracy is the
best way to do so—not the only way, and not in all circumstances the most
desirable, but by and large, the most realistic and humane.

Since "natural right" is a classic phrase that has often been used by
spokesmen for liberty and democracy, it is important to recognize that
when Spinoza employs the phrase in the pages that follow, he attaches
to it a meaning quite different from its ordinary one. He is not referring
to a kind of right that men possess whether or not society or government
has accorded it; he doesn't believe that any such right exists. Men, to be
sure, are creatures of nature, subject to nature's laws, but nature has no
moral purpose; when men call things "good" or "evil" they are simply
saying that these things serve or mis-serve their own human interests.
Accordingly, when we look at men against their natural background—
in the "state of nature" as it were—and apart from the moral principles
with which they surround themselves in their social existence, we find that
there are no moral limits to what they may do. They are simply driven
by the natural tendency to preserve themselves, and whatever serves
this purpose can be described as their "natural right." What men don't have
a "natural right" to do is simply what nature doesn't permit—what con-
travenes causal laws and therefore lies beyond their powers. Thus, when
Spinoza speaks of "natural right," the reader will understand him if he
substitutes the phrase "natural power." From Spinoza's point of view, to

have a "right" to do something, in the more normal moral connotation of the word, requires that there be an established society with customs and laws and definite procedures for enforcing them.

Is this simply to say that Machiavellianism is the only proper political philosophy? In a way, yes. But only in a way, for Spinoza doesn't draw the implications that are usually drawn from the doctrine that might makes right. Indeed, he argues, as the reader will see, that Machiavelli himself has been misinterpreted. There are limits, Spinoza points out, to what anyone can do with power, and there are consequences that follow from using it in one way or another that do not depend on our desires. So it isn't the case that if one has power, anything goes. When men and governments use power to attempt the impossible, they simply weaken themselves and cause suffering to no purpose. For example, governments regularly try to prescribe the beliefs that men should hold. But in doing so they attempt the impossible: a government can frighten men into hiding their beliefs; it can punish or eliminate those who, in its view, hold the wrong beliefs; and it no doubt has immense powers to influence the thinking of its subjects. But it cannot tell them that they must believe something, and by that command, make them believe it. A man can only believe what he thinks to be true. A moral maxim with a wholly practical base thus follows from Spinoza's realism: it is evil to try to do what one does not have the power to do. On these wholly realistic grounds, Spinoza formulates one of the most stirring defenses of freedom of thought in history.

Moreover, Spinoza draws another conclusion from his realistic premises: reason is central among the goods of life. Man as a natural being seeking to preserve himself fights constantly against the limitations of his condition. He dreams of absolute safety, or of immortality, or of the achievement of every one of his desires. But to seek such goals is to seek the impossible; it is to leave oneself a slave to one's vanities and passions, and to be condemned to a life of self-deception and complaint. Only a disengaged understanding of the inexorable natural laws that frame the human condition can release man from this bondage and give him the knowledge to achieve the firmer purposes of which he is capable. And so, when we look at governments, we must ask—and ask on realistic grounds —what they do to help or harm the cause of reason, which is man's supreme good. A government that has the power to suppress reason no doubt has the "right" to do so. This is merely to say, redundantly, that it has the power to do so, and that there is no higher law, beyond its laws, by which its actions can be declared illegitimate. But such a government cannot win a free man's approval, for it is the enemy of the crucial value in his life.

Spinoza is thus both an uncompromising political realist and an uncompromised moral idealist. He is almost unique in the history of philosophy in the degree to which he succeeds in combining these two strains of thought. He combines two similar strains in his general outlook as well. He has been called, with equal justice, an "atheist" and a "God-intoxicated" man: he is at once the surpassing spokesman of the scientific outlook and one of the most moving religious philosophers. He denies the existence of a personal God, disbelieves in miracles and the divinity of the Bible, and maintains that there is no moral design in the structure of the universe. Yet he finds in the structure of nature a logic and symmetry he thinks worthy of religious adoration, and he uses the words "God" and "Nature" interchangeably. In contemplation of the order of nature, he believes, a man can see things in their necessity; in "intellectual love" for this order a man can be released from the petty perspectives of his own ego and his narrow life. In Spinoza's masterwork, the *Ethics*, "reason" plays the same role that "love of God" plays in traditional theologies. It is not a process apart from the passions, but the supreme focusing of the passions; it is, for Spinoza, the source of the only emotion that masters a man and yet leaves him master of himself.

Spinoza was born in 1632 in Amsterdam of Portuguese-Jewish stock, and developed his heterodox religious views early in his life. By his twenties he was in trouble with the Jewish community, which at first made quiet efforts to bring him to heel, even offering him money to keep silent. But these attempts failed, and in 1656 the community, impelled both by outrage at his views and by fears that its situation as a tolerated group in Holland would be compromised, excommunicated him. Yet Spinoza was not a firebrand. He did not seek this conflict, and indeed tried to avoid it, refusing only to deny his beliefs. Nevertheless, his name became anathema not only among Jews but in the larger community. He took to grinding lenses to support himself, and it was only with the help of a few protectors that he was able to eke out a living and enjoy contact with a small circle of intellectual associates. He died in 1677. During his lifetime and for years after, "Spinozism," like "Machiavellianism," was a synonym for atheism and immorality—witness the references to Spinoza by Bishop Berkeley in his *Dialogues*, written a half century later—and Spinoza was never able to publish his philosophy openly. His major work, the *Ethics*, appeared posthumously. However, he stands today, with Socrates, as a man for whom philosophy was a personal sovereign, one who lived modestly by the rule of reason and did not flinch at accepting the consequences.

The selections that follow are from Spinoza's unfinished *Political Treatise*, and from his *Theologico-Political Treatise*, published anonymously in 1670. The latter of these works is devoted in part to the scientific study of the Bible, and its main purpose is to plead for religious and political toleration. It was banned in 1674, and when Spinoza was denounced as its author his situation became still more precarious. He was forced to move to The Hague, where he could be closer to his protectors.

The chapter from which the selection is taken is Spinoza's classic defense of freedom of speech and thought. A *Political Treatise*, apart from its intrinsic interest as a work in political philosophy, is noteworthy because it embodies conclusions Spinoza presents in his *Ethics*, and gives a first insight into the doctrines of that notable but difficult book. The translations are by R. H. H. Elwes, and were first published in 1883. I have changed the punctuation and phrasing here and there.

A Political Treatise

INTRODUCTION

Philosophers conceive of the passions which harass us as vices into which men fall by their own fault, and, therefore, generally deride, bewail, or blame them, or execrate them, if they wish to seem unusually pious. And so they think they are doing something wonderful, and reaching the pinnacle of learning, when they are clever enough to bestow manifold praise on such human nature as is nowhere to be found, and to make verbal attacks on that which, in fact, exists. For they conceive of men not as they are, but as they themselves would like them to be. Whence it has come to pass that, instead of ethics, they have generally written satire, and have never conceived a theory of politics which could be turned to use, but only such as might be taken for a chimera or might have been formed in Utopia, or in that golden age of the poets when, to be sure, there was least need of it. Accordingly, as in all sciences which have a useful application, so especially in that of politics, theory is supposed to be at variance with practice; and no men are esteemed less fit to direct public affairs than theorists or philosophers.

But statesmen, on the other hand, are suspected of plotting against mankind, rather than consulting their interests, and are thought to be more crafty than learned. No doubt nature has taught them that vices will exist as long as men do. And so, while they study to anticipate human wickedness, . . . they are thought to be enemies of religion, especially by divines, who believe that supreme authorities should handle public affairs in accordance with the same rules of piety as bind a private individual. Yet there can be no doubt that statesmen have written about politics far more happily than philosophers. For as they had experience for their mistress, they taught nothing that was inconsistent with practice. . . .

Therefore, on applying my mind to politics, I have resolved to demonstrate by a certain and undoubted course of argument, or to deduce from the very condition of human nature, not what is new and unheard of, but only such things as agree best with practice. And that I might investigate the subject-matter of this science with the same freedom of

spirit as we generally use in mathematics, I have laboured carefully, not
to mock, lament, or execrate, but to understand human actions; and to
this end I have looked upon passions, such as love, hatred, anger, envy,
ambition, pity, and the other perturbations of the mind, not in the light
of vices of human nature, but as properties just as pertinent to it as are
heat, cold, storm, thunder, and the like to the nature of the atmosphere,
which phenomena, though inconvenient, are yet necessary, and have
fixed causes. . . .

For this is certain, and we have proved its truth in our Ethics, that
men are of necessity liable to passions, and so constituted as to pity those
who are ill and envy those who are well off; and to be prone to vengeance
more than to mercy; and moreover, that every individual wishes the rest
to live after his own mind, and to approve what he approves, and reject
what he rejects. And so it comes to pass that, as all are equally eager to
be first, they fall to strife, and do their utmost mutually to oppress one
another; and he who comes out conqueror is more proud of the harm he
has done to the other than of the good he has done to himself. And although all are persuaded that religion, on the contrary, teaches every
man to love his neighbour as himself, that is, to defend another's right just
as much as his own, yet we showed that this persuasion has too little
power over the passions. It avails, indeed, in the hour of death, when
disease has subdued the very passions and man lies inert; or in temples,
where men hold no traffic; but least of all where it is most needed, in the
law-court or the palace. We showed, too, that reason can, indeed, do
much to restrain and moderate the passions, but we saw, at the same time,
that the road which reason herself points out is very steep; so that such
as persuade themselves that the multitude of men distracted by politics
can ever be induced to live according to the bare dictate of reason must
be dreaming of the poetic golden age or of a stage-play.

A dominion, then, whose well-being depends on any man's good
faith, and whose affairs cannot be properly administered unless those
who are engaged in them will act honestly, will be very unstable. On the
contrary, to insure its permanence, its public affairs should be so ordered
that those who administer them, whether guided by reason or passion,
cannot be led to act treacherously or basely. Nor does it matter to the
security of a dominion in what spirit men are led to rightly administer
its affairs. For liberality of spirit, or courage, is a private virtue; but the
virtue of a state is its security.

Lastly, inasmuch as all men, whether barbarous or civilized, everywhere frame customs, and form some kind of civil state, we must not,
therefore, look to proofs of reason for the causes and natural bases of
dominion, but derive them from the general nature or position of mankind, as I mean to do in the next chapter.

OF NATURAL RIGHT

. . . By natural right I understand the very laws or rules of nature, in accordance with which everything takes place, in other words, the power of nature itself. And so the natural right of universal nature, and consequently of every individual thing, extends as far as its power: and accordingly, whatever any man does after the laws of his nature he does by the highest natural right, and he has as much right over nature as he has power.

If then human nature had been so constituted that men should live according to the mere dictate of reason, and attempt nothing inconsistent therewith, in that case natural right, considered as special to mankind, would be determined by the power of reason only. But men are more led by blind desire than by reason: and therefore the natural power or right of human beings should be limited not by reason, but by every appetite whereby they are determined to action, or seek their own preservation. I, for my part, admit that those desires which arise not from reason are not so much actions as passive affections of man. But as we are treating here of the universal power or right of nature, we cannot here recognize any distinction between desires which are engendered in us by reason and those which are engendered by other causes; since the latter, as much as the former, are effects of nature, and display the natural impulse by which man strives to continue in existence. . . .

So we conclude that it is not in the power of any man always to use his reason, and be at the highest pitch of human liberty, and yet that everyone always, as far as in him lies, strives to preserve his own existence; and that (since each has as much right as he has power) whatever anyone, be he learned or ignorant, attempts and does, he attempts and does by supreme natural right. From which it follows that the law and ordinance of nature, under which all men are born, and for the most part live, forbids nothing but what no one wishes or is able to do, and is not opposed to strifes, hatred, anger, treachery, or, in general, anything that appetite suggests. For the bounds of nature are not the laws of human reason, which do but pursue the true interest and preservation of mankind, but other infinite laws, which regard the eternal order of universal nature, whereof man is an atom; and according to the necessity of this order only are all individual beings determined in a fixed manner to exist and operate. Whenever, then, anything in nature seems to us ridiculous, absurd, or evil, it is because we have but a partial knowledge of things and are in the main ignorant of the order and coherence of nature as a whole, and because we want everything to be arranged according to the dictate of our own reason; although, in fact, what our reason pronounces bad is not bad as regards the order and laws of universal nature, but only as regards the laws of our own nature taken separately.

Besides, it follows that everyone is so far rightfully dependent on another as he is under that other's authority, and so far independent as he is able to repel all violence, and avenge to his heart's content all damage done to him, and in general to live after his own mind. . . .

If two come together and unite their strength, they have jointly more power and consequently more right over nature than both of them separately, and the more there are that have so joined in alliance the more right they all collectively will possess.

In so far as men are tormented by anger, envy, or any passion implying hatred, they are drawn asunder and made contrary one to another, and therefore are so much the more to be feared as they are more powerful, crafty, and cunning than the other animals. And because men are in the highest degree liable to these passions, therefore men are naturally enemies. For he is my greatest enemy whom I must most fear and be on my guard against.

But inasmuch as in the state of nature each is so long independent as he can guard against oppression by another, and it is in vain for one man alone to try and guard against all, it follows hence that so long as the natural right of man is determined by the power of every individual and belongs to everyone, so long it is a nonentity existing in opinion rather than fact, since there is no assurance of making it good. And it is certain that the greater cause of fear every individual has, the less power, and consequently the less right, he possesses. To this must be added, that without mutual help men can hardly support life and cultivate the mind. And so our conclusion is, that that natural right which is special to the human race can hardly be conceived except where men have general rights, and combine to defend the possession of the lands they inhabit and cultivate, to protect themselves, to repel all violence, and to live according to the general judgment of all. For the more there are that combine together, the more right they collectively possess. And if this is why the schoolmen want to call man a sociable animal—I mean because men in the state of nature can hardly be independent—I have nothing to say against them.

Where men have general rights, and are all guided, as it were, by one mind, it is certain that every individual has the less right the more the rest collectively exceed him in power; that is, he has in fact no right over nature but that which the common law allows him. But whatever he is ordered by the general consent, he is bound to execute, or may rightfully be compelled thereto.

This right, which is determined by the power of a multitude, is generally called Dominion. And, speaking generally, he holds dominion to whom are entrusted by common consent affairs of state—such as the laying down, interpretation, and abrogation of laws, the fortification of cities, deciding on war and peace, etc. But if this charge belong to a council composed of the general multitude, then the dominion is called a democracy; if the council be composed of certain chosen persons, then it is an aristocracy; and if, lastly, the care of affairs of state and, consequently, the dominion rest with one man, then it has the name of monarchy.

From what we have proved in this chapter, it becomes clear to us that in the state of nature wrong-doing is impossible; or, if anyone does wrong, it is to himself, not to another. For no one by the law of nature is bound to please another unless he chooses, nor to hold anything to be good or evil but what he himself, according to his own temperament, pronounces to be so; and, to speak generally, nothing is forbidden by the law of nature, except what is beyond everyone's power. . . . For the ordinances of nature are the ordinances of God, which God has instituted by the liberty whereby he exists, and they follow, therefore, from the necessity of the divine nature, and, consequently, are eternal, and cannot be broken. But men are chiefly guided by appetite, without reason; yet for all this they do not disturb the course of nature, but follow it of necessity. And, therefore, a man ignorant and weak of mind is no more bound by natural law to order his life wisely than a sick man is bound to be sound of body.

Therefore wrong-doing cannot be conceived of, except under dominion —that is, where, by the general right of the whole dominion, it is decided what is good and what evil, and where no one does anything rightfully save what he does in accordance with the general decree or consent. For as we said in the last section, that is wrong-doing, which cannot lawfully be committed, or is by law forbidden. . . .

OF THE BEST STATE OF A DOMINION

. . . It is one thing to till a field by right, and another to till it in the best way. One thing, I say, to defend or preserve one's self and to pass judgment by right, and another to defend or preserve one's self in the best way and to pass the best judgment; and, consequently, it is one thing to have dominion and care of affairs of state by right, and another to exercise dominion and direct affairs of state in the best way. And so, as we have treated of the right of every commonwealth in general, it is time to treat of the best state of every dominion.

Now the quality of the state of any dominion is easily perceived from the end of the civil state, which end is nothing else but peace and security of life. And therefore that dominion is the best where men pass their lives in unity and the laws are kept unbroken. For it is certain that seditions, wars, and contempt or breach of the laws are not so much to be imputed to the wickedness of the subjects as to the bad state of a dominion. For men are not born fit for citizenship but must be made so. Besides, men's natural passions are everywhere the same; and if wickedness more prevails, and more offences are committed in one commonwealth than in another, it is certain that the former has not enough pursued the end of unity, nor framed its laws with sufficient forethought; and that, therefore, it has failed in making quite good its right as a commonwealth. For a civil state which has not done away with the causes of seditions, where war is a perpetual object of fear, and where, lastly, the laws are often broken, differs but little from the mere state of nature in which everyone lives after his own mind at the great risk of his life.

But as the vices and inordinate licence and contumacy of subjects must be imputed to the commonwealth, so, on the other hand, their virtue and constant obedience to the laws are to be ascribed in the main to the virtue and perfect right of the commonwealth. . . . And so it is deservedly reckoned to Hannibal as an extraordinary virtue that in his army there never arose a sedition.

Of a commonwealth whose subjects are but hindered by terror from taking arms, it should rather be said that it is free from war than that it has peace. For peace is not mere absence of war, but is a virtue that springs from force of character: for obedience is the constant will to execute what, by the general decree of the commonwealth, ought to be done. Besides, that commonwealth whose peace depends on the sluggishness of its subjects that are led about like sheep to learn but slavery, may more properly be called a desert than a commonwealth.

When, then, we call that dominion best where men pass their lives in unity, I understand a human life defined not by mere circulation of the blood, and other qualities common to all animals but above all by reason, the true excellence and life of the mind.

But be it remarked that by the dominion which I have said is established for this end, I intend that which has been established by a free multitude, not that which is acquired over a multitude by right of war. For a free multitude is guided more by hope than fear; a conquered one more by fear than hope: inasmuch as the former aims at making use of life, the latter but at escaping death. The former, I say, aims at living for its own ends, the latter is forced to belong to the conqueror; and so we say that the latter is enslaved but the former free. And, therefore, the end of a dominion which one gets by right of war is to be master, and have rather slaves than subjects. And so, although between the dominion created by a free multitude and that gained by right of war, if we regard only the abstract right of each, we can make no essential distinction, yet their ends, as we have already shown, and further the means to the preservation of each, are very different.

By what means a prince whose sole motive is lust of mastery should establish and maintain his dominion, the most ingenious Machiavelli has set forth at large, but with what design one can hardly be sure. If, however, he had some good design, as one should believe of a learned man, it seems to have been to show with how little foresight many attempt to remove a tyrant. For though they remove the tyrant, often the causes which make the prince a tyrant can in no wise be removed in this fashion. On the contrary, they are made so much the stronger because a prince is given more cause for his fears when the multitude has made an example of its prince, and glories in the parricide as in a thing well done. Moreover, Machiavelli perhaps wished to show how cautious a free multitude should be of entrusting its welfare absolutely to one man, who, unless in his vanity he thinks he can please everybody, must be in daily fear of plots, and so is forced to look chiefly after his own interest, and, as for the multitude, rather to plot against it than consult its good. And I am the more led to this opinion concerning that most farseeing man because it is known that he was favourable to liberty, for the maintenance of which he has besides given the most wholesome advice.

A Theologico-Political Treatise

THAT IN A FREE STATE
EVERY MAN MAY THINK WHAT HE LIKES,
AND SAY WHAT HE THINKS

If men's minds were as easily controlled as their tongues, every king would sit safely on his throne, and government by compulsion would cease; for every subject would shape his life according to the intentions of his rulers, and would esteem a thing true or false, good or evil, just or unjust, in obedience to their dictates. However, we have shown already that no man's mind can possibly lie wholly at the disposition of another, for no one can willingly transfer his natural right of free reason and judgment, or be compelled so to do. For this reason a government which attempts to control minds is accounted tyrannical, and it is considered an abuse of sovereignty and a usurpation of the rights of subjects, to seek to prescribe what shall be accepted as true, or rejected as false, or what opinions should actuate men in their worship of God. All these questions fall within a man's natural right, which he cannot abdicate even with his own consent.

I admit that the judgment can be biased in many ways and to an almost incredible degree, so that while exempt from direct external control it may be so dependent on another man's words that it may fitly be said to be ruled by him; but although this influence is carried to great lengths, it has never gone so far as to invalidate the statement that every man's understanding is his own, and that brains are as diverse as palates. . . .

However unlimited, therefore, the power of a sovereign government may be, however implicitly it is trusted as the exponent of law and religion, it can never prevent men from forming judgments according to their intellect, or being influenced by any given emotion. It is true that it has the right to treat as enemies all men whose opinions do not, on all subjects, entirely coincide with its own; but we are not discussing its strict rights, but its proper course of action. I grant that it has the right to rule in the most violent manner, and to put citizens to death for very trivial causes, but no one supposes it can do this with the approval of sound judgment. Nay, inasmuch as such things cannot be done without extreme peril to itself, we may even deny that it has the absolute power to do them, or, consequently, the absolute right; for the rights of the sovereign are limited by his power.

Since, therefore, no one can abdicate his freedom of judgment and feeling; since every man is by indefeasible natural right the master of his own thoughts, it follows that men thinking in diverse and contradictory fashions cannot, without disastrous results, be compelled to speak only according to the dictates of the supreme power. Not even the most experienced, to say nothing of the multitude, know how to keep silence. Men's common failing is to confide their plans to others, though there be need for secrecy, so that a government would be most harsh which deprived the individual of his freedom of saying and teaching what he thought; and would be moderate if such freedom were granted. Still we cannot deny that authority may be as much injured by words as by actions; hence, although the freedom we are discussing cannot be entirely denied to subjects, its unlimited concession would be most baneful; we must, therefore, now inquire, how far such freedom can and ought to be conceded without danger to the peace of the state or the power of the rulers. . . .

It follows, plainly, from the explanation given above of the foundations of a state that the ultimate aim of government is not to rule or restrain by fear, nor to exact obedience, but, contrariwise, to free every man from fear that he may live in all possible security; in other words, to strengthen his natural right to exist and work without injury to himself or others.

No, the object of government is not to change men from rational beings into beasts or puppets, but to enable them to develop their minds and bodies in security and to employ their reason unshackled; neither showing hatred, anger, or deceit, nor watched with the eyes of jealousy and injustice. In fact, the true aim of government is liberty.

Now we have seen that in forming a state the power of making laws must either be vested in the body of the citizens, or in a portion of them, or in one man. For, although men's free judgments are very diverse, each one thinking that he alone knows everything, and although complete unanimity of feeling and speech is out of the question, it is impossible to preserve peace unless individuals abdicate their right of acting entirely on their own judgment. Therefore, the individual justly cedes the right of free action, though not of free reason and judgment; no one can act against the authorities without danger to the state, though his feelings and judgment may be at variance therewith; he may even speak against them, provided that he does so from rational conviction, not from fraud, anger, or hatred, and provided that he does not attempt to introduce any change on his private authority. . . .

However, I do not deny that there are some doctrines which, while they are apparently only concerned with abstract truths and falsehoods, are yet propounded and published with unworthy motives. This question we have discussed, . . . and shown that reason should nevertheless remain unshackled. If we hold to the principle that a man's loyalty to the state should be judged, like his loyalty to God, from his actions only— namely, from his charity towards his neighbours—we cannot doubt that the best government will allow freedom of philosophical speculation no less than of religious belief. I confess that from such freedom inconveniences may sometimes arise, but what question was ever settled so wisely that no abuses could possibly spring therefrom? He who seeks to regulate everything by law is more likely to arouse vices than to reform them. It is best to grant what cannot be abolished, even though it be in itself harmful. How many evils spring from luxury, envy, avarice, drunkenness, and the like, yet these are tolerated—vices as they are—because they cannot be prevented by legal enactments. How much more then should free thought be granted, seeing that it is in itself a virtue and that it cannot be crushed! Besides, the evil results can easily be checked, as I will show, by the secular authorities, not to mention that such freedom is absolutely necessary for progress in science and the liberal arts: for no man follows such pursuits to advantage unless his judgment be entirely free and unhampered.

But let it be granted that freedom may be crushed and men be so bound down that they do not dare to utter a whisper, save at the bidding of their rulers; nevertheless this can never be carried to the pitch of making them think according to authority, so that the necessary consequences would be that men would daily be thinking one thing and saying another, to the corruption of good faith, that mainstay of government, and to the fostering of hateful flattery and perfidy, whence spring stratagems and the corruption of every good art.

It is far from possible to impose uniformity of speech, for the more rulers strive to curtail freedom of speech the more obstinately are they resisted; not indeed by the avaricious, the flatterers, and other numbskulls, who think supreme salvation consists in filling their stomachs and gloating over their money-bags, but by those whom good education, sound morality, and virtue have rendered more free. Men, as generally constituted, are most prone to resent the branding as criminal of opinions which they believe to be true, and the proscription as wicked of that which inspires them with piety towards God and man; hence they are ready to forswear the laws and conspire against the authorities, thinking it not shameful but honourable to stir up seditions and perpetuate any sort of crime with this end in view. Such being the constitution of human nature, we see that laws directed against opinions affect the generous-minded rather than the wicked, and are adapted less for coercing criminals than for irritating the upright; so that they cannot be maintained without great peril to the state.

Moreover, such laws are almost always useless, for those who hold that the opinions proscribed are sound cannot possibly obey the law; whereas those who already reject them as false accept the law as a kind of privilege, and make such boast of it, that authority is powerless to repeal it even if such a course be subsequently desired.

To these considerations may be added . . . the history of the Hebrews. And, lastly, how many schisms have arisen in the Church from the attempt of the authorities to decide by law the intricacies of theological controversy! If men were not allured by the hope of getting the law and the authorities on their side, of triumphing over their adversaries in the sight of an applauding multitude, and of acquiring honourable distinctions, they would not strive so maliciously nor would such fury sway their minds. This is taught not only by reason but by daily examples, for laws of this kind prescribing what every man shall believe and forbidding anyone to speak or write to the contrary have often been passed as sops or concessions to the anger of those who cannot tolerate men of enlightenment, and who, by such harsh and crooked enactments can easily turn the devotion of the masses into fury and direct it against whom they will.

How much better would it be to restrain popular anger and fury, instead of passing useless laws which can only be broken by those who love virtue and the liberal arts, thus paring down the state till it is too small to harbour men of talent. What greater misfortune for a state can be conceived than that honourable men should be sent like criminals into exile because they hold diverse opinions which they cannot disguise? What, I say, can be more hurtful than that men who have committed no crime or wickedness should, simply because they are enlightened, be treated as enemies and put to death, and that the scaffold, the terror of evil-doers, should become the arena where the highest examples of tolerance and virtue are displayed to the people with all the marks of ignominy that authority can devise?

He that knows himself to be upright does not fear the death of a criminal and shrinks from no punishment; his mind is not wrung with remorse for any disgraceful deed: he holds that death in a good cause is no punishment but an honour, and that death for freedom is glory.

What purpose then is served by the death of such men, what example is proclaimed? The cause for which they die is unknown to the idle and the foolish, hateful to the turbulent, loved by the upright. The only lesson we can draw from such scenes is to flatter the persecutor, or else to imitate the victim.

If formal assent is not to be esteemed above conviction, and if governments are to retain a firm hold of authority and not be compelled to yield to agitators, it is imperative that freedom of judgment should be granted, so that men may live together in harmony, however diverse or even openly contradictory their opinions may be. We cannot doubt that such is the best system of government and open to the fewest objections, since it is the one most in harmony with human nature. . . . In a democracy (the most natural form of government . . .) everyone submits to the control of authority over his actions, but not over his judgment and reason; that is, seeing that all cannot think alike, the voice of the majority has the force of law, subject to repeal if circumstances bring about a change of opinion. In proportion as the power of free judgment is withheld we depart from the natural condition of mankind, and consequently the government becomes more tyrannical. . . .

I have thus shown:—I. That it is impossible to deprive men of the liberty of saying what they think. II. That such liberty can be conceded to every man without injury to the rights and authority of the sovereign power, and that every man may retain it without injury to such rights, provided that he does not presume upon it to the extent of introducing any new rights into the state, or acting in any way contrary to the existing laws. III. That every man may enjoy this liberty without detriment to the public peace, and that no inconveniences arise therefrom which cannot easily be checked. IV. That every man may enjoy it without injury to his allegiance. V. That laws dealing with speculative problems are entirely useless. VI. Lastly, that not only may such liberty be granted without prejudice to the public peace, to loyalty, and to the rights of rulers, but that it is even necessary for their preservation. For when people try to take it away, and bring to trial not only the acts which alone are capable of offending, but also the opinions of mankind, they only succeed in surrounding their victims with an appearance of martyrdom, and raise feelings of pity and revenge rather than of terror. Uprightness and good faith are thus corrupted, flatterers and traitors are encouraged, and sectarians triumph, inasmuch as concessions have been made to their animosity, and they have gained the state sanction for the doctrines of which they are the interpreters. Hence they arrogate to themselves the state authority and rights, and do not scruple to assert that they have been directly chosen by God, and that their laws are Divine, whereas the laws of the state are human and should therefore yield obedience to the laws of God—in other words, to their own laws. Everyone must see that this is not a state of affairs conducive to public welfare. Wherefore, . . . the safest way for a state is to lay down the rule that religion is comprised solely in the exercise of charity and justice, and that the rights of rulers in sacred no less than in secular matters should merely have to do with actions, but that every man should think what he likes and say what he thinks.

I have thus fulfilled the task I set myself in this treatise. It remains only to call attention to the fact that I have written nothing which I do not most willingly submit to the examination and approval of my country's rulers; and that I am willing to retract anything which they shall decide to be repugnant to the laws, or prejudicial to the public good. I know that I am a man, and as a man liable to error, but against error I have taken scrupulous care, and have striven to keep in entire accordance with the laws of my country, with loyalty, and with morality.

George Santayana

Santayana wrote the essays that follow in the aftermath of World War I. The mood is one we should have no trouble recognizing: it is the mood of the end of an era, and then as now what is said to have died is something called "liberalism."

The reader will find that Santayana has few sympathetic words for liberalism. The equable temper and the willingness to imagine himself into another point of view which he shows when he deals with religion often desert him when he turns to politics. He looks at political creeds almost always from the outside, and tends to see them all as foolish. But his special *bête noire* is liberalism. Santayana can be seen at his worst as well as his best in these essays. There is much in them that is crabbed and bad-tempered. But Santayana's argument poses as deep a challenge to liberalism as any I know. It poses a challenge, indeed, to most contemporary political outlooks. For what he does, in effect, is to express the amused astonishment, and the scorn and despair, that an ancient Greek might feel if he were transported to the present. The "liberalism" of which he speaks is that of the nineteenth and early twentieth centuries. But he looks at that liberalism from a long perspective, and his observations transcend the moment at which he wrote and the limitations of his own prejudices.

There is, furthermore, a special fittingness in concluding this brief section on political philosophy with a selection from Santayana. The two philosophers for whom he had special sympathy were Plato and Spinoza, and the vantage point from which he looks at the modern scene is essentially a combination of Plato's moral and political ideas and Spinoza's realism. The three essays that follow are taken from a collection of Santayana's essays called *Soliloquies in England and Later Soliloquies.*

Classic Liberty

When ancient peoples defended what they called their liberty, the words stood for a plain and urgent interest of theirs: that their cities should not be destroyed, their territory pillaged, and they themselves sold into slavery. For the Greeks in particular liberty meant even more than this. Perhaps the deepest assumption of classic philosophy is that nature and the gods on the one hand and man on the other, both have a fixed character; that there is consequently a necessary piety, a true philosophy, a standard happiness, a normal art. The Greeks believed, not without reason, that they had grasped these permanent principles better than other peoples. They had largely dispelled superstition, experimented in government, and turned life into a rational art. Therefore when they defended their liberty what they defended was not merely freedom to live. It was freedom to live well, to live as other nations did not, in the public experimental study of the world and of human nature. This liberty to discover and pursue a natural happiness, this liberty to grow wise and to live in friendship with the gods and with one another, was the liberty vindicated at Thermopylae by martyrdom and at Salamis by victory.

As Greek cities stood for liberty in the world, so philosophers stood for liberty in the Greek cities. In both cases it was the same kind of liberty, not freedom to wander at hazard or to let things slip, but on the contrary freedom to legislate more precisely, at least for oneself, and to discover and codify the means to true happiness. Many of these pioneers in wisdom were audacious radicals and recoiled from no paradox. Some condemned what was most Greek: mythology, athletics, even multiplicity and physical motion. In the heart of those thriving, loquacious, festive little ant-hills, they preached impassibility and abstraction, the unanswerable scepticism of silence. Others practised a musical and priestly refinement of life, filled with metaphysical mysteries, and formed secret societies, not without a tendency to political domination. The cynics railed at the conventions, making themselves as comfortable as possible in the rôle of beggars and mocking parasites. The conservatives themselves were radical, so intelligent were they, and Plato wrote the charter of the most extreme militarism and communism, for the sake of preserving the free state. It was the swan-song of liberty, a prescription to a diseased old man to become young again and try a second life of superhuman virtue. The old man preferred simply to die.

Many laughed then, as we may be tempted to do, at all those absolute physicians of the soul, each with his panacea. Yet beneath their quarrels the wranglers had a common faith. They all believed there was a single solid natural wisdom to be found, that reason could find it, and that mankind, sobered by reason, could put it in practice. Mankind has continued to run wild and like barbarians to place freedom in their very wildness, till we can hardly conceive the classic assumption of Greek philosophers and cities, that true liberty is bound up with an institution, a corporate scientific discipline, necessary to set free the perfect man, or the god, within us.

Upon the dissolution of paganism the Christian church adopted the classic conception of liberty. Of course, the field in which the higher politics had to operate was now conceived differently, and there was a new experience of the sort of happiness appropriate and possible to man; but the assumption remained unchallenged that Providence, as well as the human soul, had a fixed discoverable scope, and that the business of education, law, and religion was to bring them to operate in harmony. The aim of life, salvation, was involved in the nature of the soul itself, and the means of salvation had been ascertained by a positive science which the church was possessed of, partly revealed and partly experimental. Salvation was simply what, on a broad view, we should see to be health, and religion was nothing but a sort of universal hygiene.

The church, therefore, little as it tolerated heretical liberty, the liberty of moral and intellectual dispersion, felt that it had come into the world to set men free, and constantly demanded liberty for itself, that it might fulfil this mission. It was divinely commissioned to teach, guide, and console all nations and all ages by the self-same means, and to promote at all costs what it conceived to be human perfection. There should be saints and as many saints as possible. The church never admitted, any more than did any sect of ancient philosophers, that its teaching might represent only an eccentric view of the world, or that its guidance and consolations might be suitable only at one stage of human development. To waver in the pursuit of the orthodox ideal could only betray frivolity and want of self-knowledge. The truth of things and the happiness of each man could not lie elsewhere than where the church, summing up all human experience and all divine revelation, had placed it once for all and for everybody. The liberty of the church to fulfil its mission was accordingly hostile to any liberty of dispersion, to any radical consecutive independence, in the life of individuals or of nations.

When it came to full fruition this orthodox freedom was far from gay; it was called sanctity. The freedom of pagan philosophers too had turned out to be rather a stiff and severe pose; but in the Christian dispensation this austerity of true happiness was less to be wondered at, since life on earth was reputed to be abnormal from the beginning, and infected with hereditary disease. The full beauty and joy of restored liberty could hardly become evident in this life. Nevertheless a certain beauty and joy did radiate visibly from the saints; and while we may well think their renunciations and penances misguided or excessive, it is certain that, like the Spartans and the philosophers, they got something for their pains. Their bodies and souls were transfigured, as none now found upon earth. If we admire without imitating them we shall perhaps have done their philosophy exact justice. Classic liberty was a sort of forced and artificial liberty, a poor perfection reserved for an ascetic aristocracy in whom heroism and refinement were touched with perversity and slowly starved themselves to death.

Since those days we have discovered how much larger the universe is, and we have lost our way in it. Any day it may come over us again that our modern liberty to drift in the dark is the most terrible negation of freedom. Nothing happens to us as we would. We want peace and make war. We need science and obey the will to believe, we love art and flounder among whimsicalities, we believe in general comfort and equality and we strain every nerve to become millionaires. After all, antiquity must have been right in thinking that reasonable self-direction must rest on having a determinate character and knowing what it is, and that only the truth about God and happiness, if we somehow found it, could make us free. But the truth is not to be found by guessing at it, as religious prophets and men of genius have done, and then damning every one who does not agree. Human nature, for all its substantial fixity, is a living thing with many varieties and variations. All diversity of opinion is therefore not founded on ignorance; it may express a legitimate change of habit or interest. The classic and Christian synthesis from which we have broken loose was certainly premature, even if the only issue of our liberal experiments should be to lead us back to some such equilibrium. Let us hope at least that the new morality, when it comes, may be more broadly based than the old on knowledge of the world, not so absolute, not so meticulous, and not chanted so much in the monotone of an abstracted sage.

Liberalism and Culture

Modern reformers, religious and political, have usually retained the classic theory of orthodoxy, namely, that there is one right or true system —democracy and free thought, for instance—which it is the reformer's duty to establish in the place of prevalent abuses. Certainly Luther and Calvin and the doctrinaires of the French revolution only meant to substitute one orthodoxy for another, and what they set forth they regarded as valid for all men and forever. Nevertheless they had a greater success in discrediting the received system than in establishing their own, and the general effect of their reforms was to introduce the modern conception of liberty, the liberty of liberalism.

This consists in limiting the prescriptions of the law to a few points, for the most part negative, leaving it to the initiative and conscience of individuals to order their life and conversation as they like, provided only they do not interfere with the same freedom in others. In practice liberal countries have never reached this ideal of peaceful anarchy, but have continued to enforce state education, monogamy, the vested rights of property, and sometimes military service. But within whatever limits, liberty is understood to lie in the individual being left alone, so that he may express his personal impulses as he pleases in word and action.

A philosopher can readily see that this liberal ideal implies a certain view about the relations of man in the universe. It implies that the ultimate environment, divine or natural, is either chaotic in itself or undiscoverable by human science, and that human nature, too, is either radically various or only determinable in a few essentials, round which individual variations play *ad libitum*. For this reason no normal religion, science, art, or way of happiness can be prescribed. These remain always open, even in their foundations, for each man to arrange for himself. The more things are essentially unsettled and optional, the more liberty of this sort there may safely be in the world and the deeper it may run.

Man, however, is a gregarious animal, and much more so in his mind than in his body. He may like to go alone for a walk, but hates to stand alone in his opinions. And he is so imitative that what he thinks he most wishes to do is whatever he sees other people doing. Hence if compulsory organization disappears a thousand free and private organizations at once take its place. Virginal liberty is good only to be surrendered at the right time to a right influence. A state in which government is limited to police duty must allow churches, universities (with millionaires to found them), public sports, private charities, masonic or monastic orders, and every other sort of party institution, to flourish within it unhindered; otherwise that state would hardly be civilized and nothing of importance would ever be done in it. Yet the prevalence of such free associations will jeopardize the perfect liberty which individuals are supposed to enjoy. Private organizations are meddlesome; if they cannot impose themselves by force, they insinuate themselves by propaganda, and no paternal government ever exerted so pervasive and indiscreet an influence as they know how to acquire. Fashions in speech or clothes are harder to evade than any laws, and religion, when it is chosen and sectarian, eats more into the soul than when it is established and conventional. In a society honeycombed by private societies a man finds his life supervised, his opportunities pre-empted, his conscience intimidated, and his pocket drained. Every one he meets informs him of a new duty and presents him with a new subscription list. At every turn he must choose between being incorporated or being ostracized. Indeed, the worst and most radical failure in his fabled liberty of choice is that he never had a choice about his environment or about his faculties, and has to take his luck as to his body, his mind, his position, his country, and his family. Even where he may cast a vote his vote is far from decisive. In electing a government, as in selecting a wife, only two or three candidates are commonly available, and the freeman's modest privilege is to declare hopefully which one he wants and then to put up with the one he gets.

If liberalism had been a primitive system, with no positive institutions behind it, it would have left human genius in the most depressed and forlorn condition. The organized part of life would have been a choice among little servitudes, and the free personal part would have been a blank. Fortunately, liberal ages have been secondary ages, inheriting the monuments, the feelings, and the social hierarchy of previous times, when men had lived in compulsory unison, having only one unquestioned religion, one style of art, one political order, one common spring of laughter and tears. Liberalism has come to remove the strain and the trammels of these traditions without as yet uprooting the traditions themselves. Most people retain their preliberal heritage and hardly remember that they are legally free to abandon it and to sample any and every other form of life. Liberalism does not go very deep; it is an adventitious principle, a mere loosening of an older structure. For that reason it brings to all who felt cramped and ill-suited such comfort and relief. It offers them an escape from all sorts of accidental tyrannies. It opens to them that sweet, scholarly, tenderly moral, critically superior attitude of mind which Matthew Arnold called culture.

Primitive, dragooned, unanimous ages cannot possess culture. What they possess is what the Germans call a *Kultur,* some type or other of manners, laws, implements, arts, religion. When these national possessions are perused and relished by some individual who does not take them for granted and who understands and judges them as if from outside, his acquaintance with them becomes an element in his culture; and if he is at home in many such forms of life and thought, his culture is the more perfect. It should ideally be culled from everywhere. Culture is a triumph of the individual over society. It is his way of profiting intellectually by a world he has not helped to make.

Culture requires liberalism for its foundation, and liberalism requires culture for its crown. It is culture that integrates in imagination the activities which liberalism so dangerously disperses in practice. Out of the public disarray of beliefs and efforts it gathers its private collection of curiosities, much as amateurs stock their museums with fragments of ancient works. It possesses a wealth of vicarious experience and historical insight which comforts it for having nothing of its own to contribute to history. The man of culture abounds in discriminating sentiments; he lives under the distant influence of exalted minds; his familiar thoughts at breakfast are intimate appreciations of poetry and art, and if his culture is really mellow, he sometimes smiles a little at his own culture.

Culture came into the modern world with the renaissance, when personal humours and remote inspiration broke in upon the consecrated mediaeval mind. Piety and learning had their intrinsic charms, but, after all, they had been cultivated for the sake of ulterior duties and benefits, and in order to appropriate and hand down the revealed wisdom which opened the way to heaven. Culture, on the contrary, had no ulterior purpose, no forced unity. It was an aroma inhaled by those who walked in the evening in the garden of life. Far from being a means to religion, it threw religion also into the context of human experience, and touched its mysteries and quarrels with judgement and elegance. It liberated the studious mind from obligatory or national discipline, and as far as possible from all bonds of time, place, utility, and co-operation, kindling sympathies by preference with what was most exotic, and compensating the mind for the ignominious necessity of having to be, in practical matters, local and partisan. Culture was courteous, open, unconscious of self; it was the joy of living every life but one's own. And its moral side—for everything has its moral side—lay in the just judgements it fostered, the clear sense it awakened of the different qualities and values of things. The scale of values established by the man of culture might sometimes be fanciful or frivolous, but he was always most scrupulous, according to his lights, in distinguishing the better from the worse. This conscientiousness, after all, is the only form of morality that a liberal society can insist upon.

The days of liberalism are numbered. First the horrors of competition discredited it, and now the trial of war, which it foolishly thought it could elude. The vogue of culture, too, has declined. We see that the man whose success is merely personal—the actor, the sophist, the millionaire, the aesthete—is incurably vulgar. The rightness of liberalism is exactly proportional to the diversity of human nature, to its vague hold on its ideals. Where this vagueness and play of variation stop, and they stop not far below the surface, the sphere of public organization should begin. It is in the subsoil of uniformity, of tradition, of dire necessity that human welfare is rooted, together with wisdom and unaffected art, and the flowers of culture that do not draw their sap from that soil are only paper flowers.

The Irony of Liberalism

To the mind of the ancients, who knew something of such matters, liberty and prosperity seemed hardly compatible, yet modern liberalism wants them together. Liberals believe that free inquiry, free invention, free association, and free trade are sure to produce prosperity. I have no doubt they are right in this; the nineteenth century, that golden age of liberalism, certainly saw a great increase in wealth, in science, and in comforts. What the ancients had before them was a different side of the question; they had no experience of liberalism; they expected to be state-ridden in their religion, their customs, and their military service; even in their personal and family morals they did not begrudge the strictest discipline; their states needed to be intensely unified, being small and in constant danger of total destruction. Under these circumstances it seemed clear to them that prosperity, however it might have been produced, was dangerous to liberty. Prosperity brought power; and when a people exercises control over other peoples its government becomes ponderous even at home; its elaborate machinery cannot be stopped, and can hardly be mended; the imperial people becomes the slave of its commitments. Moreover, prosperity requires inequalities of function and creates inequalities of fortune; and both too much work and too much wealth kill liberty in the individual. They involve subjection to *things*; and this is contrary to what the ancients, who had the pride of noble animals, called freedom. Prosperity, both for individuals and for states, means possessions; and possessions mean burdens and harness and slavery; and slavery for the mind, too, because it is not only the rich man's time that is preempted, but his affections, his judgement, and the range of his thoughts.

I often wonder, looking at my rich friends, how far their possessions are facilities and how far they are impediments. The telephone, for instance, is a facility if you wish to be in many places at once and to attend to anything that may turn up; it is an impediment if you are happy where you are and in what you are doing. Public motor-vehicles, public libraries, and public attendants (such as waiters in hotels, when they wait) are a convenience, which even the impecunious may enjoy; but private automobiles, private collections of books or pictures, and private servants are, to my thinking, an encumbrance: but then I am an old fogy and almost an ancient philosopher, and I don't count. I prize civilization, being bred in towns and liking to hear and to see what new things people are up to. I like to walk about amidst the beautiful things that adorn the world; but private wealth I should decline, or any sort of personal possessions, because they would take away my liberty.

Perhaps what liberalism aspires to marry with liberty is not so much prosperity as progress. Progress means continued change for the better; and it is obvious that liberty will conduce to progress in all those things, such as writing poetry, which a man can pursue without aid or interference from others: where aid is requisite and interference probable, as in politics, liberty conduces to progress only in so far as people are unanimous, and spontaneously wish to move in the same direction. Now what is the direction of change which seems progress to liberals? A pure liberal might reply. The direction of liberty itself: the ideal is that every man should move in whatever direction he likes, with the aid of such as agree with him, and without interfering with those who disagree. Liberty so conceived would be identical with happiness, with spontaneous life, blamelessly and safely lived; and the impulse of liberalism, to give everybody what he wants, in so far as that is possible, would be identical with simple kindness. Benevolence was one of the chief motives in liberalism in the beginning, and many a liberal is still full of kindness in his private capacity; but politically, as a liberal, he is something more than kind. The direction in which many, or even most, people would like to move fills him with disgust and indignation; he does not at all wish them to be happy, unless they can be happy on his own diet; and being a reformer and a philanthropist, he exerts himself to turn all men into the sort of men he likes, so as to be able to like them. It would be selfish, he thinks, to let people alone. They must be helped, and not merely helped to what they desire—that might really be very bad for them—but helped onwards, upwards in the *right* direction. Progress could not be rightly placed in a smaller population, a simpler economy, more moral diversity between nations, and stricter moral discipline in each of them. That would be progress backwards, and if it made people happier, it would not make the liberal so. Progress, if it is to please him, must consider in the direction in which the nineteenth century progressed, towards vast numbers, material complexity, moral uniformity, and economic interdependence. The best little boy, for instance, according to the liberal ideal, desires to be washed, to go to school, to do Swedish exercises, and to learn everything out of books. But perhaps the individual little boy (and according to the liberal philosophy his individuality is sacred, and the only judge of what is good or true for him is his own consciousness) desires to go dirty, to make mud-pies in the street, and to learn everything by experience or by report from older boys. When the philanthropist runs up to the rescue, this little in-grate snivels at him the very principle of liberal liberty, "Let me alone." To inform such an urchin that he does not know what is good for him, that he is a slave to bad habits and devilish instincts, that true freedom for him can only come of correcting himself, until he has learned to find happiness in virtue—plainly that would be to abandon liberalism, and to preach the classical doctrine that the good is not liberty but wisdom. Liberalism was a protest against just such assumptions of authority. It emphatically refused to pursue an eventual stoical freedom, absurdly so called, which was to come when we had given up everything we really wanted—the mock freedom of service. In the presence of the little boy, liberal philosophy takes a middle course. It is convinced—though it would not do to tell him so prematurely—that he must be allowed to go dirty for a time, until sufficient experience of filth teaches him how much more comfortable it is to be clean; also that he will go to school of his own ac-cord if the books have pictures enough in them, and if the teacher begins by showing him how to make superior mud-pies. As to morals and re-ligion, the boy and his companions will evolve the appropriate ones in time out of their own experience, and no others would be genuine.

Liberal philosophy, at this point, ceases to be empirical and British in order to become German and transcendental. Moral life, it now believes, is not the pursuit of liberty and happiness of all sorts by all sorts of dif-ferent creatures; it is the development of a single spirit in all life through a series of necessary phases, each higher than the preceding one. No man, accordingly, can really or ultimately desire anything but what the best people desire. This is the principle of the higher snobbery; and in fact, all earnest liberals are higher snobs. If you refuse to move in the prescribed direction, you are not simply different, you are arrested and perverse. The savage must not remain a savage, nor the nun a nun, and China must not keep its wall. If the animals remain animals it is somehow through a failure of the will in them, and very sad. Classic liberty, though only a name for stubborn independence, and obedience to one's own nature, was too free, in one way, for the modern liberal. It accepted all sorts of perfections, animal, human, and divine, as final after their kind, each the seat of a sufficient virtue and happiness. It was polytheistic. Between master and slave, between man and woman, it admitted no moral advance or development; they were, or might be, equally perfect. Inequality was honourable; amongst the humblest there could be dignity and sweetness; the higher snobbery would have been absurd, because if you were not content to be what you were now, how could you ever be content with anything? But the transcendental principle of progress is pantheistic. It requires everything to be ill at ease in its own house; no one can be really free or happy but all must be tossed, like herded emigrants, on the same compulsory voyage, to the same unhomely destination. The world came from a nebula, and to a nebula it returns. In the interval, happiness is not to be found in being a fixed star, as bright and pure as possible, even if only for a season; happiness is to flow and dissolve in sympathy with one's higher destiny.

The notion of progress is thus merged with that of universal evolution, dropping the element of liberty and even of improvement. Nevertheless, in the political expression of liberalism, liberty took the first innings. Protestants began by asserting the right of private judgement in interpreting scripture; transcendentalists ended by asserting the divine right of the individual to impose his own spirit on everything he touched. His duty to himself, which was also his deepest instinct, was to suck in from the widest possible field all that was congenial to him, and to reject, down to his very centre, whatever might thwart or offend. Sometimes he carried his consistency in egotism to the length of denying that anything he could not digest could possibly exist, or that the material world and foreign nations were more than ideal pawns in the game he played with himself for his self-development. Even when not initiated into these transcendental mysteries, he was filled with practical self-trust, the desire to give himself freedom, and the belief that he deserved it. There was no need of exploring anything he was not tempted to explore; he had an equal right to his opinion, whatever the limits of his knowledge; and he should be coerced as little as possible in his action. In specific matters, for the sake of expediency, he might be willing to yield to the majority; but only when his vote had been counted, and as a sort of insurance against being disturbed in his residual liberty.

There was a general conviction behind all these maxims, that tradition corrupts experience. All sensation—which is the test of matters of fact—is somebody's sensation; all reasoning is somebody's reasoning, and vitally persuasive as it first comes; but when transmitted the evidence loses its edge, words drop their full meaning, and inert conventions falsify the insights of those who had instituted them. Therefore, reform, revision, restatement are perpetually required: any individual, according to this view, who honestly corrected tradition was sure to improve upon it. Whatsoever was not the fresh handiwork of the soul and true to its present demand was bad for that soul. A man without traditions, if he could only be materially well equipped, would be purer, more rational, more virtuous than if he had been an heir to anything. *Weh dir, dass du ein Enkel bist!* Blessed are the orphans, for they shall deserve to have children; blessed the American! Philosophy should be transcendental, history romantic and focussed in one's own country, politics democratic, and art individual and above convention. Variety in religious dogma would only prove the truth —that is, the inwardness—of inspiration.

Yet if this transcendental freedom had been the whole of liberalism, would not the animals, such of them at least as are not gregarious, have been the most perfect liberals? Are they not ruled wholly from within? Do they not enjoy complete freedom of conscience and of expression? Does Mrs. Grundy interfere with their spontaneous actions? Are they ever compelled to fight except by their own impulse and in their private interest? Yet it was not the ideal of liberalism to return to nature; far from it. It admonished the dogs not to bark and bite, even if, in the words of the sacred poet, "it is their nature to." Dogs, according to transcendental philosophy, ought to improve their nature, and to behave better. A chief part of the liberal inspiration was the love of peace, safety, comfort, and general information; it aimed at stable wealth, it insisted on education, it venerated culture. It was wholly out of sympathy with the wilder instincts of man, with the love of foraging, of hunting, of fighting, of plotting, of carousing, or of doing penance. It had an acute, a sickening horror of suffering; to be cruel was devilish and to be hardened to pain was brutal. I am afraid liberalism was hopelessly pre-Nietzschean; it was Victorian; it was tame. In inviting every man to be free and autonomous it assumed that, once free, he would wish to be rich, to be educated, and to be demure. How could he possibly fail to covet a way of life which, in the eyes of liberals, was so obviously the best? It must have been a painful surprise to them, and most inexplicable, that hardly anybody who has had a taste of the liberal system has ever liked it.

What about liberty in love? If there is one ingenuous and winged creature among the immortals, it is Eros; the freer and more innocent love is, the more it will flutter, the farther it will range, and the higher it will soar. But at the touch of matter, of conditions, of consequences, how all its freedom shrivels, or turns into tragedy! What prohibitions, what

hypocrisies, what responsibilities, what sorrows! The progress of civilization compels love to respect the limits set to it by earlier vows, by age,
sex, class, race, religion, blood relationship, and even fictitious relationship; bounds of which the impertinent Eros himself knows nothing. Society
smothers the imp altogether in the long christening-clothes of domestic
affection and religious duty. What was once a sensuous intoxication, a
mystic rapture, an enchanted friendship, becomes all a question of money,
of habit, of children. British liberalism has been particularly cruel to love;
in the Victorian era all its amiable impulses were reputed indecent, until
a marriage certificate suddenly rendered them godly, though still un-
mentionable. And what liberty does even the latest radicalism offer to the
heart? Liberty to be divorced; divorced at great expense, with shabby
perjuries and public scandal, probably in order to be at once married
again, until the next divorce. Was it not franker and nobler to leave love,
as in Spain, to the poets; to let the stripling play the guitar as much as
he liked in the moonlight, exchange passionate glances, whisper daily at
the lattice, and then, dressing the bride in black, to dismiss free fancy at
the church door, saying: Henceforth let thy names be charity and
fidelity and obedience?

It is not politics that can bring true liberty to the soul; that must be
achieved, if at all, by philosophy; but liberalism may bring large opportunities for achievement in a man's outward life. It intensifies—because
it renders attainable—the lure of public distinction, of luxury, of love surrounded by refined pleasures. The liberal state stimulates the imagination
of an ambitious man to the highest degree. Those who have a good start
in the universal competition, or sharp wits, or audacity, will find plenty of
prizes awaiting them. With the pride of wealth, when it is great, there
comes the pride of munificence; in the suburbs of wealth there is culture,
and in its service there is science. When science can minister to wealth
and intelligence to dominion, both can be carried on the shoulders of
the plutocracy which dominates the liberal state; and they can fill it with
innumerable comforts and marvellous inventions. At the same time, nothing will hinder the weaker members of rich families from becoming
clergymen or even scholars or artists; or they may range over the five
continents, hunt whatever wild beasts remain in the jungle, and write
books about savages.

Whether these prizes offered by liberal society are worth winning,
I cannot say from experience, never having desired them; but the aspects
of modern life which any one may observe, and the analytic picture of it
which the novelists supply, are not very attractive. Wealth is always,
even when most secure, full of itch and fear; worry about health, children,
religion, marriage, servants; and the awful question of where to live,
when one may live anywhere, and yet all seems to depend on the choice.
For the politician, politics are less important than his private affairs, and

less interesting than bridge; and he has always a party, or a wicked opposition, on which to throw the blame if his careless measures turn out badly. No one in office can be a true statesman, because a true statesman is consistent, and public opinion will never long support any consistent course. What the successful man in modern society really most cares about is love; love for him is a curious mixture of sensuality, vanity, and friendship; it lights up all the world of his thought and action with its secret and unsteady flame. Even when mutual and legal, it seems to be three-quarters anxiety and sorrow; for if nothing worse happens to lovers, they grow old. I hear no laughter among the rich which is not forced and nervous. I find no sense of moral security amongst them, no happy freedom, no mastery over anything. Yet this is the very cream of liberal life, the brilliant success for the sake of which Christendom was overturned, and the dull peasantry elevated into factory-hands, shopkeepers, and chauffeurs.

When the lists are open to all, and the one aim of life is to live as much as possible like the rich, the majority must needs be discouraged. The same task is proposed to unequal strengths, and the competition emphasizes the inequality. There was more encouragement for mediocre people when happiness was set before them in mediocrity, or in excellence in some special craft. Now the mass, hopelessly out of the running in the race for wealth, falls out and drifts into squalor. Since there is liberty, the listless man will work as little and drink as much as he can; he will crawl into whatever tenement he can get cheapest, seek the society in which least effort is demanded and least shame is felt, have as many children as improvidence sends him, let himself out, at a pinch, for whatever service and whatever wages he can obtain, drift into some syndicated servitude or some great migration, or sink in solitude into the deepest misery. He then becomes a denizen of those slimy quarters, under the shadow of railway bridges, breweries, and gas-works, where the blear lights of a public-house peer through the rain at every corner, and offer him the one joy remaining in life; for joy is not to be mentioned in the same breath as the female prowling by the door, hardly less befuddled and bedraggled than the lurching idlers whom she endeavours to entice; but perhaps God does not see all this, because a pall hangs over it perpetually of impenetrable smoke. The liberal system, which sought to raise the individual, has degraded the masses; and this on so vast a scale and to so pitiable a degree, that the other element in liberalism, philanthropic zeal, has come again to the fore. Liberty go hang, say the new radicals; let us save the people. Liberal legislation, which was to have reduced government to the minimum of police control, now has undertaken public education, social reform, and even the management of industry.

This happy people can read. It supports a press conforming to the tastes of the common man, or rather to such tastes as common men can have in common; for the best in each is not diffused enough to be catered for in public. Moreover, this press is audaciously managed by some adventitious power, which guides it for its own purposes, commercial or sectarian. Superstitions old and new thrive in this infected atmosphere; they are now all treated with a curious respect, as if nobody could have anything to object to them. It is all a scramble of prejudices and rumours; whatever first catches the ear becomes a nucleus for all further presumptions and sympathies. Advertising is the modern substitute for argument, its function is to make the worse appear the better article. A confused competition of all propagandas—those insults to human nature—is carried on by the most expert psychological methods, which the art of advertising has discovered; for instance, by always repeating a lie, when it has been exposed, instead of retracting it. The world at large is deafened; but each propaganda makes its little knot of proselytes, and inspires them with a new readiness to persecute and to suffer in the sacred cause. The only question is, which propaganda can first materially reach the greatest number of persons, and can most efficaciously quench all the others. At present, it looks as if the German, the Catholic, and the communist propaganda had the best chances; but these three are divergent essentially (though against a common enemy they may work for a while together, as they did during this war), and they appeal to different weaknesses of human nature; they are alike, however, in being equally illiberal, equally "*rücksichtlos*" and "*böse*," equally regardless of the harm they may do, and accounting it all an added glory, like baiting the devil. By giving a free rein to such propagandas, and by disgusting the people with too much optimism, toleration, and neutrality, liberalism has introduced a new reign of unqualified ill-will. Hatred and wilfulness are everywhere; nations and classes are called to life on purpose to embody them; they are summoned by their leaders to shake off the lethargy of contentment and to become conscious of their existence and of their terrible wrongs. These propagandas have taken shape in the blue sky of liberalism, like so many summer clouds; they seem airships sailing under a flag of truce; but they are engines of war, and on the first occasion they will hoist their true colours, and break the peace which allowed them to cruise over us so leisurely. Each will try to establish its universal ascendancy by force, in contempt of personal freedom, or the voice of majorities. It will rely, against the apathy and vagueness of the million, on concentrated zeal in its adepts. Minorities everywhere have their way; and majorities, grown familiar with projects that at first shocked them, decide one fine morning that there may be no harm in them after all, and follow like sheep. Every trade, sect, private company, and aspiring nation, finding some one to lead it, asserts itself "ruthlessly" against every other. Incipient formations in the body politic, cutting across and subverting its old constitution, eat one another up, like different species of animals; and the combat can never cease except some day, perhaps, for lack of combatants. Liberalism has merely cleared a field in which every soul and every corporate interest may fight with every other for domination. Whoever is victorious in this struggle will make an end of liberalism; and the new order, which will deem itself saved, will have to defend itself in the following age against a new crop of rebels.

For myself, even if I could live to see it, I should not be afraid of the future domination, whatever it may be. One has to live in some age, under some fashion; I have found, in different times and places, the liberal, the Catholic, and the German air quite possible to breathe; nor, I am sure, would communism be without its advantages to a free mind, and its splendid emotions. Fanatics, as Tacitus said of the Jews or Christians, are consumed with hatred of the human race, which offends them; yet they are themselves human; and nature in them takes its revenge, and something reasonable and sweet bubbles up out of the very fountain of their madness. Once established in the world the new dispensation forms a ruling caste, a conventional morality, a standard of honour; safety and happiness soften the heart of the tyrant. Aristocracy knows how to kiss the ruddy cheeks of its tenants' children; and before mounting its thoroughbred horse at the park gates, it pats him with a gloved hand, and gives him a lump of sugar; nor does it forget to ask the groom, with a kindly interest, when he is setting out for the war. Poor flunkey! The demagogues will tell him he is a fool, to let himself be dragooned into a regiment, and marched off to endure untold privations, death, or ghastly wounds, all for some fantastic reason which is nothing to him. It is a hard fate; but can this world promise anybody anything better? For the moment he will have a smart uniform; beers and lasses will be obtainable; many comrades will march by his side; and he may return, if he is lucky, to work again in his master's stables, lounge at the public-house, and bounce his children on his knee amongst the hollyhocks before his cottage. Would the demagogues give him better prospects, or prove better masters? Would he be happier with no masters at all? Consider the demagogues themselves, and their history. They found themselves in the extreme of misery; but even this is a sort of distinction, and marks off a new species, seizing new weapons in the struggle for existence. The scum of the earth gathers itself together, becomes a criminal or a revolutionary society, finds some visionary or some cosmopolitan agitator to lead it, establishes its own code of ethics, imposes the desperate discipline of outlaws upon its members, and prepares to rend the free society that allowed it to exist. It is astonishing with what docility masses of Englishmen, supposed to be jealous of their personal liberty, will obey such a revolutionary junta, that taxes and commands them, and decrees when they shall starve and when they shall fight. I suspect that the working-people of the towns no longer have what was called the British character. Their forced unanimity in action and passion is like that of the ages of faith; its inspiration, like that of early Christianity, comes from a few apostles, perhaps foreign Jews, men who in the beginning had visions of some millennium; and the cohesion of the faithful is maintained afterwards by preaching, by custom, by persecution, and by murder. Yet it is intelligible that the most earnest liberals, who in so far as they were advocates of liberty fostered these conspiracies, in so far as they are philanthropists should applaud them, and feel the need of this new tyranny. They save liberal principles by saying that they applaud it only provisionally as a necessary means of freeing the people. But of freeing the people from what? From the consequences of freedom.

Afterword

There is a special kind of pleasure—though not everybody is equally enthusiastic about it—in leaving a warm bed in the morning and plunging into a cold mountain lake. If we can stand the shock, it wakes us up; it reminds us that we are alive, that we don't have to drag along in obedience to habit and routine, that we have some choices to make about how to live the day. That is the pleasure that philosophy brings to reflection on politics. In one way, Plato, Spinoza, and Santayana are like the rest of us where politics are concerned: they have their likes and dislikes, they adopt positions, they praise and condemn. But they do something more. They take the ideals we use when we decide where we stand, and ask whether these ideals themselves make sense.

"Democracy," for example, is a word employed by almost all of us—whether we are conservatives, liberals, or radicals—as a term of praise. But the effect of reading Plato is to make us ask why we do so. He leaves us surprised that we haven't seen some of the obvious implications of the idea. His words on democracy have a prophet's sting, a prophet's indignation at the wasting of human effort and the corrupting of human hopes. But he isn't a prophet, he is a philosopher. His indignation is directed at stupidity, at intellectual dissoluteness and vulgarity, much more than at moral dissoluteness. He finds it difficult, indeed, to separate the two. The immorality of democracy goes back to the intellectual error on which it is based. To grant every man liberty to do as he pleases is to imply that there are no right principles of conduct. To say that all men are equal is to say that all human interests and achievements are on a par, and that intelligent discrimination is unnecessary or impossible. Democracy thus makes a principle of not acting on principle. It erects systematic mindlessness into a creed.

Not that democracy isn't delightful in many ways. Plato recognizes its attractions: democracy offers a social order, he agrees, that is open, commodious, tolerant, variegated, exciting. It gives people elbowroom, and it is like a great bazaar. One can find anything one wants in it—any style of life, any way of doing business, any kind of law and disobedience to law. Everything bursts with liberty and equality; indeed, democracy is so generous, so free from any desire to discriminate against anybody, that it gives equality to equals and unequals alike. No one is ever finally told No: frauds receive as much respect as honest men, and even people convicted of crimes walk around free.

But all this is dizzying and confusing. This genial tolerance and love of variety are also the sources of the inherent weaknesses in democracy and the democratic man—spinelessness, the habit of swinging violently from one extreme to the other, receptivity to each new style, a short memory and an incapacity to exercise foresight, the inability to steer a steady course. These weaknesses can't be cured by patching up democracy here and there, or even by educating its citizens better. The democratic social order is itself a style of life, a way of educating people. And the essence of the education it gives is that everything is equal, all appetites, all ideas, all pipe dreams, and that every man's opinion as to what is good is as valid as every other man's. Democracy is the last effort of men who have lost their moral direction to live together in harmony before they fall into anarchy or tyranny.

Unless we are totally blinded by the slogans of our day, we will find it hard to escape the suasion of Plato's argument. Not only his theories but his immediate perceptions are arresting: we know what he means; we have seen it ourselves. When he recounts how the democratic man passes his days, he could be describing an account executive in Westchester: ". . . he spends his life, every day indulging the desire that comes along; now he drinks deep and tootles on the pipes, then again he drinks water and goes in for slimming; at times it is bodily exercise, at times idleness and complete carelessness, sometimes he makes a show of studying philosophy."

Plato's theories about democracy, of course, may be mistaken. His specific insights are so striking, they so often seem so exactly right, that we may leap erroneously to the conclusion that his general theories are also correct. But his insights may be quite independent of them. He is not only a theorist but an inspired poet, and he himself is wary of people who are inspired. In one of his dialogues, the *Ion*, he asks how it is that artists so often come to the right conclusion by mysterious, intuitive paths. And in *The Republic* he suggests that the intuitions of poets are essentially untrustworthy and dangerous, and that in a perfect commonwealth poets would be crowned with garlands and then ushered firmly to the gates of the city and put outside. Plato himself would have been the first to suffer this fate. He had a power of vision that was a gift of the gods, not a product of his theories.

But he does have theories, an armory of them, and they have something to do, obviously, with his capacity to pick out facts about democracy which are not peculiar to Athens. He doesn't labor these theories, for there is little pedantry in him; but merely to list them is to discover how much in what we now call "sociology" is hardly new. Plato discusses the rise and fall of democracy in terms of class struggle. He refers to the role of impoverished and embittered elements, belonging to former ruling classes, in spreading revolutionary ideas. He describes the ethic of hard work and frugality, of abstemiousness and self-restraint, that characterizes the first generation of those who accumulate wealth—a "Protestant ethic" without Protestantism. And he portrays the alienation from this ethic of the children of the affluent—their desire to drop out, to listen to the songs of the lotus-eaters. Generational conflicts, the rise and fall of elites, the difference between economic power that rests on landholding and that which derives from trade and industry, are all part of Plato's account of democracy.

Yet, for Plato, none of these sociological elements is decisive in explaining democracy. The key, in his view, is the fact that it turns upside down the principle that must govern any sound political system. The test of such a system, Plato believes, is whether it puts into power the right people, those most fit to govern; that is to say, those who know what is best for the society, and who are devoted to the public good above all else. Hence in a truly just society, philosophers, or kings trained by philosophers, would rule. For the task of philosophy is to determine what is good in everyday practice by studying the eternal Idea of the Good; and because philosophers, if they are fully philosophers, love this Good supremely and are willing for its sake to sacrifice personal advantage and possessions—to live without family, children, property, and material pleasures if these cloud their minds and make them partial in their judgments—they should have the reins of power. Plato's critique of democracy depends crucially on this conception of a good society. And if we ask whether this critique is justified, we have to ask whether this conception is defensible.

What, then, are the assumptions on which this conception rests? There are at least eight: One, an objective Good exists, quite independent of personal tastes, and knowledge of this Good constitutes a science. Two, some men are capable of mastering this science. Three, there are impartial procedures by which these men can be selected and educated. Four, once they achieve this knowledge of the Good, they will apply it impartially. Five, they will never disagree among themselves about how to apply it. Six, the Good whose implications they spell out is beneficial to everybody in the society; there are no fundamental conflicts of interest such that when some people gain, others lose. Seven, there are methods of bringing the entire society around to accepting peacefully the monopolistic exercise of power by this chosen elite. Eight, these methods aren't worse than the original disease which the new society was to cure.

These are eight stunning assumptions. Although they figure in many other political philosophies—Leninism, for example—every one of them is questionable. And if even one of them is wrong, Plato's ideal collapses. Nor is it an adequate defense of Plato to say that he is merely talking about an ideal, and isn't so foolish as to imagine that it can be put into effect. Even if this is true, as it probably is, the fact remains that he offers a standard for judging political reality that will lead us to condemn, as evil, situations that are unavoidable. His ideal state therefore points us in the wrong direction when we try to formulate our political problems or to determine a solution for them. If we think it unavoidable, for example, that even reasonable and honorable men will honestly differ over what is best for the state, then the solution does not lie in invoking the standard of a heavenly city where such disagreements don't take place. Rather, we must find practical ways by which disputes can be settled and the decision made as to who is to govern. Although the search for such practical measures may not lead us to democracy, the recognition that any political system must have a way of dealing with this problem vitiates much of Plato's denunciation of democracy as irrational or unphilosophical.

A central defect of Plato's analysis, indeed, is that he presents only a single model of good government, and treats all other models as perversions of it. The result, as his student Aristotle points out, is that he overlooks important facts. For example, when democracy declines, it doesn't always slide into tyranny; sometimes it turns into oligarchy. Aristotle suggests that it is better to admit several different models, appropriate to different conditions; and he offers three—monarchy, aristocracy, and constitutional government. When the central principle that defines a model is pushed to excess, according to him, its perversion arises: monarchy becomes tyranny, aristocracy becomes oligarchy, and constitutional government becomes democracy.

In Aristotle's view, of all these perversions, democracy is the most tolerable. Indeed, he reminds his readers that Plato himself thinks that democracy is the worst system of government when we compare systems that are working in peak form, but the best system when all are working badly. And Aristotle makes the further point that "democracy" is an ambiguous term. It may refer to "constitutional democracy," in which a basic law or constitution is supreme, or to the kind of "democracy" consisting of government by the multitude, gathered together in popular assembly and uninhibited by constitutional restrictions. If democracy is a form of government by law, this latter kind of regime should not even be called "democratic," says Aristotle.

Aristotle's critique of his master helps us to see Plato's theory, I think, in better perspective. For the most part, what people in the Western world today call "democracy" is constitutional government with an egalitarian tendency and a libertarian cast. Plato's critique, therefore, does not go to the center of the target. It is the critique of a caricature. It overlooks the role of law in democracy, the limitations on majorities, and the special powers, for better or worse, that elites—economic, hereditary, bureaucratic, or intellectual—play in the decision-making process.

Nevertheless, within its limits, Plato's is a just critique all the same.

For Plato is not the only one to caricature democracy. Democratic societies often caricature themselves. Many of democracy's adherents regularly forget that liberty and equality are workable principles only within a framework of law, and only when, side by side with these principles, there exist in the surrounding society admiration for difficult achievement and respect for trained intelligence. When liberty and equality run loose as undefined absolutes, we should not be surprised if democracies begin to accord with Plato's description of them.

In the final analysis, debating with Plato, refuting him here and adding a qualification there, is a doomed enterprise. It never quite turns back the emotional thrust of his arguments. For he is a political idealist, the paradigm of all political idealists. His appeal lies not in his answers to our niggling questions, but in the fact that he makes these questions seem ignoble. Platonic idealism, the living of one's life in pursuit of a perfection that doesn't exist, offers something that mere realism rarely offers. It brings religion's heady excitements to the sphere of politics—the sense of selflessness, of escape from a grubby compromised world, of identification with a higher reason, a greater good, than can ever be served by accommodating to things as they are.

There is at least one political realist, however, who meets Plato on his own ground. This is Spinoza. He sets a passion for the truth against Plato's passion for the ideal. And against Plato's aristocratic moral code he sets another—to do justice, to love mercy, to walk humbly with one's God. It is a homelier morality, but it is no less ardent or arduous.

In his *Ethics*, Spinoza says that those who truly love God will not expect God to love them in return. They will not entertain the self-indulgent hope that the world is organized to satisfy the boundless demands that men make upon it. The same principle stands behind his political outlook: we have to shape our demands to the possibilities; we have to assume that men think with their glands as well as their heads, and that even the wise and generous will be partial in their affections and understanding. Talking about changing such facts is like talking about making men immortal. The political problem is to start with the facts and to see what can be done to live with them and to make like tolerable just the same. For Spinoza is aware of the nether side of Platonic idealism—the ferocities it turns loose, the willfulness behind its air of impersonal devotion to the Good, the hatred of men as they are which hides behind its ostensible desire to improve their condition.

Is Spinoza too acquiescent to "necessity," too accepting of the *status quo?* The charge has been made, though it is an odd one to level at a man who suffered ostracism for his opinions. True, Spinoza, writing in trying circumstances and in an age in which tolerance was a new idea, accepts some limitations on liberty which libertarians are not in the habit of accepting today. And he thinks that the advantages of having a stable and established government are so considerable that a rational man will pause before he does anything to weaken such a government. Indeed, Spinoza regards as senseless the question, By what right does a government impose its authority on its citizens? Since no law establishing moral rights and wrongs exists outside of organized society, one can only say that a government has the "right" to do whatever it is capable of doing. But this does not mean that anything it does is right. A government so arbitrary and capricious that it increases rather than decreases the net sum of fear and distrust is subject to legitimate criticism. If it is so partisan that it concerns itself with the welfare of only a few of its subjects, and neglects or oppresses the great majority, a rational man certainly has reason to speak out. And the crucial question to ask about a government is whether it advances or retards men's best purposes. We can judge a government by its humanity, by its impact on the arts and sciences, by its respect for philosophy, and by the moral standards and intellectual horizons it makes possible for its citizens. Thus, when a government, fearing freedom of thought, punishes its most principled citizens, it exhibits itself as the worst of moral teachers. Spinoza accepts authority, but he is far from being uncritical of it. The major purpose of authority, for him, is to make possible the free life of reason.

Nor can it justly be said that Spinoza's philosophy rests on a pessimistic view of human nature. Political idealists repeatedly assert that realism like Spinoza's expresses fear of man rather than trust in him. But Spinoza's whole point is that words like "pessimism" and "optimism," and talk about the "goodness" and "badness" of human nature, lead us down useless paths. They make us look at the facts in terms of our hopes and fears instead of shaping our hopes and fears to the demands of the facts. It is silly to call men wicked because they try to stay alive, or because they fight for what they conceive to be their interests. The practical problem is to arrive at rules that allow them to live together with mutual forbearance and to act in accordance with a rational conception of their interests. And this problem, Spinoza believes, is one that can be solved. He thinks that progress is possible, that human life can be gentler and freer than it is. The one proviso is that men recognize their limitations and approach them in a neutral spirit.

The difference between Spinoza's philosophy and Plato's is caught, in the end, in the different answers they give to the same question: How is reason to be brought to bear on the affairs of state? For Plato, in *The Republic*, the solution is to get good people into government. For Spinoza, this is only part of the solution. The more important part is to surround government with other institutions, independent of it, in which rational men will have a chance to survive, to think, and to teach. The sources of self-restraint in democracy are to be found mainly in the general culture of a free society and in constitutional provisions to protect that culture. It is often said—with Plato—that the belief in liberty and democracy rests on a soft view of reality and a lax code of morals. Spinoza shows that it is possible to argue for liberty and democracy on the basis of an unillusioned realism and an austere moral code.

But if we look at modern liberal democracy in these terms, what can we conclude about its chances to survive? This is Santayana's question in the mordant essays on liberalism that we have read, and his answer is that the days of liberalism are numbered. Liberty for the Greeks, Santayana reminds us, did not not mean "freedom to wander at hazard or to let things slip." It meant virtue, disciplined power; and virtue required knowledge, an objective understanding of the structure of nature and human nature, and of the ordering of human purposes required to adjust to this structure. This sense of an objective world to which all men must accommodate is what modern liberalism has rejected. It stands for allowing men to do as they wish, while denying that there is any central core of human experience from which all men can learn, and to which they must adjust their wishes.

All that has kept modern liberalism going, indeed, is the fact that it has never been put into practice in its naked simplicity. The individual, told that he is on his own, has taken his direction from the crowd around him, accepting reigning opinion, joining this association or that, and turning his liberty into "a choice among little servitudes." And beyond this, liberalism has lived on the capital left by illiberal ages. It has stood for criticism, for greater flexibility, for individual variation, but always in relation to a larger tradition, an older orthodoxy, in the background.

Liberalism's crown is its special conception of "culture." A man of liberal culture "abounds in discriminating sentiments; he lives under the distant influence of exalted minds; his familiar thoughts at breakfast are intimate appreciations of poetry and art, and if his culture is really mellow, he sometimes smiles a little at his own culture." Such "culture," Santayana thinks, is bound to be a hothouse plant. War, commercialism, industrial requirements, and mass democracy destroy the special conditions necessary to sustain it, and thereafter another kind of culture, less artificial, more deeply rooted in orthodoxy, uniformity, tradition, is bound to reassert itself. The masses ask to be liberated from liberty, and liberalism is forced to reveal its true colors. It turns out that liberalism never quite meant what it seemed to say, but had an orthodox faith of its own, really believing, in its higher snobbery, that if men were left to find the right way for themselves, they would all end up as liberals and adherents of liberal culture. Once this belief in progress through liberty disappears, liberals turn out to be as equivocal about liberty as other people: "The liberal system, which sought to raise the individual, has degraded the masses; and this on so vast a scale

and to so pitiable a degree, that the other element in liberalism, philanthropic zeal, has come again to the fore. Liberty go hang, say the new radicals; let us save the people."

And yet, for all the sharpness and eloquence of Santayana's statement, his very prescience—his capacity to write as though he were the
witness of the travails of liberalism at this very moment—suggests that
something is wrong with his analysis. Fifty years ago, he declared the
days of liberalism numbered; but liberalism, though it has gone through
extraordinary trials, is still around. Nor have "the masses" been so universally indifferent to liberty, or so unequivocally eager to escape it, as
Santayana anticipated. Of course, no guarantee exists that liberalism will
therefore continue to survive; nevertheless, an account which fails to explain why it has so regularly fooled the prophets predicting its demise is
plainly incomplete.

There is an irony in Santayana's finding an irony in liberalism. He
is himself an exemplification of the liberal culture he dismisses; he abounds
in discriminating sentiments, lives under the distant influence of exalted
minds, and smiles a little at his own culture. The fact that he is an example of liberal culture doesn't mean that he must be a political liberal,
but it does suggest that he has avoided a crucial question. Politics, he
says rightly, cannot bring true liberty to the soul; this a man must do for
himself, and it is achieved, if at all, by philosophy. But politics can make
philosophy difficult or impossible; and can we look without regret on the
decline of a political outlook that has permitted philosophy to flourish?
For liberalism has offered other goods along with the chance to take part
in the race for worldly success.

In the end, one must ask the same question of Santayana that one
asks of Plato: If liberty is bound to collapse, what may a conscientious
man put in its place? What orthodoxy shall we adopt, what groups shall
rule, what guarantees of civilized life will remain? In answer, Santayana
offers only the silence of the mountain, plus a word of assurance, in
passing, that men will find a way to adjust to whatever new dispensation
arrives. "For myself, . . . I should not be afraid of the future domination,
whatever it may be." Well, since World War I we have seen some of the
dominations that can be. To make such a statement, one must be unduly
sanguine or innocent, which Santayana isn't, or else one is either attitudiniz-
ing or above caring. In either case, there is something remote and repugnant
in this posture. Plato, after all, is a partisan. He is opposed to liberty because
he prefers another political ideal. What political system Santayana favors is
never revealed in these essays. The most likely probability is the traditional
aristocratic society; but if that is his preference, his complaint should be not
about liberalism but about the twentieth century, which has made the aristocratic ideal, for better or worse, a hopeless anachronism.

And yet as with Plato, so with Santayana: he accomplishes his work not because he supports our beliefs but because he upsets them. And he upsets them because he helps us to recognize what, in fact, these beliefs are, and to see that the very things we complain about are actually consequences of them. Santayana is like another Platonic and Catholic moralist, Dante, who portrays the inhabitants of Hell as men and women who have got what they wished; they do in Hell precisely what they most wanted to do on earth, and all that makes Hell hellish is that they realize, in its full meaning, what it is they did want. Santayana writes: "Nothing happens to us as we would. We want peace and make war. We need science and obey the will to believe [i.e., we believe what we want to believe], we love art and flounder among whimsicalities, we believe in general comfort and equality and we strain every nerve to become millionaires." But these very contradictions, if Santayana is right, are what we want. For we have sought to have our cake and eat it too—to live as we please while we drift in the dark, to adopt, each of us on his own, a way of life, while imagining that the world exacts no price from us for what we adopt. And so, feeling free to choose anything, we have in fact made a considered choice of nothing; and we have got everything and nothing.

We may think Santayana overstates the case. Nevertheless, if we care for liberty, his central point is vital—more vital, indeed, than if we share his apparent indifference to liberty's fate. If liberty comes to mean the freedom to live as though no one ever lived before, if liberty becomes a cult which contemplates that the world's business can be carried on while each man's duty is merely "to suck in . . . all that [is] congenial to him, and to reject, down to his very centre, whatever might thwart or offend," then liberty is a name for inanity. One need not be an orthodox believer to recognize that there are such things as heresies against the experience of the human race. Santayana's fundamental insight, taken from the Greeks, is correct; if liberty is to endure, it must be accompanied by what the Greeks called virtue—a social discipline, willingly accepted, that rests on a prudent regard for objective facts. This condition makes the survival of liberty depend on a big *if*, and it explains why the condition of liberalism is always precarious.

It may also suggest the utility of philosophy to politics. There are people who want philosophy to tell them that, despite appearances, there really isn't anything to worry about: the nature of things is on their side. And there are philosophers who have responded to this call for help. But the greater service that philosophers can render—and the incomparably livelier pleasure that they can give—is to make us more aware of the peculiar character of our ideals and of the price we must pay, in effort and candor, if we want to maintain them. This is what Plato, Spinoza, and Santayana do, and it is why they speak to us whether or not we agree with them.

3. Philosophy and the Ideal of Reason

*B*ehind all the philosophies we have so far considered there is the presumption that men can come to an understanding of the universe as it is and not read into it their own preconceptions. Plato hopes that political systems can be reshaped in the image of an objective idea of the Good. Santayana thinks that "our modern liberty to drift in the dark is the most terrible negation of freedom." Similarly, though Diderot, Berkeley, and Santayana disagree on many things with regard to religion, they agree that there is a difference between living in the dark and living in the light, between pursuing falsehoods and knowing what is true. And Spinoza, of course, is a supreme apostle of reason, who regards it as the keystone of man's highest achievements.

But is there a way by which the limited human creature, weighed down by the terrors of his environment and bedeviled by impulses within him of whose sources he is unaware, can see truth without prejudice? If there is a central question in philosophy, this is it. Repeatedly, from Plato on, philosophers have come forward offering the same hope in the realm of the intellect that revolutionaries offer in the world of politics. They claim that they have found a method—the method—for washing the human mind clean. If it is followed, they say, the heritage of past errors can be eliminated, the rise of new falsehoods can be prevented, and the human mind will finally be set on the firm path to truth.

In this section we shall have a chance to look at three classic efforts to map a new and proper course for human reason—the ambitious proposal of René Descartes, a seventeenth-century French mathematician, the more restrained and skeptical recommendation of an eighteenth-century Scot, David Hume, and the down-to-earth notions of a late-nineteenth-century American, Charles Peirce.

René Descartes

In 1619, while he was serving with the French army on the Danube, René Descartes went off by himself and plunged into a study of what he called "the chaos" of geometry as it existed in his day. This was Descartes' style —making a solo voyage to remap an entire intellectual terrain, shutting himself off from outside distractions while he rethought an entire subject for himself and put it into logical order. The outcome of this particular undertaking was his invention of what we now know as analytic geometry, which unites geometry and algebra. Subsequently, Descartes had three dreams in which, he believed, it was revealed to him that "the Spirit of Truth" had opened to him "the treasures of all the sciences." He reflected that if an admirable general-purpose tool like analytic geometry could be developed, clarifying large parts of the physical sciences, then a similar method of thinking, adapted to the more general needs of philosophy and human life, could accomplish an intellectual revolution.

The selection from Descartes' work that we are about to read is the story of his attempt to realize this project. It is taken from a brief book, published in 1636, whose title indicates its purpose exactly: *Discourse on the Method of Rightly Conducting the Reason and Seeking Truth in the Sciences*. No one was ever more aware than Descartes of the play of ego, convention, and sheer stupid habit in what passes for human thinking. And he has a proposal for dealing with these encumbrances: let us clear the field, let us doubt everything, and then, using a method of thinking with built-in guarantees against bias and illusion, let us construct a purely rational view of the world. He was a man, as the reader will see, who rather disliked the fact that we have to be children before we become adults; our minds are deformed, filled with all sorts of fancies and delusions, before we have a chance to defend ourselves. That damage must be undone, and Descartes thought he had found the way to do so. He was a man with a message.

But he was also a prudent one. He lived between 1596 and 1650, in an age of royal absolutism and religious intolerance. He meant to keep his skirts clean so that he could pursue what he thought—and had good reason to think—was his own important purpose. He believed that one who wants to make a revolution should decide where it is to occur and concentrate his attention there. And if the contemplated revolution is intellectual—a revolution in men's minds—he should be careful to live, so far as externals go, by the conventions. He won't attack religion; he will take care to announce that he doesn't advocate tearing down existing regimes; and in fact, even though he may think that all beliefs should be taken apart piece by piece and put together again in a rational manner, he won't say so in so many words. Conducting himself in this way, a man will be freed from external pressures and will enjoy greater, not less, spiritual freedom. Descartes never says in his *Discourse* that he wants others to follow his lead. He presents himself simply as an individual reciting a fragment of his autobiography, telling his own story and not preaching to anyone else.

Rarely, however, has a man succeeded in preaching more successfully. The *Discourse on Method* seems for the most part a disarmingly simple, almost innocent, account of one person's schooling and intellectual wanderings. In fact, however, it presents a radically original way of looking at the whole process of growing up and being educated; the picture it offers of how the individual should relate himself to tradition was, in its time, almost entirely new. It is not new to us mainly because, since Descartes' time, schoolboys and grown men have relived Descartes' story, imitating him without knowing it.

The very first words of the *Discourse,* which seem almost banal, are the announcement of a tidal change in men's image of themselves. Good sense, Descartes says, is of all things the most equally distributed among men. Does he mean it? Doesn't he suspect that he himself is brighter than others? Very probably; but the reader should note what he says next—that good sense *must* be equally distributed because even those who complain that they haven't received a fair share of other good things rarely claim that they haven't received enough good sense. Indeed, how can they? They would have to trust their good sense if they came to the judgment that they didn't have enough good sense. A man has no alternative but to use his own judgment when he decides what is true and false; even if he resolves to accept the opinions of others or to accede to authority, he has to make *that* decision for himself. In half a dozen apparently harmless sentences, Descartes has thus subverted the doctrine that some individuals should have unquestioned intellectual authority over others, and that people should believe what they are told because those who do the telling are preternaturally wiser than they. The entire tradition that upholds the authority of tradition is thus questioned at the very start. Descartes has transposed his readers to another world and another era, in which men will take as a good starting hypothesis the view that the reigning wisdom is merely the conventional wisdom.

It should not be surprising, then, that Descartes' account of his education has a contemporary ring. He is one of the first to have put forth the very idea of being "contemporary," of freeing oneself from the past and thinking things out in the light of one's own experience. Thus, he tells us that he was just an ordinary fellow, no more intelligent than others, and that, like other men, he went to school hoping to learn something. But all that he really learned was that there was no rhyme or reason to his schooling. What he was taught was usually only established opinion or foolish reverence for the past. Nothing was really proved, and nothing was relevant to his central need, which was to learn how to distinguish the true from the false, and to conduct his life rightly.

The schools, Descartes says, pay too much attention to the past and leave students ignorant of the present; and they assume that the student learns best in the classroom, when, in fact, he will probably do better outside school, studying "the great book of the world." Learned men, scholars in their studies, are deformed by the lives they lead: they know only abstractions and never have to test them in real life. "I should find much more truth," says Descartes, "in the reasonings of each individual with reference to the affairs in which he is personally interested, and the issue of which must presently punish him if he has judged amiss, than in those conducted by a man of letters in his study, regarding speculative matters that are of no practical moment, and followed by no consequences to himself, farther, perhaps, than that they foster his vanity. . . ."

The whole litany of complaints about education with which we are familiar today can be found in Descartes' reflections on his schooling. But he offers something more than complaints. He admires mathematics and believes in close, careful, systematic thought. He worships lucidity, articulateness, orderly reasoning. His simple, straightforward French testifies to his belief in the value of everyday clarity, and his prose style has had an influence on the development of modern French comparable to the influence of the King James Bible on English. And most to the point, he thinks that there is a discipline, a proper method, by which the human mind should conduct its business, and that education should teach this discipline. For there is a supreme truth to be found which is the same for all men, and this method leads to it.

This is what the *Discourse on Method* is about. If we are going to work our way to the truth, says Descartes, we must first clear our minds of all the false ideas that clutter them. And just to be sure that we are doing the job thoroughly, let us eliminate all opinions whatsoever: let us doubt everything, even what seems overwhelmingly obvious, and assume nothing. If we do, we shall be left with only one thing we cannot doubt—that there is a self, an "I," that is doing the doubting. From this sure premise we can go on, he asserts, and build up our beliefs again on sound foundations. We shall see, for example, that there is a God, that He has given us a guarantee that mathematics is a reliable guide to the nature of His creation, and that the new mathematical physics gives a true account of the world and is in fact the model for discovering the truth in general.

There is no better way to find out what "intellectual individualism" means at its most uncompromising than to become acquainted with Descartes' philosophy. He thinks that buildings and cities are better when they are the work of one man; and he thinks that a man's mind is at its best when he has shaped it for himself—all of it, from beginning to end—so that it is not composed of shreds and patches of opinion picked up here and there. At the center of Descartes' vision is always his own thinking mind. It is good to travel and to read history, he agrees, because we learn not to assume "that everything contrary to our customs is ridiculous and irrational." But even these activities can be overdone: too much travel leads to ignorance of one's own country, too much history leads to ignorance of the present. And too much attention to the opinions of others leads to the failure to use one's own intelligence.

Descartes is a philosopher who speaks supremely to those for whom the main rule of life is not to be deceived—those who resist being taken in by "the system" and want to go it alone. Reading his philosophy is, for that reason, like engaging in a mental and moral experiment. His attitude toward the world is one that many others also take, but he adopts it unflinchingly and develops it as far as he can. He thus allows us to perceive its logic and its full consequences. That is one of the instructive delights a philosopher can give us. We may think him odd and extravagant, but what we see in him is only our own oddity and extravagance in sharper silhouette.

The translation of the *Discourse on Method* used here is by John Veitch.

Discourse on the Method
of Rightly Conducting the Reason
and Seeking Truth in the Sciences

PART I

Good sense is, of all things among men, the most equally distributed; for everyone thinks himself so abundantly provided with it, that those even who are the most difficult to satisfy in everything else, do not usually desire a larger measure of this quality than they already possess. And in this it is not likely that all are mistaken; the conviction is rather to be held as testifying that the power of judging aright and of distinguishing truth from error, which is properly what is called good sense or reason, is by nature equal in all men; and that the diversity of our opinions, consequently, does not arise from some being endowed with a larger share of reason than others, but solely from this, that we conduct our thoughts along different ways, and do not fix our attention on the same objects. For to be possessed of a vigorous mind is not enough; the prime requisite is rightly to apply it. The greatest minds, as they are capable of the highest excellences, are open likewise to the greatest aberrations; and those who travel very slowly may yet make far greater progress, provided they keep always to the straight road, than those who, while they run, forsake it.

For myself, I have never fancied my mind to be in any respect more perfect than those of the generality; on the contrary, I have often wished that I were equal to some others in promptitude of thought, or in clearness and distinctness of imagination, or in fullness and readiness of memory. . . .

I will not hesitate, however, to avow my belief that it has been my singular good fortune to have very early in life fallen in with certain tracks which have conducted me to considerations and maxims, of which I have formed a method that gives me the means, as I think, of gradually augmenting my knowledge, and of raising it by little and little to the highest point which the mediocrity of my talents and the brief duration of my life will permit me to reach. . . .

My present design, then, is not to teach the method which each ought to follow for the right conduct of his reason, but solely to describe the way in which I have endeavored to conduct my own. They who set themselves to give precept must of course regard themselves as possessed of greater skill than those to whom they prescribe; and if they err in the slightest particular, they subject themselves to censure. But as this tract is put forth merely as a history, or if you will, as a tale, in which, amid some examples worthy of imitation, there will be found, perhaps, as many more which it were advisable not to follow, I hope it will prove useful to some without being hurtful to any, and that my openness will find some favor with all.

From my childhood, I have been familiar with letters; and as I was given to believe that by their help a clear and certain knowledge of all that is useful in life might be acquired, I was ardently desirous of instruction. But as soon as I had finished the entire course of study, at the close of which it is customary to be admitted into the order of the learned, I completely changed my opinion. For I found myself involved in so many doubts and errors that I was convinced I had advanced no farther in all my attempts at learning than the discovery at every turn of my own ignorance. And yet I was studying in one of the most celebrated schools in Europe, in which I thought there must be learned men, if such were anywhere to be found. . . .

I still continued, however, to hold in esteem the studies of the schools. I was aware that the languages taught in them are necessary to the understanding of the writings of the ancients; that the grace of fable stirs the mind; that the memorable deeds of history elevate it, and if read with discretion, aid in forming the judgment; that the perusal of all excellent books is, as it were, to interview with the noblest men of past ages, who have written them, and even a studied interview, in which are discovered to us only their choicest thoughts; that eloquence has incomparable force and beauty; that poesy has its ravishing graces and delights; that in mathematics there are many refined discoveries eminently suited to gratify the inquisitive, as well as further all the arts and lessen the labor of man; that numerous highly useful precepts and exhortations to virtue are contained in treatises on morals; that theology points out the path to heaven; that philosophy affords the means of discoursing with an appearance of truth on all matters, and commands the admiration of the more simple; that jurisprudence, medicine, and the other sciences secure for their cultivators honors and riches; and in fine, that it is useful to bestow some attention upon all, even upon those abounding the most in superstition and error, that we may be in a position to determine their real value, and guard against being deceived.

But I believed that I had already given sufficient time to languages, and likewise to the reading of the writings of the ancients, to their histories and fables. For to hold converse with those of other ages and to travel are almost the same thing. It is useful to know something of the manners of different nations, that we may be enabled to form a more correct judgment regarding our own, and be prevented from thinking that everything contrary to our customs is ridiculous and irrational—a conclusion usually come to by those whose experience has been limited to their own country. On the other hand, when too much time is occupied in traveling we become strangers to our native country; and the over-curious in the customs of the past are generally ignorant of those of the present. . . .

I was especially delighted with mathematics, on account of the certitude and evidence of its reasoning; but I had not as yet a precise knowledge of its true use; and thinking that it but contributed to the advancement of the mechanical arts, I was astonished that its foundations, so strong and solid, should have had no loftier superstructure reared on them. On the other hand, I compared the disquisitions of the ancient moralists to very towering and magnificent palaces with no better foundation than sand and mud: they laud the virtues very highly, and exhibit them as estimable far above anything on earth; but they give us no adequate criterion of virtue, and frequently that which they designate with so fine a name is but apathy, or pride, or despair, or parricide.

I revered our theology, and aspired as much as anyone to reach heaven: but being given assuredly to understand that the way is not less open to the most ignorant than to the most learned, and that the revealed truths which lead to heaven are above our comprehension, I did not presume to subject them to the impotency of my reason; and I thought that in order competently to undertake their examination, there was need of some special help from heaven, and of being more than man.

Of philosophy I will say nothing, except that when I saw that it had been cultivated for many ages by the most distinguished men, and that yet there is not a single matter within its sphere which is not still in dispute, and nothing, therefore, which is above doubt, I did not presume to anticipate that my success would be greater in it than that of others; and further, when I considered the number of conflicting opinions touching a single matter that may be upheld by learned men, while there can be but one true, I reckoned as well-nigh false all that was only probable.

As to the other sciences, inasmuch as these borrow their principles from philosophy, I judged that no solid superstructures could be reared on foundations so infirm; and neither the honor nor the gain held out by them was sufficient to determine me to their cultivation: for I was not, thank Heaven, in a condition which compelled me to make merchandise of science for the bettering of my fortune. . . .

For these reasons, as soon as my age permitted me to pass from under the control of my instructors, I entirely abandoned the study of letters, and resolved no longer to seek any other science than the knowledge of myself, or of the great book of the world. I spent the remainder of my youth in traveling, in visiting courts and armies, in holding intercourse with men of different dispositions and ranks, in collecting varied experience, in proving myself in the different situations into which fortune threw me, and above all, in making such reflection on the matter of my experience as to secure my improvement. For it occurred to me that I should find much more truth in the reasonings of each individual with reference to the affairs in which he is personally interested, and the issue of which must presently punish him if he has judged amiss, than in those conducted by a man of letters in his study, regarding speculative matters that are of no practical moment, and followed by no consequences to himself, farther, perhaps, than that they foster his vanity the better the more remote they are from common sense; requiring, as they must in this case, the exercise of greater ingenuity and art to render them probable. In addition, I had always a most earnest desire to know how to distinguish the true from the false, in order that I might be able clearly to discriminate the right path in life, and proceed in it with confidence.

It is true that, while busied only in considering the manners of other men, I found here, too, scarce any ground for settled conviction, and remarked hardly less contradiction among them than in the opinions of the philosophers. So that the greatest advantage I derived from the study consisted in this, that, observing many things which, however extravagant and ridiculous to our apprehension, are yet by common consent received and approved by other great nations, I learned to entertain too decided a belief in regard to nothing of the truth of which I had been persuaded merely by example and custom; and thus I gradually extricated myself from many errors powerful enough to darken our natural intelligence and incapacitate us in great measure from listening to reason. But after I had been occupied several years in thus studying the book of the world, and in essaying to gather some experience, I at length resolved to make myself an object of study, and to employ all the powers of my mind in choosing the paths I ought to follow, an undertaking which was accompanied with greater success than it would have been had I never quitted my country or my books.

PART II

I was then in Germany, attracted thither by the wars in that country, which have not yet been brought to a termination; and as I was returning to the army from the coronation of the emperor, the setting in of winter arrested me in a locality where, as I found no society to interest me, and was besides fortunately undisturbed by any cares or passions, I remained the whole day in seclusion, with full opportunity to occupy my attention with my own thoughts. Of these one of the very first that occurred to me was that there is seldom so much perfection in works composed of many separate parts, upon which different hands had been employed, as in those completed by a single master. Thus it is observable that the buildings which a single architect has planned and executed are generally more elegant and commodious than those which several have attempted to improve by making old walls serve for purposes for which they were not originally built. Thus also, those ancient cities which, from being at first only villages, have become, in course of time, large towns, are usually but ill laid out compared with the regularly constructed towns which a professional architect has freely planned on an open plain; so that although the several buildings of the former may often equal or surpass in beauty those of the latter, yet when one observes their indiscriminate juxtaposition, there a large one and here a small, and the consequent crookedness and irregularity of the streets, one is disposed to allege that chance rather than any human will guided by reason must have led to such an arrangement. And if we consider that nevertheless there have been at all times certain officers whose duty it was to see that private buildings contributed to public ornament, the difficulty of reaching high perfection with but the materials of others to operate on will be readily acknowledged. . . . In the same way I thought that the sciences contained in books (such of them at least as are made up of probable reasonings, without demonstrations), composed as they are of the opinions of many different individuals massed together, are farther removed from truth than the simple inferences which a man of good sense using his natural and unprejudiced judgment draws respecting the matters of his experience. And because we have all to pass through a state of infancy to manhood, and have been of necessity, for a length of time, governed by our desires and preceptors (whose dictates were frequently conflicting, while neither perhaps always counseled us for the best), I farther concluded that it is almost impossible that our judgments can be so correct or solid as they would have been had our reason been mature from the moment of our birth and had we always been guided by it alone.

It is true, however, that it is not customary to pull down all the houses of a town with the single design of rebuilding them differently and thereby rendering the streets more handsome; but it often happens that a private individual takes down his own with the view of erecting it anew, and that people are even sometimes constrained to this when their houses are in danger of falling from age, or when the foundations are insecure. With this before me by way of example, I was persuaded that it would indeed be preposterous for a private individual to think of reforming a state by fundamentally changing it throughout and overturning it in order to set it up amended; and the same I thought was true of any similar project for reforming the body of sciences, or the order of teaching them established in the schools; but as for the opinions which up to that time I had embraced, I thought that I could not do better than resolve at once to sweep them wholly away, that I might afterward be in a position to admit either others more correct, or even perhaps the same when they had undergone the scrutiny of reason. I firmly believed that in this way I should much better succeed in the conduct of my life than if I built upon old foundations and leaned upon principles which, in my youth, I had taken upon trust. . . .

But like one walking alone and in the dark, I resolve to proceed so slowly and with such circumspection that if I did not advance far, I would at least guard against falling. I did not even choose to dismiss summarily any of the opinions that had crept into my belief without having been introduced by reason, but first of all took sufficient time carefully to satisfy myself of the general nature of the task I was setting myself, and ascertain the true method by which to arrive at the knowledge of whatever lay within the compass of my powers.

. . . And as a multitude of laws often only hampers justice, so that a state is best governed when, with few laws, these are rigidly administered; in like manner, instead of the great number of precepts of which logic is composed, I believed that the four following would prove perfectly sufficient for me, provided I took the firm and unwavering resolution never in a single instance to fail in observing them.

The *first* was never to accept anything for true which I did not clearly know to be such; that is to say, carefully to avoid precipitancy and prejudice, and to comprise nothing more in my judgment than what was presented to my mind so clearly and distinctly as to exclude all ground of doubt.

The *second*, to divide each of the difficulties under examination into as many parts as possible, and as might be necessary for its adequate solution.

The *third*, to conduct my thoughts in such order that, by commencing with objects the simplest and easiest to know, I might ascend by little and little, and as it were, step by step, to the knowledge of the more complex; assigning in thought a certain order even to those objects which in their own nature do not stand in a relation of antecedence and sequence.

And the *last*, in every case to make enumerations so complete, and reviews so general, that I might be assured that nothing was omitted. . . .

And, in point of fact, the accurate observance of these few precepts gave me, I take the liberty of saying, such ease in unraveling all the questions embraced in [geometrical analysis and algebra] that in the two or three months I devoted to their examination, not only did I reach solutions of questions I had formerly deemed exceedingly difficult, but even as regards questions of the solution of which I continued ignorant, I was enabled, as it appeared to me, to determine the means whereby, and the extent to which, a solution was possible; results attributable to the circumstance that I commenced with the simplest and most general truths, and that thus each truth discovered was a rule available in the discovery of subsequent ones. . . .

But the chief ground of my satisfaction with this method was the assurance I had of thereby exercising my reason in all matters, if not with absolute perfection, at least with the greatest attainable by me: besides, I was conscious that by its use my mind was becoming gradually habituated to clearer and more distinct conceptions of its objects: and I hoped also, from not having restricted this method to any particular matter, to apply it to the difficulties of the other sciences, with not less success than to those of algebra. I should not, however, on this account have ventured at once on the examination of all the difficulties of the sciences which presented themselves to me, for this would have been contrary to the order prescribed in the method; but observing that the knowledge of such is dependent on principles borrowed from philosophy, in which I found nothing certain. I thought it necessary first of all to endeavor to establish its principles. And because I observed, besides, that an inquiry of this kind was of all others of the greatest moment, and one in which precipitancy and anticipation in judgment were most to be dreaded, I thought that I ought not to approach it till I had reached a more mature age (being at that time but twenty-three), and had first of all employed much of my time in preparation for the work, as well by eradicating from my mind all the erroneous opinions I had up to that moment accepted, as by amassing variety of experience to afford materials for my reasonings, and by continually exercising myself in my chosen method with a view to increased skill in its application. . . .

PART IV

I am in doubt as to the propriety of making my first meditations . . . matter of discourse; for these are so metaphysical, and so uncommon, as not perhaps to be acceptable to everyone. And yet, that it may be determined whether the foundations that I have laid are sufficiently secure, I find myself in a measure constrained to advert to them. I had long before remarked that in relation to practice, it is sometimes necessary to adopt, as if above doubt, opinions which we discern to be highly uncertain, as has been already said; but as I then desired to give my attention solely to the search after truth, I thought that a procedure exactly the opposite was called for, and that I ought to reject as absolutely false all opinions in regard to which I could suppose the least ground for doubt, in order to ascertain whether after that there remained aught in my belief that was wholly indubitable. Accordingly, seeing that our senses sometimes deceive us, I was willing to suppose that there existed nothing really such as they presented to us; and because some men err in reasoning, and fall into paralogisms, even on the simplest matters of geometry, I, convinced that I was as open to error as any other, rejected as false all the reasonings I had hitherto taken for demonstrations; and finally, when I considered that the very same thoughts which we experience when awake may also be experienced when we are asleep, while there is at that time not one of them true, I supposed that all the objects that had ever entered into my mind when awake had in them no more truth than the illusions of my dreams. But immediately upon this I observed that, whilst I thus wished to think that all was false, it was absolutely necessary that I, who thus thought, should be somewhat; and as I observed that this truth, *I think, hence I am,* was so certain and of such evidence, that no ground of doubt, however extravagant, could be alleged by the skeptics capable of shaking it, I concluded that I might, without scruple, accept it as the first principle of which I was in search.

In the next place, I attentively examined what I was; and as I observed that I could suppose that I had no body, and that there was no world nor any place in which I might be; but that I could not therefore suppose that I was not; and that, on the contrary, from the very circumstance that I thought to doubt of the truth of other things, it most clearly and certainly followed that I was; while, on the other hand, if I had only ceased to think, although all the other objects which I had ever imagined had been in reality existent, I would have had no reason to believe that I existed; I thence concluded that I was a substance whose whole essence or nature consists only in thinking, and which, that it may exist, has need of no place, nor is dependent on any material thing; so that "I," that is to say, the mind by which I am what I am, is wholly distinct from the body, and is even more easily known than the latter, and is such that although the latter were not, it would still continue to be all that it is.

After this I inquired in general into what is essential to the truth and certainty of a proposition; for since I had discovered one which I knew to be true, I thought that I must likewise be able to discover the ground of this certitude. And as I observed that in the words *I think, hence I am* there is nothing at all which gives me assurance of their truth beyond this, that I see very clearly that in order to think it is necessary to exist, I concluded that I might take, as a general rule, the principle that all the things which we very clearly and distinctly conceive are true, only observing, however, that there is some difficulty in rightly determining the objects which we distinctly conceive.

In the next place, from reflecting on the circumstance that I doubted, and that consequently my being was not wholly perfect (for I clearly saw that it was a greater perfection to know than to doubt), I was led to inquire whence I had learned to think of something more perfect than myself; and I clearly recognized that I must hold this notion from some nature which in reality was more perfect. As for the thoughts of many other objects external to me, as of the sky, the earth, light, heat, and a thousand more, I was less at a loss to know whence these came; for since I remarked in them nothing which seemed to render them superior to myself, I could believe that if these were true, they were dependencies on my own nature, insofar as it possessed a certain perfection, and if they were false, that I held them from nothing, that is to say, that they were in me because of a certain imperfection of my nature. But this could not be the case with the idea of a nature more perfect than myself; for to receive it from nothing was a thing manifestly impossible; and because it is not less repugnant that the more perfect should be an effect of, and dependence on, the less perfect than that something should proceed from nothing, it was equally impossible that I could hold it from myself; accordingly, it but remained that it had been placed in me by a nature which was in reality more perfect than mine, and which even possessed within itself all the perfections of which I could form any idea; that is to say, in a single word, which was God. . . .

Finally, if there be still persons who are not sufficiently persuaded of the existence of God and of the soul, by the reasons I have adduced, I am desirous that they should know that all the other propositions, of the truth of which they deem themselves perhaps more assured, as that we have a body, and that there exist stars and an earth, and such like, are less certain; for, although we have a moral assurance of these things, which is so strong that there is an appearance of extravagance in doubting of their existence, yet at the same time no one, unless his intellect is impaired, can deny,

when the question relates to a metaphysical certitude, that there is sufficient reason to exclude entire assurance in the observation that when asleep
we can in the same way imagine ourselves possessed of another body and
that we see other stars and another earth, when there is nothing of the
kind. For how do we know that the thoughts which occur in dreaming
are false rather than those other which we experience when awake, since
the former are often not less vivid and distinct than the latter? And though
men of the highest genius study this question as long as they please, I do
not believe that they will be able to give any reason which can be sufficient
to remove this doubt, unless they presuppose the existence of God. For,
in the first place, even the principle which I have already taken as a rule,
viz., that all the things which we clearly and distinctly conceive are true,
is certain only because God is or exists and because He is a Perfect Being,
and because all that we possess is derived from Him; whence it follows
that our ideas or notions, which to the extent of their clearness and distinctness are real, and proceed from God, must to that extent be true. Accordingly, whereas we not unfrequently have ideas or notions in which
some falsity is contained, this can only be the case with such as are to
some extent confused and obscure, and in this proceed from nothing, that
is, exist in us thus confused because we are not wholly perfect. And it is
evident that it is not less repugnant that falsity or imperfection, insofar
as it is imperfection, should proceed from God than that truth or perfection
should proceed from nothing. But if we did not know that all which we
possess of real and true proceeds from a Perfect and Infinite Being, however clear and distinct our ideas might be, we should have no ground on
that account for the assurance that they possessed the perfection of being
true. . . .

David Hume

For all his differences with Descartes, David Hume begins where Descartes begins. In his first book he writes that "disputes are multiplied, as if everything was uncertain, and these disputes are managed with the greatest warmth, as if everything was certain." His hope, like Descartes', is to find a method that will bring order out of this disorder, and allow men to know when they can be certain and when they can't. But Hume approaches the problem from the other end than does Descartes. Above all, he believes, we must be aware that human knowledge is *human* knowledge. Accordingly, if we want to understand its logic, and determine the sphere in which the search for knowledge can be successful, we ought to begin by looking at human nature. Only by examining the way the human mind and human sentiments actually work can we determine what man is capable of knowing and what lies beyond his powers. Hence, the title of his first book—*A Treatise of Human Nature*.

In contrast with Descartes' high speculations, Hume takes a homely approach. He believes that the simple example of a child who, after burning his finger at a candle, treats candles with caution, gives a sounder insight into the logic of human beliefs and the rules by which we ought to regulate our thinking than do speculations on mathematics, God, and the existence of the self. Indeed, if Hume is correct, then one of the principal barriers to the right conduct of human reason is the kind of excessive hope which Descartes turned loose, the hope that men can free their minds entirely from the trammels of their limiting experience and attain infallible knowledge. Probably the majority of Hume's readers, and certainly the majority of philosophers, have not liked his conclusions. Nevertheless, he is the intellectual conscience of modern philosophy. For two centuries most philosophers have been looking over their shoulders to see if Hume was watching them. They have known that, in the end, they were going to have to face his arguments, and make their peace with his clear-eyed doubts.

Hume's central interest is to discover and evaluate the principles which, in actual practice, lead men to say that one belief is true and another is false. His single most compelling discussion of this question is presented in the pages that follow. At its heart is a distinction between two different kinds of thinking in which men engage. Sometimes they think about what Hume calls "relations of ideas." Sometimes they think about what he calls "matters of fact." The difference between these is very great, and when we fail to keep the distinction in mind, Hume believes, we fall into fallacy after fallacy.

What is a "relation of ideas"? Well, if we know, for example, that a man is a husband, we know he must have a wife; the very meaning of the term "husband" links it to the concept "wife." And because we draw such an inference simply by inspecting the meaning of the terms used, we can demonstrate its truth, as Hume says, "*a priori.*" We don't need to go out and collect husbands and wives and report that, Yes, indeed, each husband has a wife. Such activity would be silly, for we know in advance that *if* a man is a husband, he necessarily has a wife. This is the kind of truth, Hume reminds us, in which mathematics specializes. If one knows what "straight line" means, what "circle" means, and so on, one is logically compelled to accept step by step the theorems in Euclid's geometry. Such knowledge, as Hume says, is "demonstratively certain" because one cannot deny the conclusions it yields without falling into self-contradiction: to say, for example, that a man is a husband but doesn't have a wife, is to say that he both is and isn't a husband.

The point may seem almost trivial. Yet, in Hume's view it provides the ultimate refutation of Descartes' belief that man can achieve knowledge that is certain. For *only* "relations of ideas"—purely verbal statements—can be proved by applying the test of noncontradiction. To spell out the meanings, without self-contradiction, of terms such as "husband" and "wife," or "straight line" and "circle," doesn't begin to prove that there are in the world any actual husbands, wives, straight lines, or circles. To ascertain their existence, we must go out and look, for then we are trying to determine not a "relation of ideas," but a "matter of fact," and we cannot prove a matter of fact by subjecting it to the test of the principle of noncontradiction. There is nothing self-contradictory in saying that the Alps don't exist. The statement is false, but we can discover that it is false only by observation, not simply by inspecting the meaning of the words.

But what, then, do our beliefs about matters of fact depend on? Here we come to the central argument of the succeeding pages, and I shall only set the stage. When we conclude that something is a "fact," Hume says, what we have done is to place it within a chain of cause and effect. If we regard it as a fact, for example, that the house we left in the morning is still in its place even though we don't see it, we do so because we know that the house is made of wood and stone, that these have certain properties, and that the house, therefore, won't just blow away in the wind. Nor will our absence cause these properties to change. In other words, we assume the regular working of certain causal laws. In constrast, if we think we see a pink elephant climbing the wall, we—or those still sober around us—are inclined to dismiss this experience as a hallucination; pink elephants who defy the laws of gravity contravene our notions about the regular relations between certain causes and certain effects. Correspondingly, we conclude that what is really taking place is a hallucination, because we know that certain causes—for example, excessive alcohol in the system—produce hallucinations, and we believe these causes to be present.

What, then, is the basis of our knowledge of cause and effect? Hume says that such knowledge has no ultimate logical defense, but rests merely on habits of mind; philosophers ever since have found this answer disturbing, and because of it they have accused him of bottomless skepticism. But Hume himself seems not to have thought that his ideas were quite as skeptical in their effects as others have painted them. As the reader will see, he rejects "Pyrrhonism"—the doctrine that man can never know the truth about anything—as "excessive." He seems mainly to have wanted to cut philosophers down to size. Like Berkeley, he distrusts vague abstractions, and believes that men think best when they are guided by their experience and don't attempt to go beyond it.

Hume was born in 1711 and died in 1776. He was a master of the prose essay, a successful historian, and a writer on politics and economics as well as on the nature of human reasoning. His greatest passion was for literary fame. He achieved a reputation only after considerable difficulty, but he is now regarded as probably the most important philosopher to have written in the English language, and certainly one of the great masters of English prose. The concluding paragraphs of his autobiography, written a few months before he died, communicate his special personal charm:

In spring 1775, I was struck with a disorder in my bowels, which at first gave me no alarm, but has since, as I apprehend it, become mortal and incurable. I now reckon upon a speedy dissolution. I have suffered very little pain from my disorder and, what is more strange, have, notwithstanding the great decline of my person, never suffered a moment's abatement of my spirits, insomuch that were I to name the period of my life which I should most choose to pass over again, I might be tempted to point to this later period. I possess the same ardor as ever in study, and the same gaiety in company. I consider, besides, that a man of sixty-five, by dying, cuts off only a few years of infirmities; and though I see many symptoms of my literary reputation's breaking out at last with additional luster, I knew that I could have but few years to enjoy it. It is difficult to be more detached from life than I am at present.

To conclude historically with my own character, I am, or rather was (for that is the style I must now use in speaking of myself, which emboldens me the more to speak my sentiments)—I was, I say, a man of mild dispositions, of command of temper, of an open, social, and cheerful humor, capable of attachment, but little susceptible of enmity, and of great moderation in all my passions. Even my love of literary fame, my ruling passion, never soured my temper, notwithstanding my frequent disappointments. My company was not unacceptable to the young and careless, as well as to the studious and literary; and as I took particular pleasure in the company of modest women, I had no reason to be displeased with the reception I met with from them. In a word, though most men anywise eminent have found reason to complain of calumny, I never was touched or even attacked by her baleful tooth; and though I wantonly exposed myself to the rage of both civil and religious factions, they seemed to be disarmed in my behalf of their wonted fury. My friends never had occasion to vindicate any one circumstance of my character and conduct; not but that the zealots, we may well suppose, would have been glad to invent and propagate any story to my disadvantage, but they could never find any which they thought would wear the face of probability. I cannot say there is no vanity in making this funeral oration of myself, but I hope it is not a misplaced one; and this is a matter of fact which is easily cleared and ascertained.

Some resist Hume for the same reason that others find him appealing. His friend, the great economist Adam Smith, said of him that he had the most "happily balanced" temperament of any man he had ever known, and approached "as nearly to the idea of a perfectly wise and virtuous man as the nature of human frailty will permit." But Hume, though he was generous, witty, equable, and self-disciplined, lacked one quality—a talent for what the eighteenth century called, with distrust, "enthusiasm." If anything provoked him it was zealotry. His philosophy is an attack on the "airy sciences" and "abstruse philosophy" which, he believed, served as the shields behind which zealots protected their superstitions. Zealots, therefore, have never found anything appealing in Hume. He speaks to those who think of philosophy not as an intoxicant, but as a disintoxicant.

The selection that follows is taken from Hume's *Enquiry Concerning Human Understanding*, a shortened version of his earlier *Treatise*, which he published in 1746 to repair the failure of the *Treatise* to reach a wide audience. Many philosophers believe that Hume in the *Enquiry* sacrificed the superior qualities of the *Treatise* in the effort to write a popular book. However, it was the *Enquiry* which awakened one of the other preeminent philosophers of the modern world, Immanuel Kant, from what he described as "dogmatic slumbers." This should be enough to recommend it as a solid piece of work.

An Enquiry Concerning Human Understanding

OF THE DIFFERENT SPECIES OF PHILOSOPHY

Moral philosophy, or the science of human nature, may be treated after two different manners; each of which has its peculiar merit, and may contribute to the entertainment, instruction, and reformation of mankind. The one considers man chiefly as born for action; and as influenced in his measures by taste and sentiment; pursuing one object, and avoiding another, according to the value which these objects seem to possess, and according to the light in which they present themselves. As virtue, of all objects, is allowed to be the most valuable, this species of philosophers paint her in the most amiable colors; borrowing all helps from poetry and eloquence, and treating their subject in an easy and obvious manner, and such as is best fitted to please the imagination, and engage the affections. . . .

The other species of philosophers consider man in the light of a reasonable rather than an active being, and endeavor to form his understanding more than cultivate his manners. They regard human nature as a subject of speculation; and with a narrow scrutiny examine it, in order to find those principles, which regulate our understanding, excite our sentiments, and make us to approve or blame any particular object, action, or behavior. They think it a reproach to all literature, that philosophy should not yet have fixed, beyond controversy, the foundation of morals, reasoning, and criticism; and should for ever talk of truth and falsehood, vice and virtue, beauty and deformity, without being able to determine the source of the distinctions. . . .

It is certain that the easy and obvious philosophy will always, with the generality of mankind, have the preference above the accurate and abstruse; and by many will be recommended, not only as more agreeable, but more useful than the other. It enters more into common life; molds the heart and affections; and, by touching those principles which actuate men, reforms their conduct, and brings them nearer to that model of perfection which it describes. On the contrary, the abstruse philosophy, being founded on a turn of mind, which cannot enter into business and action, vanishes when the philosopher leaves the shade, and comes into open day; nor can its principles easily retain any influence over our conduct and behavior. The feelings of our heart, the agitation of our passions, the vehemence of our affections, dissipate all its conclusions, and reduce the profound philosopher to a mere plebeian. . . .

But this obscurity in the profound and abstract philosophy, is objected to, not only as painful and fatiguing, but as the inevitable source of uncertainty and error. Here indeed lies the justest and most plausible objection against a considerable part of metaphysics, that they are not properly a science; but arise either from the fruitless efforts of human vanity, which would penetrate into subjects utterly inaccessible to the understanding, or from the craft of popular superstitions, which, unable to defend themselves on fair ground, raise these entangling brambles to cover and protect their weakness. Chased from the open country, these robbers fly into the forest, and lie in wait to break in upon every unguarded avenue of the mind, and overwhelm it with religious fears and prejudices. The stoutest antagonist, if he remit his watch a moment, is oppressed. And many, through cowardice and folly, open the gates to the enemies, and willingly receive them with reverence and submission, as their legal sovereigns.

But is this a sufficient reason, why philosophers should desist from such researches, and leave superstition still in possession of her retreat? Is it not proper to draw an opposite conclusion, and perceive the necessity of carrying the war into the most secret recesses of the enemy? In vain do we hope, that men, from frequent disappointment, will at last abandon such airy sciences, and discover the proper province of human reason. . . . Each adventurous genius will leap at the arduous prize, and find himself stimulated, rather than discouraged, by the failures of his predecessors; while he hopes that the glory of achieving so hard an adventure is reserved for him alone. The only method of freeing learning, at once, from these abstruse questions, is to inquire seriously into the nature of human understanding, and show, from an exact analysis of its powers and capacity, that it is by no means fitted for such remote and abstruse subjects. . . . Accurate and just reasoning is the only catholic remedy, fitted for all persons and all dispositions; and is alone able to subvert that abstruse philosophy and metaphysical jargon, which, being mixed up with popular superstition, renders it in a manner impenetrable to careless reasoners, and gives it the air of science and wisdom. . . .

SCEPTICAL DOUBTS CONCERNING THE
OPERATIONS OF THE UNDERSTANDING

PART I

All the objects of human reason or inquiry may naturally be divided into two kinds, to wit, *relations of ideas,* and *matters of fact.* Of the first kind are the sciences of geometry, algebra, and arithmetic; and in short, every affirmation which is either intuitively or demonstratively certain. *That the square of the hypothenuse is equal to the squares of the two sides,* is a proposition which expresses a relation between these figures. *That three times five is equal to the half of thirty,* expresses a relation between these numbers. Propositions of this kind are discoverable by the mere operation of thought, without dependence on what is anywhere existent in the universe. Though there never were a circle or triangle in nature, the truths demonstrated by Euclid would for ever retain their certainty and evidence.

Matters of fact, which are the second objects of human reason, are not ascertained in the same manner; nor is our evidence of their truth, however great, of a like nature with the foregoing. The contrary of every matter of fact is still possible; because it can never imply a contradiction, and is conceived by the mind with the same facility and distinctness, as if ever so conformable to reality. *That the sun will not rise tomorrow* is no less intelligible a proposition, and implies no more contradiction than the affirmation, *that it will rise.* We should in vain, therefore, attempt to demonstrate its falsehood. Were it demonstratively false, it would imply a contradiction, and could never be distinctly conceived by the mind.

It may, therefore, be a subject worthy of curiosity, to inquire what is the nature of that evidence which assures us of any real existence and matter of fact, beyond the present testimony of our senses, or the records of our memory. . . .

All reasonings concerning matter of fact seem to be founded on the relation of *cause and effect.* By means of that relation alone we can go beyond the evidence of our memory and senses. If you were to ask a man, why he believes any matter of fact, which is absent; for instance, that his friend is in the country, or in France; he would give you a reason; and this reason would be some other fact; as a letter received from him, or the knowledge of his former resolutions and promises. A man finding a watch or any other machine in a desert island, would conclude that there had once been men in that island. All our reasonings concerning fact are of the same nature. And here it is constantly supposed that there is a connection between the present fact and that which is inferred from it. Were there nothing to bind them together, the inference would be entirely precarious. The hearing of an articulate voice and rational discourse in the dark assures us of the presence of some person: Why? because these are the effects of the human make and fabric, and closely connected with it. If we anatomize all the other reasonings of this nature, we shall find that they are founded on the relation of cause and effect, and that this relation is either near or remote, direct or collateral. Heat and light are collateral effects of fire, and the one effect may justly be inferred from the other.

If we would satisfy ourselves, therefore, concerning the nature of that evidence, which assures us of matters of fact, we must inquire how we arrive at the knowledge of cause and effect.

I shall venture to affirm, as a general proposition, which admits of no exception, that the knowledge of this relation is not, in any instance, attained by reasonings *a priori;* but arises entirely from experience, when we find that any particular objects are constantly conjoined with each other. Let an object be presented to a man of ever so strong natural reason and abilities; if that object be entirely new to him, he will not be able, by the most accurate examination of its sensible qualities, to discover any of its causes or effects. Adam, though his rational faculties be supposed, at the very first, entirely perfect, could not have inferred from the fluidity and transparency of water that it would suffocate him, or from the light and warmth of fire that it would consume him. No object ever discovers, by the qualities which appear to the senses, either the causes which produced it, or the effects which will arise from it; nor can our reason, unassisted by experience, ever draw any inference concerning real existence and matter of fact.

This proposition, *that causes and effects are discoverable, not by reason but by experience,* will readily be admitted with regard to such objects, as we remember to have once been altogether unknown to us; since we must be conscious of the utter inability, which we then lay under, of foretelling what would arise from them. Present two smooth pieces of marble to a man who has no tincture of natural philosophy; he will never discover that they will adhere together in such a manner as to require great force to separate them in a direct line, while they make so small a resistance to a lateral pressure. Such events, as bear little analogy to the common course of nature, are also readily confessed to be known only by experience; nor does any man imagine that the explosion of gunpowder, or the attraction of a loadstone, could ever be discovered by arguments *a priori*. In like manner, when an effect is supposed to depend upon an intricate machinery or secret structure of parts, we make no difficulty in attributing all our knowledge of it to experience. Who will assert that he can give the ultimate reason, why milk or bread is proper nourishment for a man, not for a lion or a tiger?

But the same truth may not appear, at first sight, to have the same evidence with regard to events, which have become familiar to us from our first appearance in the world, which bear a close analogy to the whole course of nature, and which are supposed to depend on the simple qualities of objects, without any secret structure of parts. We are apt to imagine that we could discover these effects by the mere operation of our reason, without experience. We fancy, that were we brought on a sudden into this world, we could at first have inferred that one billiard ball would communicate motion to another upon impulse; and that we needed not to have waited for the event, in order to pronounce with certainty concerning it. Such is the influence of custom, that, where it is strongest, it not only covers our natural ignorance, but even conceals itself, and seems not to take place, merely because it is found in the highest degree.

But to convince us that all the laws of nature, and all the operations of bodies without exception, are known only by experience, the following reflections may, perhaps, suffice. Were any object presented to us, and were we required to pronounce concerning the effect, which will result from it, without consulting past observation; after what manner, I beseech you, must the mind proceed in this operation? It must invent or imagine some event, which it ascribes to the object as its effect; and it is plain that this invention must be entirely arbitrary. The mind can never possibly find the effect in the supposed cause, by the most accurate scrutiny and examination. For the effect is totally different from the cause, and consequently can never be discovered in it. Motion in the second billiard ball is a quite distinct event from motion in the first: nor is there anything in the one to suggest the smallest hint of the other. A stone or piece of metal raised into the air, and left without any support, immediately falls: but to consider the matter *a priori*, is there anything we discover in this situation which can beget the idea of a downward, rather than an upward, or any other motion, in the stone or metal? . . .

Hence we may discover the reason why no philosopher who is rational and modest has ever pretended to assign the ultimate cause of any natural operation, or to show distinctly the action of that power, which produces any single effect in the universe. It is confessed, that the utmost effort of human reason is to reduce the principles, productive of natural phenomena, to a greater simplicity, and to resolve the many particular effects into a few general causes, by means of reasonings from analogy, experience, and observation. But as to the causes of these general causes, we should in vain attempt their discovery; nor shall we ever be able to satisfy ourselves, by any particular explication of them. These ultimate springs and principles are totally shut up from human curiosity and inquiry. Elasticity, gravity, cohesion of parts, communication of motion by impulse; these are probably the ultimate causes and principles which we ever discover in nature; and we may esteem ourselves sufficiently happy, if, by accurate inquiry and reasoning, we can trace up the particular phenomena to, or near to, these general principles. The most perfect philosophy of the natural kind only staves off our ignorance a little longer: as perhaps the most perfect philosophy of the moral or metaphysical kind serves only to discover larger portions of it. Thus the observation of human blindness and weakness is the result of all philosophy, and meets us at every turn, in spite of our endeavors to elude or avoid it. . . .

PART II

But we have not yet attained any tolerable satisfaction with regard to the question first proposed. Each solution still gives rise to a new question as difficult as the foregoing, and leads us on to farther inquiries. When it is asked, *What is the nature of all our reasonings concerning matter of fact?* the proper answer seems to be, that they are founded on the relation of cause and effect. When again it is asked, *What is the foundation of all our reasonings and conclusions concerning that relation?* it may be replied in one word, *experience*. But if we still carry on our sifting humor, and ask, *What is the foundation of all conclusions from experience?* this implies a new question, which may be of more difficult solution and explication. Philosophers, that give themselves airs of superior wisdom and sufficiency have a hard task when they encounter persons of inquisitive dispositions who push them from every corner to which they retreat, and who are sure at last to bring them to some dangerous dilemma. The best expedient to prevent this confusion is to be modest in our pretensions; and even to discover the difficulty ourselves before it is objected to us. By this means, we may make a kind of merit of our very ignorance.

I shall content myself, in this section, with an easy task, and shall pretend only to give a negative answer to the question here proposed. I say then, that, even after we have experience of the operations of cause and effect, our conclusions from that experience are *not* founded on reasoning, or any process of the understanding. This answer we must endeavor both to explain and to defend.

. . . If a body of like color and consistence with that bread which we have formerly eaten be presented to us, we make no scruple of repeating the experiment, and foresee, with certainty, like nourishment and support. Now this is a process of the mind or thought of which I would willingly know the foundation. It is allowed on all hands that there is no known connection between the sensible qualities and the secret powers; and consequently, that the mind is not led to form such a conclusion concerning their constant and regular conjunction, by anything which it knows of their nature. As to past *experience*, it can be allowed to give *direct* and *certain* information of those precise objects only, and that precise period of time, which fell under its cognizance: but why this experience should be extended to future times, and to other objects, which, for aught we know, may be only in appearance similar; this is the main question on which I would insist. The bread, which I formerly ate, nourished me; that is, a body of such sensible qualities was, at that time, endued with such secret powers: but does it follow, that other bread must also nourish me at another time, and that like sensible qualities must always be attended with like secret powers? The consequence seems no wise necessary. At least, it must be acknowledged that there is here a consequence drawn by the mind; that there is a certain step taken; a process of thought, and an inference, which wants to be explained. These two propositions are far from being the same, *I have found that such an object has always been attended with such an effect*, and *I forsee, that other objects, which are, in appearance, similar, will be attended with similar effects*. I shall allow, if you please, that the one proposition may justly be inferred from the other; I know, in fact, that it always is inferred. But if you insist that the inference is made by a chain of reasoning, I desire you to produce that reasoning. The connection between these propositions is not intuitive. There is required a medium which may enable the mind to draw such an inference, if indeed it be drawn by reasoning and argument. What that medium is, I must confess, passes my comprehension; and it is incumbent on those to produce it who assert that it really exists, and is the origin of all our conclusions concerning matter of fact.

. . . For all inferences from experience suppose, as their foundation, that the future will resemble the past, and that similar powers will be conjoined with similar sensible qualities. If there be any suspicion that the course of nature may change, and that the past may be no rule for the future, all experience becomes useless, and can give rise to no inference or conclusion. It is impossible, therefore, that any arguments from experience can prove this resemblance of the past to the future; since all these arguments are founded on the supposition of that resemblance. Let the course of things be allowed hitherto ever so regular; that alone, without some new argument or inference, proves not that, for the future, it will continue so. In vain do you pretend to have learned the nature of bodies from your past experience. Their secret nature, and consequently all their effects and in-fluence, may change, without any change in their sensible qualities. This happens sometimes, and with regard to some objects: Why may it not happen always, and with regard to all objects? What logic, what process of argument secures you against this supposition? My practice, you say, refutes my doubts. But you mistake the purport of my question. As an agent, I am quite satisfied in the point; but as a philosopher, who has some share of curiosity, I will not say scepticism, I want to learn the foundation of this inference. No reading, no inquiry has yet been able to remove my difficulty, or to give me satisfaction in a matter of such importance. Can I do better than propose the difficulty to the public, even though, perhaps, I have small hopes of obtaining a solution? We shall, at least, by this means, be sensible of our ignorance, if we do not augment our knowledge.

I must confess that a man is guilty of unpardonable arrogance who concludes, because an argument has escaped his own investigation, that therefore it does not really exist. I must also confess that, though all the learned, for several ages, should have employed themselves in fruitless search upon any subject, it may still, perhaps, be rash to conclude positively that the subject must, therefore, pass all human comprehension. Even though we examine all the sources of our knowledge, and conclude them unfit for such a subject, there may still remain a suspicion, that the enumera-tion is not complete, or the examination not accurate. But with regard to the present subject, there are some considerations which seem to remove all this accusation of arrogance or suspicion of mistake.

It is certain that the most ignorant and stupid peasants—nay infants, nay even brute beasts—improve by experience, and learn the qualities of natural objects, by observing the effects which result from them. When a child has felt the sensation of pain from touching the flame of a candle, he will be careful not to put his hand near any candle; but will expect a similar effect from a cause which is similar in its sensible qualities and appearance. If you assert, therefore, that the understanding of the child is led into this conclusion by any process of argument or ratiocination, I may justly require you to produce that argument; nor have you any pre-tense to refuse so equitable a demand. You cannot say that the argument is abstruse and may possibly escape your inquiry; since you confess that it is obvious to the capacity of a mere infant. If you hesitate, therefore, a moment, or if, after reflection, you produce any intricate or profound argument, you, in a manner, give up the question, and confess that it is not reasoning which engages us to suppose the past resembling the future, and to expect similar effects from causes which are, to appearance, similar. This is the proposition which I intended to enforce in the present section. If I be right, I pretend not to have made any mighty discovery. And if I be wrong, I must acknowledge myself to be indeed a very backward scholar; since I cannot now discover an argument which, it seems, was perfectly familiar to me long before I was out of my cradle.

OF THE ACADEMICAL
OR SCEPTICAL PHILOSOPHY
PART I

. . . What is meant by a sceptic? And how far is it possible to push these philosophical principles of doubt and uncertainty?

There is a species of scepticism, *antecedent* to all study and philosophy, which is much inculcated by Descartes and others, as a sovereign preservative against error and precipitate judgment. It recommends an universal doubt, not only of all our former opinions and principles, but also of our very faculties; of whose veracity, say they, we must assure ourselves, by a chain of reasoning, deduced from some original principle, which cannot possibly be fallacious or deceitful. But neither is there any such original principle, which has a prerogative above others that are self-evident and convincing: or if there were, could we advance a step beyond it, but by the use of those very faculties, of which we are supposed to be already diffident. The Cartesian doubt, therefore, were it ever possible to be attained by any human creature (as it plainly is not) would be entirely incurable; and no reasoning could ever bring us to a state of assurance and conviction upon any subject.

It must, however, be confessed, that this species of scepticism, when more moderate, may be understood in a very reasonable sense, and is a necessary preparative to the study of philosophy, by preserving a proper impartiality in our judgments, and weaning our mind from all those prejudices, which we may have imbibed from education or rash opinion. To begin with clear and self-evident principles, to advance by timorous and sure steps, to review frequently our conclusions, and examine accurately all their consequences; though by these means we shall make both a slow and a short progress in our systems; are the only methods, by which we can ever hope to reach truth, and attain a proper stability and certainty in our determinations. . . .

PART II

. . . The chief and most confounding objection to *excessive* scepticism, [is] that no durable good can ever result from it while it remains in its full force and vigor. We need only ask such a sceptic, *What his meaning is? And what he proposes by all these curious researches?* He is immediately at a loss, and knows not what to answer. . . . On the contrary, he must acknowledge, if he will acknowledge anything, that all human life must perish were his principles universally and steadily to prevail. All discourse, all action would immediately cease; and men remain in a total lethargy, till the necessities of nature, unsatisfied, put an end to their miserable existence. It is true; so fatal an event is very little to be dreaded. Nature is always too strong for principle. And though a Pyrrhonian may throw himself or others into a momentary amazement and confusion by his profound reasonings, the first and most trivial event in life will put to flight all his doubts and scruples, and leave him the same, in every point of action and speculation, with the philosophers of every other sect, or with those who never concerned themselves in any philosophical researches. When he awakes from his dream, he will be the first to join in the laugh against himself, and to confess, that all his objections are mere amusement, and can have no other tendency than to show the whimsical condition of mankind, who must act and reason and believe; though they are not able, by their most diligent inquiry, to satisfy themselves concerning the foundation of these operations, or to remove the objections, which may be raised against them.

PART III

There is, indeed, a more *mitigated* scepticism or *academical* philosophy, which may be both durable and useful, and which may, in part, be the result of this Pyrrhonism, or *excessive* scepticism, when its undistinguished doubts are, in some measure, corrected by common sense and reflection. The greater part of mankind are naturally apt to be affirmative and dogmatical in their opinions; and while they see objects only on one side, and have no idea of any counterpoising argument, they throw themselves precipitately into the principles, to which they are inclined; nor have they any indulgence for those who entertain opposite sentiments. To hesitate or balance perplexes their understanding, checks their passion, and suspends their action. They are, therefore, impatient till they escape from a state, which to them is so uneasy: and they think, that they could never remove themselves far enough from it, by the violence of their affirmations and obstinacy of their belief. But could such dogmatical reasoners become sensible of the strange infirmities of human understanding, even in its most perfect state, and when most accurate and cautious in its determinations; such a reflection would naturally inspire them with more modesty and reserve, and diminish their fond opinion of themselves, and their prejudice against antagonists. . . . In general, there is a degree of doubt, and caution, and modesty, which, in all kinds of scrutiny and decision, ought forever to accompany a just reasoner.

Another species of *mitigated* scepticism which may be of advantage to mankind, and which may be the natural result of the Pyrrhonian doubts and scruples, is the limitation of our inquiries to such subjects as are best adapted to the narrow capacity of human understanding. The *imagination* of man is naturally sublime, delighted with whatever is remote and extraordinary, and running, without control, into the most distant parts of space and time in order to avoid the objects, which custom has rendered too familiar to it. A correct *judgment* observes a contrary method, and avoiding all distant and high inquiries, confines itself to common life, and to such subjects as fall under daily practice and experience; leaving the more sublime topics to the embellishment of poets and orators, or to the arts of priests and politicians. To bring us to so salutary a determination, nothing can be more serviceable, than to be once thoroughly convinced of the force of the Pyrrhonian doubt, and of the impossibility, that anything, but the strong power of natural instinct, could free us from it. Those who have a propensity to philosophy, will still continue their researches; because they reflect, that, besides the immediate pleasure, attending such an occupation, philosophical decisions are nothing but the reflections of common life, methodized and corrected. But they will never be tempted to go beyond common life, so long as they consider the imperfection of those faculties which they employ, their narrow reach, and their inaccurate operations. While we cannot give a satisfactory reason, why we believe, after a thousand experiments, that a stone will fall, or fire burn; can we ever satisfy ourselves concerning any determination, which we may form, with regard to the origin of worlds, and the situation of nature, from, and to eternity?

This narrow limitation, indeed, of our inquiries, is, in every respect, so reasonable, that it suffices to make the slightest examination into the natural powers of the human mind and to compare them with their objects, in order to recommend it to us. We shall then find what are the proper subjects of science and inquiry. . . .

The existence . . . of any being can only be proved by arguments from its cause or its effect; and these arguments are founded entirely on experience. If we reason *a priori*, anything may appear able to produce anything. The falling of a pebble may, for aught we know, extinguish the sun; or the wish of a man control the planets in their orbits. It is only experience, which teaches us the nature and bounds of cause and effect, and enables us to infer the existence of one object from that of another. . . .

When we run over libraries, persuaded of these principles, what havoc must we make? If we take in our hand any volume; of divinity or school metaphysics, for instance; let us ask, *Does it contain any abstract reasoning concerning quantity or number?* No. *Does it contain any experimental reasoning concerning matter of fact and existence?* No. Commit it then to the flames: for it can contain nothing but sophistry and illusion.

Charles Peirce

Charles Peirce is generally recognized today as the originator of some of the most powerful ideas in modern philosophy, but during his lifetime he seemed, to himself and to his friends, a failure. His friend William James described Peirce vividly in a letter he wrote to his brother Henry James after hearing that the two were dining together in Paris:

I am amused that you should have fallen into the arms of C. S. Peirce, whom I imagine you find a rather uncomfortable bedfellow, thorny and spinous, but the way to treat him is after the fabled "nettle" receipt: grasp firmly, contradict, push hard, make fun of him, and he is as pleasant as anyone; but be overawed by his sententious manner and his paradoxical and obscure statements—wait upon him, as it were, for light to dawn—and you will never get a feeling of ease with him any more than I did for years, until I changed my course and treated him more or less chaffingly. I confess I like him very much in spite of all his peculiarities, for he is a man of genius, and there's always something in that to compel one's sympathy.[1]

But if we may judge from Peirce's writings—particularly his essays on the nature of human reasoning and on logic and the philosophy of science—some of his difficulties came not at all from the fact that he was paradoxical and obscure, but rather from the fact that he had a disconcerting way of brushing old intellectual formalities aside and getting right to the point—and of finding that point to be not at all where centuries of discussion had placed it. Peirce was both a mathematician and an experimental scientist. He could bring to the philosophical discussion of the grounds of sound belief two qualities which do not often come together— a trained philosopher's sophistication and a trained scientist's knowledge, from the inside, of the way careful, controlled human thinking actually takes place. Furthermore, Peirce had an original idea: he thought that the questions about human reason that Descartes, Hume, and so many others had pursued should be recast, that they should be approached from a biological point of view.

Peirce's life spanned the years 1839–1914. The great intellectual event of this period was Darwin's formulation of the theory of evolution. The idea of biological adaptation dominated Peirce's era just as the new mathematical

1. Quoted by Gay Wilson Allen, *William James* (New York, Viking Press, 1967), pp. 204–5.

physics dominated Descartes' day. And what Peirce does is to apply this idea to the issues we have been examining. Descartes makes *doubt*—an extreme, all-embracing doubt—the starting point of his philosophy. Hume asks about the grounds of human *belief*, and finds that the nature of these grounds condemns all our knowledge to being merely probable. Peirce takes these concepts—*doubt* and *belief*—and suggests that the questions surrounding them become entirely different if we think of doubt and belief as the names for phases in a biological process, for events in the life of a creature trying to accomplish his purposes in a given environment. "Doubt" now stands for a specific perplexity, an unsettled frame of mind that comes from having the smooth flow of one's activities blocked. It is therefore always particular, an irritation with specific causes. When this irritation arises, a process—*inquiry*—begins. And inquiry stops when the specific irritation is removed; then we have what we know as "belief," the absence of doubt. When, in due course, we doubt a belief, genuinely doubt it, there are specific reasons why we do so, and inquiry starts again in an effort to remove the doubt.

But if belief is simply a peaceful, untroubled state of mind, why are not all beliefs on a par? So long as they don't trouble us, isn't that enough? And why isn't any method that keeps them from troubling us—narcosis, psychic or political repression, wishful or fallacious thinking—a perfectly satisfactory one? How can we distinguish among our beliefs, separating the better from the worse? Is there some method which allows us to arrive at *true* beliefs? This is the question to which Peirce's epoch-making essay, "The Fixation of Belief," is addressed. Most of that essay follows, and the reader can judge for himself the strength of Peirce's proposal. The importance of the essay, however, lies as much in the radically new way in which Peirce reformulates old questions as it does in the specific answer he gives to them. Note, for example, that he dismisses Descartes' all-embracing doubt as a self-deception; he thinks that doubt of this kind is not really possible. And instead of trying to begin at rock bottom, as Descartes does, and build up a sure method for conducting the reason properly, he begins by assuming that men can't get back to absolutely first principles. They are mortal animals, caught in the middle of the stream of life and inevitably inheritors of a social tradition. So, in contrast to Descartes, Peirce conducts his search for a correct method of thought by canvassing the various methods that men have actually used, and then indicating why he thinks that one of them is superior to the others.

In many ways, Peirce is close to Hume. Hume points out that "Pyrrhonism"—mere doubting for doubting's sake—is not an outlook that anybody can really maintain in his behavior. He points out, too, that our beliefs about matters of fact reflect mere habits of the mind, and that men, for practical reasons, have to rely on these habits. But Peirce carries Hume's philosophy one step farther. He asks the kind of questions about human thinking that a biologist would ask about other natural processes: What starts it off? What function does it serve? When does it stop? What are the conditions under which it serves its function best? The result is that Hume's arguments are converted by Peirce from an invitation to skepticism into a cure for that malady. It turns out, if Peirce is right, that there is no reason for us to be disturbed by the fact that our beliefs are inevitably fallible. Beliefs that are admittedly fallible are subject to criticism and improvement, and this makes them preferable to beliefs that claim to be certain. Nor should we be disturbed, or tempted by skepticism, because we can't find any ultimate logical defense of our habits of mind. The best test of them is also the simplest—do these habits lead to true beliefs? If they do, let us keep them. If not, let us throw them out.

But the import of this whole train of reasoning depends, it must be obvious, on what we mean by "true beliefs." So let us turn to Peirce. The reader will find that, whatever Peirce's differences from Descartes and Hume, he is also like them. He too is searching for a method that will eliminate obscurity and self-deception, and lead the mind economically to such truths as it is capable of discovering. And he too has a disarming way of saying, in clear, ordinary prose, most unprosaic things. Not least, what he says has implications, as in the case of Descartes and Hume, that go beyond the immediate purposes of his essay. Peirce is thinking as a logician when he comments on what he calls "the method of authority." But his words have considerable bearing on political issues: "Wherever you are, let it be known that you seriously hold a tabooed belief, and you may be perfectly sure of being treated with a cruelty no less brutal but more refined than hunting you like a wolf. Thus, the greatest intellectual benefactors of mankind have never dared, and dare not now, to utter the whole of their thought; and thus a shade of *prima facie* doubt is cast upon every proposition which is considered essential to the security of society."

"The Fixation of Belief" is the first of a series of essays Peirce wrote to outline his new approach to logic and intellectual method. It appeared in *Popular Science Monthly* in 1877.

The Fixation of Belief

. . . We generally know when we wish to ask a question and when we wish to pronounce a judgment, for there is a dissimilarity between the sensation of doubting and that of believing.

But this is not all which distinguishes doubt from belief. There is a practical difference. Our beliefs guide our desires and shape our actions. The Assassins, or followers of the Old Man of the Mountain, used to rush into death at his least command, because they believed that obedience to him would insure everlasting felicity. Had they doubted this, they would not have acted as they did. So it is with every belief, according to its degree. The feeling of believing is a more or less sure indication of there being established in our nature some habit which will determine our actions. Doubt never has such an effect.

Nor must we overlook a third point of difference. Doubt is an uneasy and dissatisfied state from which we struggle to free ourselves and pass into the state of belief; while the latter is a calm and satisfactory state which we do not wish to avoid, or to change to a belief in anything else.[1] On the contrary, we cling tenaciously, not merely to believing, but to believing just what we do believe.

Thus, both doubt and belief have positive effects upon us, though very different ones. Belief does not make us act at once, but puts us into such a condition that we shall behave in a certain way, when the occasion arises. Doubt has not the least effect of this sort, but stimulates us to action until it is destroyed. This reminds us of the irritation of a nerve and the reflex action produced thereby; while for the analogue of belief, in the nervous system, we must look to what are called nervous associations—for example, to that habit of the nerves in consequence of which the smell of a peach will make the mouth water.

The irritation of doubt causes a struggle to attain a state of belief. I shall term this struggle *inquiry*, though it must be admitted that this is sometimes not a very apt designation.

The irritation of doubt is the only immediate motive for the struggle to attain belief. It is certainly best for us that our beliefs should be such as may truly guide our actions so as to satisfy our desires; and this reflection will make us reject any belief which does not seem to have been so formed as to insure this result. But it will only do so by creating a doubt in the place of that belief. With the doubt, therefore, the struggle begins, and with the cessation of doubt it ends. Hence, the sole object of inquiry is the settlement of opinion. We may fancy that this is not enough for us, and that we seek not merely an opinion, but a true opinion. But put this fancy to the test and it proves groundless; for as soon as a firm belief is reached we are entirely satisfied, whether the belief be false or true. And it is clear that nothing out of the sphere of our knowledge can be our object, for nothing which does not affect the mind can be a motive for a mental effort. The most that can be maintained is that we seek for a belief that we shall *think* to be true. But we think each one of our beliefs to be true, and, indeed, it is mere tautology to say so.

That the settlement of opinion is the sole end of inquiry is a very

1. I am not speaking of secondary effects occasionally produced by the interference of other impulses.—*Author.*

important proposition. It sweeps away, at once, various vague and erroneous conceptions of proof. A few of these may be noticed here.

1. Some philosophers have imagined that to start an inquiry it was only necessary to utter or question or set it down on paper, and have even recommended us to begin our studies with questioning everything! But the mere putting of a proposition into the interrogative form does not stimulate the mind to any struggle after belief. There must be a real and living doubt, and without all this, discussion is idle.

2. It is a very common idea that a demonstration must rest on some ultimate and absolutely indubitable propositions. These, according to one school, are first principles of a general nature; according to another, are first sensations. But, in point of fact, an inquiry, to have that completely satisfactory result called demonstration, has only to start with propositions perfectly free from all actual doubt. If the premises are not in fact doubted at all, they cannot be more satisfactory than they are.

3. Some people seem to love to argue a point after all the world is fully convinced of it. But no further advance can be made. When doubt ceases, mental action on the subject comes to an end; and, if it did go on, it would be without a purpose. . . .

If the settlement of opinion is the sole object of inquiry, and if belief is of the nature of a habit, why should we not attain the desired end, by taking any answer to a question, which we may fancy, and constantly re-iterating it to ourselves, dwelling on all which may conduce to that belief, and learning to turn with contempt and hatred from anything which might disturb it? This simple and direct method is really pursued by many men. I remember once being entreated not to read a certain newspaper lest it might change my opinion upon free trade. "Lest I might be entrapped by its fallacies and misstatements" was the form of expression. "You are not," my friend said, "a special student of political economy. You might, there-fore, easily be deceived by fallacious arguments upon the subject. You might, then, if you read this paper, be led to believe in protection. But you admit that free trade is the true doctrine; and you do not wish to believe what is not true." I have often known this system to be deliberately adopted.

Still oftener, the instinctive dislike of an undecided state of mind, exag-gerated into a vague dread of doubt, makes men cling spasmodically to the views they already take. The man feels that if he only holds to his belief without wavering, it will be entirely satisfactory. Nor can it be denied that a steady and immovable faith yields great peace of mind. It may, indeed, give rise to inconveniences, as if a man should resolutely continue to be-lieve that fire would not burn him, or that he would be eternally damned if he received his *ingesta* otherwise than through a stomach pump. But then the man who adopts this method will not allow that its inconveniences are greater than its advantages. He will say, "I hold steadfastly to the truth and the truth is always wholesome." And in many cases it may very well be that the pleasure he derives from his calm faith overbalances any inconveniences resulting from its deceptive character. Thus, if it be true that death is annihilation, then the man who believes that he will certainly go straight to heaven when he dies, provided he will have fulfilled certain simple observances in this life, has a cheap pleasure which will not be followed by the least disappointment.

A similar consideration seems to have weight with many persons in religious topics, for we frequently hear it said, "Oh, I could not believe so-and-so, because I should be wretched if I did." When an ostrich buries its head in the sand when danger approaches, it very likely takes the happiest course. It hides the danger, and then calmly says there is no danger; and, if it feels perfectly sure there is none, why should it raise its head to see? A man may go through life, systematically keeping out of view all that might cause a change in his opinions, and if he only succeeds—basing his method, as he does, on two fundamental psychological laws—I do not see what can be said against his doing so. It would be an egotistical impertinence to object that his procedure is irrational, for that only amounts to saying that his method of settling belief is not ours. He does not propose to himself to be rational, and indeed, will often talk with scorn of man's weak and illusive reason. So let him think as he pleases.

But this method of fixing belief, which may be called the method of tenacity, will be unable to hold its ground in practice. The social impulse is against it. The man who adopts it will find that other men think differently from him, and it will be apt to occur to him in some saner moment that their opinions are quite as good as his own, and this will shake his confidence in his belief. This conception, that another man's thought or sentiment may be equivalent to one's own, is a distinctly new step, and a highly important one. It arises from an impulse too strong in man to be suppressed, without danger of destroying the human species. Unless we make ourselves hermits, we shall necessarily influence each other's opinions; so that the problem becomes how to fix belief, not in the individual merely, but in the community.

Let the will of the state act, then, instead of that of the individual. Let an institution be created which shall have for its object to keep correct doctrines before the attention of the people, to reiterate them perpetually, and to teach them to the young; having at the same time power to prevent contrary doctrines from being taught, advocated, or expressed. Let all possible causes of a change of mind be removed from men's apprehensions. Let them be kept ignorant, lest they should learn of some reason to think otherwise than they do. Let their passions be enlisted, so that they may regard private and unusual opinions with hatred and horror. Then, let all men who reject the established belief be terrified into silence. Let the people turn out and tar and feather such men, or let inquisitions be made into the manner of thinking of suspected persons, and, when they are found guilty of forbidden beliefs, let them be subjected to some signal punishment. When complete agreement could not otherwise be reached, a general massacre of all who have not thought in a certain way has proved a very effective means of settling opinion in a country. If the power to do this be wanting, let a list of opinions be drawn up, to which no man of the least independence of thought can assent, and let the faithful be required to accept all these propositions, in order to segregate them as radically as possible from the influence of the rest of the world.

This method has, from the earliest times, been one of the chief means of upholding correct theological and political doctrines, and of preserving their universal or catholic character. In Rome, especially, it has been practiced from the days of Numa Pompilius to those of Pius Nonus. This is the most perfect example in history; but wherever there is a priesthood—and no religion has been without one—this method has been more or less made use of. Wherever there is aristocracy, or a guild, or any association of a class of men whose interests depend or are supposed to depend on certain propositions, there will be inevitably found some traces of this natural product of social feeling. Cruelties always accompany this system; and when it is consistently carried out, they become atrocities of the most horrible kind in the eyes of any rational man. Nor should this occasion surprise, for the officer of a society does not feel justified in surrendering the interests of that society for the sake of mercy, as he might of his own private interests. It is natural, therefore, that sympathy and fellowship should thus produce a most ruthless power.

In judging this method of fixing belief, which may be called the method of authority, we must, in the first place, allow its immeasurable mental and moral superiority to the method of tenacity. Its success is proportionally greater; and in fact it has over and over again worked the most majestic results. The mere structures of stone which it has caused to be put together —in Siam, for example, in Egypt, and in Europe—have many of them a sublimity hardly more than rivaled by the greatest works of nature. And, except the geological epochs, there are no periods of time so vast as those which are measured by some of these organized faiths. If we scrutinize the matter closely, we shall find that there has not been one of their creeds which has remained always the same; yet the change is so slow as to be imperceptible during one person's life, so that individual belief remains sensibly fixed. For the mass of mankind, then, there is perhaps no better method than this. If it is their highest impulse to be intellectual slaves, then slaves they ought to remain.

But no institution can undertake to regulate opinions upon every subject. Only the most important ones can be attended to, and on the rest men's minds must be left to the action of the natural causes. This imperfection will be no source of weakness so long as men are in such a state of culture that one opinion does not influence another—that is, so long as they cannot put two and two together. But in the most priest-ridden states some individuals will be found who are raised above that condition. These men possess a wider sort of social feeling; they see that men in other countries and in other ages have held to very different doctrines from those which they themselves have been brought up to believe; and they cannot help seeing that it is the mere accident of their having been taught as they have, and of their having been surrounded with the manners and associations they have, that has caused them to believe as they do and not far differently. And their candor cannot resist the reflection that there is no reason to rate their own views at a higher value than those of other nations and other centuries; and this gives rise to doubts in their minds.

They will further perceive that such doubts as these must exist in their minds with reference to every belief which seems to be determined by the caprice either of themselves or of those who originated the popular opinions. The willful adherence to a belief, and the arbitrary forcing of it upon others, must, therefore, both be given up and a new method of settling opinions must be adopted, which shall not only produce an impulse to believe, but shall also decide what proposition it is which is to be believed. Let the action of natural preferences be unimpeded, then, and under their influence let men conversing together and regarding matters in different lights, gradually develop beliefs in harmony with natural causes. This method resembles that by which conceptions of art have been brought to maturity. The most perfect example of it is to be found in the history of metaphysical philosophy. Systems of this sort have not usually rested upon observed facts, at least not in any great degree. They have been chiefly adopted because their fundamental propositions seemed "agreeable to reason." This is an apt expression; it does not mean that which agrees with experience, but that which we find ourselves inclined to believe. Plato, for example, finds it agreeable to reason that the distances of the celestial spheres from one another should be proportional to the different lengths of strings which produce harmonious chords. Many philosophers have been led to their main conclusions by considerations like this; but this is the lowest and least developed form which the method takes, for it is clear that another man might find Kepler's theory, that the celestial spheres are proportional to the inscribed and circumscribed spheres of the different regular solids, more agreeable to *his* reason. But the shock of opinions will soon lead men to rest on preferences of a far more universal nature. Take, for example, the doctrine that man only acts selfishly—that is, from the consideration that acting in one way will afford him more pleasure than acting in another. This rests on no fact in the world, but it has a wide acceptance as being the only reasonable theory.

This method is far more intellectual and respectable from the point of view of reason than either of the others which we have noticed. But its failure has been the most manifest. It makes of inquiry something similar to the development of taste; but taste, unfortunately, is always more or less a matter of fashion, and accordingly, metaphysicians have never come to any fixed agreement, but the pendulum has swung backward and forward between a more material and a more spiritual philosophy, from the earliest times to the latest. And so from this, which has been called the *a priori* method, we are driven, in Lord Bacon's phrase, to a true induction. We have examined into this *a priori* method as something which promised to deliver our opinions from their accidental and capricious element. But development, while it is a process which eliminates the effect of some casual circumstances, only magnifies that of others. This method, therefore, does not differ in a very essential way from that of authority. The government may not have lifted its finger to influence my convictions; I may have been left outwardly quite free to choose, we will say, between monogamy and polygamy, and appealing to my conscience only, I may have concluded that the latter practice is in itself licentious. But when I come to see that the chief obstacle to the spread of Christianity among a people of as high culture as Hindus has been a conviction of the immorality of our way of treating women, I cannot help seeing that, though governments do not interfere, sentiments in their development will be very greatly determined by accidental causes. Now there are some people, among whom I must suppose that my reader is to be found, who, when they see that any belief of theirs is determined by any circumstance extraneous to the facts, will from that moment not merely admit in words that that belief is doubtful but will experience a real doubt of it, so that it ceases in some degree at least to be a belief.

To satisfy our doubts, therefore, it is necessary that a method should be found by which our beliefs may be caused by nothing human, but by some external permanency—by something upon which our thinking has no effect. Some mystics imagine that they have such a method in a private inspiration from on high. But that is only a form of the method of tenacity, in which the conception of truth as something public is not yet developed. Our external permanency would not be external, in our sense, if it was restricted in its influence to one individual. It must be something which affects, or might affect, every man. And, though these affections are necessarily as various as are individual conditions, yet the method must be such that the ultimate conclusion of every man shall be the same, or would be the same if inquiry were sufficiently persisted in. Such is the method of science. Its fundamental hypothesis, restated in more familiar language, is this: There are real things, whose characters are entirely independent of our opinions about them; those realities affect our senses according to regular laws, and, though our sensations are as different as our relations to the objects, yet, by taking advantage of the laws of perception, we can ascertain by reasoning how things really are, and any man, if he have sufficient experience and reason enough about it, will be led to the one true conclusion.

The new conception here involved is that of reality. It may be asked how I know that there are any realities. If this hypothesis is the sole support of my method of inquiry, my method of inquiry must not be used to support my hypothesis. The reply is this: 1. If investigation cannot be regarded as proving that there are real things, it at least does not lead to a contrary conclusion; but the method and the conception on which it is based remain ever in harmony. No doubts of the method, therefore, necessarily arise from its practice, as is the case with all the others. 2. The feeling which gives rise to any method of fixing belief is a dissatisfaction at two repugnant propositions. But here already is a vague concession that there is some *one* thing to which a proposition should conform. Nobody, therefore, can really doubt that there are realities, or, if he did, doubt would not be a source of dissatisfaction. The hypothesis, therefore, is one which every mind admits. So that the social impulse does not cause me to doubt it. 3. Everybody uses the scientific method about a great many things, and only ceases to use it when he does not know how to apply it. 4. Experience of the method has not led me to doubt it, but, on the contrary, scientific investigation has had the most wonderful triumphs in the way of settling opinion. These afford the explanation of my not doubting the method or the hypothesis which it supposes; and not having any doubt, nor believing that anybody else whom I could influence has, it would be the merest babble for me to say more about it. If there be anybody with a living doubt upon the subject, let him consider it. . . .

This is the only one of the four methods which presents any distinction of a right and a wrong way. If I adopt the method of tenacity and shut myself out from all influences, whatever I think necessary to doing this is necessary according to that method. So with the method of authority: the state may try to put down heresy by means which, from a scientific point of view, seem very ill calculated to accomplish its purposes; but the only test *on that method* is what the state thinks, so that it cannot pursue the method wrongly. So with the *a priori* method. The very essence of it is to think as one is inclined to think. All metaphysicians will be sure to do that, however they may be inclined to judge each other to be perversely wrong. . . . But with the scientific method the case is different. I may start with known and observed facts to proceed to the unknown; and yet the rules which I follow in doing so may not be such as investigation would approve. The test of whether I am truly following the method is not an immediate appeal to my feelings and purposes, but, on the contrary, itself involves the application of the method. Hence it is that bad reasoning as well as good reasoning is possible; and this fact is the foundation of the practical side of logic.

It is not to be supposed that the first three methods of settling opinion present no advantage whatever over the scientific method. On the contrary, each has some peculiar convenience of its own. The *a priori* method is distinguished for its comfortable conclusions. It is the nature of the process to adopt whatever belief we are inclined to, and there are certain flatteries to one's vanities which we all believe by nature, until we are awakened from our pleasing dream by rough facts. The method of authority will always govern the mass of mankind; and those who wield the various forms of organized force in the state will never be convinced that dangerous reasoning ought not to be suppressed in some way. If liberty of speech is to be untrammeled from the grosser forms of constraint, then uniformity of opinion will be secure by a moral terrorism to which the respectability of society will give its thorough approval.

Following the method of authority is the path of peace. Certain nonconformities are permitted; certain others (considered unsafe) are forbidden. These are different in different countries and in different ages; but, wherever you are, let it be known that you seriously hold a tabooed belief, and you may be perfectly sure of being treated with a cruelty no less brutal but more refined than hunting you like a wolf. Thus, the greatest intellectual benefactors of mankind have never dared, and dare not now, to utter the whole of their thought; and thus a shade of *prima facie* doubt is cast upon every proposition which is considered essential to the security of society. Singularly enough, the persecution does not all come from without; but a man torments himself and is oftentimes most distressed at finding himself believing propositions which he has been brought up to regard with aversion.

The peaceful and sympathetic man will, therefore, find it hard to resist the temptation to submit his opinions to authority. But most of all I admire the method of tenacity for its strength, simplicity, and directness. Men who pursue it are distinguished for their decision of character, which becomes very easy with such a mental rule. They do not waste time in trying to make up their minds to what they want, but, fastening like lightning upon whatever alternative comes first, they hold to it to the end, whatever happens, without an instant's irresolution. This is one of the splendid qualities which generally accompany brilliant, unlasting success. It is impossible not to envy the man who can dismiss reason, although we know how it must turn out at last.

Such are the advantages which the other methods of settling opinions have over scientific investigation. A man should consider well of them; and then he should consider that, after all, he wishes his opinions to coincide with the fact, and that there is no reason why the results of those first three methods should do so. To bring about this effect is the prerogative of the method of science. Upon such considerations he has to make his choice— a choice which is far more than the adoption of any intellectual opinion, which is one of the ruling decisions of his life, to which when once made he is bound to adhere. The force of habit will sometimes cause a man to hold on to old beliefs after he is in a condition to see that they have no sound basis. But reflection upon the state of the case will overcome these habits, and he ought to allow reflection full weight.

People sometimes shrink from doing this, having an idea that beliefs are wholesome which they cannot help feeling rest on nothing. But let such persons suppose an analogous though different case from their own. Let them ask themselves what they would say to a reformed Mussulman who should hesitate to give up his old notions in regard to the relations of the sexes; or to a reformed Catholic who should still shrink from the Bible. Would they not say that these persons ought to consider the matter fully, and clearly understand the new doctrine, and then ought to embrace it in its entirety? But, above all, let it be considered that what is more wholesome than any particular belief is integrity of belief; and that to avoid looking into the support of any belief from a fear that it may turn out rotten is quite as immoral as it is disadvantageous. The person who confesses that there is such a thing as truth, which is distinguished from falsehood simply by this, that if acted on it should, on full consideration, carry us to the point we aim at and not astray, and then, though convinced of this, dares not know the truth and seeks to avoid it, is in a sorry state of mind indeed.

Yes, the other methods do have their merits: a clear logical conscience does cost something—just as all that we cherish, costs us dear. But, we should not desire it to be otherwise. The genius of a man's logical method should be loved and reverenced as his bride, whom he has chosen from all the world. He need not condemn the others; on the contrary, he may honor them deeply, and in doing so he only honors her the more. But she is the one that he has chosen, and he knows that he was right in making that choice. And having made it, he will work and fight for her, and will not complain that there are blows to take, hoping that there may be as many and as hard to give, and will strive to be the worthy knight and champion of her from the blaze of whose splendors he draws his inspiration and his courage.

Afterword

One of the great themes of the modern novel, stretching from Don Quixote to Stendhal's Julian Sorel and F. Scott Fitzgerald's Jay Gatsby, is that of the man who cuts himself loose from his past and tries to journey through the world wholly on his own terms, inventing his own name and career, and quite literally making himself up. Descartes' philosophy has the quality of these romances: it is the same story, transposed to the realm of the mind. The experiment in which he invites us to join is that of seeing whether an individual, by himself, can cut through the prejudices that hang like a veil between the mind and the world, and, depending only on his own resources, discover the truth for himself.

Does he succeed? To have provided three centuries of philosophy with some of its major preoccupations is no small thing. But he does not, I think, accomplish what he sets out to do.

Descartes uses the root idea which he cannot doubt—*I think, hence I am*—as the model against which he measures other ideas. He observes that it is conceived "clearly and distinctly." Even the attempt to reject it reaffirms it. For him, therefore, the question to be answered is this: If there are other ideas that are clear and distinct in the same way, are we justified in believing that they, too, are true? It is with this question in mind that Descartes introduces his argument for the existence of God. We have an idea of God, and since our imperfect minds could not by themselves give rise to the idea of a perfect being, God must exist. And since it is incompatible with the nature of a perfect being that He should give us a powerful inclination to accept clear and distinct ideas as true, and then make these ideas false, we can accept clarity and distinctness as criteria of truth. The clarity and distinctness of ideas such as those to be found in mathematics are God's signals to us to accept them; if we adhere faithfully to these signals, and only to them, we cannot go wrong.

But the argument limps. It is notorious that what is clear and distinct to one person can seem vague and obscure, even mad, to another. Descartes' test is intuitive, essentially personal, despite its resemblance, in his view, to the methods of mathematical proof. And there are, besides, grave internal flaws in his argument. In proving the existence of God, for example, he confuses two quite different things—the idea of perfection and the perfect idea. We can have quite imperfect ideas of a perfect being. In fact, that is the kind we normally do have. But if these ideas are imperfect, there is no problem about how an imperfect being can have them. He isn't exceeding his limitations at all. Moreover, what is impossible about a lesser being thinking of a greater one? Can't a pigmy imagine a giant, or a dachshund a Great Dane? Descartes says that a "less perfect" thing cannot give rise to the idea of a "more perfect" thing: to assume the contrary, we would have to suppose that "something should proceed from nothing." But there is nothing clear and distinct about these propositions; even the meaning of their language is not plain. And in any event, Descartes can't use them, within the ground rules of his own argument, without begging the question. For even if we say that they are clear and distinct we have accomplished nothing, since the entire purpose of his argument is rather to prove that clear and distinct ideas are true.

The paradox, indeed, is that these propositions that Descartes uses to make his point, were part of the traditional conventional wisdom of Descartes' day. He took them over unconsciously from the stock of medieval ideas descended from Plato's metaphysics. Descartes did not manage to break loose from his heritage. Like Robinson Crusoe, he could start anew only by using at least a few pieces of lumber salvaged from the wreckage of the ship that had failed him. If we take Descartes as an example, we may conclude that the effort to find the truth by a process of lonely introspection, in which we search our minds and adopt the ideas we find indubitable, seems to be simply an unwitting way of justifying ideas we are strongly disposed to accept.

But his effort raises a question that is perhaps even more fundamental: Why should we look for a method for conducting the reason which is controlled by an intellectual ideal irrelevant to most of the issues with which reason concerns itself? Most of our judgments are about matters of fact or about what course of conduct we ought to adopt. In such judgments, absolute logical certainty is conspicuous by its absence. Even mathematics is one thing when it is pure, and another when it is applied. A surveyor who uses a Euclidean theorem to calculate the size of an area has to give a concrete meaning to the concept of a "straight line": he must say, for example, that the concept will refer to the path of light rays moving from a distant object to his glass. Applied mathematics requires the interpretation of its terms, and this interpretation is separate from the mathematics itself; accordingly, we enter a realm where the certainties of mathematics no longer exist. It seems a mistake, then, to adopt the idea of logical certainty as the standard to be employed in our matter-of-fact judgments.

This, in essence, is the issue that Hume raises. One way to go wrong in using our reason, he suggests, is to follow Descartes' road and try to attain true ideas by reasoning from self-evident principles. In so doing, we spin a web of words around ourselves, but do not come to any knowledge about matters of fact. In the acquisition of the latter kind of knowledge, the evidence of the senses is the *sine qua non*. For example, we cannot determine through logic what will occur when one billiard ball strikes another; there would be nothing self-contradictory in both balls coming to a complete rest, or in one disintegrating, or in something different happening each time. The only basis for our actual expectations about their behavior is our past observation of what occurs when they collide.

But what, then, is the basis, the logical foundation, for the inferences we draw from our observations? These inferences, as Hume points out, are all based on the assumption of causal relations. We have observed that water quenches thirst, and so, when we see a man drinking water, we confidently infer that his thirst will be quenched. And here Hume comes to the point which troubles him. Our beliefs about the regular operation of causal laws are founded upon past experience. But when we ask for the basis of the assumption that what has happened in the past will happen in the future, the only answer we can give is that, in the past, the future has resembled the past. And this is circular reasoning. Our knowledge and vaunted powers of reason thus turn out, if Hume is right, to be curious affairs. Even the beliefs of which we are proudest and surest are simply habits of the mind, "tendencies to feign," to leap ahead and assume a regularity in the world which we cannot logically demonstrate.

This is the so-called "problem of induction," which has worried and fascinated many philosophers since Hume's time. Admitting that he could not refute Hume, Bertrand Russell said: "I cannot but hope that something less skeptical than Hume's system may be discoverable. . . . If not, there is no intellectual difference between sanity and insanity. The lunatic who believes that he is a poached egg is to be condemned solely on the ground that he is in a minority, or rather—since we must not assume democracy— on the ground that the government does not agree with him. This is a desperate point of view, and it must be hoped that there is some way of escaping from it." [1]

Is this imputation of unlimited skepticism to Hume fair? Hume himself, it must be admitted, was troubled by the possibility that he was taking a "desperate point of view." Only "carelessness and inattention," he said, protected human beings from the corrosive doubts that emerge when we look carefully at the basis of our beliefs. Our animal requirements keep us going, and turn us away from skepticism. But it is only animal vitality, and not inexorable logic, that does so. As he said in his *Treatise*, " 'Tis not solely in poetry and music we must follow our taste and sentiment, but likewise in philosophy. When I am convinced of any principle, 'tis only an idea which strikes more strongly upon me."

Nevertheless, extreme skepticism does not necessarily follow from Hume's view. Russell says: "[Hume] arrives at the disastrous conclusion that from experience and observation nothing is to be learnt. There is no

1. *A History of Western Philosophy* (New York, Simon and Schuster, 1945), pp. 659, 673.

such thing as a rational belief: 'If we believe that fire warms, or water refreshes, 'tis only because it costs us too much pains to think otherwise.' " [2] But the response to Russell is that this quotation from Hume *defines* Hume's conception of "rational belief." We believe that fire warms and water refreshes because it does indeed cost pain to think otherwise—not only the pain of changing a settled habit of thought, but the pain of cold and thirst. Even if we say that our beliefs are merely habits, we may recognize that some of our mental habits are better than others, just as the physical habit of eating a variety of foods is better than that of just eating sweets. Why can't we sift and choose our beliefs, and criticize them, just as we pass judgment on our other habits?

In essence, I think, this is the method Hume proposes for distinguishing sound ideas from unsound ones. It may seem almost too obvious to need the support of all the arguments he produces. But it is in fact, as he believed, a position of the greatest importance. If it is correct, our most lofty notions must meet the same test that our homely everyday ideas meet. Hume is the great democratizer of thought. He resists the notion that some ideas are more equal than others—that there is a special category set apart for disciplines like "metaphysics" or "theology" and that people engaged in them can rise above the limitations otherwise encountered by human thought. In saying that a meaningful piece of reasoning is either about "relations of ideas" or about "matters of fact," and that if it is neither it is worthless, Hume exposes the pretensions of an entire tradition of thought, stretching back through Descartes to Plato, which has claimed to be able to provide us with *a priori* knowledge of matters of fact. If his point is valid, all beliefs, without exception, should be subjected to the ordinary tests of experience. If we ever adopted such a program consistently and seriously, we would have to abandon, or hold with considerably more skepticism, a very large portion of our ideas about morals, politics, education, "human nature," and numberless other subjects. A practical revolution in human thinking would take place, at least as profound as that envisaged by Descartes.

The depth of the resistance aroused by Hume's position is suggested by the history of the opposition to it. Few men have ever had at once a profounder influence on philosophy and fewer disciples. Many of the most prestigious philosophers of the two hundred years since his death—Immanuel Kant, G. W. F. Hegel, Bertrand Russell—have gained their reputations at least in part in consequence of their efforts to refute Hume or to circumvent him. One of the most revealing and significant of these attempts was made by Immanuel Kant (1724–1804).

Some twelve years after he first read the *Enquiry*, Kant came to see that Hume had raised questions that called for the renovation of philosophy. Kant accepted Hume's position that all knowledge based on experience is

2. *Ibid.*, p. 672.

doomed to be merely probable. But he thought he saw in this doctrine the clue to a response to Hume: in the very fact that man could know that his experience was limited, Kant argued, he transcended the limits of his experience. In fact, Hume was wrong to think that *all* our knowledge of matters of fact rests on observation. For we know some things about all possible human experience without depending on observation: we know in advance, for example, that our experience will have spatial and temporal dimensions, and that its parts will be causally connected. It is impossible for us to think about experience in any other way. No matter how we try, we come back to the categories of space, time, and causation as the containers or frames in which we know, eyes shut, that our experience will be presented to us.

To Kant, the existence of this special kind of *a priori* knowledge compels at least three conclusions. First, our minds have a certain unavoidable structure: we see things in temporal, spatial, and causal frameworks because our minds are so constituted that we must, just as our eyes are so constituted that we see red and green while other animals may see only blacks, whites, and grays. Second, this indicates that the universe's own structure—the character of "things-in-themselves"—is something which our observations as such can throw no light on. Science, based on observations, is true so far as it goes, but it only goes so far. Third, we thus have a right to take other data of our experience—the insights we derive from our conscience, for example—and draw conclusions from them. Just as we presuppose space and time when we engage in scientific investigation, so we have to presuppose the free will of the individual when we make our moral judgments. Accordingly, even though science is "deterministic," and denies freedom in its sphere, we have the right to suppose that in the separate sphere of morals free will is a reality.

Kant, I think, is on less sure ground than Hume. We learn little if anything, for example, when we are told that all things are perceived in spatial categories. The question is what spatial framework to use—that of Euclidean geometry or of some non-Euclidean geometry—and this cannot be settled *a priori*, but only by a process of experimental inquiry. However, to discuss Kant's carefully orchestrated and lengthy arguments, and to compare their validity with that of Hume's, would take us far afield. The interesting fact is that Kant, though he described his own *Critique of Pure Reason* as "dry, obscure, opposed to all ordinary notions, and moreover long-winded," and compared its qualities invidiously to the "subtlety" and "grace" that he found in Hume, has had by far the lion's share of followers. It is not from Hume but from Kant that Protestant theologians, "existentialists," "philosophical idealists," and most contemporary legal and moral philosophers draw their main impulse. Hume, in contrast, is regularly dismissed as too "negative" and "skeptical."

There does exist, however, a constructive line of development out of

Hume. Philosophers like Kant or Russell find Hume's position unsatisfactory because they have a special notion of what a "rational belief" must be. They think that when we reason from the past to the future, for example, such a process of thought can be shown to be "rational" only if it depends, in Russell's words, on "an independent principle not based on experience." [3] But aren't we being led to a dead end? If we could find such a principle, how could we justify *it?* Presumably, only by logically deducing it from a higher principle. And this principle in its turn would have to be deduced from a still higher one. So we should either be involved in an infinite regress, or we should have to stop at some point arbitrarily. Hume can be interpreted as saying that this Cartesian game makes no sense. Not only can't we find a *general* principle to justify our reasoning about matters of fact, but we don't need one. The justification can always be specific—this particular habit of the mind or that one, which takes us where we expect to go, and is appropriate as long as it does.

When a basketball player makes a basket and scores two points, we do not criticize him because he didn't make a touchdown and score six points. That would be to impose on him standards taken from a different game with different objectives. The thrust of Hume's argument is that a similarly fallacious procedure goes on with respect to judging the powers and possibilities of the human mind. He suggests, in effect, that we should redefine "rationality" so that the word is applicable to the behavior and thinking of a creature who is governed by his habits and needs and whose knowledge is fallible; our definition of rationality or reasonableness should not impose on man a standard appropriate to angels or gods. When we seek to explain a particular causal relation, the best we can do is to appeal to a more embracing set of causal laws. But eventually we reach the end of what we know, and can only say that these laws happen to be what they are. The pursuit of knowledge always culminates, therefore, not in the recognition that everything can be explained, but in the recognition that we have run out of explanations. Thus, for Hume, the most perfect science "only staves off our ignorance a little longer," and the most perfect philosophy "serves only to discover larger portions of it."

This is the cue that Peirce takes. But for him it is a cue not to skepticism, but to what he came to call "fallibilism." The recognition that all human beliefs are fallible is the first condition for exercising some control over what we believe. If we choose a method which rests on the assumption that all beliefs are fallible, and which institutes procedures by which they are regularly corrected, we have the only method capable of guiding men to sound beliefs. In presenting his answer to the question, How can I give a rational proof that the method for reasoning which I propose is more rational than any other? Peirce seeks to avoid circularity not as Descartes does, by trying to start from bedrock, but by looking at the various

3. *Ibid.*, p. 674.

approaches that men have employed, and asking what we want in a method of fixing our beliefs. *If* we want a procedure that can itself be used to correct the results which it has obtained, then the methods of logic and science must win our allegiance. They alone do this; they alone are consistent with the principle that all human belief is liable to error.

By taking a biological and social approach to human inquiry, Peirce offers a way of escaping the puzzles into which Descartes, Kant, and Russell lead us. Nevertheless, there are inevitably questions to be asked about his approach. Why should we assume that because a method corrects its own results, these "corrections" take us closer to the truth? What do we mean by a "true" belief? Is it simply a belief on which we can act without running into surprises or objections? But then it may be true today and false tomorrow, which seems odd. Moreover, we may run into no surprises simply because our habits of mind do not allow us to observe the surprises; and if others do not object to our beliefs that may be only because they happen to share our peculiar habits of mind.

Against those who, with Peirce, assert the special reliability of scientific method as a path of truth, the counterargument has repeatedly been made that science itself is a system of shared prejudices. Indeed, it has been said that a position like Peirce's simply sanctifies this system. Science, Peirce asserts, is the best method for fixing our beliefs because it does not merely put our doubts to rest but brings our minds to bear on the facts, on realities. But what are these "facts" or "realities"? These, it appears, are states of affairs which we come to believe in as a consequence of properly conducted scientific inquiries. The argument seems circular.

I think that there are ways of responding satisfactorily to such objections. Nevertheless, they exist, and they are put forward by men who speak out of a long tradition. Such men are often inclined to think, indeed, that Peirce, Hume, and Descartes, despite the disagreements among them, are victims of a common illusion—the belief that human reason, if it will only adopt the correct method, can arrive, all by itself, at the truth about the universe. Descartes, Hume, and Peirce suspect the nonrational and the irrational in human thought: they believe that we should use logic, mathematics, and experimental methods to protect ourselves against the superstitions and illusions that our emotions and instincts are likely to impose on us.

But is it possible that logic, mathematics, and experimental methods are themselves instruments of illusion? This is a view that has been held by some of the most powerful thinkers our civilization has known. Let us turn to what some of these men say.

4. Philosophy

and the

Irrational

Is the human mind formed in such a way that it is capable of finding the truth by relying on its own powers? Is there a place for the promptings of instinct, "the reasons of the heart," revelation, or mystical insight? Isn't man, in the main, an unreasoning animal? And is his effort to find a rational order in the world perhaps his greatest act of faith? Is he perhaps insisting, against the evidence, that the universe must conform to the rules his limited mind has imposed upon it?

In this section we turn to some classic attacks on the ideal of reason—the views of those who are aware not of man's rationality but of his irrationality, not of the order in the universe but of its impenetrability to human reason.

We begin with a man who was canonized as a saint though he never pretended to saintliness and who was profoundly skeptical about the powers of human reason though himself one of the great reasoners in human history —Augustine. We next move on to a philosophical novelist, Dostoyevsky, and then to an individual who, as he would have wished it, is unclassifiable— Friedrich Nietzsche. Finally, there is a selection from the work of Henri Bergson, the early-twentieth-century French philosopher who found in Darwin's theories reinforcement for a kind of mysticism that antedates Plato.

St. Augustine

St. Augustine, the bishop of Hippo, a provincial town in North Africa, has exercised an influence on Christianity second only to that of Jesus. His administrative and political ideas as well as his theology provided the foundation on which the Catholic Church was organized for a millennium. And he is also a central figure in the history of Protestantism, for Protestant reformers from John Calvin to Reinhold Niebuhr have regularly returned to Augustine's thought in their efforts to restore Christianity to its "essence." Much has been added to Christian doctrine since Augustine's time, but his philosophy is still the basic expression of the Christian outlook, and new ideas, if they are to be accepted as Christian, still have to be adjusted to it.

But Augustine's influence extends far beyond Christianity. Perhaps no one except Plato has given Western thought so many of its central themes. On one side, the West owes to Augustine its conception of human history as the story of mankind's progress toward a goal. On the other, it owes to Augustine its preoccupation with introspection and the inner history of the individual soul. The novels and plays of Kafka, Camus, and Beckett, the "nausea" and "agony" around which the atheistic philosophy of Sartre turns, the ideas of psychoanalysis, the political notions of Hobbes, Marx, and Lenin, are all Augustinian or quasi-Augustinian in character. Augustine, indeed, was the originator of a major literary genre—the self-analytic autobiography. His *Confessions* is the first great literary creation of this sort in Western history.

Augustine takes us into a mood, an emotional environment, different from that of any of the philosophers we have read so far. He is more tortured and puzzled, more profoundly uncertain, and yet more dogmatic. It is useful to realize that he wrote against the background of what one historian has called "the worst catastrophe recorded in the whole history of the Western world." [1] When he was born in 354, the Roman Empire still seemed impregnable, but during his lifetime the Visigoths under Alaric captured Rome. He died in 430 in Hippo while a Vandal army was besieging the city. He wrote for an age stunned by the collapse of an empire that had ruled most of the known world for five hundred years and was the repository of a civilization that stretched back for a thousand. To such an age it must have seemed that the sky had fallen. The despair, the perplexity, the agonized desire to assert a faith, that mark Augustine's writing come

1. G. G. Coulton, *Medieval Panorama* (New York, Macmillan, 1944), p. 8.

from his effort to persuade his contemporaries—and to persuade himself—
that the sky, the true sky, is still in place. The lesson of Rome's collapse, according to Augustine, is that purely secular institutions, depending wholly
on man's natural powers, are bound to fail. Behind that failure can be seen
the eruption into history of a supernatural Judgment, the unfolding of God's
plan for the spiritual salvation of mankind.

Augustine finds in his personal life the same essential story, in mi-
crocosm, that is revealed in the collapse of Rome. His mother was a devout
Christian, but he fell away from the faith as a youth, and did not return to
it until he was in his thirties and had gone through much inner travail.
Augustine sees in himself a man who was beaten by his own spiritual pride,
and was unable to find, within himself, a way to recover. And yet he did recover. The recovery, he is convinced, was God's work, not his. In his
Confessions he tells this story, offering the testimony of a man who believes
he has learned from his own experience that human reason, divorced from
truths that lie beyond reason, corrupts even rational truths.

The passages that follow are taken from Book XI of Augustine's *Confessions*, in the translation by John K. Ryan. "What is time?" Augustine
asks. The very experience of living in time generates puzzles, he says, which
reveal the limits of human reason. Plato, who believed that the visible world
was a deformed copy of a perfect world of finished Ideas, faced but never
resolved to his own satisfaction the problem of how Ideas that are eternal
ever come to take their warped, temporal shape. This problem, as Augustine
recognizes, is even greater for a believing Christian. Plato could treat time
and change as a kind of accident, a sort of lapse of attention in the workings
of the cosmos. But Augustine has to explain how God, who knows all things
and makes all things, can have entered into the very process of creating an
imperfect world in which change and death are the dominant facts.

Augustine approaches these questions as we have learned to expect that
a philosopher will. He asks whether they are the right questions, whether
they may rest on a false premise. What do we mean by "time"? Do we not
measure time by our human standards? Are not these standards relative and
variable? And when we look closely at the process of time, does it not seem
to disappear before our eyes? So perhaps the paradoxes we think we see in
God's Creation are paradoxes created by our own limited minds. Perhaps
time itself is the illusion.

In short, Augustine turns the questions about time back on those who
ask them. The questioners regard time, change, and imperfection as the
unimpeachable realities, and so they are puzzled about how anything can
be eternal and how God can be perfect and still part of the world. But time
is the mystery, not eternity. The very effort to understand it shows that it is
a paradoxical and unintelligible notion, and a product of our own corrupted
minds. In God's mind, Augustine concludes, all things are present simultaneously. In His perspective, from which nothing is hidden, change does

not take place, and there is no beginning or end, no expectation or memory, no time or sense of time. All is at rest, and only the restlessness of a fallen creature like man makes this difficult to comprehend.

Augustine was a Christian theologian, but it would be a mistake to think that the problem of time as he discusses it is of interest only to Christian theology. Doubts about the reality of time, and the desire to transcend time, are constant themes of poetry and philosophy, and occur as well in the mystical traditions of many different civilizations. They have regularly preoccupied men who have looked closely at what seems to be the most inescapable aspect of their lives—the remorseless killing of each moment by the next, the irresistible movement into nothingness—and who have felt, in consequence, that all their experience is shadowed by meaninglessness. It is the sense of the intrinsic elusiveness of time, its paradoxical character, its "absurdity," that has led contemporary philosophers like Heidegger and Sartre to puzzle about the relation of "essence" to "existence," and of "being" to "nothingness." But Augustine's reflections on these questions are more personal and poignant, and move more directly to the heart of the issue.

Time and Eternity

CHAPTER 1
FOR LOVE OF LOVE

(1) Lord, since eternity is yours, are you ignorant of the things that I say to you, or do you see only at a certain time what is done in time? Why then do I set out in order before you this account of so many deeds? In truth, it is not that you may learn to know these matters from me, but that I may rouse up towards you my own affections, and those of other men who read this, so that all of us may say: "The Lord is great, and exceedingly to be praised." I have already said this, and I will say it again: for love of your love I perform this task. . . .

CHAPTER 10
A SKEPTICAL OBJECTION

(12) Lo, are not those men full of their old carnal nature who say to us, "What was God doing before he made heaven and earth?" "For if," they say, "he took his ease and did nothing, why did he not continue in this way henceforth and forever, just as previously he always refrained from work? If any new motion arise in God, or a new will is formed in him, to the end of establishing creation, which he had never established previously, how then would there be true eternity, when a will arises that previously was not there? . . ."

CHAPTER 12
A FRIVOLOUS ANSWER

(14) See, I answer the man who says, "What did God do before he made heaven and earth?" I do not give the answer that someone is said to have given, evading by a joke the force of the objection: "He was preparing hell," he said, "for those prying into such deep subjects." It is one thing to see the objection; it is another to make a joke of it. I do not answer in this way. I would rather respond, "I do not know," concerning what I do not know rather than say something for which a man inquiring about such profound matters is laughed at, while the one giving a false answer is praised.

I say that you, our God, are the creator of every creature, and, if by the phrase heaven and earth all creation is understood, I boldly say, "Before God made heaven and earth, he did not make anything." If he made anything, what else did he make except a creature? Would that I knew all I want to know that is for my good in the same way that I know that no creature was made before any creature was made.

CHAPTER 13
BEFORE ALL TIME

(15) If any flighty mind wanders among mental pictures of past times, and wonders that you, the all-great, all-creating, and all-sustaining God, maker of heaven and earth, should for countless ages have refrained from doing so great a work before actually doing it, let him awake and realize that he wonders at falsities. How could they pass by, those countless ages, which you had not made, although you are the author and creator of all ages? Or what times would there be, times not been made by you? Or how did they pass by, if they never were? Therefore, since you are the maker of all times, if there was a time before you made heaven and earth, why do they say that you rested from work? You made that very time, and no times could pass by before you made those times. But if there was no time before heaven and earth, why do they ask what you did then? There was no "then," where there was no time. . . .

CHAPTER 14
WHAT IS TIME?

(17) At no time, therefore, did you do nothing, since you had made time itself. No times are coeternal with you, because you are permanent, whereas if they were permanent, they would not be times. What is time? Who can easily and briefly explain this? Who can comprehend this even in thought, so as to express it in a word? Yet what do we discuss more famil-

iarly and knowingly in conversation than time? Surely we understand it when we talk about it, and also understand it when we hear others talk about it.

What, then, is time? If no one asks me, I know; if I want to explain it to someone who does ask me, I do not know. Yet I state confidently that I know this: if nothing were passing away, there would be no past time, and if nothing were coming, there would be no future time, and if nothing existed, there would be no present time. How, then, can these two kinds of time, the past and the future, be, when the past no longer is and the future as yet does not be? But if the present were always present, and would not pass into the past, it would no longer be time, but eternity. Therefore, if the present, so as to be time, must be so constituted that it passes into the past, how can we say that it is, since the cause of its being is the fact that it will cease to be? Does it not follow that we can truly say that it is time only because it tends towards non-being?

CHAPTER 21

MEASURES OF TIME

(27) I said just a while ago that we measure passing times, so that we can say that this tract of time is double that single one, or that this one is just as long as the other, and whatever else as to periods of time we can describe by our measurements. Therefore, as I was saying, we measure passing times. If someone says to me, "How do you know this?" I may answer, "I know this because we make such measurements, and we cannot measure things that do not exist, and neither past nor future things exist." Yet how do we measure present time, since it has no extent? Therefore, it is measured as it passes by, but once it has passed by, it is not measured, for what would be measured will no longer exist. But from where, and on what path, and to what place does it pass, as it is measured? From where, except from the future? By what path, except by the present? To what place, except into the past? Therefore, it is from that which does not yet exist, by that which lacks space, and into that which no longer exists.

But what do we measure if time is not in a certain space? We do not say single, or double, or threefold, or equal, or anything else of this sort in the order of time, except with regard to tracts of time. In what space, then, do we measure passing time? In the future, out of which it passes? But we do not measure what does not yet exist. Or in the present, by which it passes? We do not measure what is without space. Or in the past, into which it passes? We do not measure what no longer exists.

CHAPTER 23
BODILY MOTION AS TIME

(29) I have heard from a certain learned man that the movements of the sun, moon, and stars constitute time, but I did not agree with him. Why should not rather the movement of all bodies be times? In fact, if the lights of heaven should stop, while a potter's wheel was kept moving, would there be no time by which we might measure those rotations? Would we say either that it moved with equal speeds, or, if it sometimes moved more slowly and sometimes more swiftly, that some turns were longer and others shorter? Or while we were saying this, would we not also be speaking in time? Or would there be in our words some long syllables and others short, except for the fact that some were sounded for a longer and others for a shorter time? Grant to men, O God, that they may see in a little matter evidence common to things both small and great. The stars and the lights of heaven are "for signs, and for seasons, and for days, and for years." Truly they are such. Yet I should not say that the turning of that little wooden wheel constitutes a day, nor under those conditions should that learned man say that there is no time.

(30) I desire to know the power and the nature of time, by which we measure bodily movements, and say, for instance, that this movement is twice as long as that. I put this question: "Since a day is defined not only as the sun's time over the earth—according to which usage, day is one thing and night another—but also as its entire circuit from east to east—and accordingly we say 'So many days have passed,' for they are termed 'so many days' with their nights included and are not reckoned as days apart from the night hours—since, then, a day is completed by the sun's movement and its circuit from east to east, I ask whether the movement itself constitutes a day, or the period in which the movement is performed, or both together?"

If the first were a day, then there would be a day even if the sun completed its course in a period of time such as an hour. If the second, then there would not be a day, if from one sunrise to another there were as brief a period as an hour, whereas the sun would have to go around twenty-four times to complete a day. If both, it could not be called a day if the sun ran its entire course in the space of an hour, nor if, while the sun stood still, just so much time passed by as the sun usually takes to complete its entire course from morning to morning.

Therefore, I will not now ask what is it that is called a day, but rather what is time, by which we would measure the sun's circuit and say that it was completed in half the time it usually takes, if it were finished in a period like twelve hours. Comparing both times, we should call the one a single period, the other a double period, even if the sun ran its course from east to east sometimes in the single period and sometimes in the double.

Let no man tell me, then, that movements of the heavenly bodies constitute periods of time. When at the prayer of a certain man, the sun stood still until he could achieve victory in battle, the sun indeed stood still, but time went on. That battle was waged and brought to an end during its own tract of time, which was sufficient for it. Therefore, I see that time is a kind of distention. Yet do I see this, or do I only seem to myself to see it? You, O Light, will show this to me.

CHAPTER 27
WHERE TIME IS MEASURED

. . . (36) It is in you, O my mind, that I measure my times. Do not interrupt me by crying that time is. Do not interrupt yourself with the noisy mobs of your prejudices. It is in you, I say, that I measure tracts of time. The impression that passing things make upon you remains, even after those things have passed. That present state is what I measure, not the things which pass away so that it be made. That is what I measure when I measure tracts of time. Therefore, either this is time, or I do not measure time. . . .

CHAPTER 31
UNCHANGING THOUGHT, UNCHANGING ACT

(41) O Lord my God, how deep are your secret places, and how far from them have the consequences of my sins cast me! Heal my eyes, and let me share in the joy of your light. Surely, if there is a mind possessed of such great knowledge and foreknowledge, so that to it are known all things past and future, just as I know one well-known psalm, then supremely marvelous is that mind and wondrous and fearsome. From it whatever there is of ages past and of ages to come is no more hidden than there are hidden from me as I sing that psalm what and how much preceded from its beginning and what and how much remains to the end.

But far be it that you, creator of the universe, creator of souls and bodies, far be it that in such wise you should know future and past. Far, far more wonderfully, far more deeply do you know them! It is not as emotions are changed or senses filled up by expectation of words to come and memory of those past in one who sings well-known psalms or hears a familiar psalm. Not so does it befall you who are unchangeably eternal, that is, truly eternal, the creator of minds. Therefore, just as in the beginning you have known heaven and earth without change in your knowledge, so too "in the beginning you made heaven and earth" without any difference in your activity. Whosoever understands this, let him confess it to you, and whosoever does not understand it, let him confess it to you. O how exalted are you, and yet the humble of heart are your dwelling place! You "lift up them that are cast down," and they do not fall down, whose place aloft is you!

Fyodor Dostoyevsky

The British philosopher John Stuart Mill was the outstanding spokesman in nineteenth-century England for the scientific outlook. Yet when he was a young man he asked himself what his feelings would be if all the ideals for which he strove were achieved, and if the human scene were to be ruled as rationally as he wished it to be. His answer was that his life would be vacant, and that nothing would seem worth enduring. It was an answer that led Mill to a long-drawn-out period of acute depression, in which he questioned the worthwhileness of all effort and hope, and—as he wrote in his *Autobiography*—even tears were impossible for him. Eventually he recovered and returned to the rationalist fold; but he retained for the rest of his days a tempered view of the attractiveness of a life conducted entirely in accordance with reason.

In Russia, one of Mill's contemporaries, the novelist Fyodor Dostoyevsky, asked much the same question. But he asked it both early and late, and his answer was radically different from Mill's. In *The Writer's Diary*, it takes this form: "What if all knowledge, the scientific discoveries which our sages don't even dream of, were suddenly disclosed to mankind? . . . At first they would feel that they had been showered with blessings. . . . I doubt, however, if all these ecstasies would last for one generation. Men would suddenly discover that they had no life, no freedom of spirit, no freedom of will and personality . . . , and man would realize that he had become a brute. Man would be covered with festering sores and would bite his tongue in torment when he saw that life had been taken from him for bread, for 'stones made into bread.' . . . Then perhaps men would cry out to God: 'Thou art right, O Lord. Man shall not live by bread alone.'"

Dostoyevsky's own life could have been the creation of Dostoyevsky the novelist. He was born in Moscow in 1821, the son of a former army doctor. His mother died when he was young, and his alcoholic father, who neglected him, was murdered by peasants. At the age of twenty-four Dostoyevsky wrote a novel, *Poor People*, which was a great success, but his fortunes turned downward precipitously almost immediately thereafter. His subsequent novels did not win the same acclaim, he drifted into editing and other work, and he joined a group of Russian social critics—the so-called Petrashevsky circle—which was attached to the ideas of the French utopian socialist Fourier. The Petrashevsky circle fell afoul of the Czarist authorities, and Dostoyevsky and other members of the group were arrested in 1849. Following months in a St. Petersburg prison, they were sentenced to death. After waiting for their execution for a month, they were taken to the execution grounds and tied to stakes, and the firing squads were made ready. Only at the ultimate moment were they told that it was all a trick; they had in fact been reprieved, and had been sentenced to prison in Siberia.

Dostoyevsky spent four years as a convict, and remained in exile in Siberia, mainly in military service, until 1859. The works for which he is known—*The House of the Dead, Crime and Punishment, The Idiot, The Possessed, The Brothers Karamazov*—all belong to the period after his return. Heavily in debt, plagued by epilepsy, addicted to gambling, exploited by editors who paid him low rates, he produced these books at a furious pace in an effort to keep his head above water. In the last few years of his life his reputation and fortunes were somewhat restored, and when he died in 1881, there was widespread public mourning in Russia.

The selection that follows is from Dostoyevsky's *Letters from the Underworld*, which he published in 1864. The translation is by C. J. Hogarth, and most of the first part is presented. For all its marvelous, almost reckless, air of spontaneity, it offers a shrewd and adroit attack on fundamental articles of faith in the rationalist creed. Is there an objective truth to be found? Yes, Dostoyevsky says, but reason isn't the way to find it, for reason is simply the mask that men wear when they want to hide their prejudices from themselves. Is reason at least the best instrument available to man for mastering the world and serving human interests? The question would make more sense, replies Dostoyevsky, if men wanted to satisfy what are regarded as their interests, but they also have an invincible interest in self-destruction. "The more I have recognised what is good," says his antihero, "and what constitutes 'the great and the beautiful,' the deeper I have plunged into the mire."

In fact, "reason" is an impossible sovereign; for if we give our final allegiance to it then we must believe there is an inevitable order to the universe, a network of causes and effects to which we are subject; and thus, the single thing we value most, our free will, is denied. Men would rather be unreasonable and unhappy than surrender their souls in this act of self-annihilation which "reason" demands. All the statistics, all the theories of human engineering, all the dreams of a scientific Golden Palace in which men will be prosperous and gentle, loving and tame, come down in pieces in the face of this fundamental fact.

But there is more than argument, obviously, in these pages. There is a Dostoyevskean creation: a full-bodied character, vivid, unique, with the gift of gab, stinking—like Smerdyakov in *The Brothers Karamazov*—of bad health and malice, who speaks a truth we don't like to hear, and who turns out, when we look at him closely, to be a brother of ours. Dostoyevsky's portrait of this "underworld" man has been a major source of the anti-heros in many modern novels, and of the vision of man to be found in contemporary antirationalist philosophy.

Letters from the Underworld

I

I am ill; I am full of spleen and repellent. I conceive there to be something wrong with my liver, for I cannot even think for the aching of my head. Yet what my complaint is I do not know. Medicine I cannot, I never could, take, although for medicine and doctors I have much reverence. Also, I am extremely superstitious: which, it may be, is why I cherish such a respect for the medical profession. I am well-educated, and therefore might have risen superior to such fancies, yet of them I am full to the core.

Also, I have no real desire to be cured of my ill-humour. I suppose you cannot understand this? No, I thought not; but *I* can understand it, although it would puzzle me to tell you exactly whom I am vexed with. I only know that I do not choose to offend the doctors by telling them that I am unable to accept their treatment. Also, I know—better than any one else can do—that I alone am my worst enemy, and that I am my own worst enemy far more than I am any one else's. However, if I am not to be cured, so much the worse for me and my evil passions. If my liver is out of order, so much the worse for my liver.

I have been living like this for a long while now—for fully twenty years. I am forty years old, and, in my day, have been a civil servant. But I am a civil servant no longer. Moreover, I was a bad civil servant at that. I used to offend every one, and to take pleasure in doing so. Yet never once did I accept a bribe, though it would have been easy enough for me to have feathered my nest in that way. This may seem to you a poor sort of a witticism, yet I will not erase it. I had written it down in the belief that it would wear rather a clever air when indited, yet I will not—no, not even now, when I see that I was but playing a buffoon—alter the *mot* by a single iota.

Whenever people approached my office table to ask for information, or what not, I used to grind my teeth at them, and invariably to feel pleased when I had offended their dignity. I seldom failed in my aim. Men, for the most part, are timid creatures—and we all of us know the sort of men favour-seekers are. Of such dolts there was one in particular—an officer—whom I could not bear, for he refused to defer to me at all, and always kicked up a most disgusting clatter with his sword. For a year and a half we joined battle over that sword; but it was I who won the victory, I who caused him to cease clattering his precious weapon. All this happened during my early manhood.

Do you wish to know wherein the sting of my evil temper has always lain? It has always lain (and therein also has always lain its peculiar offensiveness) in the fact that, even at moments of my bitterest spleen, I have been forced to acknowledge with shame that not only am I not at all bad-tempered, but also I have never received any real cause of offence—that I have been but roaring to frighten away sparrows, and amusing myself with doing so. Foam though I might at the mouth, I needed but to be given a doll to play with, or a cup of sweet tea to drink, and at once I sank to quiescence. Yes, I have always grown calm for the moment—even though, later, I have gnashed my teeth at myself, and suffered from months of insomnia. Such has invariably been my way.

For a long time past I have been belying my own personality by calling myself an irascible fellow. It has been pure rancour that has made me tell that lie against myself. As a matter of fact, I only played, so to speak, with my office callers, and with that officer, while all the while it was impossible for me to lose my temper. Every day I keep discovering in myself elements of the most opposite order conceivable, and can feel them swarming within me, and am aware that, to the very end of my life, they will continue so to swarm. Yet, often as they have striven to manifest themselves outwardly, I have never allowed them to do so. Of set purpose I always prevent that from happening, even though they torture me shamefully with their presence, and sometimes throw me into convulsions of ennui—ah, of how much ennui indeed! Would not all this lead you, gentlemen, to suppose that I am expressing a sort of regret—that I am asking, as it were, your pardon? I am sure that you think so? Well, I can only say that I do not care a rap for your opinion.

No, I am not really bad-tempered. Rather, the fact is that I have never succeeded in being anything at all—whether kind-hearted or cruel, a villain or a saint, a hero or an insect. . . .

II

I wish to tell you, gentlemen (no matter whether you care to hear it or not), why I have never even been able to become an insect. I solemnly declare to you that I have often *wished* to become an insect, but could never attain my desire. I swear to you, gentlemen, that to be overcharged with sensibility is an actual malady—a real, a grievous malady. For humanity's daily needs mere ordinary human sensibility ought to suffice, or about one-half or one-quarter of the sensibility which falls to the lot of the average educated man of our miserable nineteenth century, if he has the additional misfortune to reside in St. Petersburg (the most abstract, the most deviously-minded, city on this terrestrial sphere of ours, where towns, in their psychology, may be complex or non-complex). At all events such sensibility as falls to the lot of (for instance) the generality of so-called independent persons and men of action ought to suffice. I dare wager, now, that you think that I am writing this with my tongue in my cheek, and solely to make fun of men of action; that you think that it is sheer bad taste that is making me rattle my sword in the way that that officer used to do? Yet, to tell the truth, gentlemen, who would be vain of one's weaknesses while at the same time one is using them as a means for poking fun at others?

Yet why should I *not* do this? All men do it. All men are proud of their weaknesses, and I, perhaps, more so than my fellows. Let us not quarrel about it. It may be that I have used an awkward expression. Yet I am persuaded that not only is excess of sensibility, but also sensibility of any kind whatsoever, a malady. Of that I have not the smallest doubt in the world. For the moment, however, let us drop the point. Tell me this: how is it that always, and of set purpose, as it were, and at the very moment—yes, at the very moment—when I have appeared to be most in a position to appreciate the finer shades of "the great and the beautiful" (to use the term once current amongst us), I have not only invariably failed to recognise as unseemly, but also have never failed to commit, actions which—well, in a word, actions which all men commit, but which I have always perpetrated just when I was most acutely sensible that I ought not to do them? The more I have recognised what is good and what constitutes "the great and the beautiful," the deeper I have plunged into the mire, and the more I have been ready to smear myself over with the sticky stuff.

But the most curious point of all is this—that the mood which I have described never seemed to be a mere fortuitous happening with me, but my permanent, my normal, condition, and therefore neither a weakness nor a vice. Consequently I have gradually come to lose all desire to combat this failing of mine. Indeed, things have reached the point that I almost believe (I might almost say, I *wholly* believe) that it is my normal condition. At first, however—*i. e.* at the actual beginning of things—I suffered terrible pangs in the struggle against my weakness, for I never could bring myself to believe that other men were not in the same position as I. Yet I kept the fact a secret close-locked in my breast, for I was ashamed of it then, and am ashamed of it now—yes, ashamed of the fact that I used to experience a sort of mysterious, abnormal, base gratification in recalling to my memory (say) some filthy nocturnal revel in St. Petersburg, and in recognising that once again I had acted foully, but that what had been done could never be undone. Inwardly and secretly I often licked my lips at the thought of these revels, and chewed the cud of my recollections until their bitterness turned to a sort of base, accursed sweetness, and then to an actual, an assured, sensation of delight. Yes, I say of delight, of delight. I insist upon that. I often told myself that I would greatly like to know whether the same delight fell to the lot of other men.

First of all, however, let me explain to you wherein that delight lay.

It lay in a clear consciousness of my degradation—in a feeling that I had reached the last wall, and that the whole thing was base, and could never be otherwise, and that no escape therefrom was to be looked for, and that it was not possible for me to become a different man, and that, even if I still retained sufficient faith and energy to become a different man, I should not wish to become so, but that I would rather do nothing at all in the matter, since to undergo such a change might not be worth my while. And the chief thing about it was that one felt that the process was ruled by the normal, the fundamental, laws of acute sensibility, added to the inertia which arises from the working of those laws; wherefore one was never likely to alter, nor yet to lift a finger to effect an alteration. Hence may be deduced the fact that over-sensibility causes a villain to hug his villainy to himself if he really *perceives* that he is a villain. . . .

v

How could any man respect himself who wilfully takes pleasure in a consciousness of his self-abasement? I do not say this out of any feeling of puling regret, for never at any time have I found it possible to say, "Father, forgive me, and I will sin no more." This is not so much because I have actually felt myself *incapable* of uttering the words as because they have always come too easily to my lips. And whenever I have said them, what has happened next? Why, that, as though bound to fall, I have plunged straight into sin, when all the time I have been innocent both in thought and intent. A worse thing could not be. Next I have felt softened in heart, and shed tears, and reproved myself, and seen things as they were, and felt unclean of soul. Yet for this I cannot very well blame the laws of Nature, since to offend against them has been the chief, the constant, occupation of my life. It is a degrading fact to have to recall, but the fact remains. Then, a moment or two later, I have always angrily reminded myself that my whole conduct has been false—horribly, gratuitously false (by "it," of course, I mean all my regrets, my softenings of heart, my vows of regeneration).

So I would ask you, gentlemen—what caused me to rack and torture myself in this way? Well, the answer is that I always found it irksome merely to sit with folded hands. That is why I have given myself up to so much wrongdoing. Mark what I say, gentlemen, for what I say is true, and will give you the key to the whole business. . . . The sole cause of it all, gentlemen, is *ennui;* yes, the sole cause of it all is *ennui.* The fact is that one comes to feel crushed with the tedium, the conscious folding of the hands in contemplation, which is the direct, the inevitable, the automatic outcome of sensibility. Of this I have spoken above. I repeat, therefore, I earnestly repeat, that all men of independence and action—men who are men of action because they are *prone* to action—are both gross and limited in their purview.

How is this to be explained? Thus. Such men are led by their limitations to mistake approximate and secondary causes for primary, and so to persuade themselves, more easily and more readily than other men do, that they have an assured basis for their action, and therefore may cease to trouble themselves further. That is the truth, and the whole truth, of the matter. To embark upon action one must first of all feel perfectly sure of oneself, so that no doubts as to the wisdom of that action may remain. . . . Perhaps, in despair of finding a first cause for action, one shrugs one's shoulders? Well, my advice is blindly and unthinkingly to leave first causes alone, and to give oneself up to one's impulses, and, for once in a while, to let volition lie altogether in abeyance. That is to say, either hate or love, but in any case do anything rather than sit with folded hands. . . .

VII

. . . Who was it first said, first propounded the theory, that man does evil only because he is blind to his own interests, but that if he were enlightened, if his eyes were opened to his real, his normal interests, he would at once cease to do evil, and become virtuous and noble for the reason that, being now enlightened and brought to understand what is best for him, he would discern his true advantage only in what is good (since it is a known thing that no man of set purpose acts against his own interests), and therefore would of necessity also *do* what is good? Oh, the simplicity of the youth who said this! Oh, the utter artlessness of the prattler!

To begin with, since when, during these thousands of years, has man ever acted solely in accordance with his own interests? What about the millions of facts which go to show that only too often man knowingly (that is to say, with a full comprehension of what is his true advantage) puts that advantage aside in favour of some other plan, and betakes himself to a road, to risks, to the unknown, to which no agent nor agency has compelled him, as though, unwilling to follow the appointed path, he preferred to essay a difficult and awkward road along which he must feel his way in darkness? Would it not almost seem as though the directness, the voluntariness, of such a course had for him a greater attraction than any advantage? Advantage, indeed? What, after all, *is* advantage? Would *you*, gentlemen, undertake exactly to define wherein human advantage consists? What if human advantage not only *may*, but *does*, consist of the fact that, on certain occasions, man may desire, not what is good for him, but what is bad? And if this be so, if this really be so, the rule falls to the ground at once.

What is your opinion about it? Can it be so? I see you smiling. Well, smile away, gentlemen, but also answer me this: Can human interests *ever* be properly reckoned up? May there not always remain interests which never have been, never can be, included in any classification? You, gentlemen, take your lists of human interests from averages furnished by statistics and economic formulæ. Your lists of interests include only prosperity, riches, freedom, tranquillity, and so forth, and any one who openly and knowingly disagreed with those lists would, in your opinion (as in mine also, for that matter), be either an obscurantist or a madman. Would he not? But the most surprising point is this—that statists, savants, and lovers of the human race never fail, in their summing up of human interests, to overlook *one interest in particular*. This interest is never taken into account in the shape in which it ought to be taken; and this fact vitiates all their calculations. Yet, were they to add this interest to their summaries, no great harm would be done. The mischief lies in the fact that this particular interest declines to fall under any particular heading, or to enter into any particular schedule.

For instance, I might have a friend—as also might you yourselves, gentlemen (for who has not?)—who, when about to embark upon a given piece of work, might tell one, clearly and grandiloquently, that he intends to proceed strictly on lines of truth and reason. He might even go so far as to speak with emotion and enthusiasm of the nature of true, normal human interests, and with a smile to inveigh against shortsighted dolts who do not understand either their own interests or the proper meaning of virtue. Yet within only a quarter of an hour, and without any sudden, unforeseen event having arisen—merely in accordance with something which is stronger than all his other interests put together—this same man may cut straight across what he himself has said—that is to say, cut straight across both the dictates of reason and his own true interests and everything else! Yet this friend of mine is but one of a type; wherefore the fault cannot be laid at his door alone.

May there not, therefore, exist something which to most men is even dearer than their true interests? Or, not to infringe the logical sequence, may there not exist some supreme interest of interests (the additional interest of which I am speaking) which is greater and more absorbing than any other interest, and for which man, if the need should arise, is ready to contravene every law, and to lose sight alike of common sense, honour, prosperity, and ease—in a word, of all the things which are fair and expedient—if haply he can gain for himself that primal, that supreme, advantage which he conceives to be the dearest thing on earth?

"Ah well, there are interests and interests," you might interrupt me at this point. Pardon me, gentlemen, but I ought to make it clear that, not to juggle with words, this interest of which I am speaking is a notable one, and escapes all classification, and shatters every system which has ever been established by lovers of the human race for that race's improvement. In short, let it be understood that it is an interest which introduces general confusion into everything. Before naming to you that interest I should like to damn myself for ever in your eyes by telling you bluntly that all those fine systems of, and schemes for, demonstrating to mankind its true, its normal, interests, and for explaining to it that, so long as it strives to attain its true interests, it will ever grow better and more noble, are so much dialectic. Yes, I say so much dialectic. To maintain theories of renovating the human race through systems of classification of true interests is, in my opinion, about the same thing as—well, about the same thing as to maintain that man grows milder with civilisation, and, consequently, less bloodthirsty, less addicted to fighting. Logically, perhaps, that *does* happen; yet he is so prone to systems and to abstract deductions that he is for ever ready to mutilate the truth, to be blind to what he sees, and deaf to what he hears, so long only as he can succeed in vindicating his logic.

Of this let me give an example which will be clear to all. Look around you at the world. Everywhere you will see blood flowing in streams, and as merrily as champagne. Look at our nineteenth century; look at Napoleon—the great Napoleon and the modern one; look at North America, with its everlasting "Union"; look at the present caricature of Schleswig-Holstein. What has civilisation done to instil greater mildness into our bosoms? Civilisation develops in man nothing but an added capacity for receiving impressions. That is all. And the growth of that capacity further augments man's tendency to seek pleasure in blood-letting. Nothing else has civilisation conferred upon him. You may have noticed that the most enthusiastic blood-letters have almost invariably been the most civilised of men—men whose shoes even Attila and Stenka Razin [1] would have been unworthy to unloose; and if such men as the former have not bulked in the public eye quite so largely as have Attila and Stenka Razin, it is only because the former have been too numerous, too transitory.

At all events civilisation has rendered man, if not more bloodthirsty, at least a worse (in the sense of a meaner) thirster after blood than before. Once upon a time he considered blood-letting to be just retribution, and could therefore, with a quiet conscience, exterminate any one whom he wanted to; but now we account blood-letting a crime—and indulge in that crime even more than in former days. Which, then, is the worst of the two? Well, judge for yourselves. It is said that Cleopatra (if I may take an instance from Roman history) loved to thrust golden pins into the breasts of her slaves, and took pleasure in the cries and contortions of her victims.

Possibly you may say that all this happened in a comparatively barbarous age—that even at the present day the times are barbarous—that golden pins are still being thrust into people's breasts—that though man, in many things, has learnt to see clearer now than he used to do in *more* barbarous ages, he has not yet learnt to act wholly as reason and science

1. Leader of a Cossack rebellion during the reign of Catherine the Great.—*Translator.*

would have him do. Yet all the while, I know, you are persuaded in your own minds that man is bound to improve as soon as ever he has dropped some old, bad customs of his, and allowed science and healthy thought alone to nourish, to act as the normal directors of, human nature. Yes, I know that you are persuaded that eventually man will cease to err *of set purpose,* or to let his will clash with his normal interests. On the contrary (say you), science will in time show man (though, in our opinion, it is superfluous to do so) that he does not possess *any* will or initiative of his own, and never has done, but that he is as the keyboard of a piano, or as the handle of a hurdy-gurdy. Above all, science will show him that in the world there exist certain laws of nature which cause everything to be done, not of man's volition, but of nature's, and in accordance with her laws. Consequently, say you, those laws will only need to be *explained* to man, and at once he will become divested of all responsibility, and find life a much easier thing to deal with. All human acts will then be mathematically computed according to nature's laws, and entered in tables of logarithms which extend to about the 108,000th degree, and can be combined into a calendar. Better still, there will be published certain carefully revised editions of this calendar (after the manner of modern encyclopædias) in which everything will be enumerated and set down so exactly that henceforth the world will cease to know wrong-doing, or any occasion for the same.

Then (I am supposing *you* still to be speaking) there will arise new economic relations—relations all ready for use, and calculated with mathematical precision, so that in a flash all possible questions will come to an end, for the reason that to all possible questions there will have been compiled a store of all possible answers. Then there will arise the Golden Palace of the legends. Then—well, *then,* in a word, there will dawn the millennium! Of course, though (it is *I* who am now speaking), you cannot very well guarantee that things will not have come to be excessively dull, seeing that there will be nothing left for us to do when everything has been computed beforehand and tabulated? By this I do not mean to say that things will not also be excessively *regular.* I only mean to say, is there anything which dullness will not lead men to devise? For instance, out of sheer *ennui,* golden pins may again be inserted into victims' breasts.

That is all. It is shameful to have to think that into everything which is goodly man loves to thrust golden pins! Yes, he is a gross animal, phenomenally gross. Rather, he is not so much gross as ungrateful to a degree which nothing else in the world can equal. For instance, I should not be surprised if, amid all this order and regularity of the future, there should suddenly arise, from some quarter or another, some gentleman of lowborn—or, rather, of retrograde and cynical—demeanour who, setting his arms akimbo, should say to you all: "How now, gentlemen? Would it not be a good thing if, with one consent, we were to kick all this solemn wisdom to the winds, and to send those logarithms to the devil, and to begin to live our lives again according to our own stupid whims?" Yet this would be as nothing; the really shameful part of the business would be that this gentleman would find a goodly number of adherents. Such is always man's way. And he might act thus for the shallowest of reasons; for a reason which is not worth mentioning; for the reason that, always, and everywhere, and no matter what his station, man loves to act as he *likes*, and not necessarily as reason and self-interest would have him do.

Yes, he will even act straight against his own interests. Indeed, he is sometimes *bound* to do so. Such, at least, is my notion of the matter. His own will, free and unfettered; his own untutored whims; his own fancies, sometimes amounting almost to a madness—here we have that superadded interest of interests which enters into no classification, which for ever consigns systems and theories to the devil. Whence do savants have it that man needs a normal, a virtuous, will? What, in particular, has made these pundits imagine that what man most needs is a will which is acutely alive to man's interests? Why, what man most needs is an *independent* will—no matter what the cost of such independence of volition, nor what it may lead to. Yet the devil only knows what man's will——

VIII

. . . Consequently, I would ask you—what are we to expect from man, seeing that he is a creature endowed with such strange qualities? You may heap upon him every earthly blessing, you may submerge him in well-being until the bubbles shoot to the surface of his prosperity as though it were a pond, you may give him such economic success that nothing will be left for him to do but to sleep and to eat dainties and to prate about the continuity of the world's history; yes, you may do all this, but none the less, out of sheer ingratitude, sheer devilment, he will end by playing you some dirty trick. He will imperil his comfort, and purposely desiderate for himself deleterious rubbish, some improvident trash, for the sole purpose that he may alloy all the solemn good sense which has been lavished upon him with a portion of the futile, fantastical element which forms part of his very composition.

Yes, it is these same fantastical dreams, this same debased stupidity, that he most wishes to retain in order to feel assured of the one thing with which he cannot dispense—namely, of the knowledge that men are still men, and not keyboards of pianos over which the hands of Nature may play at their own sweet will, and continue so to play until they threaten to deprive him of all volition, save by rote and according to calendars. Moreover, even if man *were* the keyboard of a piano, and could be convinced that the laws of nature and of mathematics had made him so, he would still decline to change. On the contrary, he would once more, out of

sheer ingratitude, attempt the perpetration of something which would enable him to insist upon himself; and if he could not effect this, he would
then proceed to introduce chaos and disruption into everything, and to
devise enormities of all kinds, for the sole purpose, as before, of asserting
his personality. He would need but to launch a single curse upon the world,
and the mere fact that man alone is able to utter curses (the one privilege
by which he is differentiated from the other animals) would, through the
very act of commination, effect his purpose for him—namely, the purpose of
convincing himself that he really *is* a man, and not the keyboard of a piano.

But if you were to tell me that all this could be set down in tables—
I mean the chaos, and the confusion, and the curses, and all the rest of it—
so that the possibility of computing everything might remain, and reason
continue to rule the roost—well, in that case, I believe, man would *purposely* become a lunatic, in order to become devoid of reason, and therefore able to insist upon himself. I believe this, and I am ready to vouch for
this, simply for the reason that every human act arises out of the circumstance that man is for ever striving to prove to his own satisfaction that he
is a man and not an organ-handle. And, however devious his methods, he
has succeeded in proving it; however troglodyte-like his mode of working
may have been, he *has* succeeded in proving it. So in future, perhaps, you
will refrain from asserting that this particular interest of his is nugatory, or
that his volition depends upon anything at all? . . .

I X

. . . Why, then, are you so absolutely, so portentously, certain that one
thing, and one thing only, is normal and positive—in a word, good—for
mankind? Does reason never err in estimating what is advantageous? May it
not be that man occasionally loves something besides prosperity? May it
not be that he also loves *adversity?* And may not adversity be as good for
him as is happiness? Certainly there are times when man *does* love adversity, and love it passionately; so do not resort to history for your justification, but, rather, put the question to *yourselves,* if you are men, and
have had any experience of life.

For my part, I look upon undivided love of prosperity as something
almost indecent; for to cause an occasional catastrophe, come weal come
woe, seems to me a very pleasant thing to do. Yet I am not altogether for
adversity, any more than I am altogether for prosperity; what I most
stand for is my personal freewill, and for what it can do for me when I feel
in the right mood to use it. I know that adversity is not thought acceptable
in vaudeville plays, and that in the Palace of Crystal [2] it would be a thing
quite unthinkable, for the reason that, since adversity connotes a denial
and a doubt, no edifice of the kind could exist where in a doubt was har-

2. Russian expression for the millennium.—*Translator.*

boured. Nevertheless, I feel certain that man never wholly rejects adversity (in the sense of chaos and disruption of his schemes); for adversity is the mainspring of self-realisation. When beginning these letters I said that, in my opinion, self-realisation is, for man, a supreme misfortune; yet I am sure that he loves it dearly, and that he would not exchange it for any other sort of delight. . . .

. . . Again I see you smiling. Well, smile away. I take your smiles for what they are worth, for at least I am not in the habit of saying that I am surfeited when I am hungry, or that I do not know that my hopes are based upon something better than a mere compromise, an ever-recurring nought, which the laws of nature may (and, indeed, *do*) allow to exist. The crown of my desires is not a block of flats, with its tenements let as offices to dentists, or as homes to poor lodgers on thousand-year leases; but if you were to annul my volition, to erase my ideals, and to show me something *better,* I might then come to fall in with your views. To this you might reply that to convince me would not be worth your while; whereupon I might make a similar retort: after which we might solemnly discuss the matter a little further, until finally you decided that I was not deserving of your attention. I should not greatly care. For me there will always remain the underworld.

Meanwhile, I go on living, and exercising my volition: and may my hand wither ere ever I use it to add so much as a brick to any block of tenements! Never mind that only a short while ago I rejected the idea of a crystal edifice, for the sole reason that I should not be able to put out my tongue at it. What I then said I did not say because I am fond of putting out my tongue at things, but because, of all buildings, an edifice whereat no one can mock is the only one that has not yet come into existence. On the contrary, of sheer gratitude I would cut out my tongue if matters could be so arranged that I should never at any time feel a desire to protrude that member. What care I that an edifice of such a kind is impossible, and that I must rest content with my present lodgings? Why should such desires occur to me at all? Merely in order that, eventually, I may come to the conclusion that my whole organisation is a fraud? Is that the object of it all? I do not believe it.

Yet of one thing I am certain—namely, that a denizen of the underworld ought always to ride himself upon the bit; for although for forty years he may sit silently in his den, let him once issue into the light of day, and straightway he will take the bit in his teeth, and continue talking, and talking, and talking.

XI

So at length, gentlemen, we have reached the conclusion that the best thing for us to do is to do nothing at all, but to sink into a state of contemplative inertia. For that purpose all hail the underworld! True, I said above that I profoundly envy the normal man; yet, under the conditions in which I see him placed, I have no wish to be he. That is to say, though I envy him, I find the underworld better, since at least one can—— Yet I am lying. I am lying because, even as I know that two and two make four, so do I know that it is not the underworld which is so much better, but something else, something else—something for which I am hungry, but which I shall never find. Ah no! To the devil with the underworld! . . .

Friedrich Nietzsche

Probably the most shattering intellectual event of the nineteenth century was the publication, in 1859, of Charles Darwin's *Origin of Species*. Through most of Western history the dominant view had been that the world, in its essential features, was fixed and unchanging. The animals, in their existing form, were the animals that had been created by God; human nature as it displayed itself in the present was what it had always been; and the rules by which men should live were eternal rules, as valid at one time as they were at any other. Darwin's theories cast the gravest doubt on all these assumptions. Friedrich Nietzsche is one of the most important, and certainly the most flamboyant, of the nineteenth-century philosophers who, in response to the idea of evolution, attempted to develop a new world outlook.

Looking back on human history from the standpoint of the idea of eternal change, Nietzsche propounds the view that men's efforts to lay down eternal principles of truth and conduct have been efforts, conscious or unconscious, to hold back the development of the human species. Philosophers in particular, with their never-ending talk about the eternal verities, have been on the side of stagnation rather than change. They have been spokesmen for death, not for life. The great secret of history lies in man's attempt to surpass himself, to break through the old bounds. Western philosophy has been an unwitting conspiracy against this attempt.

As developed by the classic philosophers, the very idea of "reason," Nietzsche asserts, embodies a slavish point of view. "Reason" sets down uniform standards by which men should think and live; and these standards, at any given time, merely codify the conventional notions which men at their existing level of development happen to think are right. But the task of taking the human species to a new and higher stage of development can never be performed by men in the mass; it is always the work of exceptional individuals who break through the stereotypes and assert their own idiosyncratic selves. In consequence, the men who carry the evolutionary drive in them are bound to seem unreasonable to their fellows, and to be unreasonable by existing standards. They do not speak, as too many philosophers have spoken, about the virtues of balance and moderation, and they do not seek agreement with others. They speak for the virtue of a concentrated and eccentric vision, for ecstasy, and for the power of an original mind to draw the world after it. Indeed, Nietzsche goes beyond Darwin, who sees evolution as the product of chance variations. Nietzsche sees it as the product of the exceptional individuals' drive to be different, as a consequence of their will to power.

Nietzsche began his career as a classical scholar, and he used these ideas about evolution to produce a new interpretation of Greek thought and culture. He agrees with the general view that the origins of the Western ideal of reason lie in Greek philosophy. But there was in Greek culture, Nietzsche asserts, another strain, which the worshipers of Greek rationalism overlook. This is the Greek admiration for the unrestrained, instinctual, Dionysian element in human life, and it is this Dionysian element, much more than the Apollonian tradition of rationalism represented by Socrates and Plato, which was responsible for Greece's greatest achievements. Indeed, the Apollonian was the enemy of the Dionysian. In his first book, *The Birth of Tragedy*, Nietzsche argues that the art of tragedy originated in music, a nonverbal, profoundly instinctual mode of expression, and that the rationalism of a generation corrupted by Socrates' idolatry of words and argument was responsible for the destruction of this art in Greece.

In his later books Nietzsche extends this critique to the entire tradition of Western philosophy and to the central ideals of the Western heritage. The philosophical pursuit of reason, the religious outlook of Christianity, the regard paid to contemplation and resignation, the distrust of the body, are all, in his view, flights from the hard but noble task of the human species to replace itself with something better. Those who perform this task don't speak in the tones of reason and humility. They are moved by visions whose sources lie below consciousness, and they speak with the confidence of men who know that they are the carriers of a life drive larger than themselves.

Nietzsche's work is easily misinterpreted. Almost from the beginning of his career as a writer he suffered from bad health and loneliness, and the effects show in his style. He expresses himself in florid metaphors, and rarely puts together a connected argument. His books, for the most part, are collections of aphorisms, and these are sometimes so succinct as to be opaque. But probably the greatest reason why Nietzsche is misinterpreted is that people try to categorize a man who fits no categories. And the fact that no labels fit him is his greatest triumph. For above all, he is categorically opposed to categorizers. Human advance, the entire creative process of evolution, is the work, he is convinced, of those who refuse to be classified. It is the excellent man—the man who stands apart from, who rises above, the normal, the standard, the regular—whom he admires. And he writes in a style—impetuous, irreverent, unapologetically opinionated—appropriate to this attitude.

Nietzsche was born in Röcken, Germany, in 1844, and after a brilliant career as a student became a professor of classical philology at Basel, Switzerland. He left his academic work temporarily to serve as a medical orderly in the Franco-Prussian War, and returned with his health severely damaged, but he nevertheless produced a long series of books over the next decade. In 1879, his health still bad, he resigned from the university to devote himself entirely to his writing. During most of this time he was largely ignored and friendless, but in the late eighties his reputation gradually began to grow. In the fall of 1888 Nietzsche finally came into the public eye when the well-known Danish critic Georg Brandes delivered a series of lectures on his philosophy in Copenhagen. However, he did not enjoy his fame for long. In January, 1889, he fell helplessly insane, and he spent the rest of his life in the care of his mother and sister. He died in 1900.

The following selections are taken from Nietzsche's *Twilight of the Idols*, which he wrote in 1888, a few months before his breakdown. The book has the quality of the calm before the storm: in comparison with most of his other writing, it is tranquil and controlled. It comes as close as any of Nietzsche's works to epitomizing his views. The translation is by Walter Kaufmann.

The portrait which Nietzsche draws of Socrates in *Twilight of the Idols* is based on Plato's description of his teacher as a physically ugly man, a mocker of himself and others, and a master of irony. But Nietzsche turns Plato's representation inside out: he draws Socrates as a buffoon who for some reason was taken seriously, a mocker of courage, idiosyncrasy, strong convictions, nobility, a man plebeian in spirit as well as in his actual origins who invented the art of logical analysis in order to destroy fresh ideas and original visions. And from this "patron saint of moral twaddle," as Nietzsche describes Socrates elsewhere, philosophy has taken the cue that has made it the ally of decadence. It has been the enemy of the instincts even though "as long as life is *ascending*, happiness equals instinct." Struggling against the instinct for life and novelty, philosophy has cast doubt on the reality of time and change, and has taken the objects of men's noblest aspirations—truth, justice, beauty—and dehumanized them by turning them into impersonal laws of nature. Thus it has spread contempt for what is best in man. For truth, justice, and beauty are advanced only when men realize that they are human creations, and only when eccentric men lay rude hands on the ideals that exist and shatter them to make way for new ones.

Twilight of the Idols

THE PROBLEM OF SOCRATES

1

Concerning life, the wisest men of all ages have judged alike: *it is no good*. Always and everywhere one has heard the same sound from their mouths—a sound full of doubt, full of melancholy, full of weariness of life, full of resistance to life. Even Socrates said, as he died: "To live— that means to be sick a long time: I owe Asclepius the Savior a rooster." Even Socrates was tired of it. What does that evidence? What does it evince? Formerly one would have said (—oh, it has been said, and loud enough, and especially by our pessimists): "At least something of all this must be true! The consensus of the sages evidences the truth." Shall we still talk like that today? *May* we? "At least something must be *sick* here," *we* retort. These wisest men of all ages—they should first be scrutinized closely. Were they all perhaps shaky on their legs? late? tottery? decadents? Could it be that wisdom appears on earth as a raven, inspired by a little whiff of carrion?

2

This irreverent thought that the great sages are *types of decline* first occurred to me precisely in a case where it is most strongly opposed by both scholarly and unscholarly prejudice: I recognized Socrates and Plato to be symptoms of degeneration, tools of the Greek dissolution, pseudo-Greek, anti-Greek (*The Birth of Tragedy*, 1872). The consensus of the sages—I comprehended this ever more clearly—proves least of all that they were right in what they agreed on: it shows rather that they themselves, these wisest men, agreed in some *physiological* respect, and hence adopted the same negative attitude to life—*had to* adopt it. Judgments, judgments of value, concerning life, for it or against it, can, in the end, never be true: they have value only as symptoms, they are worthy of consideration only as symptoms; in themselves such judgments are stupidities. One must by all means stretch out one's fingers and make the attempt to grasp this amazing finesse, *that the value of life cannot be estimated.* Not by the living, for they are an interested party, even a bone of contention, and not judges; not by the dead, for a different reason. For a philosopher to see a problem in the value of life is thus an objection to him, a question mark concerning his wisdom, an un-wisdom. Indeed? All these great wise men—they were not only decadents but not wise at all? But I return to the problem of Socrates.

3

In origin, Socrates belonged to the lowest class: Socrates was plebs. We know, we can still see for ourselves, how ugly he was. But ugliness, in itself an objection, is among the Greeks almost a refutation. Was Socrates a Greek at all? Ugliness is often enough the expression of a development that has been crossed, *thwarted* by crossing. Or it appears as *declining* development. The anthropologists among the criminologists tell us that the typical criminal is ugly: *monstrum in fronte, monstrum in animo*. But the criminal is a decadent. Was Socrates a typical criminal? At least that would not be contradicted by the famous judgment of the physiognomist which sounded so offensive to the friends of Socrates. A foreigner who knew about faces once passed through Athens and told Socrates to his face that he *was* a *monstrum*—that he harbored in himself all the bad vices and appetites. And Socrates merely answered: "You know me, sir!"

4

Socrates' decadence is suggested not only by the admitted wantonness and anarchy of his instincts, but also by the hypertrophy of the logical faculty and that *sarcasm of the rachitic* which distinguishes him. Nor should we forget those auditory hallucinations which, as "the *daimonion* of Socrates," have been interpreted religiously. Everything in him is exaggerated, *buffo*, a caricature; everything is at the same time concealed, ulterior, subterranean. I seek to comprehend what idiosyncrasy begot that Socratic equation of reason, virtue, and happiness: that most bizarre of all equations, which, moreover, is opposed to all the instincts of the earlier Greeks.

5

With Socrates, Greek taste changes in favor of dialectics. What really happened there? Above all, a *noble* taste is thus vanquished; with dialectics the plebs come to the top. Before Socrates, dialectic manners were repudiated in good society: they were considered bad manners, they were compromising. The young were warned against them. Furthermore, all such presentations of one's reasons were distrusted. Honest things, like honest men, do not carry their reasons in their hands like that. It is indecent to show all five fingers. What must first be proved is worth little. Wherever authority still forms part of good bearing, where one does not give reasons but commands, the dialectician is a kind of buffoon: one laughs at him, one does not take him seriously. Socrates was the buffoon who *got himself taken seriously:* what really happened there?

6

One chooses dialectic only when one has no other means. One knows that one arouses mistrust with it, that it is not very persuasive. Nothing is easier to erase than a dialectical effect: the experience of every meeting at which there are speeches proves this. It can only be *self-defense* for those who no longer have other weapons. One must have to *enforce* one's right: until one reaches that point, one makes no use of it. The Jews were dialecticians for that reason; Reynard the Fox was one—and Socrates too?

7

Is the irony of Socrates an expression of revolt? Of plebeian *ressentiment?* Does he, as one oppressed, enjoy his own ferocity in the knife-thrusts of his syllogisms? Does he *avenge* himself on the noble people whom he fascinates? As a dialectician, one holds a merciless tool in one's hand; one can become a tyrant by means of it; one compromises those one conquers. The dialectician leaves it to his opponent to prove that he is no idiot: he makes one furious and helpless at the same time. The dialectician renders the intellect of his opponent powerless. Indeed? Is dialectic only a form of *revenge* in Socrates?

8

I have given to understand how it was that Socrates could repel: it is therefore all the more necessary to explain his fascination. That he discovered a new kind of *agon* [contest], that he became its first fencing master for the noble circles of Athens, is one point. He fascinated by appealing to the agnostic impulse of the Greeks—he introduced a variation into the wrestling match between young men and youths. Socrates was also a great *erotic*.

9

But Socrates guessed even more. He saw *through* his noble Athenians; he comprehended that his own case, his idiosyncrasy, was no longer exceptional. The same kind of degeneration was quietly developing everywhere: old Athens was coming to an end. And Socrates understood that all the world *needed* him—his means, his cure, his personal artifice of self-preservation. Everywhere the instincts were in anarchy; everywhere one was within five paces of excess: *monstrum in animo* was the general danger. "The impulses want to play the tyrant; one must invent a *counter-tyrant* who is stronger." When the physiognomist had revealed to Socrates who he was—a cave of bad appetites—the great master of irony let slip another word which is the key to his character. "This is true," he said, "but I mastered them all." *How* did Socrates become master over *himself?* His case was, at bottom, merely the extreme case, only the most striking instance of what was then beginning to be a universal distress: no one was any longer master over himself, the instincts turned *against* each other. He fascinated, being this extreme case; his awe-inspiring ugliness proclaimed him as such to all who could see: he fascinated, of course, even more as an answer, a solution, an apparent *cure* of this case.

10

When one finds it necessary to turn *reason* into a tyrant, as Socrates did, the danger cannot be slight that something else will play the tyrant. Rationality was then hit upon as the savior; neither Socrates nor his "patients" had any choice about being rational: it was *de rigeur*, it was their last resort. The fanaticism with which all Greek reflection throws itself upon rationality betrays a desperate situation; there was danger, there was but one choice: either to perish or—to be *absurdly rational*. The moralism of the Greek philosophers from Plato on is pathologically conditioned; so is their esteem of dialectics. Reason-virtue-happiness, that means merely that one must imitate Socrates and counter the dark appetites with a permanent daylight —the daylight of reason. One must be clever, clear, bright at any price: any concession to the instincts, to the unconscious, leads *downward*.

11

I have given to understand how it was that Socrates fascinated: he seemed to be a physician, a savior. Is it necessary to go on to demonstrate the error in his faith in "rationality at any price"? It is a self-deception on the part of philosophers and moralists if they believe that they are extricating themselves from decadence when they merely wage war against it. Extrication lies beyond their strength: what they choose as a means, as salvation, is itself but another expression of decadence; they change its expression, but they do not get rid of decadence itself. Socrates was a misunderstanding; *the whole improvement-morality, including the Christian, was a misunderstanding.* The most blinding daylight; rationality at any price; life, bright, cold, cautious, conscious, without instinct, in opposition to the instincts—all this too was a mere disease, another disease, and by no means a return to "virtue," to "health," to happiness. To *have* to fight the instincts—that is the formula of decadence: as long as life is *ascending*, happiness equals instinct.

12

Did he himself still comprehend this, this most brilliant of all self-out-witters? Was this what he said to himself in the end, in the *wisdom* of his courage to die? Socrates *wanted* to die: not Athens, but he himself chose the hemlock; he forced Athens to sentence him. "Socrates is no physician," he said softly to himself; "here death alone is the physician. Socrates himself has merely been sick a long time."

"REASON" IN PHILOSOPHY

1

You ask me which of the philosophers' traits are really idiosyncrasies? For example, their lack of historical sense, their hatred of the very idea of becoming, their Egypticism. They think that they show their respect for a subject when they de-historicize it, *sub specie aeterni*—when they turn it into a mummy. All that philosophers have handled for thousands of years have been concept-mummies; nothing real escaped their grasp alive. When these honorable idolators of concepts worship something, they kill it and stuff it; they threaten the life of everything they worship. Death, change, old age, as well as procreation and growth, are to their minds objections— even refutations. Whatever has being does not become; whatever becomes does not have being. Now they all believe, desperately even, in what has being. But since they never grasp it, they seek for reasons why it is kept from them. "There must be mere appearance, there must be some deception which prevents us from perceiving that which has being: where is the deceiver?"

"We have found him," they cry ecstatically; "it is the senses! These senses, which are so immoral in other ways too, deceive us concerning the *true* world. Moral: let us free ourselves from the deception of the senses, from becoming, from history, from lies; history is nothing but faith in the senses, faith in lies. Moral: let us say No to all who have faith in the senses, to all the rest of mankind; they are all 'mob.' Let us be philosophers! Let us be mummies! Let us represent monotono-theism by adopting the expression of a gravedigger! And above all, away with the body, this wretched *idée fixe* of the senses, disfigured by all the fallacies of logic, refuted, even impossible, although it is impudent enough to behave as if it were real!"

3

And what magnificent instruments of observation we possess in our senses! This nose, for example, of which no philosopher has yet spoken with reverence and gratitude, is actually the most delicate instrument so far at our disposal: it is able to detect minimal differences of motion which even a spectroscope cannot detect. Today we possess science precisely to the extent to which we have decided to *accept* the testimony of the senses— to the extent to which we sharpen them further, arm them, and have learned to think them through. The rest is miscarriage and not-yet-science —in other words, metaphysics, theology, psychology, epistemology—or formal science, a doctrine of signs, such as logic and that applied logic which is called mathematics. In them reality is not encountered at all, not even as a problem—no more than the question of the value of such a sign convention as logic.

4

The other idiosyncrasy of the philosophers is no less dangerous; it consists in confusing the last and the first. They place that which comes at the end—unfortunately! for it ought not to come at all!—namely, the "highest concepts," which means the most general, the emptiest concepts, the last smoke of evaporating reality, in the beginning, *as* the beginning. This again is nothing but their way of showing reverence: the higher *may* not grow out of the lower, may not have grown at all. Moral: whatever is of the first rank must be *causa sui*. Origin out of something else is considered an objection, a questioning of value. All the highest values are of the first rank; all the highest concepts, that which has being, the unconditional, the good, the true, the perfect—all these cannot have become and must therefore be *causa sui*. All these, moreover, cannot be unlike each other or in contradiction to each other. Thus they arrive at their stupendous concept, "God." That which is last, thinnest, and emptiest is put first, as *the* cause, as *ens realissimum*. Why did mankind have to take seriously the brain afflictions of sick web-spinners? They have paid dearly for it!

6

It will be appreciated if I condense so essential and so new an insight into four theses. In that way I facilitate comprehension; in that way I provoke contradiction.

First proposition. The reasons for which "this" world has been characterized as "apparent" are the very reasons which indicate its reality; any other kind of reality is absolutely indemonstrable.

Second proposition. The criteria which have been bestowed on the "true being" of things are the criteria of not-being, of *naught;* the "true world" has been constructed out of contradiction to the actual world: indeed an apparent world, insofar as it is merely a moral-optical illusion.

Third proposition. To invent fables about a world "other" than this one has no meaning at all, unless an instinct of slander, detraction, and suspicion against life has gained the upper hand in us: in that case, we avenge ourselves against life with a phantasmagoria of "another," a "better" life.

Fourth proposition. Any distinction between a "true" and an "apparent" world—whether in the Christian manner or in the manner of Kant (in the end, an underhanded Christian)—is only a suggestion of decadence, a symptom of the *decline of life.* That the artist esteems appearance higher than reality is no objection to this proposition. For "appearance" in this case means reality *once more,* only by way of selection, reinforcement, and correction. The tragic artist is no pessimist: he is precisely the one who says Yes to everything questionable, even to the terrible—he is *Dionysian.*

WHAT I OWE TO THE ANCIENTS

1

In conclusion, a word about that world to which I sought approaches, to which I have perhaps found a new approach—the ancient world. My taste, which may be the opposite of a tolerant taste, is in this case too far from saying Yes indiscriminately: it does not like to say Yes; rather even No; but best of all, nothing. That applies to whole cultures, it applies to books—also to places and landscapes. At bottom it is a very small number of ancient books that counts in my life; the most famous are not among them. . . .

Nor was my experience any different in my first contact with Horace. To this day, no other poet has given me the same artistic delight that a Horatian ode gave me from the first. In certain languages that which has been achieved here could not even be attempted. This mosaic of words, in which every word—as sound, as place, as concept—pours out its strength right and left and over the whole, this *minimum* in the extent and number of the signs, and the maximum thereby attained in the energy of the signs— all that is Roman and, if one will believe me, *noble* par excellence. All the rest of poetry becomes, in contrast, something too popular—a mere gar- rulity of feelings.

2

To the Greeks I do not by any means owe similarly strong impressions; and—to come right out with it—they *cannot* mean as much to us as the Romans. One does not *learn* from the Greeks—their manner is too foreign, and too fluid, to have an imperative, a "classical" effect. Who could ever have learned to write from a Greek? Who could ever have learned it *with- out* the Romans?

For heaven's sake, do not throw Plato at me. I am a complete skeptic about Plato, and I have never been able to join in the admiration for the *artist* Plato which is customary among scholars. In the end, the subtlest judges of taste among the ancients themselves are here on my side. Plato, it seems to me, throws all stylistic forms together and is thus a first-rate decadent in style: his responsibility is thus comparable to that of the Cynics, who invented the *satura Menippea*. To be attracted by the Platonic dialogue, this horribly self-satisfied and childish kind of dialectic, one must never have read good French writers—Fontenelle, for example. Plato is boring. In the end, my mistrust of Plato goes deep: he represents such an aberration from all the basic instincts of the Hellene, is so moralistic, so pre-existently Christian—he already takes the concept "good" for the highest concept— that for the whole phenomenon Plato I would sooner use the harsh phrase "higher swindle," or, if it sounds better, "idealism," than any other. We have paid dearly for the fact that this Athenian got his schooling from the Egyp- tians (or from the Jews in Egypt?). In that great calamity, Christianity, Plato represents that ambiguity and fascination, called an "ideal," which made it possible for the nobler spirits of antiquity to misunderstand them- selves and to set foot on the bridge leading to the cross. And how much Plato there still is in the concept "church," in the construction, system, and practice of the church!

My recreation, my preference, my *cure* from all Platonism has always been *Thucydides*. Thucydides and, perhaps, Machiavelli's *Principe* are most closely related to myself by the unconditional will not to gull oneself and to see reason in *reality*—not in "reason," still less in "morality." For the wretched embellishment of the Greeks into an ideal, which the "classically educated" youth carries into life as a prize for his classroom drill, there is no more complete cure than Thucydides. One must follow him line by line and read no less clearly between the lines: there are few thinkers who say so much between the lines. With him the culture of the Sophists, by which

I mean the culture of the realists, reaches its perfect expression—this inestimable movement amid the moralistic and idealistic swindle set loose on all sides by the Socratic schools. Greek philosophy: the decadence of the Greek instinct. Thucydides: the great sum, the last revelation of that strong, severe, hard factuality which was instinctive with the older Hellenes. In the end, it is *courage* in the face of reality that distinguishes a man like Thucydides from Plato: Plato is a coward before reality, consequently he flees into the ideal; Thucydides has control of *himself*, consequently he also maintains control of things.

3

To smell out "beautiful souls," "golden means," and other perfections in the Greeks, or to admire their calm in greatness, their ideal cast of mind, their noble simplicity—the psychologist in me protected me against such "noble simplicity," a *naiiserie allemande* anyway. I saw their strongest instinct, the will to power; I saw them tremble before the indomitable force of this drive—I saw how all their institutions grew out of preventive measures taken to protect each other against their inner explosives. This tremendous inward tension then discharged itself in terrible and ruthless hostility to the outside world: the city-states tore each other to pieces so that the citizens of each might find peace from themselves. One needed to be strong: danger was near, it lurked everywhere. The magnificent physical suppleness, the audacious realism and immoralism which distinguished the Hellene constituted a *need*, not "nature." It only resulted, it was not there from the start. And with festivals and the arts they also aimed at nothing other than to feel *on top*, to *show* themselves on top. These are means of glorifying oneself, and in certain cases, of inspiring fear of oneself.

How could one possibly judge the Greeks by their philosophers, as the Germans have done, and use the Philistine moralism of the Socratic schools as a clue to what was basically Hellenic! After all, the philosophers are the decadents of Greek culture, the counter-movement to the ancient, noble taste (to the agonistic instinct, to the *polis*, to the value of race, to the authority of descent). The Socratic virtues were preached because the Greeks had lost them: excitable, timid, fickle comedians, every one of them, they had a few reasons too many for having morals preached to them. Not that it did any good—but big words and attitudes suit decadents so well.

4

I was the first to take seriously, for the understanding of the older, the still rich and even overflowing Hellenic instinct, that wonderful phenomenon which bears the name of Dionysus: it is explicable only in terms of an *excess* of force. Whoever followed the Greeks, like that most profound student of their culture in our time, Jacob Burckhardt in Basel, knew immediately that something had been accomplished thereby; and Burckhardt added a special section on this phenomenon to his *Civilization of the Greeks*. To see the opposite, one should look at the almost amusing poverty of instinct among the German philologists when they approach the Dionysian. The famous Lobeck, above all, crawled into this world of mysterious states with all the venerable sureness of a worm dried up between books, and persuaded himself that it was scientific of him to be glib and childish to the point of nausea—and with the utmost erudition, Lobeck gave us to understand that all these curiosities really did not amount to anything. In fact, the priests could have told the participants in such orgies some not altogether worthless things; for example, that wine excites lust, that man can under certain circumstances live on fruit, that plants bloom in the spring and wilt in the fall. As regards the astonishing wealth of rites, symbols, and myths of an orgiastic origin, with which the ancient world is literally overrun, this gave Lobeck an opportunity to become still more ingenious. "The Greeks," he said (*Aglaophamus I*, 672), "when they had nothing else to do, laughed, jumped, and ran around; or, since man sometimes feels that urge too, they sat down, cried, and lamented. *Others* came later on and sought some reason for this spectacular behavior; and thus there originated, as explanations for these customs, countless traditions concerning feasts and myths. On the other hand, it was believed that this *droll ado*, which took place on the feast days after all, must also form a necessary part of the festival and therefore it was maintained as an indispensable feature of the religious service." This is contemptible prattle; a Lobeck simply cannot be taken seriously for a moment.

We have quite a different feeling when we examine the concept "Greek" which was developed by Winckelmann and Goethe, and find it incompatible with that element out of which Dionysian art grows—the orgiastic. Indeed I do not doubt that as a matter of principle Goethe excluded anything of the sort from the possibilities of the Greek soul. *Consequently Goethe did not understand the Greeks*. For it is only in the Dionysian mysteries, in the psychology of the Dionysian state, that the *basic fact* of the Hellenic instinct finds expression—its "will to life." What was it that the Hellene guaranteed himself by means of these mysteries? *Eternal* life, the eternal return of life; the future promised and hallowed in the past; the triumphant Yes to life beyond all death and change; *true* life as the overall continuation of life through procreation, through the mysteries of sexuality. For the Greeks the *sexual* symbol was therefore the venerable symbol par excellence, the real profundity in the whole of ancient piety. Every single element in the act of procreation, of pregnancy, and of birth aroused the highest and most solemn feelings. In the doctrine of the mysteries, *pain* is pronounced holy: the pangs of the woman giving birth hallow all pain; all becoming and growing—all that guarantees a future—involves pain. That there may be the eternal joy of creating, that the will to life may eternally affirm itself, the agony of the woman giving birth *must* also be there eternally.

All this is meant by the word Dionysus: I know no higher symbolism than this *Greek* symbolism of the Dionysian festivals. Here the most profound instinct of life, that directed toward the future of life, the eternity of life, is experienced religiously—and the way to life, procreation, as the *holy* way. It was Christianity, with its *ressentiment* against life at the bottom of its heart, which first made something unclean of sexuality: it threw *filth* on the origin, on the presupposition of our life.

Henri Bergson

French philosophy has produced many figures who set out to battle with Descartes by arguing, with great clarity and distinctness, that the search for clarity and distinctness is a mistake. Henri Bergson is one of these—a Cartesian in spite of himself, a man who uses words luminously to say that words are inexact instruments of communication. He believes that logic and argument, by the very way they function, may deform reality and mislead men as to its nature.

His philosophy is in large part a reflection on the meaning of human evolution. He was born in 1859, the year Darwin's *Origin of Species* was published, and the theory of evolution raised a series of old and tormenting questions, now in a more challenging form than before. Was man simply a passive victim of an inexorable process? Did he have the freedom to work against this process or to affect its direction? Darwin himself was disturbed by these questions; Peirce and Nietzsche as well as Bergson were preoccupied by them.

But to these questions Bergson added another, which is as old as the Greeks, but which he made peculiarly his own. The traditional view has been that human reason, when it seeks the truth, attempts to grasp the unchanging structure underlying all things. But if everything is in flux, as the theory of evolution appears to suggest, is not the traditional effort to grasp an unchanging, abstract reality fundamentally misconceived? Bergson came to believe that human history is the scene of a contest between two kinds of forces—one essentially static and conservative, expressed in laws, social pressure, and conscious human cerebration; the other essentially creative, and closer to the mystery of things, expressing itself in art, prophecy, and the personalities of charismatic individuals. Bergson's philosophy is an extended exploration of the deeper reasonableness that can be found in what is mistaken for unreason.

The following selection is from Bergson's brief book *An Introduction to Metaphysics*, first published in 1903, and translated by T. E. Hulme in 1912. In it Bergson, like Descartes, tries to build a philosophy from an intuition of the self, of the "I." But his is not the "I" of Descartes, the "I" which thinks and analyzes. It is the "I" of which we are aware intuitively, without analysis or thought—the self inside us that moves and flows, that is various and yet continuous, and that proves its ultimate reality by its resistance to all efforts to characterize it in abstract words. We *intuit* it; and we intuit all realities, even more remote ones, in a similar fashion: we grasp them by penetrating into them in an act of intellectual sympathy. When we try to conceptualize them we leave out what is unique about them; when we analyze them we break apart in thought what is indivisible in fact. Science, therefore, though it may be of practical use to us, gives us purely relative knowledge. And philosophies written in the tradition of Descartes or of Hume, of Plato or of Spinoza—the tradition that takes mathematics or science to be the model of knowledge—are therefore fundamentally misleading.

Bergson is suave, modest, soft-spoken, but his objective is an overturning of inherited standards of rationality. The intellectual revolution he contemplates is as radical as any that Descartes or Nietzsche contemplated. He hopes to free the human mind from its cage of language and symbols. He wishes to use words to go beyond words, to find images and metaphors that will echo, as it were, to the sounds of silence, to the absolute reality that lies beyond all speaking or logic or analysis. In brief, the task of philosophy —of what Bergson calls "metaphysics"—is the task of pointing beyond itself to mystic insight.

Bergson was the most noted French philosopher of his day. He died in wartime France in 1941.

An Introduction to Metaphysics

A comparison of the definitions of metaphysics and the various conceptions of the absolute leads to the discovery that philosophers, in spite of their apparent divergencies, agree in distinguishing two profoundly different ways of knowing a thing. The first implies that we move round the object; the second that we enter into it. The first depends on the point of view at which we are placed and on the symbols by which we express ourselves. The second neither depends on a point of view nor relies on any symbol. The first kind of knowledge may be said to stop at the *relative;* the second, in those cases where it is possible, to attain the *absolute.*

Consider, for example, the movement of an object in space. My perception of the motion will vary with the point of view, moving or stationary, from which I observe it. My expression of it will vary with the systems of axes, or the points of reference, to which I relate it; that is, with the symbols by which I translate it. For this double reason I call such motion *relative:* in the one case, as in the other, I am placed outside the object itself. But when I speak of an *absolute* movement, I am attributing to the moving object an interior and, so to speak, states of mind; I also imply that I am in sympathy with those states, and that I insert myself in them by an effort of imagination. Then, according as the object is moving or stationary, according as it adopts one movement or another, what I experience will vary. And what I experience will depend neither on the point of view I may take up in regard to the object, since I am inside the object itself, nor on the symbols by which I may translate the motion, since I have rejected all translations in order to possess the original. In short, I shall no longer grasp the movement from without, remaining where I am, but from where it is, from within, as it is in itself. I shall possess an absolute.

Consider, again, a character whose adventures are related to me in a novel. The author may multiply the traits of his hero's character, may make him speak and act as much as he pleases, but all this can never be equivalent to the simple and indivisible feeling which I should experience if I were able for an instant to identify myself with the person of the hero himself. Out of that indivisible feeling, as from a spring, all the words, gestures, and actions of the man would appear to me to flow naturally. They would no longer be accidents which, added to the idea I had already formed of the character, continually enriched that idea, without ever completing it. The character would be given to me all at once, in its entirety, and the thousand incidents which manifest it, instead of adding themselves to the idea and so enriching it, would seem to me, on the contrary, to detach themselves from it, without, however, exhausting it or impoverishing its essence. All the things I am told about the man provide me with so many points of view from which I can observe him. All the traits which describe him, and which can make him known to me only by so many comparisons with persons or things I know already, are signs by which he is expressed more or less symbolically. Symbols and points of view, therefore, place me outside him; they give me only what he has in common with others, and not what belongs to him and to him alone. But that which is properly himself, that which constitutes his essence, cannot be perceived from without, being internal by definition, nor be expressed by symbols, being incommensurable with everything else. Description, history, and analysis leave me here in the relative. Coincidence with the person himself would alone give me the absolute. . . .

It follows from this that an absolute could only be given in an *intuition*, whilst everything else falls within the province of *analysis*. By intuition is meant the kind of *intellectual sympathy* by which one places oneself within an object in order to coincide with what is unique in it and consequently inexpressible. Analysis, on the contrary, is the operation which reduces the object to elements already known, that is, to elements common both to it and other objects. To analyze, therefore, is to express a thing as a function of something other than itself. All analysis is thus a translation, a development into symbols, a representation taken from successive points of view from which we note as many resemblances as possible between the new object which we are studying and others which we believe we know already. In its eternally unsatisfied desire to embrace the object around which it is compelled to turn, analysis multiplies without end the number of its points of view in order to complete its always incomplete representation, and ceaselessly varies its symbols that it may perfect the always imperfect translation. It goes on, therefore, to infinity. But intuition, if intuition is possible, is a simple act.

Now it is easy to see that the ordinary function of positive science is analysis. Positive science works, then, above all, with symbols. Even the most concrete of the natural sciences, those concerned with life, confine themselves to the visible form of living beings, their organs and anatomical elements. They make comparisons between these forms, they reduce the more complex to the more simple; in short, they study the workings of life in what is, so to speak, only its visual symbol. If there exists any means of possessing a reality absolutely instead of knowing it relatively, of placing oneself within it instead of looking at it from outside points of view, of having the intuition instead of making the analysis: in short, of seizing it without any expression, translation, or symbolic representation—metaphysics is that means. *Metaphysics, then, is the science which claims to dispense with symbols.*

There is one reality, at least, which we all seize from within, by intuition and not by simple analysis. It is our own personality in its flowing through time—our self which endures. We may sympathize intellectually with nothing else, but we certainly sympathize with our own selves.

When I direct my attention inward to contemplate my own self (supposed for the moment to be inactive), I perceive at first, as a crust solidified on the surface, all the perceptions which come to it from the material world. These perceptions are clear, distinct, juxtaposed or juxtaposable one with another; they tend to group themselves into objects. Next, I notice the memories which more or less adhere to these perceptions and which serve to interpret them. These memories have been detached, as it were, from the depth of my personality, drawn to the surface by the perceptions which resemble them; they rest on the surface of my mind without being absolutely myself. Lastly, I feel the stir of tendencies and motor habits—a crowd of virtual actions, more or less firmly bound to these perceptions and memories. All these clearly defined elements appear more distinct from me, the more distinct they are from each other. Radiating, as they do, from within outwards, they form, collectively, the surface of a sphere which tends to grow larger and lose itself in the exterior world. But if I draw myself in from the periphery towards the centre, if I search in the depth of my being that which is most uniformly, most constantly, and most enduringly myself, I find an altogether different thing.

There is, beneath these sharply cut crystals and this frozen surface, a continuous flux which is not comparable to any flux I have ever seen. There is a succession of states, each of which announces that which follows and contains that which precedes it. They can, properly speaking, only be said to form multiple states when I have already passed them and turn back to observe their track. Whilst I was experiencing them they were so solidly organized, so profoundly animated with a common life, that I could not have said where any one of them finished or where another commenced. In reality no one of them begins or ends, but all extend into each other. . . .

Every comparison will be insufficient, because the unrolling of our duration resembles in some of its aspects the unity of an advancing movement and in others the multiplicity of expanding states; and, clearly, no metaphor can express one of these two aspects without sacrificing the other. If I use the comparison of the spectrum with its thousand shades, I have before me a thing already made, whilst duration is continually in the making. If I think of an elastic which is being stretched, or of a spring which is extended or relaxed, I forget the richness of color, characteristic of duration that is lived, to see only the simple movement by which consciousness passes from one shade to another. The inner life is all this at once: variety of qualities, continuity of progress, and unity of direction. It cannot be represented by images.

But it is even less possible to represent it by *concepts*, that is by abstract, general, or simple ideas. It is true that no image can reproduce exactly the original feeling I have of the flow of my own conscious life. But it is not even necessary that I should attempt to render it. If a man is incapable of getting for himself the intuition of the constitutive duration of his own being, nothing will ever give it to him, concepts no more than images. Here the single aim of the philosopher should be to promote a certain effort, which in most men is usually fettered by habits of mind more useful to life. Now the image has at least this advantage, that it keeps us in the concrete. No image can replace the intuition of duration, but many diverse images, borrowed from very different orders of things, may, by the convergence of their action, direct consciousness to the precise point where there is a certain intuition to be seized. . . .

Concepts on the contrary—especially if they are simple—have the disadvantage of being in reality symbols substituted for the object they symbolize, and demand no effort on our part. Examined closely, each of them, it would be seen, retains only that part of the object which is common to it and to others, and expresses, still more than the image does, a *comparison* between the object and others which resemble it. But as the comparison has made manifest a resemblance, as the resemblance is a property of the object, and as a property has every appearance of being a *part* of the object which possesses it, we easily persuade ourselves that by setting concept beside concept we are reconstructing the whole of the object with its parts, thus obtaining, so to speak, its intellectual equivalent. In this way we believe that we can form a faithful representation of duration by setting in line the concepts of unity, multiplicity, continuity, finite or infinite divisibility, etc. There precisely is the illusion. There also is the danger. Just in so far as abstract ideas can render service to analysis, that is, to the scientific study of the object in its relations to other objects, so far are they incapable of replacing intuition, that is, the metaphysical investigation of what is essential and unique in the object. For on the one hand these concepts, laid side by side, never actually give us more than an artificial reconstruction of the object, of which they can only symbolize certain general, and, in a way, impersonal aspects; it is therefore useless to believe that with them we can seize a reality of which they present to us the shadow alone. And, on the other hand, besides the illusion there is also a very serious danger. For the concept generalizes at the same time as it abstracts. The concept can only symbolize a particular property by making it common to an infinity of things. It therefore always more or less deforms the property by the extension it gives to it. . . .

Either metaphysics is only this play of ideas, or else, if it is a serious occupation of the mind, if it is a science and not simply an exercise, it must transcend concepts in order to reach intuition. Certainly, concepts are necessary to it, for all the other sciences work as a rule with concepts, and metaphysics cannot dispense with the other sciences. But it is only truly itself when it goes beyond the concept, or at least when it frees itself from rigid and ready-made concepts in order to create a kind very different from those which we habitually use; I mean supple, mobile, and almost fluid representations, always ready to mould themselves on the fleeting forms of intuition. . . .

Afterword

The appeal of Augustine, Bergson, Nietzsche, and Dostoyevsky lies in the gnawing themes on which they touch: the frustration, and what seems like the ultimate insoluble riddle, of man's entrapment in time and accident; the dangers of human language, and its magic; the circuitousness of the human mind, and the impossibility of pinning down its resources in any formula; man's propensity for working against himself, his aversion to the good. "This is the law of all times, past, present and future," says Sophocles in the *Antigone:* "Everything that is great enters into the realm of mortals with a curse." The writers in this section instruct us to think of human logic and intelligence, and of the philosopher's quest for objectivity, as cursed. Before we consider whether they succeed in demonstrating what they have set out to prove, let us ask why the attitude they take seems to make such sense.

Obviously, they write well—with a surge of feeling and an intensity of conviction that carry the reader along. But they do something more: they bring to the surface of our minds doubts and self-doubts that are likely to haunt the thoughts of any man not wholly immersed in his everyday busyness. Consider Augustine's observations on time—not the logic, but as it were, the psychologic of what he says. Time is the insistent pulse of our experience; mortality and change give their tone to all we do. And these are phenomena at which our minds—or our instincts—boggle. For the past, in which we lived and suffered and hoped, is irretrievably gone, and the future, for which we are living, is only an image in our minds. After it has arrived, it will in its turn disappear. All that really exists, then, is the present. And yet when we look for it, this present, too, is not there. It goes by us as we try to fix it. Time thus seems a nothingness, and all our preoccupation with temporal things a preoccupation with nothingness.

Can anything in human life be of value, then, if there is nothing beyond time and death? To Augustine the situation of man is intelligible and tolerable only if the poison of time can be escaped or overcome. His argument is an effort to show that time is, in fact, only a human fiction, a product or "distention" of our minds which shows their limited and corrupted state. If we were capable of seeing things unwaveringly, as they are seen by a Being to whom all is present at once, the illusion of time would disappear. There would be only an unshifting, timeless present. The procession of things that come into being and pass away would be seen not as a procession but as a single, unmoving spectacle.

It is possible to say, of course, in reaction to Augustine's torments about time, that they merely express the sickly attitude of one man—unfortunately a very influential man—toward the inevitable human condition. Time and change aren't problems. Things die, the world fleets by, and that is that. Indeed, why should we consider mortality an unmixed evil? Isn't it a consolation that some of our yesterdays have disappeared?

But Augustine's paradoxes point to a fact about the human condition which resists the thrust of such questions. Most of us, if we are reflective, and no matter if we are mystical or rationalist in temper, "idealistic" or "realistic" in moral outlook, tend to live, in William James's phrase, in "a two-story world." On one level, we accept the circumstance that we are what our heredity, environment, and fortune have made us. But on another level, we find it inane that we should be constrained and constricted by this roll of the dice, by these accidents of place and time and fate. For we also live with meanings and ideals. We think, or want to think, that what counts about our lives is not the chance set of happenings making up our biographies, but the unique potency that is in us, the essential aspiration that has moved us, the truths we have discovered or the experiences we have had that can be valued for themselves. In these resides the justification, if there is any, for our having lived at all. And from this point of view, time and change aren't merely sad but unavoidable facts. They hide the most important truth about us. To be so immersed in the accidental circumstances of one's life as not to see their oddity and evanescence is to have no independent life, no separate soul of one's own. It is something like this, I think, that Augustine is saying, once we strip away the special theology and dialectic in which he couches his position.

Although time is for Bergson the fundamental reality, he speaks to the same point. In an essay on laughter, he argues that the essence of the comic is the spectacle of human behavior turned mechanistic and predictable. Thus we laugh at a pratfall because the victim is moved not from within, but merely in response to external physical laws. And we laugh at the characters in Molière's plays because each is in the grip of an *idée fixe* which makes him act like a puppet on a string. Correspondingly, in the end, words and abstractions are dangerous because they attempt to pin down the flow of reality. They categorize what is unique, and seek to catch in the net of language what inevitably overflows all generalizations. To mistake for vehicles of genuine knowledge the science and philosophy that lean on words and concepts is to put the mind in a straitjacket, and quite literally to take the life out of things.

Bergson is perusasive because his philosophy seems to have a thousand immediate applications. Any man whose mind is more than a telegraph network knows that language is often inadequate to express his feelings and experiences, and that for many purposes, there are better means of communication than words. Bergson expresses the conviction—he is one of those responsible for its being so widespread—that modern society, organized in the interests of efficiency and verbal communication, has rendered life arid. A screen of theory and technology has come down between us and the physical universe; bureaucratic rules, social roles, managerial techniques, separate us from other human beings. Our experience is "rationalized," and so it is indirect, cerebral, stereotyped, ideological. "Reason" has been achieved at a heavy price. In the end, Descartes' view of reason, Hume's, Peirce's, are all the same in one respect. They present reason as a process that seeks principles, uniformities, regularities, laws. But significant human achievement is always the product of an idiosyncratic vision or an exceptional act. Reason, which makes a principle of being guided by principle, can thus be little more than a sanctimonious excuse for adhering to the routine and mediocre.

This is a large part of what Bergson has to say, and it is Nietzsche's central thesis. The human mind, Nietzsche reminds us, rises to its greatest achievements when it seems to be taken over by forces that lie below the level of conscious ratiocination. He considers Descartes' root idea—"I think, hence I am"—a formula for self-delusion. A man's best thoughts don't come to him at his bidding. They occur *to* him. He is not their agent, but their recipient. The thought, in a sense, thinks him, focusses, captures, animates him. Philosophers, in their worship of reason, have distorted both the actual way in which the mind works and the natural order of things. They have turned conscious reason into the plan of the universe and the mainspring of its evolution. But nature has its own quite different order: power, will, the Dionysian life of the instincts, are primary.

Dostoyevsky is, if anything, even more explicit, more extreme. "Reason" isn't simply the enemy of instinct, it is instinct denatured and dishonest, and those who think that reason can be the guide of life are engaged in a moral deception. They recommend reason on the ground that it serves man's interests, but the recommendation rests on a prettified picture of these interests. For man welcomes pain, he enjoys abasing himself, he has an evident, daily, industrious interest in working against his own interests. Indeed, man will reject reason if only to protect his own sense of inner freedom. For to live in accordance with reason is to deal with one's problems by putting them in a deterministic framework. It is to concern oneself with causes and effects, statistics, the predictable. And man would rather be evil, or lunatic, than accept the notion that he is simply a passive keyboard on which nature plays its tunes.

Is it possible, then, for philosophers to achieve the goal of rationality which they set for themselves? Is the pursuit of such a goal even desirable? Dostoyevsky's answer to these questions is a profoundly negative one. Reason—shining, tidy, hygienic—cannot possibly triumph in human affairs. But if it could, it would create a brave new world in which men's freedom would be lost and their lives bare of meaning. And in one way or another, Augustine, Bergson, and Nietzsche have the same essential message for us.

Need we accept it? I wish that this question weren't as difficult to answer as it is. It is difficult not only because it poses some challenging intellectual issues but also because, when one disagrees with Augustine, Bergson, Nietzsche, and Dostoyevsky, one can sound like a fool, or like someone who has been anesthetized to the human condition, unless one expresses one's disagreement with great care. There is too much substance in what they say. Nevertheless, their position, it seems to me, is a combination of important truths and deceptive untruths.

Let us go back and look again, for example, at Augustine's paradoxes about time. They call our attention, in a peculiarly arresting way, to a moral and psychological truth of considerable importance: if an individual is preoccupied only with things that come and go, if nothing counts for him but the powers and dominations of this world or the fleeting surfaces of his experience, he is likely to end by finding emptiness in the pit of his being. There are limitations, Augustine makes indelibly plain, in a wholly time-bound, exclusively utilitarian, approach to the business of human life. In an important sense, therefore, we may speak of time's "illusory" character.

But the sense is a metaphorical one. It doesn't follow from this moral truth that the concept of time represents an insoluble logical paradox, or that human reason, when it wrestles with this concept, is exposed in all its weakness. The kind of puzzle that Augustine raises about time has been presented again and again by philosophers and laymen. It rests on two principal points: our measurements of time are relative, depending on the standards we use; and they concern something that doesn't seem entirely there to be measured, since all its parts aren't present. But the fact that our measurements of time are relative doesn't prove that time itself is a product of our own invention. No matter how we measure it, we cannot help noticing that events have a before-and-after quality, that they occur in sequence and that the sequence can't be reversed. Processes like aging take place; Napoleon I comes before Napoleon III. We may describe these phenomena of sequentiality on one time scale or another, but the phenomena themselves are not hallucinations.

Nor is there an unfathomable enigma in the fact that when we measure time, the past and the future aren't present before us. To be sure, when we deal with space, all the parts of what we are measuring *are* present. We can determine the length of a road by starting at one end and then proceeding to the other, and all along the road we know that the end toward which we are moving is there, right now. Obviously, we can't do this with time: we can't go back to yesterday or even to half a minute ago, and we can't, here and now, move into next year if it is to remain next year. But this is simply to say that time is different from space; there is a mystery about how we can measure it only if we adopt as the proper model for this process the kind of operation we perform when we measure space. The source of Augustine's paradoxes about time lies in the fact that there lurks in his mind, as there lurks in the mind of many of us, a half-conscious notion that time has a spatial character, that it is like a container that expands, a scroll that unfolds, or a finger that moves across a page. Once we get rid of such erroneous spatial analogies, Augustine's paradoxes lose their force. They retain their provocative flavor and their moral interest, but they do not show the inexorable limitations of human reason. They show only the implications of a mistake in reasoning.

When we turn to Bergson's warnings about the dangers of abstraction we come to another example, I believe, of a sound general observation that has been pushed too far. Bergson reminds us that there is more to life, certainly more to a sane life, than theorizing and analyzing. And surely even a man who believes in living in accordance with reason will agree, unless he is mad, that it would be quite irrational to try to behave like a thinking machine. Such a course would be an invitation to aridity, defeat, and despair. To live rationally does not mean to live by constant ratiocination. It means adopting intelligent standards, including standards that very often call for spontaneity, uncalculated actions, and some intuitiveness and imaginative sympathy in personal relations.

But Bergson says more than this, much more. He says that reasoning, in the conventional sense of the term, has something inherently deceptive about it. It analyzes, breaks apart, what is a living unity; it uses words and symbols, and these can never be identical with what they refer to. But if reasoning is analytic and abstract, that doesn't prove it to be deceptive. Indeed, the virtue of words and symbols lies precisely in the fact that they are not identical with what they point to. A map of a mountain is useful to us because it is a separate thing from the mountain. If it weren't, it wouldn't show us the way to the top. And conversely, union with what is outside us, immersion in its flow, and sympathetic identification with it, aren't knowledge of it. At best, they are only knowledge's prelude. A doctor who sneezes, coughs, and suffers with us may comfort us, but he hasn't diagnosed our ailment. And he may in fact be identifying with pains that he attributes to us but that we don't have.

Bergson reminds us, properly, that we aren't divine, and that even our most sophisticated processes of reasoning still remain those of a limited biological creature with practical interests and inevitable prejudices. But why is this not true of our intuitions as well? And the problem with intuitions, as against the more explicit processes of reasoning, is that they aren't out in the open where they can be criticized. The standards to be applied to them are either purely personal or nonexistent. There isn't anything to hold them down or correct them. In sum, one can make the point that there are other values besides logic and science without disparaging these as inferior forms of mental activity. Nor does one have to overpraise imagination, sympathy, and intuition, describing them as sources of insight that take us beyond our human limitations, in order to affirm the immense values that they possess.

But do not men, by sudden, inexplicable leaps of the mind, make discoveries that they rarely or never make by moving step by step, in an orderly progression, from premise to conclusion? Undeniably, this is the case. It is what lends persuasiveness to Bergson's position, and it is probably the heart of the matter when we turn to Nietzsche. When we eliminate the more *ad hominem* features of Nietzsche's attack on Socrates, it comes down to the accusation that Socrates elevated a debater's view of reason into a cult, and thereby discouraged his contemporaries from relying on their deeper instinctual powers, which alone could have allowed them to develop a new faith to replace the ones that were moribund. So far as Socrates is concerned, the accusation is unpersuasive, for he does seem to have stimulated some new faiths, for example Plato's. But Nietzsche's general point is sound: dialectic alone is not a substitute for believing in something, and argument by itself is not sufficient to persuade a man to commit himself to an ideal. Ideals, values, commitments, must have an emotional source and an emotional contagion; logic and evidence are useful only for criticizing and clarifying them.

Nevertheless, this is a use. If a new faith has been generated, does it not have to be evaluated? Or is any faith acceptable, provided only that it is put forward with the imperious confidence that Nietzsche admires? Socrates' dialectic, Nietzsche says, was a plebeian substitute for nobler forms of contest. Perhaps so. Still, with respect to questions of truth and falsity, consistency and inconsistency, dialectic has a more obvious utility than dueling, and it has the additional advantage that it sheds less blood.

In sum, it is necessary to distinguish between the paths by which men discover truths or arrive at their visions and the methods by which we evaluate these truths or visions. If this distinction is kept in mind, we can accept many of Nietzsche's general points without concluding that the ideal of reason has to be abandoned. Nietzsche's position, indeed, turns out to be not too far from Hume's: men's beliefs express their "tendency to feign"; as vital creatures, they leap ahead of the evidence—and they must; human reason, though it can try to bring order to human emotions, is nevertheless rooted in them, and remains, in Hume's phrase, "the slave of the passions." If we interpret Nietzsche in this way, he is not an apostle of unreason, but only a critic of notions of reason which deny its animal origins and functions. His attack on past philosophers for having disguised their all-too-human points of view as the pronouncements of impersonal reason is simply a melodramatic way of reminding philosophers that if they were more frankly personal they might also find it easier to be more objective.

But what of Dostoyevsky's description of this animal, man? Does it not make rationalist philosophies seem juvenile? In speaking of the portrayals of man as overwhelmingly selfish, Hume once remarked, "The descriptions which certain philosophers delight so much to form of mankind in this particular are as wide of nature as any accounts of monsters which we meet with in fables and romances." At the very least, Hume argued, men's feelings for their families, and the influence on them of social institutions, redeemed them from utter, uncontrolled self-interest. Self-love might be the strongest single emotion in them; but in most men their other emotions, taken together, frequently overbalanced it. Surely Hume's insight belongs as much as Dostoyevsky's in a complete portrait of "human nature."

In what kind of process are we engaged, indeed, when we offer general portraits of "human nature"? The best of such portraits are likely to be both true and treacherous. For they merely point to the propensities of men, and these show themselves differently in different situations. Hume is right about human nature, but there are also situations in which Dostoyevsky is right. When institutions and manners collapse, when families lose their solidity, when the individual stands alone and unguided, it is not so rare to encounter men who resemble the monsters we meet in fables. Dostoyevsky reminds us that civilization is a thin and fragile covering, and that beneath its surface there waits a predatory and involuted underworld creature, who takes a perverse joy in destruction and in self-destruction. To those who think that there will come a time when man won't be a principal cause of his own woes, Dostoyevsky offers an irrefutable response.

But his response merely underscores the significance of the ideal of reason. To be rational—to discriminate among the options presented to us, and to try to be clear about the principles we use when we discriminate—is necessary precisely because our desires can be self-destructive. As Bertrand Russell once remarked, "Rationality in practice may be defined as the habit of remembering all our relevant desires, and not only the one which happens at the moment to be strongest." The crucial premise on which Dostoyevsky's entire argument rests is that men prize their sense of free will, of being the cause of their own behavior and having responsibility for it, and that this is why they are bound to resist science and reason, which deny their freedom. But to act freely, to choose what one wants and to do it, is possible only if the world has a certain predictable structure and if we can foresee the probable outcome of the choices we make. Rationality is incompatible with freedom only if we mean by "freedom" ignorance or indifference to causes and effects. This confuses freedom with random or careless behavior.

There is a sense, however, in which Dostoyevsky, given his premises, is right. The view of freedom which associates it with knowledgeable, uncoerced choice of causes and consequences leaves man still embedded in the network of causes and consequences. He still can't escape from his own skin; even if he is the kind of man who, by force of character, can change his character and alter his wants, this ability arises from a personal endowment with which he started. And thus, while we can call him "free" in relation to this or that particular act of choice, we cannot, on this view of freedom, call him free before his Maker. He doesn't have total, unconditional responsibility for his being what he is. And it is this total, unconditional power to choose to be anything one wants, and one's total responsibility before God for the choice one makes, that Dostoyevsky has in mind when he speaks of "freedom."

In the final analysis, the disagreement between men like Descartes, Hume, and Peirce and men like Augustine and Dostoyevsky turns, I think, on this difference in perspective. Despite appearances, they aren't disagreeing, in the main, about the facts of human nature. The difference is one of values. They are using dissimilar standards to measure the adequacy of human moral and intellectual capacities. Descartes, Hume, and Peirce are interested in attaining reliable knowledge of the natural world and information as to the best ways to achieve constructive purposes in that world. Augustine and Dostoyevsky condemn reason because such limited purposes are not what they have in mind.

"I have no wish to be [the normal man]," says Dostoyevsky; even the underworld is better. "Yet," he cries, "I am lying. . . . I know that it is not the underworld which is so much better, but something else, something else—something for which I am hungry, but which I shall never find." The genius of Dostoyevsky and Augustine is to show us our middling world as it looks to those who live only on its edge. Their territory is the underworld and an overworld for which they are hungry. There is Satan and there is God, and only shadows lie between. And time, logic, and the precarious achievements of human civility and reason all disappear into these shadows.

In the end, philosophical irrationalists like Augustine, Bergson, and Dostoyevsky belong to the tradition of the early Church Father who said, "I blush when I remember that I have a body." What they want is release from the constraints of their bodies. They seek the conversion of their souls. Anyone who is impelled to believe that man can escape the consequences of being a creature of mortal circumstance will be compelled to recognize, as Augustine and Dostoyevsky do, that reason cannot serve his purpose; he must go beyond it, as they do, to faith.

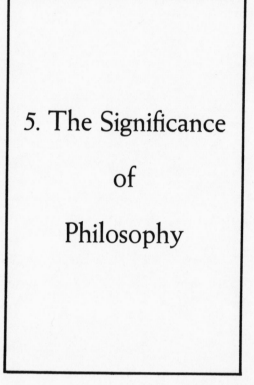

5. The Significance

of

Philosophy

*W*hat, *beyond giving immediate pleasure, does philosophy accomplish?
What does the continuance of the philosophic enterprise mean to human
civilization? F. H. Bradley, the nineteenth-century British philosopher, said
that metaphysics is the seeking of bad reasons for what we believe on
instinct. At times philosophy looks almost like a joke that philosophers play
on themselves. Each major philosopher enters the lists thinking or hoping
that he has finally found the argument to end all arguments; in a sense,
each major philosopher sets out to put an end to philosophy. And yet each
one fails, and the arguments continue. Why does this happen? Does it
mean that philosophy itself is a failure? What does philosophy achieve, if
anything, beyond all its arguments and counterarguments?*

*These are the questions to which, in this concluding section, William
James, Bertrand Russell, Josiah Royce, Friedrich Waismann, and Plato
address themselves. Their reflections will give us the opportunity to look at
philosophy philosophically.*

William James

William James was the brother of the novelist Henry James. It was said of them that Henry wrote novels like a philosopher and William wrote philosophy like a novelist. William's exuberant prose and philosophical optimism, however, were hard won. He lived through an extended period of depression in his youth, and throughout his life he had special sympathy for those he called "the sick-souled": he wondered what made them sick, whether they saw truths that others missed, and whether he could speak to their despair and interpret the world in such a way as to reflect the facts of their experience. Yet he also wished to remain faithful to the spirit of science and the laboratory. His philosophy was a means of therapy, for himself and for others. And he saw in philosophy the clash of temperamental differences that he felt in himself.

James was born in 1842 in New York. He tried his hand at painting and medicine before he turned to psychology and philosophy, and was in his forties when he published the work that made his reputation—his *Psychology*. This book took twelve years of agonizing writing, but in its finished form it reads as though it had been produced effortlessly, almost spontaneously. It helped change the basis of psychology from speculation and introspection to experimentation. Subsequently, James gave steadily more attention to philosophy, and became known as the leading spokeman for pragmatism, a philosophy whose invention he attributed to his friend Charles Peirce. But Peirce refused to take the credit—or the blame—for James's views. Peirce's interest in pragmatism—he came to call it "pragmaticism" to stress the difference—was a logician's: he saw in it possibilities for controlling thinking so that it could reach clear and reliable conclusions. James, in contrast, had a psychological and medical interest in "pragmatism": he thought of it as a way of choosing between ideas from the point of view of their life-enhancing effects.

James was at the center of the remarkable group of men, including Josiah Royce and George Santayana (whose teacher he had been), who taught philosophy at Harvard at the turn of the century. His warmth of heart and infectious spirits, as well as his intellectual brilliance, made him, indeed, the central figure in American philosophy in his day, and he remains even now probably the most widely read American philosopher abroad. He died in 1910.

The following selection is from the first chapter of James's book *Prag-*

matism: A New Name for Some Old Ways of Thinking, which was based on public lectures he delivered in Boston and New York in 1906–1907. I have retitled the selection "Temperament and Philosophy."

Temperament and Philosophy

In the preface to that admirable collection of essays of his called 'Heretics,' Mr. Chesterton writes these words: "There are some people— and I am one of them—who think that the most practical and important thing about a man is still his view of the universe. We think that for a landlady considering a lodger it is important to know his income, but still more important to know his philosophy. We think that for a general about to fight an enemy it is important to know the enemy's numbers, but still more important to know the enemy's philosophy. We think the question is not whether the theory of the cosmos affects matters, but whether in the long run anything else affects them."

I think with Mr. Chesterton in this matter. I know that you, ladies and gentlemen, have a philosophy, each and all of you, and that the most interesting and important thing about you is the way in which it determines the perspective in your several worlds. You know the same of me. And yet I confess to a certain tremor at the audacity of the enterprise which I am about to begin. For the philosophy which is so important in each of us is not a technical matter; it is our more or less dumb sense of what life honestly and deeply means. It is only partly got from books; it is our individual way of just seeing and feeling the total push and pressure of the cosmos. . . .

The history of philosophy is to a great extent that of a certain clash of human temperaments. Undignified as such a treatment may seem to some of my colleagues, I shall have to take account of this clash and explain a good many of the divergencies of philosophers by it. Of whatever temperament a professional philosopher is, he tries, when philosophizing, to sink the fact of his temperament. Temperament is no conventionally recognized reason, so he urges impersonal reasons only for his conclusions. Yet his temperament really gives him a stronger bias than any of his more strictly objective premises. It loads the evidence for him one way or the other, making for a more sentimental or a more hard-hearted view of the universe, just as this fact or that principle would. He *trusts* his temperament. Wanting a universe that suits it, he believes in any representation of the universe that does suit it. He feels men of opposite temper to be out of key with the world's character, and in his heart considers them incompetent and 'not in it,' in the philosophic business, even though they may far excel him in dialectical ability.

Yet in the forum he can make no claim, on the bare ground of his temperament, to superior discernment or authority. There arises thus a certain insincerity in our philosophic discussions: the potentest of all our premises is never mentioned. I am sure it would contribute to clearness if . . . we should break this rule and mention it, and I accordingly feel free to do so.

Of course I am talking here of very positively marked men, men of radical idiosyncracy, who have set their stamp and likeness on philosophy and figure in its history. Plato, Locke, Hegel, Spencer, are such temperamental thinkers. Most of us have, of course, no very definite intellectual temperament, we are a mixture of opposite ingredients, each one present very moderately. We hardly know our own preferences in abstract matters; some of us are easily talked out of them, and end by following the fashion or taking up with the beliefs of the most impressive philosopher in our neighborhood, whoever he may be. But the one thing that has *counted* so far in philosophy is that a man should *see* things, see them straight in his own peculiar way, and be dissatisfied with any opposite way of seeing them. There is no reason to suppose that this strong temperamental vision is from now onward to count no longer in the history of man's beliefs.

Now the particular difference of temperament that I have in mind in making these remarks is one that has counted in literature, art, government, and manners as well as in philosophy. In manners we find formalists and free-and-easy persons. In government, authoritarians and anarchists. In literature, purists or academicals, and realists. In art, classics and romantics. You recognize these contrasts as familiar; well, in philosophy we have a very similar contrast expressed in the pair of terms 'rationalist' and 'empiricist,' 'empiricist' meaning your lover of facts in all their crude variety, 'rationalist' meaning your devotee to abstract and eternal principles. No one can live an hour without both facts and principles, so it is a difference rather of emphasis; yet it breeds antipathies of the most pungent character between those who lay the emphasis differently; and we shall find it extraordinarily convenient to express a certain contrast in men's ways of taking their universe, by talking of the 'empiricist' and of the 'rationalist' temper. These terms make the contrast simple and massive.

More simple and massive than are usually the men of whom the terms are predicated. For every sort of permutation and combination is possible in human nature; and if I now proceed to define more fully what I have in mind when I speak of rationalists and empiricists, by adding to each of those titles some secondary qualifying characteristics, I beg you to regard my conduct as to a certain extent arbitrary. I select types of combination that nature offers very frequently, but by no means uniformly, and I select them solely for their convenience in helping me to my ulterior purpose of characterizing pragmatism. Historically we find the terms 'intellectualism' and 'sensationalism' used as synonyms of 'rationalism' and 'empiricism.' Well, nature seems to combine most frequently with intellectualism an idealistic and optimistic tendency. Empiricists on the other hand are not uncommonly materialistic, and their optimism is apt to be decidedly conditional and tremulous. Rationalism is always monistic. It starts from wholes and universals, and makes much of the unity of things. Empiricism starts from the parts, and makes of the whole a collection—is not averse therefore to calling itself pluralistic. Rationalism usually considers itself more religious than empiricism, but there is much to say about this claim, so I merely mention it. It is a true claim when the individual rationalist is what is called a man of feeling, and when the individual empiricist prides himself on being hard-headed. In that case the rationalist will usually also be in favor of what is called free-will, and the empiricist will be a fatalist—I use the terms most popularly current. The rationalist finally will be of dogmatic temper in his affirmations, while the empiricist may be more sceptical and open to discussion.

I will write these traits down in two columns. I think you will practically recognize the two types of mental make-up that I mean if I head the columns by the titles 'tender-minded' and 'tough-minded' respectively.

The Tender-minded	*The Tough-minded*
Rationalistic (going	Empiricist (going
by 'principles'),	by 'facts'),
Intellectualistic,	Sensationalistic,
Idealistic,	Materialistic,
Optimistic,	Pessimistic,
Religious,	Irreligious,
Free-willist,	Fatalistic,
Monistic,	Pluralistic,
Dogmatical.	Sceptical.

Pray postpone for a moment the question whether the two contrasted mixtures which I have written down are each inwardly coherent and self-consistent or not—I shall very soon have a good deal to say on that point. It suffices for our immediate purpose that tender-minded and tough-minded people, characterized as I have written them down, do both exist. Each of you probably knows some well-marked example of each type, and you know what each example thinks of the example on the other side of the line. They have a low opinion of each other. Their antagonism, whenever as individuals their temperaments have been intense, has formed in all ages a part of the philosophic atmosphere of the time. It forms a part of the philosophic atmosphere to-day. The tough think of the tender as sentimentalists and soft-heads. The tender feel the tough to be unrefined, callous, or brutal. Their mutual reaction is very much like that that takes place when Bostonian tourists mingle with a population like that of Cripple Creek. Each type believes the other to be inferior to itself; but disdain in the one case is mingled with amusement, in the other it has a dash of fear.

Now, as I have already insisted, few of us are tenderfoot Bostonians pure and simple, and few are typical Rocky Mountain toughs, in philosophy. Most of us have a hankering for the good things on both sides of the line. Facts are good, of course—give us lots of facts. Principles are good—give us plenty of principles. The world is indubitably one if you look at it in one way, but as indubitably is it many, if you look at it in another. It is both one and many—let us adopt a sort of pluralistic monism. Everything of course is necessarily determined, and yet of course our wills are free: a sort of free-will determinism is the true philosophy. The evil of the parts is undeniable, but the whole can't be evil: so practical pessimism may be combined with metaphysical optimism. And so forth—your ordinary philosophic layman never being a radical, never straightening out his system, but living vaguely in one plausible compartment of it or another to suit the temptations of successive hours.

But some of us are more than mere laymen in philosophy. We are worthy of the name of amateur athletes, and are vexed by too much inconsistency and vacillation in our creed. We cannot preserve a good intellectual conscience so long as we keep mixing incompatibles from opposite sides of the line. . . .

If any of you here are professional philosophers, and some of you I know to be such, you will doubtless have felt my discourse so far to have been crude in an unpardonable, nay, in an almost incredible degree. Tender-minded and tough-minded, what a barbaric disjunction! And, in general, when philosophy is all compacted of delicate intellectualities and subtleties and scrupulosities, and when every possible sort of combination and transition obtains within its bounds, what a brutal caricature and reduction of highest things to the lowest possible expression is it to represent its field of conflict as a sort of rough-and-tumble fight between two hostile temperaments! What a childishly external view! . . .

Believe me, I feel the full force of the indictment. The picture I have given is indeed monstrously oversimplified and rude. But like all abstractions, it will prove to have its use. If philosophers can treat the life of the universe abstractly, they must not complain of an abstract treatment of the life of philosophy itself. In point of fact the picture I have given is, however coarse and sketchy, literally true. Temperaments with their cravings and refusals do determine men in their philosophies, and always will. The details of systems may be reasoned out piecemeal, and when the student is working at a system, he may often forget the forest for the single tree. But when the labor is accomplished, the mind always performs its big summarizing act, and the system forthwith stands over against one like a living thing, with that strange simple note of individuality which haunts our memory, like the wraith of the man, when a friend or enemy of ours is dead.

Not only Walt Whitman could write 'who touches this book touches a man.' The books of all the great philosophers are like so many men. Our sense of an essential personal flavor in each one of them, typical but indescribable, is the finest fruit of our own accomplished philosophic education. What the system pretends to be is a picture of the great universe of God. What it is,—and oh so flagrantly!—is the revelation of how intensely odd the personal flavor of some fellow creature is. Once reduced to these terms (and all our philosophies get reduced to them in minds made critical by learning) our commerce with the systems reverts to the informal, to the instinctive human reaction of satisfaction or dislike. We grow as peremptory in our rejection or admission, as when a person presents himself as a candidate for our favor; our verdicts are couched in as simple adjectives of praise or dispraise. We measure the total character of the universe as we feel it, against the flavor of the philosophy proffered us, and one word is enough. . . .

Our work over the details of his system is indeed what gives us our resultant impression of the philosopher, but it is on the resultant impression itself that we react. Expertness in philosophy is measured by the definiteness of our summarizing reactions, by the immediate perceptive epithet with which the expert hits such complex objects off. But great expertness is not necessary for the epithet to come. Few people have definitely articulated philosophies of their own. But almost every one has his own peculiar sense of a certain total character in the universe, and of the inadequacy fully to match it of the peculiar systems that he knows. They don't just cover *his* world. One will be too dapper, another too pedantic, a third too much of a job-lot of opinions, a fourth too morbid, and a fifth too artificial, or what not. At any rate he and we know off-hand that such philosophies are out of plumb and out of key and out of 'whack,' and have no business to speak up in the universe's name. Plato, Locke, Spinoza, Mill, Caird, Hegel—I prudently avoid names nearer home!—I am sure that to many of you, my hearers, these names are little more than reminders of as many curious personal ways of falling short. It would be an obvious absurdity if such ways of taking the universe were actually true.

We philosophers have to reckon with such feelings on your part. In the last resort, I repeat, it will be by them that all our philosophies shall ultimately be judged. The finally victorious way of looking at things will be the most completely *impressive* way to the normal run of minds. . . .

Bertrand Russell

Bertrand Russell, one of the master philosophers of this century, said that two passions dominated his life—the desire for certainty in knowledge and the desire for justice in human affairs. He satisfied neither of these, but he obviously had an enormously good time failing. He lived almost ninety-eight years (1872–1970), evidently demonstrating the effectiveness in his own case of his recipe for longevity: to find things one doesn't like and fight them.

Yet for all his involvement in public controversies, Russell also, like Plato or Spinoza, valued philosophy for the detachment that it brings. He thought that philosophy should give men a perspective allowing them to look beyond the battle, and to attach themselves to truths more enduring than the partisan attitudes of the moment. Indeed, his reputation as a partisan, like his reputation as a skeptic and doubter, is in part undeserved. He held, it is true, unconventional opinions on many subjects, and in philosophy he changed his views many times and never came to a final position with regard to some of the most important questions with which he grappled. But Russell's "skepticism" is in many ways like Descartes'. He doubts received opinions, but he never wavers in the belief that men should try to find a kind of truth that is immune to possible doubt. His philosophy, though different in fundamental respects from Descartes', has the same suspicion of obscurantism, the same paradoxical combination of wide-eyed candor and worldly wisdom, and the same respect for clear and distinct ideas—and most particularly for his own. In short, he is not only a skeptic, and not only this century's most eloquent spokesman for the scientific outlook and the ideal of reason, but also the kind of man the French call an *illuminé*—a man subject to bouts of inner certainty, and searching for a way to embody this certainty in an embracing vision.

Thus, Russell is peculiarly well qualified to discuss the two impulses —the mystical and the scientific-logical—that so frequently exist side by side in philosophy. Russell distrusts mysticism, but he can understand it. In the essay that follows he discusses time and eternity, evolution, the validity of intuition, the possibility of objectivity—issues which, as we have seen, are also discussed by St. Augustine, Nietzsche, Bergson, and Spinoza. But Russell expresses his dissatisfaction with the mystical and irrationalist approach only in passing, concentrating his attention on explaining why mystics think as they do, and why what they think is of value to philosophy. He believes that a completely committed scientific approach to philosophy offers the most complete satisfaction of the mystical drive, for it is like mysticism in certain respects.

No comment about Russell begins to be adequate, however, if it is restricted to his work as a philosopher and as a public figure. He was, among other things, a man of spontaneous high spirits, and a satirist and wit in the tradition of Voltaire. In 1937, at sixty-five, Russell wrote an obituary for himself. It conveys his qualities better than any secondhand description can.

OBITUARY[1]

By the death of the Third Earl Russell (or Bertrand Russell, as he preferred to call himself) at the age of ninety,[2] a link with a very distant past is severed. His grandfather, Lord John Russell, the Victorian Prime Minister, visited Napoleon in Elba; his maternal grandmother was a friend of the Young Pretender's widow. In his youth he did work of importance in mathematical logic, but his eccentric attitude during the First World War [3] revealed a lack of balanced judgment which increasingly infected his later writings. Perhaps this is attributable, at least in part, to the fact that he did not enjoy the advantages of a public school education, but was taught at home by tutors until the age of 18, when he entered Trinity College, Cambridge becoming 7th Wrangler in 1893 and a Fellow in 1895. During the fifteen years that followed, he produced the books upon which his reputation in the learned world was based: *The Foundations of Geometry, The Philosophy of Leibniz, The Principles of Mathematics,* and (in collaboration with Dr. A. N. Whitehead) *Principia Mathematica.*[4] The last work, which was of great importance in its day, doubtless owed much of its superiority to Dr. (afterwards Professor) Whitehead, a man who, as his subsequent writings showed, was possessed of that insight and spiritual depth so notably absent in Russell; for Russell's argumentation, ingenious and clever as it is, ignores those higher considerations that transcend mere logic.

This lack of spiritual depth became painfully evident during the First World War, when Russell, although (to do him justice) he never minimized the wrong done to Belgium, perversely maintained that, war being an evil, the aim of statesmanship should have been to bring the war to an end as soon as possible, which would have been achieved by British neutrality and a German victory. It must be supposed that mathematical studies had caused him to take a wrongly quantitative view which ignored the question of principle involved. Throughout the war, he continued to urge that it should be ended, on no matter what terms. Trinity College, very properly, deprived him of his lectureship, and for some months of 1918 he was in prison.

In 1920 he paid a brief visit to Russia, whose government did not impress

1. This obituary will (or will not) be published in *The Times* for June 1, 1962, on the occasion of my lamented but belated death. It was printed prophetically in *The Listener* in 1937.—*Author.*

2. Russell, of course, underestimated himself: he lived, and was active, almost a decade longer.—*Editor.*

3. Russell opposed British participation in World War I, and went to prison for a short time.—*Editor.*

4. The classic work in modern mathematical logic. Whitehead subsequently went on to become a speculative philosopher of the kind that Russell abominated.—*Editor.*

him favorably, and a longer visit to China, where he enjoyed the rationalism of the traditional civilization, with its still surviving flavor of the eighteenth century. In subsequent years his energies were dissipated in writings advocating socialism, educational reform, and a less rigid code of morals as regards marriage. At times, however, he returned to less topical subjects. His historical writings, by their style and their wit, conceal from careless readers the superficiality of the antiquated rationalism which he professed to the end.

In the Second World War he took no public part, having escaped to a neutral country just before its outbreak.[5] In private conversation he was wont to say that homicidal lunatics were well employed in killing each other, but that sensible men would keep out of their way while they were doing it. Fortunately this outlook, which is reminiscent of Bentham, has become rare in this age, which recognizes that heroism has a value independent of its utility. True, much of what was once the civilized world lies in ruins; but no right-thinking person can admit that those who died for the right in the great struggle have died in vain.

His life, for all its waywardness, had a certain anachronistic consistency, reminiscent of that of the aristocratic rebels of the early nineteenth century. His principles were curious, but, such as they were, they governed his actions. In private life he showed none of the acerbity which marred his writings, but was a genial conversationalist and not devoid of human sympathy. He had many friends, but had survived almost all of them. Nevertheless, to those who remained he appeared, in extreme old age, full of enjoyment, no doubt owing, in large measure, to his invariable health, for politically, during his last years, he was as isolated as Milton after the Restoration. He was the last survivor of a dead epoch.

The following selection presents the bulk of Russell's essay "Mysticism and Logic," which was first published in July, 1914, and was subsequently reprinted in *Mysticism and Logic and Other Essays* (1925).

Mysticism and Logic

Metaphysics, or the attempt to conceive the world as a whole by means of thought, has been developed, from the first, by the union and conflict of two very different human impulses, the one urging men towards mysticism, the other urging them towards science. Some men have achieved greatness through one of these impulses alone, others through the other alone: in Hume, for example, the scientific impulse reigns quite unchecked, while in Blake [1] a strong hostility to science co-exists with profound mystic insight. But the greatest men who have been philosophers have felt the need both of science and of mysticism: the attempt to harmonise the two was what made their life, and what always must, for all its arduous uncertainty, make philosophy, to some minds, a greater thing than either science or religion. . . .

5. Russell, as it turned out, stayed in England, and supported the struggle against the Nazis.—*Editor.*
1. The eighteenth-century English poet William Blake.—*Editor.*

Mystical philosophy, in all ages and in all parts of the world, is characterized by certain beliefs. . . .

There is, first, the belief in insight as against discursive analytic knowledge: the belief in a way of wisdom, sudden, penetrating, coercive, which is contrasted with the slow and fallible study of outward appearance by a science relying wholly upon the senses. All who are capable of absorption in an inward passion must have experienced at times the strange feeling of unreality in common objects, the loss of contact with daily things, in which the solidity of the outer world is lost, and the soul seems, in utter loneliness, to bring forth, out of its own depths, the mad dance of fantastic phantoms which have hitherto appeared as independently real and living. This is the negative side of the mystic's initiation: the doubt concerning common knowledge, preparing the way for the reception of what seems a higher wisdom. Many men to whom this negative experience is familiar do not pass beyond it, but for the mystic it is merely the gateway to an ampler world.

The mystic insight begins with the sense of a mystery unveiled, of a hidden wisdom now suddenly become certain beyond the possibility of a doubt. The sense of certainty and revelation comes earlier than any definite belief. The definite beliefs at which mystics arrive are the result of reflection upon the inarticulate experience gained in the moment of insight. Often, beliefs which have no real connection with this moment become subsequently attracted into the central nucleus; thus in addition to the convictions which all mystics share, we find, in many of them, other convictions of a more local and temporary character, which no doubt become amalgamated with what was essentially mystical in virtue of their subjective certainty. We may ignore such inessential accretions, and confine ourselves to the beliefs which all mystics share.

The first and most direct outcome of the moment of illumination is belief in the possibility of a way of knowledge which may be called revelation or insight or intuition, as contrasted with sense, reason, and analysis, which are regarded as blind guides leading to the morass of illusion. Closely connected with this belief is the conception of a Reality behind the world of appearance and utterly different from it. This Reality is regarded with an admiration often amounting to worship; it is felt to be always and everywhere close at hand, thinly veiled by the shows of sense, ready, for the receptive mind, to shine in its glory even through the apparent folly and wickedness of Man. The poet, the artist, and the lover are seekers after that glory: the haunting beauty that they pursue is the faint reflection of its sun. But the mystic lives in the full light of the vision: what others dimly seek he knows, with a knowledge beside which all other knowledge is ignorance.

The second characteristic of mysticism is its belief in unity, and its refusal to admit opposition or division anywhere. We found Heraclitus saying "good and ill are one"; and again he says, "the way up and the way down is one and the same." The same attitude appears in the simultaneous assertion of contradictory propositions, such as: "We step and do not step into the same rivers; we are and are not." The assertion of Parmenides, that reality is one and indivisible, comes from the same impulse towards unity.[2] In Plato, this impulse is less prominent, being held in check by his theory of ideas; but it reappears, so far as his logic permits, in the doctrine of the primacy of the Good.

A third mark of almost all mystical metaphysics is the denial of the reality of Time. This is an outcome of the denial of division; if all is one, the distinction of past and future must be illusory. We have seen this doctrine prominent in Parmenides; and among moderns it is fundamental in the systems of Spinoza and Hegel.

The last of the doctrines of mysticism which we have to consider is its belief that all evil is mere appearance, an illusion produced by the divisions and oppositions of the analytic intellect. Mysticism does not maintain that such things as cruelty, for example, are good, but it denies that they are real: they belong to that lower world of phantoms from which we are to be liberated by the insight of the vision. Sometimes— for example in Hegel, and at least verbally in Spinoza—not only evil, but good also, is regarded as illusory, though nevertheless the emotional attitude towards what is held to be Reality is such as would naturally be associated with the belief that Reality is good. What is, in all cases, ethically characteristic of mysticism is absence of indignation or protest, acceptance with joy, disbelief in the ultimate truth of the division into two hostile camps, the good and the bad. This attitude is a direct outcome of the nature of the mystical experience: with its sense of unity is associated a feeling of infinite peace. Indeed it may be suspected that the feeling of peace produces, as feelings do in dreams, the whole system of associated beliefs which make up the body of mystic doctrine. But this is a difficult question, and one on which it cannot be hoped that mankind will reach agreement.

Four questions thus arise in considering the truth or falsehood of mysticism, namely:

I. Are there two ways of knowing, which may be called respectively reason and intuition? And if so, is either to be preferred to the other?

II. Is all plurality and division illusory?

III. Is time unreal?

IV. What kind of reality belongs to good and evil?

On all four of these questions, while fully developed mysticism seems to me mistaken, I yet believe that, by sufficient restraint, there is an element of wisdom to be learned from the mystical way of feeling,

2. Heraclitus and Parmenides were the two most important philosophical thinkers in Greece before Socrates.—*Editor.*

which does not seem to be attainable in any other manner. If this is the truth, mysticism is to be commended as an attitude towards life, not as a creed about the world. The metaphysical creed, I shall maintain, is a mistaken outcome of the emotion, although this emotion, as colouring and informing all other thoughts and feelings, is the inspirer of whatever is best in Man. Even the cautious and patient investigation of truth by science, which seems the very antithesis of the mystic's swift certainty, may be fostered and nourished by that very spirit of reverence in which mysticism lives and moves.

I. REASON AND INTUITION

Of the reality or unreality of the mystic's world I know nothing. I have no wish to deny it, nor even to declare that the insight which reveals it is not a genuine insight. What I do wish to maintain—and it is here that the scientific attitude becomes imperative—is that insight, untested and unsupported, is an insufficient guarantee of truth, in spite of the fact that much of the most important truth is first suggested by its means. It is common to speak of an opposition between instinct and reason; in the eighteenth century, the opposition was drawn in favour of reason, but under the influence of Rousseau and the romantic movement instinct was given the preference, first by those who rebelled against artificial forms of government and thought, and then, as the purely rationalistic defence of traditional theology became increasingly difficult, by all who felt in science a menace to creeds which they associated with a spiritual outlook on life and the world. Bergson, under the name of "intuition," has raised instinct to the position of sole arbiter of metaphysical truth. But in fact the opposition of instinct and reason is mainly illusory. Instinct, intuition, or insight is what first leads to the beliefs which subsequent reason confirms or confutes; but the confirmation, where it is possible, consists, in the last analysis, of agreement with other beliefs no less instinctive. Reason is a harmonising, controlling force rather than a creative one. Even in the most purely logical realm, it is insight that first arrives at what is new.

Where instinct and reason do sometimes conflict is in regard to single beliefs, held instinctively, and held with such determination that no degree of inconsistency with other beliefs leads to their abandonment. Instinct, like all human faculties, is liable to error. Those in whom reason is weak are often unwilling to admit this as regards themselves, though all admit it in regard to others. Where instinct is least liable to error is in practical matters as to which right judgment is a help to survival: friendship and hostility in others, for instance, are often felt with extraordinary discrimination through very careful disguises. But even in such matters a wrong impression may be given by reserve or flattery; and in matters less directly practical, such as philosophy deals with, very strong instinctive beliefs are sometimes wholly mistaken, as we may come to know through their perceived inconsistency with other equally strong beliefs. It is such considerations that necessitate the harmonising mediation of reason, which tests our beliefs by their mutual compatibility, and examines, in doubtful cases, the possible sources of error on the one side and on the other. In this there is no opposition to instinct as a whole, but only to blind reliance upon some one interesting aspect of instinct to the exclusion of other more commonplace but not less trustworthy aspects. It is such one-sidedness, not instinct itself, that reason aims at correcting. . . .

The theoretical understanding of the world, which is the aim of philosophy, is not a matter of great practical importance to animals, or to savages, or even to most civilised men. It is hardly to be supposed, therefore, that the rapid, rough and ready methods of instinct or intuition will find in this field a favourable ground for their application. It is the older kinds of activity, which bring out our kinship with remote generations of animal and semi-human ancestors, that show intuition at its best. In such matters as self-preservation and love, intuition will act sometimes (though not always) with a swiftness and precision which are astonishing to the critical intellect. But philosophy is not one of the pursuits which illustrate our affinity with the past: it is a highly refined, highly civilised pursuit, demanding, for its success, a certain liberation from the life of instinct, and even, at times, a certain aloofness from all mundane hopes and fears. It is not in philosophy, therefore, that we can hope to see intuition at its best. On the contrary, since the true objects of philosophy, and the habit of thought demanded for their apprehension, are strange, unusual, and remote, it is here, more almost than anywhere else, that intellect proves superior to intuition, and that quick unanalysed convictions are least deserving of uncritical acceptance.

In advocating the scientific restraint and balance, as against the self-assertion of a confident reliance upon intuition, we are only urging, in the sphere of knowledge, that largeness of contemplation, that impersonal disinterestedness, and that freedom from practical preoccupations which have been inculcated by all the great religions of the world. Thus our conclusion, however it may conflict with the explicit beliefs of many mystics, is, in essence, not contrary to the spirit which inspires those beliefs, but rather the outcome of this very spirit as applied in the realm of thought.

II. UNITY AND PLURALITY

One of the most convincing aspects of the mystic illumination is the apparent revelation of the oneness of all things, giving rise to pantheism in religion and to monism in philosophy. An elaborate logic, beginning with Parmenides, and culminating in Hegel and his followers, has been gradually developed, to prove that the universe is one indivisible Whole, and that what seem to be its parts, if considered as substantial and self-existing, are mere illusion. The conception of a Reality quite other than the world of appearance, a reality one, indivisible, and unchanging, was introduced into Western philosophy by Parmenides, not, nominally at least, for mystical or religious reasons, but on the basis of a logical argument as to the impossibility of not-being, and most subsequent metaphysical systems are the outcome of this fundamental idea.

The logic used in defence of mysticism seems to be faulty as logic, and open to technical criticisms, which I have explained elsewhere. I shall not here repeat these criticisms, since they are lengthy and difficult, but shall instead attempt an analysis of the state of mind from which mystical logic has arisen.

Belief in a reality quite different from what appears to the senses arises with irresistible force in certain moods, which are the source of most mysticism, and of most metaphysics. While such a mood is dominant, the need of logic is not felt, and accordingly the more thoroughgoing mystics do not employ logic, but appeal directly to the immediate deliverance of their insight. But such fully developed mysticism is rare in the West. When the intensity of emotional conviction subsides, a man who is in the habit of reasoning will search for logical grounds in favour of the belief which he finds in himself. But since the belief already exists, he will be very hospitable to any ground that suggests itself. The paradoxes apparently proved by his logic are really the paradoxes of mysticism, and are the goal which he feels his logic must reach if it is to be in accordance with insight. The resulting logic has rendered most philosophers incapable of giving any account of the world of science and daily life. If they had been anxious to give such an account, they would probably have discovered the errors of their logic; but most of them were less anxious to understand the world of science and daily life than to convict it of unreality in the interests of a super-sensible "real" world. . . .

Such an attitude naturally does not tend to the best results. Everyone knows that to read an author simply in order to refute him is not the way to understand him; and to read the book of Nature with a conviction that it is all illusion is just as unlikely to lead to understanding. If our logic is to find the common world intelligible, it must not be hostile, but must be inspired by a genuine acceptance such as is not usually to be found among metaphysicians.

III. TIME

The unreality of time is a cardinal doctrine of many metaphysical systems, often nominally based, as already by Parmenides, upon logical arguments, but originally derived, at any rate in the founders of new systems, from the certainty which is born in the moment of mystic insight. As a Persian Sufi poet says:

> Past and future are what veil God from our sight.
> Burn up both of them with fire! How long
> Wilt thou be partitioned by these segments as a reed?

The belief that what is ultimately real must be immutable is a very common one: it gave rise to the metaphysical notion of substance, and finds, even now, a wholly illegitimate satisfaction in such scientific doctrines as the conservation of energy and mass.

It is difficult to disentangle the truth and the error in this view. The arguments for the contention that time is unreal and that the world of sense is illusory must, I think, be regarded as fallacious. Nevertheless there is some sense—easier to feel than to state—in which time is an unimportant and superficial characteristic of reality. Past and future must be acknowledged to be as real as the present, and a certain emancipation from slavery to time is essential to philosophic thought. The importance of time is rather practical than theoretical, rather in relation to our desires than in relation to truth. A truer image of the world, I think, is obtained by picturing things as entering into the stream of time from an eternal world outside, than from a view which regards time as the devouring tyrant of all that is. Both in thought and in feeling, even though time be real, to realise the unimportance of time is the gate of wisdom.

That this is the case may be seen at once by asking ourselves why our feelings towards the past are so different from our feelings towards the future. The reason for this difference is wholly practical: our wishes can affect the future but not the past, the future is to some extent subject to our power, while the past is unalterably fixed. But every future will some day be past: if we see the past truly now, it must, when it was still future, have been just what we now see it to be, and what is now future must be just what we shall see it to be when it has become past. The felt difference of quality between past and future, therefore, is not an intrinsic difference, but only a difference in relation to us; to impartial contemplation, it ceases to exist. And impartiality of contemplation is, in the intellectual sphere, that very same virtue of disinterestedness which, in the sphere of action, appears as justice and unselfishness. Whoever wishes to see the world truly, to rise in thought above the tyranny of practical desires, must learn to overcome the difference of attitude towards past and future, and to survey the whole stream of time in one comprehensive vision.

The kind of way in which, as it seems to me, time ought not to enter into our theoretic philosophical thought, may be illustrated by the philosophy which has become associated with the idea of evolution, and which is exemplified by Nietzsche, pragmatism, and Bergson. This philosophy, on the basis of the development which has led from the lowest forms of life up to man, sees in *progress* the fundamental law of the universe, and thus admits the difference between *earlier* and *later* into the very citadel of its contemplative outlook. With its past and future history of the world, conjectural as it is, I do not wish to quarrel. But I think that, in the intoxication of a quick success, much that is required for a true understanding of the universe has been forgotten. Something of Hellenism, something, too, of Oriental resignation, must be combined with its hurrying Western self-assertion before it can emerge from the ardour of youth into the mature wisdom of manhood. . . .

Life, in this [evolutionist] philosophy, is a continuous stream, in which all divisions are artificial and unreal. Seperate things, beginnings and endings, are mere convenient fictions: there is only smooth unbroken transition. The beliefs of to-day may count as true to-day, if they carry us along the stream; but to-morrow they will be false, and must be replaced by new beliefs to meet the new situation. All our thinking consists of convenient fictions, imaginary congealings of the stream: reality flows on in spite of all our fictions, and though it can be lived, it cannot be conceived in thought. Somehow, without explicit statement, the assurance is slipped in that the future, though we cannot foresee it, will be better than the past or the present: the reader is like the child which expects a sweet because it has been told to open its mouth and shut its eyes. Logic, mathematics, physics disappear in this philosophy, because they are too "static"; what is real is an impulse and movement towards a goal which, like the rainbow, recedes as we advance, and makes every place different when it reaches it from what it appeared to be at a distance.

I do not propose to enter upon a technical examination of this philosophy. I wish only to maintain that the motives and interests which inspire it are so exclusively practical, and the problems with which it deals are so special, that it can hardly be regarded as touching any of the questions that, to my mind, constitute genuine philosophy.

The predominant interest of evolutionism is in the question of human destiny, or at least of the destiny of Life. It is more interested in morality and happiness than in knowledge for its own sake. It must be admitted that the same may be said of many other philosophies, and that a desire for the kind of knowledge which philosophy can give is very rare. But if philosophy is to attain truth, it is necessary first and foremost that philosophers should acquire the distinterested intellectual curiosity which characterises the genuine man of science. Knowledge concerning the future—which is the kind of knowledge that must be sought if we are to know about human destiny—is possible within certain narrow limits. It is impossible to say how much the limits may be enlarged with the progress of science. But what is evident is that any proposition about the future belongs by its subject-matter to some particular science, and is to be ascertained, if at all, by the methods of that science. Philosophy is not a short cut to the same kind of results as those of the other sciences: if it is to be a genuine study, it must have a province of its own, and aim at results which the other sciences can neither prove nor disprove.

Evolutionism, in basing itself upon the notion of *progress*, which is change from the worse to the better, allows the notion of time, as it seems to me, to become its tyrant rather than its servant, and thereby loses that impartiality of contemplation which is the source of all that is best in philosophic thought and feeling. Metaphysicians, as we saw, have frequently denied altogether the reality of time. I do not wish to do this; I wish only to preserve the mental outlook which inspired the denial, the attitude which, in thought, regards the past as having the same reality as the present and the same importance as the future. "In so far," says Spinoza, "as the mind conceives a thing according to the dictate of reason, it will be equally affected whether the idea is that of a future, past, or present thing." It is this "conceiving according to the dictate of reason" that I find lacking in the philosophy which is based on evolution.

IV. GOOD AND EVIL

Mysticism maintains that all evil is illusory, and sometimes maintains the same view as regards good, but more often holds that all Reality is good. . . . The possibility of this universal love and joy in all that exists is of supreme importance for the conduct and happiness of life, and gives inestimable value to the mystic emotion, apart from any creeds which may be built upon it. But if we are not to be led into false beliefs, it is necessary to realise exactly *what* the mystic emotion reveals. It reveals a possibility of human nature—a possibility of a nobler, happier, freer life than any that can be otherwise achieved. But it does not reveal anything about the non-human, or about the nature of the universe in general. Good and bad, and even the higher good that mysticism finds everywhere, are the reflections of our own emotions on other things, not part of the substance of things as they are in themselves. And therefore an impartial contemplation, freed from all pre-occupation with Self, will not judge things good or bad, although it is very easily combined with that feeling of universal love which leads the mystic to say that the whole world is good. . . .

I believe . . . that the elimination of ethical considerations from philosophy is both scientifically necessary and—though this may seem a paradox—an ethical advance. Both these contentions must be briefly defended.

The hope of satisfaction to our more human desires—the hope of demonstrating that the world has this or that desirable ethical characteristic—is not one which, so far as I can see, a scientific philosophy can do anything whatever to satisfy. The difference between a good world and a bad one is a difference in the particular characteristics of the particular things that exist in these worlds: it is not a sufficiently abstract difference to come within the province of philosophy. Love and hate, for example, are ethical opposites, but to philosophy they are closely analogous attitudes towards objects. The general form and structure of those attitudes towards objects which constitute mental phenomena is a problem for philosophy, but the difference between love and hate is not a difference of form or structure, and therefore belongs rather to the special science of psychology than to philosophy. Thus the ethical interests which have often inspired philosophers must remain in the background: some kind of ethical interest may inspire the whole study, but none must obtrude in the detail or be expected in the special results which are sought.

If this view seems at first sight disappointing, we may remind ourselves that a similar change has been found necessary in all the other sciences. The physicist or chemist is not now required to prove the ethical importance of his ions or atoms; the biologist is not expected to prove the utility of the plants or animals which he dissects . . . In psychology, the scientific attitude is even more recent and more difficult than in the physical sciences: it is natural to consider that human nature is either good or bad, and to suppose that the difference between good and bad, so all-important in practice, must be important in theory also. It is only during the last century that an ethically neutral psychology has grown up; and here too, ethical neutrality has been essential to scientific success.

In philosophy, hitherto, ethical neutrality has been seldom sought and hardly ever achieved. Men have remembered their wishes, and have judged philosophies in relation to their wishes. Driven from the particular sciences, the belief that the notions of good and evil must afford a key to the understanding of the world has sought a refuge in philosophy. But even from this last refuge, if philosophy is not to remain a set of pleasing dreams, this belief must be driven forth. It is a commonplace that happiness is not best achieved by those who seek it directly; and it would seem that the same is true of the good. In thought, at any rate, those who forget good and evil and seek only to know the facts are more likely to achieve good than those who view the world through the distorting medium of their own desires.

We are thus brought back to our seeming paradox, that a philosophy which does not seek to impose upon the world its own conceptions of good and evil is not only more likely to achieve truth, but is also the outcome of a higher ethical standpoint than one which, like evolutionism and most traditional systems, is perpetually appraising the universe and seeking to find in it an embodiment of present ideals. In religion, and in every deeply serious view of the world and of human destiny, there is an element of submission, a realisation of the limits of human power, which is somewhat lacking in the modern world, with its quick material successes and its insolent belief in the boundless possibilities of progress. "He that loveth his life shall lose it"; and there is danger lest, through a too confident love of life, life itself should lose much of what gives it its highest worth. The submission which religion inculcates in action is essentially the same in spirit as that which science teaches in thought; and the ethical neutrality by which its victories have been achieved is the outcome of that submission.

The good which it concerns us to remember is the good which it lies in our power to create—the good in our own lives and in our attitude towards the world. Insistence on belief in an external realisation of the good is a form of self-assertion, which, while it cannot secure the external good which it desires, can seriously impair the inward good which lies within our power, and destroy that reverence towards fact which constitutes both what is valuable in humility and what is fruitful in the scientific temper.

Human beings cannot, of course, wholly transcend human nature; something subjective, if only the interest that determines the direction of our attention, must remain in all our thought. But scientific philosophy comes nearer to objectivity than any other human pursuit, and gives us, therefore, the closest constant and the most intimate relation with the outer world that it is possible to achieve. To the primitive mind, everything is either friendly or hostile; but experience has shown that friendliness and hostility are not the conceptions by which the world is to be understood. Scientific philosophy thus represents, though as yet only in a nascent condition, a higher form of thought than any pre-scientific belief or imagination, and, like every approach to self-transcendence, it brings with it a rich reward in increase of scope and breadth and comprehension. Evolutionism, in spite of its appeals to particular scientific facts, fails to be a truly scientific philosophy because of its slavery to time, its ethical preoccupations, and its predominant interest in our mundane concerns and destiny. A truly scientific philosophy will be more humble, more piecemeal, more arduous, offering less glitter of outward mirage to flatter fallacious hopes, but more indifferent to fate, and more capable of accepting the world without the tyrannous imposition of our human and temporary demands.

Josiah Royce

Josiah Royce was William James's colleague at Harvard, and his good friend. He might also be said to have been, in Arnold Toynbee's language, the "challenge" to which James's philosophy was a "response." James spent most of his philosophical career trying to get rid of the Absolute—trying to show that the world is as full of discordance and unplanned chanciness as it seems to be, and that the effort of "tender-minded" rationalists to prove that everything is tidy and logical in the universe was mistaken. In immediate personal terms, this meant that James spent a good deal of his time debating with Royce. For Royce was the most eloquent spokesman America has had for the outlook, descended from Hegel, known as "philosophical idealism," which asserts that the universe, properly comprehended, is a single, harmonious, logical whole, the embodiment of an Absolute Mind. Royce's outlook is an excellent example of the kind of philosophy which Russell describes as an effort to use logic to prove the truth of the mystic's view of the world.

Royce is also an excellent example of the truth that a two-sided mind makes for philosophy. Born in a mining town in California in 1855, he entered the newly established University of California planning to become an engineer. But two teachers excited his interest, one a geologist and the other a poet, and Royce became a philosopher. A man with a literary bent—he began his teaching career as an instructor in English at California, and he once wrote a novel, *The Feud of Oakland Creek*—he also had talents as a logician and as a student of the sciences. Under the influence of Charles Peirce, he developed an interest in mathematical logic and made contributions to this subject. With the encouragement and support of James, Royce moved to Harvard in 1882, and became a professor of the history of philosophy. Thereafter, his learning and eloquence made him one of America's best-known and most influential teachers. George Santayana, looking back on his days as a student at Harvard, said that Royce at first made a greater impact on him even than James. Royce died in 1916.

Despite the philosophical differences between Royce and James, the two men have much in common. They are vivid writers; they are interested in the psychological sources of philosophy, and have a talent for evoking the feelings and attitudes that lie behind philosophical doctrines; and they consider that philosophy should be not only a specialist's subject but a discipline useful to laymen seeking guidance in life. But Royce, perhaps because of his desire for an embracing system, is more interested than James in the ways that various philosophies, though they seem different on the surface, supplement one another at a deeper level. And he stresses, more than James does, the role of the philosopher as the articulator of the ideals of his society, and as a social and cultural critic.

These are the themes that Royce develops in the selection that follows. Believing that there is a single embracing truth to be found, and that it is the task of philosophy to move toward this truth, Royce is naturally sensitive to the questions, Is the whole history of philosophy a history of failure? Why do philosophers continue to disagree? His answer suggests that philosophers, though they usually accomplish less than they wish, often accomplish much more than they realize.

The selection is taken from the introductory chapter of Royce's book *The Spirit of Modern Philosophy*, which was based on a series of lectures to a general audience. I have retitled it, using a phrase that Royce himself employs in describing his purpose, "The Human Significance of Philosophers."

The Human Significance of Philosophers

I

The assumption upon which these lectures are based is one that I may as well set forth at the very beginning. It is the assumption that Philosophy, in the proper sense of the term, is not a presumptuous effort to explain the mysteries of the world by means of any superhuman insight or extraordinary cunning, but has its origin and value in an attempt to give a reasonable account of our own personal attitude towards the more serious business of life. You philosophize when you reflect critically upon what you are actually doing in your world. What you are doing is of course, in the first place, living. And life involves passions, faiths, doubts, and courage. The critical inquiry into what all these things mean and imply is philosophy. We have our faith in life; we want reflectively to estimate this faith. We feel ourselves in a world of law and of significance. Yet why we feel this homelike sense of the reality and the worth of our world is a matter for criticism. Such a criticism of life, made elaborate and thorough-going, is a philosophy.

If this assumption of mine be well-founded, it follows that healthy philosophizing, or thorough-going self-criticism, is a very human and natural business, in which you are all occasionally, if not frequently engaged, and for which you will therefore from the start have a certain sympathy. Whether we will it or no, we all of us do philosophize. The difference between the temperament which loves technical philosophy and the temperament which can make nothing of so-called metaphysics is rather one of degree than of kind. The moral order, the evils of life, the authority of conscience, the intentions of God, how often have I not heard them discussed, and with a wise and critical skepticism, too, by men who seldom looked into books. The professional student of philosophy does, as his constant business, precisely what all other people do at moments. In the life of non-metaphysical people, reflection on destiny and the deepest truths of life occupies much the same place as music occupies in the lives of appreciative, but much distracted amateurs. The constant student of philosophy is merely the professional musician of reflective thought. He daily plays his scales in the form of what the scoffers call "chopping logic." He takes, in short, a delight in the technical subtleties of his art which makes his enthusiasm often incomprehensible to less devoted analysts of life. But his love for speculation is merely their own natural taste somewhat specialized. . . .

I I

All this, however, by way of mere opening suggestion. What you wish to know further . . . is, how this natural tendency to reflect critically upon life leads men to frame elaborate systems of philosophy, why it is that these systems have been so numerous and so varied in the past, and whether or no it seems to be true, as many hold, that the outcome of all this long and arduous labor of the philosophers has so far been nothing but doubtful speculation and hopeless variety of opinion. I suppose that a student who knows little as yet of the details of philosophic study feels as his greatest difficulty, when he approaches the topic for the first time, the confusing variety of the doctrines of the philosophers, joined as it is with the elaborateness and the obscurity that seem so characteristic of technical speculation. So much labor, you say, and all thus far in vain! For if the thinkers really aimed to bring to pass an agreement amongst enlightened persons about the great truths that are to be at the basis of human life, how sadly, you will say, they seemed to have failed! . . . They aimed, each one in his own private way, at the absolute, and so, if they failed, they must, you will think, have failed utterly. Each one raised, all alone, his own temple to his own god, declared that he, the first of men, possessed the long-sought truth, and undertook to initiate the world into his own mysteries. Hence it is that so many temples lie in ruins and so many images of false gods are shattered to fragments. I put the case thus strongly against the philosophers, because I am anxious to have you comprehend from the start how we are to face this significant preliminary difficulty of our topic. It may be true that the philosophers deal with life, and that, too, after a fashion known and occasionally tried by all of us. But is not their dealing founded upon vain pretense? How much better, you may say, to live nobly than to inquire thus learnedly and ineffectually into the mysteries of life? As the "Imitation of Christ" so skillfully states the case against philosophy, speaking indeed from the point of view of simple faith, but using words that doubters, too, can understand, "What doth it profit thee to enter into deep discussion concerning the Holy Trinity, if thou lack humility, and be thus displeasing to the Trinity? For verily it is not deep words that make a man holy and upright. I had rather feel contrition than be skillful in the definition thereof." . . .

Well, if such is the somewhat portentous case against philosophy, what can we say for philosophy? I answer first, that the irony of fate treats all human enterprises in precisely this way, if one has regard to the immediate intent of the men engaged in them. Philosophy is not alone in missing her directly sought aim. But true success lies often in serving ends that were higher than the ones we intended to serve. Surely no statesman ever founded an enduring social order; nay, one may add that no statesman ever produced even temporarily the precise social order that he meant to found. No poet ever gave us just the song that in his best moments he had meant and hoped to sing. No human life ever attained the fulfillment of the glorious dreams of its youth. And as for passing away, and being forgotten, and having one's mouth stopped with dust, surely one is not obliged to be either a saint or a sage to have that fate awaiting one. But still the saints and sages are not total failures, even if they are forgotten. There was an enduring element about them. They did not wholly die.

In view of all this, what we need to learn concerning philosophy is, not whether its leaders have in any sense failed or not, but whether its enterprise has been essentially a worthy one, one through which the human spirit has gained; whether the dark tower before which these Rolands have ended their pilgrimage has contained treasures in any way worthy of their quest. For a worthy quest always leaves good traces behind it, and more treasures are won by heroes than they visibly bring home in their own day. A more careful examination of the true office of philosophy may serve to show us, in fact, both why final success in it has been unattainable and why the partial successes have been worth the cost. Let such an examination be our next business.

III

The task of humanity, to wit, the task of organizing here on earth a worthy social life, is in one sense a hopelessly complex one. These are our endlessly numerous material foes, our environment, our diseases, our weaknesses. There are amongst us men ourselves, our rivalries, our selfish passions, our anarchical impulses, our blindness, our weak wills, our short and careful lives. These things all stand in the way of progress. For progress, for organization, for life, for spirituality, stand, as the best forces, our healthier social instincts, our courage, our endurance, and our insight. Civilization depends upon these. How hopeless every task of humanity, were not instinct often on the side of order and of spirituality. How quick would come our failure, were not courage and endurance ours. How blindly chance would drive us, did we not love insight for its own sake, and cultivate contemplation even when we know not yet what use we can make of it. And so, these three, if you will, to wit, healthy instinct, enduring courage, and contemplative insight, rule the civilized world. He who wants life to prosper longs to have these things alike honored and cultivated. They are brethren, these forces of human spirituality; they cannot do without one another; they are all needed.

Well, what I have called contemplative insight, that disposition and power of our minds whereby we study and enjoy truth, expresses itself early and late, as you know, in the form of a searching curiosity about our world and about life, a curiosity to which you in vain endeavor to set bounds. As the infant that studies its fist in the field of vision does not know as yet why this curiosity about space and about its own movements will be of service to it, so throughout life there is something unpractical, wayward, if so you choose to call it, in all our curious questionings concerning our world. The value of higher insight is seldom immediate. Science has an element of noble play about it. It is not the activity, it is the often remote outcome of science, that is of practical service. Insight is an ally of the moral nature of man, an ally of our higher social instincts, of our loyalty, of our courage, of our devotion; but the alliance is not always one intended directly by the spirit of curious inquiry itself. A singular craft of our nature links the most theoretical sorts of inquiry by unexpected ties with men's daily business. One plays with silk and glass and amber, with kites that one flies beneath thunder clouds, with frogs' legs and with acids. The play is a mere expression of a curiosity that former centuries might have called idle. But the result of this play recreates an industrial world. And so it is everywhere with our deeper curiosity. There is a sense in which it is all superfluous. Its immediate results seem but vanity. One could surely live without them; yet for the future, and for the spiritual life of mankind, these results are destined to become of vast import. Without this cunning contrivance of our busy brains, with their tireless curiosity and their unpractical wonderings, what could even sound instinct and the enduring heart have done to create the world of the civilized man?

Of all sorts of curiosity one of the most human and the most singular is the reflective curiosity whose highest expression is philosophy itself. This form of curiosity scrutinizes our own lives, our deepest instincts, our most characteristic responses to the world in which we live, our typical "reflex actions." It tries to bring us to a self-consciousness as to our temperaments. Our temperaments, our instincts, are in one sense fatal. We cannot directly alter them. What philosophy does is to find them out, to bring them to the light, to speak in words the very essence of them. And so the historical office of the greatest philosophers has always been to reword, as it were, the meaning and the form of the most significant life, temperaments, and instincts of their own age. As man is social, as no man lives alone, as your temperament is simply the sum total of your social "reflex actions," is just your typical bearing towards your fellows, the great philosopher, in reflecting on his own deepest instincts and faiths, inevitably describes, in the terms of his system, the characteristic attitude of his age and people. So, for instance, Plato and Aristotle, taken together, express for us, in their philosophical writings, the essence of the highest Greek faith and life. The Greek love of the beautiful and reverence for the state, the Greek union of intellectual freedom with conventional bondage to the forms of politics and of religion, the whole Greek attitude towards the universe, in so far as the Athens of that age could embody it, are made articulate in enduring form in the speculations of these representative men. They consciously interpret this Hellenic life,—they do also more: they criticise it. Plato especially is in some of his work a fairly destructive analyst of his nation's faith. And yet it is just this faith, incorporated as it was into his own temperament, bred into his every fibre, that he must needs somehow express in his doctrine. And now perhaps you may already see why there is of necessity nothing absolute, nothing final, about much that a Plato himself may have looked upon as absolute and as final in his work. Greek life was not all of human life; Greek life was doomed to pass away; Greek instincts and limitations could not be eternal. . . . If philosophy criticises, estimates, and to that end rewords life, if the great philosopher expresses in his system the most characteristic faiths and passions of his age, then indeed the limitation of the age will be in a sense the limitation of the philosophy; and with the life whose temperament it reflectively embodied the philosophy will pass away. It will pass away, but it will not be lost. A future humanity will, if civilization healthily progresses, inherit the old kingdom, and reëmbody the truly essential and immortal soul of its old life. This new humanity, including in itself the spirit of the old, will need something, at least, of the old philosophy to express in reflective fashion its own attitude towards the universe. . . . No, the philosopher's work is not lost when, in one sense, his system seems to have been refuted by death, and when time seems to have scattered to scorn the words of his dust-filled mouth. His immediate end may have been unattained; but thousands of years may not be long enough to develop for humanity the full significance of his reflective thought.

Insight, this curious scrutiny of ours into the truth, keeps here, as you will see, its immediately unpractical, its ultimately significant character. There is indeed a sense in which life has no need of the philosopher. He does not invent life, nor does he lead in its race; he follows after; he looks on; he is no prophet to inspire men; he has a certain air of the playful about him. Plato, in a famous passage, makes sport of the men of the world, who are driven by business, who are oppressed by the law courts, whose only amusement is evil gossip about their neighbors. The philosopher, on the contrary, according to Plato, has infinite leisure, and accordingly thinks of the infinite, but does not know who his next neighbor is, and never dreams of the law courts, or of finishing his business at any fixed hour. His life is a sort of artistic game; his are not the passions of the world; his is the reflection that comprehends the world. The Thracian servant maids laugh at him, as the one in the story laughed at Thales, because he stares at the heavens, and hence occasionally falls into wells. But what is he in the sight of the gods, and what are the servant maids? When *they* are some day asked to look into the heavens, and to answer concerning the truth, what scorn will not be their lot? After some such fashion does Plato seek to glorify the contemplative separation from the pettiness of life which shall give to the philosopher his freedom. And yet, as we know, this freedom, this sublime playfulness, of even a Plato, does not suggest the real justification of his work. This game of reflection is like all the rest of our insight, indirectly valuable because from it all there is a return to life possible, and in case of a great thinker like Plato, certain to occur. The coming humanity shall learn from the critic who, standing indeed outside of life, embodied in his reflection the meaning of it.

Thus far, then, my thought has been simply this. Humanity depends, for its spirituality and its whole civilization, upon faiths and passions that are in the first place instinctive, inarticulate, and in part unconscious. The philosopher tries to formulate and to criticise these instincts. What he does will always have a two-fold limitation. It will, on the one hand, be criticism from the point of view of a single man, of a single age, of a single group of ideals, as Plato or Aristotle embodied the faith of but one great age of Greek life, and did that from a somewhat private and personal point of view. This first necessary limitation of the philosopher's work makes his system less absolute, less truthful, less final than he had meant it to be. Another humanity will have a new faith, a new temperament, and in so far will need a new philosophy. Only the final and absolute humanity, only the ultimate and perfect civilization, would possess, were such a civilization possible on earth, the final and absolute philosophy. But this limitation, as we have seen, while it dooms a philosopher to one kind of defeat, doesn't deprive his work of worth. His philosophy is capable of becoming and remaining just as permanently significant as is his civilization and its temperament; his reflective work will enter into future thought in just the same fashion as the deeper passions of his age will beget the spiritual temper of those who are to come after.

There remains as second limitation, so we have seen, the always seemingly unfruitful critical attitude of the philosopher. He speculates, but does not prophesy; he criticises, but does not create. Yet this limitation he shares with all theory, with all insight; and the limitation is itself only partial and in great measure illusory. Criticism means self-consciousness, and self-consciousness means renewed activity on a higher plane. The reflective play of one age becomes the passion of another. Plato creates Utopias, and the Christian faith of Europe afterwards gives them meaning. Contemplation gives birth to future conduct, and so the philosopher also becomes, in his own fashion, a world-builder.

I V

But now, having said so much for the philosopher, I may venture to say yet more, that if his work is not lost in so far as it enters into the life of the humanity which comes after him, there is yet another and a deeper sense in which his labor is not in vain. For truth is once for all manifold, and especially is the truth about man's relation to the universe manifold. The most fleeting passion, if so be it is only deep and humane, may reveal to us some aspect of truth which no other moment of life can fully express. I know how difficult it is to comprehend that seemingly opposing assertions about the world may, in a deeper sense, turn out to be equally true. . . . Young thinkers always find refutation easy, and old doctrines not hard to transcend; and yet what if the soul of the old doctrines should be true just because the new doctrines seemingly oppose, but actually complete them? Our reflective insights, in following our life, will find now this, now that aspect of things prominent. What if all the aspects should contain truth? What if our failure thus far to find and to state the absolute philosophy were due to the fact, not that all the philosophies thus far have been essentially false, but that the truth is so wealthy as to need not only these, but yet other and future expressions to exhaust its treasury? . . .

In fact the reason why there is as yet no one final philosophy may be very closely allied to the reason why there is no final and complete poem. Life is throughout a complicated thing; the truth of the spirit remains an inexhaustible treasure house of experience; and hence no individual experience, whether it be the momentary insight of genius recorded in the lyric poem, or the patient accumulation of years of professional plodding through the problems of philosophy, will ever fully tell all the secrets which life has to reveal.

It is for just this reason, so I now suggest, that when you study philosophy, you have to be tolerant, receptive, willing to look at the world from many sides, fearless as to the examination of what seem to be even dangerous doctrines, patient in listening to views that look even abhorrent to common sense. It is useless to expect a simple and easy account of so paradoxical an affair as this our universe and our life. When you first look into philosophy you are puzzled and perhaps frightened by those manifold opinions of the philosophers of which we have thus far had so much to say. "If they, who have thought so deeply, differ so much," you say, "then what hope is there that the truth can ever be known?" But if you examine further you find that this variety, better studied, is on its more human side largely an expression of the liveliness and individuality of the spiritual temperaments of strong men. The truth is not in this case "in the middle." The truth is rather "the whole." . . . For grant that the philosophers are all in fact expressing not dead truth, but the essence of human life, then because this life is many-sided, the individual expressions cannot perfectly agree. It is the union of many such insights that will be the one true view of life. Or again, using the bolder phrases, let us say that all these thinkers are trying to comprehend a little of the life of the one World Spirit who lives and moves in all things. Then surely this life, which in our world needs both the antelopes and the tigers to embody its endless vigor, that life which the frost and cold, the ice and snow, do bless and magnify, is not a life which any one experience can exhaust. All the philosophers are needed, not merely to make jarring assertions about it, but to give us embodiments now of this, now of that fragment of its wealth and its eternity. And in saying this I don't counsel you in your study of philosophy merely to jumble together all sorts of sayings of this thinker and of that, and then to declare, as makers of eclectic essays and of books of extracts love to say, "This is all somehow great and true." What I mean is that, apart from the private whims and the non-essential accidents of each great philosopher, his doctrine will contain for the critical student an element of permanent truth about life, a truth which in its isolation may indeed contradict the view of his equally worthy co-workers, but which, in union, in synthesis, in vital connection with its very bitterest opposing doctrines, may turn out to be an organic portion of the genuine treasure of humanity. . . .

v

Thus far I have spoken of the various opinions and of the general human significance of the philosophers. I called attention, also, a little while since, to the apparently unpractical attitude that they assume towards life. In this connection I have already suggested that their criticism of life has often its destructive side. In these present days, when

philosophy is frequently so negative, it is precisely this destructive, this
skeptically critical character of philosophy, that to the minds of many constitutes its best-known character, and its most obvious danger. It is not
mine to defend recent philosophy from the charge of being often cruelly
critical. To many of us it might, indeed, in pity be said: "Mayest thou never
know what thou art." I have myself more than once felt the pang, as I have
studied philosophy, of finding out to my sorrow what I am. I have, therefore, many times lamented that philosopsy is indeed often so sternly and
so negatively critical of many things that our hearts have loved and prized.
If any one fears the pangs of self-consciousness, it is not my office to
counsel him to get it. But I must, indeed, point out here that when a wise
philosophy is destructive, the true fault lies not with the critic who finds
the wound in our faith, but with the faith that has secretly nursed its own
wounds in unconsciousness. Philosophy, in the true sense of that word,
never destroys an ideal that is worth preserving. Coming to consciousness
of yourself can only bring to light weakness in case the weakness already
exists in you. If you fear, I say, the pang of such a discovery,—and, as I
can assure you, the pang is often keen,—then do not try philosophy. For
the rest, however, this relation of philosophy to positive faith is one whereof
I may speak in yet a very few words before I leave it. Let me point out
in what sense philosophy is critical, but in what sense also it can hope to
be constructive.

Of course philosophy, as thus far described, is sure to begin at once,
if it can, with inquiries into the largest and most significant instincts, the
deepest faiths of humanity. These, when it discovers them, it will single out
and criticise. Hence, indeed, the philosophers are always talking of such
problems as duty and God. Hence they inquire how we can come to know
whether there is any external world at all, and, if so, whether this world
is to be treated as dead matter, or as live mind. Hence they are curious to
study our ideas of natural law, of moral freedom, of time, of space, of
causation, of self. They pry into the concerns of faith as if these were theirs
by divine right. They are not only prying, they are on one side of their
activity merciless, skeptical, paradoxical, inconsiderate. They don't ask,
it would seem, how dear your faith is to you; they analyze it, as they would
the reflex action of a starfish, or the behavior of a pigeon; and then they try
to estimate faith objectively, as an editor looks critically at a love-sonnet
which somebody has sent him (a sonnet written with the author's heart's
blood), and weighs it coolly and cruelly before he will consent to find it
available. Even so the philosopher has his standard of the availability of
human faiths. You have to satisfy this with your creed before he will
approve you. All this sometimes seems cynical, just as the editor's coolness
may become provoking. But then, as you know, the editor, with all his
apparent cruelty, is a man of sympathy and of more than negative aims. He
has to consider what he calls availability, because he has his critical public

to please. And the philosopher—he, too, has to be critical and to seem cruel, because he also has a public to please with his estimate; and his chosen public ought to be no less than the absolute judge, the world spirit himself, in whose eyes the philosopher can find favor only if he be able to sift the truth from the error. That is why he is rigid. Nothing but an absolute critical standard ought to satisfy him, because he wants nothing short of the truth itself. He will fail to get it, but then, as I have said, we all of us fail more or less in some career or other; and the metaphysician, with his one talent of critical estimate, must do what he can.

Yet I hasten to correct this seemingly too lifeless a picture of the philosopher's cruel analysis of passion, by a reference to the thoughts upon which I have already dwelt. From the often disheartening difficulties and incompleteness of the human search for absolute truth, we who read philosophy continually find ourselves returning, hand to hand with the author himself, to the world of the concrete passions which he criticises. We find this world at each return more fair and yet more serious, because we know it better. . . . We have criticised, so much the more cheerfully may we enjoy. I once saw something of a pair of literary lovers, friends of mine, who, being a trifle reflective, were prone to amuse themselves by affecting to treat each other's productions with a certain editorial coldness and severity of critical estimate. They wrote poems to each other, suppressing or changing of course the names, and then each, wholly ignoring whom this poem might be intended to mean, used to pick the other's work to pieces with an air of gentle and pathetic disdain. "Here the sentiment somehow failed to justify its object, being expressed unmusically. There the experiment was a clever one, but the lines were such as a dispassionate observer (like either of us who should happen not to be the author) could not approve, might even smile at." These people never precisely quarreled, to my knowledge, at least over their literary criticism. I was not able to make out altogether why they did this sort of thing, but, so far as I could discover, they both liked it, and were the better lovers for it. I conjecture that their delight must have resembled the kind of joy that philosophical students take in analyzing life. Let me admit frankly: it is indeed the joy, if you like, of playing cat and mouse with your dearest other self. It is even somewhat like the joy, if so you choose to declare, which infants take in that primitive form of hide and seek that is suited to their months. "Where is my truth, my life, my faith, my temperament?" says the philosopher. And if, some volumes further on in the exposition of his system, he says, "Oh! *there* it is," the healthy babies will be on his side in declaring that such reflections are not wholly without their rational value. But why do I thus apparently degrade speculation by again deliberately comparing it with a game? Because, I answer, in one sense, all consciousness is a game, a series of longings and of reflections which it is easy to call superfluous if witnessed from without. The justification of consciousness is the having of it. And this magnificent play of the spirit with itself, this infantile love of rewinning its own wealth ever anew through deliberate loss, through seeking, and through joyous recognition, what is this, indeed, but the pastime of the divine life itself? We enter into the world of the spirit just when even the tragedy of life becomes for our sight as much a divine game as a divine tragedy, when we know that the world is not only serious, terrible, cruel, but is also a world where a certain grim humor of the gods is at home; when we see in it a world, too, where a serene and childlike confidence is justified, a world where courage is in place as well as reverence, and sport as well as seriousness; where, above all, the genius of reflection, expressing at once vast experience of life and a certain infantile cheerfulness or even sportiveness of mood, rightfully lets itself loose in the freest form, now assuming a stern and critical air, now demurely analyzing, as if there were nothing else to do, now prying into men's hearts like a roguish boy playing with precious jewels, now pretending that all faith is dead, now serenely demonstrating unexpected truths, and, last of all, plunging back again into life with the shout of them that triumph.

VI

. . . There is a great deal in every noteworthy metaphysical treatise which can be grasped only by special study. . . . [But] I confess to you that, although I myself often take a certain personal delight in the mere subtleties of speculation, although I also enjoy at times that miserliness which makes the professional student hoard up the jewels of reflection for the sake of gloating over their mere hardness and glitter, I find always that when I come to think of the thing fairly, there is, after all, no beauty in a metaphysical system, which does not spring from its value as a record of a spiritual experience. I love the variety of the philosophers, as I love the variety of the thoughtful looks which light up earnest young faces. I love all these because they express passion, wonder, truth. But alas for me if ever I have for professional reasons to study a book behind whose technical subtleties I can catch no glimpse of the manly heart of its author. His conclusions may be sound. I shall then hate him only the more for that. Error may be dull if it chooses; but there is no artistic blasphemy equal to so placing the harp of truth as to make it sound harsh and wooden when you strike it fairly. Philosophical books I have read, with whose doctrines, as doctrines, I have even been forced in great measure to agree; and yet, so lifeless, so bloodless, were their authors, so reptilian were the cold and slowly writhing sentences in which their thought was expressed, that I have laid down such volumes with a sense of disgrace and rebellion, "bitterly ashamed," as a friend of mine has expressed the same feeling in my hearing, "bitterly ashamed to find myself living in a universe whose truth could possibly be made so inefficacious and uninteresting." To be sure, in saying all this I am far from desiring to make technical metaphysics easy, for the study is a laborious one; and there are many topics in logic, in the theory of the sciences, and in ethics, to whose comprehension there is no royal road. But then, once your eyes opened, and you will indeed find subjects that at first seemed dry and inhuman full of life and even of passion; as, for instance, few sciences are in their elementary truths more enticing to the initiated, more coy and baffling to the reflective philosophical student, in fact, more romantic, than is the Differential Calculus. But if such matters lie far beyond our present field, I mention them only to show that even the hardest and least popular reflective researches are to be justified, in the long run, by their bearings upon life.

Friedrich Waismann

A search for the meaning and use of philosophy leads one to ask, What is philosophy? The problem has long been a favorite subject for philosophers. One way of approaching it is to consider the various philosophies simply as expressions of different temperaments. So conceived, philosophy becomes a form of literature, and whether or not philosophers agree is then beside the point.

And yet, while there is much to be said for this interpretation of the nature of philosophy, it is not entirely satisfactory. For philosophy is also plainly a discipline, an exchange not simply of reactions to the world but of arguments. Philosophers give every appearance of seeking convergence of opinion, and of trying to compel others, by force of reason, to agree with them. But is philosophy then to be construed as a science? This definition, too, runs into difficulties. For if philosophy is a science, why is it so hard to produce examples of arguments that every competent philosopher will accept?

This is the problem to which Friedrich Waismann addresses himself in the fascinating essay that follows. He takes an unexpected approach to the issue. Philosophers do argue, he says, and their arguments are of the greatest importance. But it is a mistake to imagine that philosophers prove anything. Proof, in fact, isn't their real business. And yet they aren't merely expressing personal reactions to the world, and the choice among philosophies isn't just based on individual preference. Philosophies are concerned with vision or insight, and there are ways of distinguishing between those visions and insights that aid the search for knowledge and self-awareness and those that don't. Thus, philosophy is part of man's quest for truth, even though philosophies themselves cannot, in the main, be called true or false.

Waismann was born in Vienna in 1896 and was an associate of Moritz Schlick, one of the central figures in the famed Vienna circle, which developed the philosophy of "logical positivism," or "logical empiricism." Waismann fled central Europe under Hitler to settle in England, and became a member of a vigorous community of philosophers at Oxford, where he taught until his death in 1959.

The members of the Vienna circle were mainly men with a strong scientific background—Waismann's was in mathematics—and they were well trained in the methods of modern logic. They used these methods to explore the logical structure of the sciences, and to introduce greater precision and clarity into the discussion of old philosophical issues. On the whole, this predilection for logic made them suspicious of classic types of speculative philosophy, and gave their work a pronounced quality of antagonism, resembling Hume's, toward airy and abstruse ideas that could not be formulated in clear logical form or given a definite experimental content. Most of the members of the Vienna circle rejected the efforts of traditional philosophers to discuss the character of a world that lies beyond human observation, and some of them, in this vein, declared that "metaphysics is nonsense."

Among the approaches that developed as an expression of this point of view was one that is known as "therapeutic positivism." In this approach philosophical problems are depicted as the consequences of unconscious confusions of thought that are embedded in our language and mental habits, and the task of the philosopher, it is held, is to dispel these confusions. Accordingly, philosophical problems are not so much to be solved as *dissolved*: they are puzzles which come from mistaken analogies, like the implicit analogy that St. Augustine draws between space and time, or from assuming that a word which has a meaning in one setting has the very same meaning in another setting. For example, the word "cause" as it is used in physics doesn't have the same meaning that it has when one says, "My concern for justice causes me to impose a punishment on you." The failure to see the shift in the meaning of "cause" can lead to puzzles about the possibility of free choice and to other philosophical paradoxes. Once such intellectual tangles are unraveled, the answer to a philosophical question turns out to be that it isn't a well-conceived question. It represents a trick with words, or rather it is a consequence of the tricks that words play on their users.

In the first stage of his philosophical career Ludwig Wittgenstein, who exercised a great influence on Waismann, developed this therapeutic positivism. But he went beyond this approach, and so does Waismann. As Waismann argues in the essay we are about to read, "dissolving" St. Augustine's puzzle about time doesn't reduce it to worthlessness. The propounding of the question has itself had important effects—an uprooting of stodgy mental habits, the communication of a radical and fresh insight— that make it foolish to call it simply a linguistic error. Indeed, some of the leading philosophers who are known as logical empiricists are anything but unequivocal devotees of reason and scientific method. Wittgenstein has a pronounced mystical strain: he admires the visionary Kierkegaard above all other nineteenth-century philosophers. And Waismann, too, has great sympathy for mysticism, and refuses to rule out mystical illumination as a source of valid insight into the truth.

Moreover, the early interest of Waismann and other linguistic philosophers in the mistakes into which language can lead us was gradually transformed into an interest in the truths which may also be hidden in language's structure. A number of such philosophers came to use methods of linguistic analysis not simply for the purpose of dismissing old metaphysical questions, but for the purpose of finding clues to new answers to them. At Oxford, Waismann became a critic of the earlier preoccupation of the Vienna circle with "clarity," and with artificial, deliberately constructed, logical languages. He stressed that ordinary language, the language of everyday speech, is a far richer medium of thought. It has an "open texture," a flexibility and suppleness that allows men to use it in relation to the unpredictable intricacies of their daily affairs. Accordingly, serious mistakes in philosophy are likely to occur, he argues, when the attempt is made to fit human thought, as it takes shape in ordinary speech, to the Procrustean bed of a formal logical system. One reason that philosophy can't "prove" anything is that its instrument of proof—ordinary language—has too elusive a structure to permit sharp, unambiguous demonstrations in the style of geometry or mathematical logic. But this absence of precision doesn't mean that philosophy has no function. It is an instrument for breaking through existing language- or thought-forms, and thus bringing hitherto unnoticed resources of language to the surface.

Logical empiricism and linguistic philosophy are often denounced as approaches which substitute semantic qubbles for philosophic vision. This criticism applies to some of the second-rate representatives of these tendencies; similarly, second-rate representatives of the tradition of William James can sound like exponents of faith cures, and second-rate disciples of Josiah Royce like publicists for the power of positive thinking. But this essay by Waismann shows, I think, that the popular disparaging views of logical empiricism and linguistic philosophy do an injustice to the better representatives of these approaches. Indeed, Waismann is not simply the "representative" of an approach to philosophy. He is an idiosyncratic thinker with a mind of his own.

Waismann wrote this essay as a contribution to a symposium, *Contemporary British Philosophy,* third series, edited by H. D. Lewis and published in 1956. The editor had asked him, "What is philosophy?" Waismann's answer follows.

How I See Philosophy

I

What Philosophy is? I don't know, nor have I a set formula to offer. Immediately I sit down to contemplate the question I am flooded with so many ideas, tumbling over one another, that I cannot do justice to all of them. I can merely make an attempt, a very inadequate one, to sketch with a few strokes what the lie of the land seems to me to be, tracing some lines of thought without entering upon a close-knit argument.

It is, perhaps, easier to say what philosophy is not than what it is. The first thing, then, I should like to say is that philosophy, as it is practised today, is very unlike science; and this in three respects: in philosophy there are no proofs; there are no theorems; and there are no questions which can be decided, Yes or No. In saying that there are no proofs I do not mean to say that there are no arguments. Arguments certainly there are, and first-rate philosophers are recognized by the originality of their arguments; only these do not work in the sort of way they do in mathematics or in the sciences.

There are many things beyond proof: the existence of material objects, of other minds, indeed of the external world, the validity of induction, and so on. Gone are the days when philosophers were trying to prove all sorts of things: that the soul is immortal, that this is the best of all possible worlds and the rest, or to refute, by "irrefutable" argument and with relish, materialism, positivism and what not. Proof, refutation—these are dying words in philosophy (though G. E. Moore still "proved" to a puzzled world that it exists. What can one say to this—save, perhaps, that he is a great prover before the Lord?).

But can it be *proved* that there are no proofs in philosophy? No; for one thing, such a proof, if it were possible, would by its very existence establish what it was meant to confute. But why suppose the philosopher to have an I.Q. so low as to be unable to learn from the past? Just as the constant failure of attempts at constructing a perpetual motion has in the end led to something positive in physics, so the efforts to construct a philosophical "system," going on for centuries and going out of fashion fairly recently, tell their tale. This, I think, is part of the reason why philosophers today are getting weaned from casting their ideas into deductive moulds, in the grand style of Spinoza.

What I want to show in this article is that it is quite wrong to look at philosophy as though it had for its aim to provide theorems but had lamentably failed to do so. The whole conception changes when one comes to realize that what philosophers are concerned with is something different —neither discovering new propositions nor refuting false ones nor checking and re-checking them as scientists do. For one thing, proofs require premisses. Whenever such premisses have been set up in the past, even tentatively, the discussion at once challenged them and shifted to a deeper level. Where there are no proofs there are no theorems either. (To write down lists of propositions "proved" by Plato or Kant: a pastime strongly to be recommended.) Yet the failure to establish a sort of Euclidean system of philosophy based on some suitable "axioms" is, I submit, neither a mere accident nor a scandal but deeply founded in the nature of philosophy.

Yet there are questions; (and arguments). Indeed, a philosopher is a man who senses as it were hidden crevices in the build of our concepts where others only see the smooth path of commonplaceness before them.

Questions but no answers? Decidedly odd. The oddness may lessen when we take a look at them at closer range. Consider two famous examples: Achilles and the tortoise, and the astonishment of St. Augustine when confronted with the fact of memory. He is amazed, not at some striking feat of memory, but at there being such a thing as memory at all. A sense-impression, say a smell or a taste, floats before us and disappears. One moment it is here and the next it is gone. But in the galleries of the memory pale copies of it are stored up after its death. From there I can drag them out when and as often as I wish, like, and yet strangely unlike, the original—unlike in that they are not perishable like the momentary impression: what was transitory has been arrested and has achieved duration. But who can say how this change comes about?

Here the very fact of memory feels mystifying in a way in which ordinary questions asking for information do not; and *of course* it is not a factual question. What is it?

From Plato to Schopenhauer philosophers are agreed that the source of their philosophizing is wonder. What gives rise to it is nothing recondite and rare but precisely those things which stare us in the face: memory, motion, general ideas. (Plato: What does "horse" mean? A single particular horse? No, for it may refer to *any* horse; *all* the horses, the total class? No, for we may speak of this or that horse. But if it means neither a single horse nor all horses, what *does* it mean?) The idealist is shaken in just the same way when he comes to reflect that he has, in Schopenhauer's words, "no knowledge of the sun but only of an eye that sees a sun, and no knowledge of the earth but only of a hand that feels an earth." Can it be, then, that nothing whatever is known to us except our own consciousness?

In looking at such questions, it seems as if the mind's eye were growing dim and as if everything, even that which ought to be absolutely clear, was becoming oddly puzzling and unlike its usual self. To bring out what seems to be peculiar to these questions one might say that they are not so much questions as tokens of a profound uneasiness of mind. Try for a moment to put yourself into the frame of mind of which Augustine was possessed when he asked: How is it possible to measure time? Time consists of past, present and future. The past can't be measured, it is gone; the future can't be measured, it is not yet here; and the present can't be measured, it has no extension. Augustine knew of course how time is measured and this was not his concern. What puzzled him was how it is *possible* to measure time, seeing that the past hour cannot be lifted out and placed alongside the present hour for comparison. Or look at it this way: what is measured is in the past, the measuring in the present: how can that be?

The philosopher as he ponders over some such problem has the appearance of a man who is deeply disquieted. He seems to be straining to grasp something which is beyond his powers. The words in which such a question presents itself do not quite bring out into the open the real point—which may, perhaps more aptly, be described as the recoil from the incomprehensible. If, on a straight railway journey, you suddenly come in sight of the very station you have just left behind, there will be terror, accompanied perhaps by slight giddiness. That is exactly how the philosopher feels when he says to himself, "Of course time can be measured; but how *can* it?" It is as though, up to now, he had been passing heedlessly over the difficulties, and now, all of a sudden, he notices them and asks himself in alarm, "But how can that be?" That is a sort of question which we only ask when it is the very facts themselves which confound us, when something about them strikes us as preposterous.

Kant, I fancy, must have felt something of the sort when he suddenly found the existence of geometry a puzzle. Here we have propositions as clear and transparent as one would wish, prior, it seems, to all experience; at the same time they apply miraculously to the real world. How is that possible? Can the mind, unaided by experience, in some dark manner actually fathom the properties of real things? Looked upon in this way, geometry takes on a disturbing air.

We all have our moments when something quite ordinary suddenly strikes us as queer—for instance, when time appears to us as a curious thing. Not that we are often in this frame of mind; but on some occasions, when we look at things in a certain way, unexpectedly they seem to change as though by magic: they stare at us with a puzzling expression, and we begin to wonder whether they can possibly be the things we have known all our lives.

"Time flows" we say—a natural and innocent expression, and yet one pregnant with danger. It flows "equably," in Newton's phrase, at an even rate. What can this mean? When something moves, it moves with a definite speed (and speed means: rate of change in time). To ask with what speed time moves, i.e. to ask how quickly time changes in time, is to ask the unaskable. It also flows, again in Newton's phrase, "without relation to anything external." How are we to figure that? Does time flow on irrespective of what happens in the world? Would it flow on even if everything in heaven and on earth came to a sudden standstill as Schopenhauer believed? For if this were not so, he said, time would have to stop with the stopping of the clock and move with the clock's movement. How odd: time flows at the same rate and yet without speed; and perhaps even without anything to occur in it? The expression is puzzling in another way. "I can never catch myself being in the past or in the future," someone might say; "whenever I think or perceive or breathe the word 'now,' I am in the present; therefore I am *always* in the present." In saying this, he may think of the present moment as a bridge as it were from which he is looking down at the "river of time." Time is gliding along underneath the bridge, but the "now" does not take part in the motion. What was future passes into the present (is just below the bridge) and then into the past, while the onlooker, the "self" or the "I," is always in the present. "Time flows *through* the 'now,'" he may feel to be a quite expressive metaphor. Yes, it sounds all right—until he suddenly comes to his senses and, with a start, realizes, "But surely the moment flies?" (Query: How to succeed in wasting time? Answer: In this way, for instance—by trying, with eyes closed or staring vacantly in front of oneself, to catch the present moment as it is flitting by.) He may come now to look at matters in a different way. He sees himself advancing through time towards the future, and with this goes a suggestion of being active, just as at other times he may see himself floating down the stream whether he likes it or not. "What exactly is it that is moving—the events in time or the present moment?" he may wonder. In the first case, it looks to him as if time were moving while he stands still; in the second case as if he were moving through time. "How exactly is it," he may say in a dubious voice, "am I always in the present? Is the present always eluding me?" Both ring true in a way; but they contradict each other. Again, does it make sense to ask, "At what time is the present moment?" Yes, no doubt; but how *can* it, if the "now" is but the fixed point from which the dating of any event ultimately receives its sense?

So he is pulled to and fro: "I am always in the present, yet it slips through my fingers; I am going forward in time—no, I am carried down the stream." He is using different pictures, each in its way quite appropriate to the occasion; yet when he tries to apply them jointly they clash. "What a queer thing time must be," he may say to himself with a puzzled look on his face, "what after all *is* time?"—expecting, half-expecting perhaps, that the answer will reveal to him time's hidden essence. Ranged beyond the intellectual are deeper levels of uneasiness—terror of the inevitability of time's passage, with all the reflections upon life that this forces upon us. Now all these anxious doubts release themselves in the question, "What is time?" (*En passant* this is a hint that *one* answer will never do—will never remove all these doubts that break out afresh on different levels and yet are expressed in the same form of words.)

As we all know what time is and yet cannot say what it is it feels mystifying; and precisely because of its elusiveness it catches our imagination. The more we look at it the more we are puzzled: it seems charged with paradoxes. "What is time? What is this being made up of movement only without anything that is moving?" (Schopenhauer). How funny to have it bottled up! "I've got here in my hand the most potent, the most enigmatic, the most fleeting of all essences—Time." (Logan Pearsall Smith of an hour-glass.) For Shelley it is an "unfathomable sea! whose waves are years," a "shoreless flood," for Proust—well, why not leave something to the reader?

But isn't the answer to this that what mystifies us lies in the *noun* form "the time"? Having a notion embodied in the form of a noun almost irresistibly makes us turn round to look for what it is "the name of." We are trying to catch the shadows cast by the opacities of speech. A wrong analogy absorbed into the forms of our language produces mental discomfort; (and the feeling of discomfort, when it refers to language, is a profound one). "All sounds, all colors . . . evoke indefinite and yet precise emotions, or, as I prefer to think call down among us certain disembodied powers whose footsteps over our hearts we call emotions" (W. B. Yeats).

Yet the answer is a prosaic one: don't ask what time is but how the *word* "time" is being used. Easier said than done; for if the philosopher rectifies the use of language, ordinary language has "the advantage of being in possession of declensions" to speak with Lichtenberg, and thus renews its spell over him, luring him on into the shadow chase. It is perhaps only when we turn to languages of a widely different grammatical structure that the way towards such possibilities of interpretation is entirely barred. "It is highly probable that philosophers within the domain of the Ural-Altaic languages (where the subject-concept is least developed) will look differently 'into the world' and be found on paths of thought different from those of the Indo-Europeans or Mussulmans" (Nietzsche).

II

It may be well at this point to remind ourselves that the words "question" and "answer," "problem" and "solution" are not always used in their most trite sense. It is quite obvious that we often have to do something very different to find the way out of a difficulty. A problem of politics is solved by adopting a certain line of action, the problems of novelists perhaps by the invention of devices for presenting the inmost thoughts and feelings of their characters; there is the painter's problem of how to suggest depth or movement on the canvas, the stylistic problem of expressing things not yet current, not yet turned into cliché; there are a thousand questions of technology which are answered, not by the discovery of some truth, but by a practical achievement; and there is of course the "social question." In philosophy, the real problem is not to find the answer to a given question but to find a sense for it. . . .

Many are the types of bewilderment: there is the obsessional doubt— can I ever know that other people have experiences, that they see, hear and feel as I do? Can I be sure that memory does not always deceive me? Are there really material objects and not only sense-impressions "of" them? There is the doubtlike uneasiness—what sort of being is possessed by numbers? There is the anxiety-doubt—are we really free? This doubt has taken many different forms one of which I shall single out for discussion— the question, namely, whether the law of excluded middle, when it refers to statements in the future tense, forces us into a sort of logical Predestination. A typical argument is this. If it is true now that I shall do a certain thing tomorrow, say, jump into the Thames, then no matter how fiercely I resist, strike out with hands and feet like a madman, when the day comes I cannot help jumping into the water; whereas, if this prediction is false now, then whatever efforts I may make, however many times I may nerve and brace myself, look down at the water and say to myself, One, two, three—," it is impossible for me to spring. Yet that the prediction is either true or false is itself a necessary truth, asserted by the law of excluded middle. From this the startling consequence seems to follow that it is already now decided what I shall do tomorrow, that indeed the entire future is somehow fixed, logically preordained. Whatever I do and whichever way I decide, I am merely moving along lines clearly marked in advance which lead me towards my appointed lot. We are all, in fact, marionettes. If we are not prepared to swallow *that*, then—and there is a glimmer of hope in the "then"—there is an alternative open to us. We need only renounce the law of excluded middle for statements of this kind, and with it the validity of ordinary logic, and all will be well. Descriptions of what will happen are, at present, neither true nor false. (This sort of argument was actually propounded by Lukasiewicz in favor of a three-valued logic with "possible" as a third truth-value alongside "true" and "false.")

The way out is clear enough. The asker of the question has fallen into the error of so many philosophers: of giving an answer before stopping to consider the question. For is he clear what he is asking? He seems to suppose that a statement referring to an event in the future is at present undecided, neither true nor false, but that when the event happens the proposition enters into a sort of new state, that of being true. But how are we to figure the change from "undecided" to "true"? Is it sudden or gradual? At what moment does the statement "it will rain tomorrow" begin to be true? When the first drop falls to the ground? And supposing that it will not rain, when will the statement begin to be false? Just at the end of the day, at 12 P.M. sharp? Supposing that the event *has* happened, that the statement *is* true, will it remain so for ever? If so, in what way? Does it remain uninterruptedly true, at every moment of day and night? Even if there were no one about to give it any thought? Or is it true only at the moments when it is being thought of? In that case, how long does it remain true? For the duration of the thought? We wouldn't know how to answer these questions; this is due not to any particular ignorance or stupidity on our part but to the fact that something has gone wrong with the way the words "true" and "false" are applied here.

If I say, "It is true that I was in America," I am saying that I was in America and no more. That in uttering the words "It is true that—" I take responsibility upon myself is a different matter that does not concern the present argument. The point is that in making a statement prefaced by the words "It is true that" I do not *add* anything to the factual information I give you. *Saying* that something is true is not *making* it true: cp. the criminal lying in court, yet every time he is telling a lie protesting, his hand on his heart, that he is telling the truth.

What is characteristic of the use of the words "true" and "false" and what the pleader of logical determinism has failed to notice is this. "It is true" and "it is false," while they certainly have the force of asserting and denying, are not descriptive. Suppose that someone says, "It is true that the sun will rise tomorrow" all it means is that the sun will rise tomorrow: he is not regaling us with an extra-description of the trueness of what he says. But supposing that he were to say instead, "It is true *now* that the sun will rise tomorrow," this would boil down to something like "The sun will rise tomorrow now"; which is nonsense. To ask, as the puzzle-poser does, "Is it true or false *now* that such-and-such will happen in the future?" is not the sort of question to which an answer can be given: which *is* the answer.

This sheds light on what has, rather solemnly, been termed the "timelessness of truth." It lies in this that the clause "it is true that—" does not allow of inserting a date. To say of a proposition like "Diamond is pure carbon" that it is true on Christmas Eve would be just as poor a joke as to say that it is true in Paris and not in Timbuctoo. (This does not mean that we cannot say in certain circumstances, "Yes, it was true in those days" as this can clearly be paraphrased without using the word "true.")

Now it begins to look a bit less paradoxical to say that when a philosopher wants to dispose of a question the one thing he must not do is: to give an answer. A philosophic question is not solved: it *dis*solves. And in what does the "dissolving" consist? In making the meaning of the words used in putting the question so clear to ourselves that we are released from the spell it casts on us. Confusion was removed by calling to mind the use of language or, so far as the use *can* be distilled into rules, the rules: it therefore *was* a confusion about the use of language, or a confusion about rules. It is here that philosophy and grammar meet. . . .

But isn't the result of this that philosophy itself "dissolves"? Philosophy eliminates those questions which *can* be eliminated by such a treatment. Not all of them, though: the metaphysician's craving that a ray of light may fall on the mystery of the existence of this world, or on the incomprehensible fact that it is comprehensible, or on the "meaning of life"—even if such questions *could* be shown to lack a clear meaning or to be devoid of meaning altogether, they are *not silenced*. It does nothing to lessen the dismay they rouse in us. There is something cheap in "debunking" them. The heart's unrest is not to be stilled by logic. Yet philosophy is not dissolved. It derives its weight, its grandeur, from the significance of the questions it destroys. It overthrows idols, and it is the importance of these idols which gives philosophy its importance.

Now it can perhaps be seen why the search for answers fitting the moulds of the questions fails, is *bound* to fail. They are not real questions asking for infomation but "muddles felt as problems" (Wittgenstein) which wither away when the ground is cleared. If philosophy advances, it is not by adding new propositions to its list, but rather by transforming the whole intellectual scene and, as a consequence of this, by reducing the number of questions which befog and bedevil us. Philosophy so construed is one of the great liberating forces. Its task is, in the words of Frege, "to free the spirit from the tyranny of words by exposing the delusions which arise, almost inevitably, through the use of a word language."

III

What, only criticism and no meat? The philosopher a fog dispeller? If that were all he was capable of I would be sorry for him and leave him to his devices. Fortunately, this is not so. For one thing, a philosophic question, if pursued far enough, may lead to something positive—for instance, to a more profound understanding of language. Take the sceptical doubts as to material objects, other minds, etc. The first reaction is perhaps to say: these doubts are idle. Ordinarily, when I doubt whether I shall finish this article, after a time my doubt comes to an end. I cannot go on doubting for ever. It's the destiny of doubt to die. But the doubts raised by the sceptic never die. Are they doubts? Are they pseudo-questions? They appear so only when judged by the twin standards of common sense and common speech. The real trouble lies deeper: it arises from the sceptic casting doubt on the very facts which underlie the use of language, those permanent features of experience which make concept formation possible, which in fact are precipitated in the use of our most common words. Suppose that you see an object in front of you quite clearly, say, a pipe, and when you are going to pick it up it melts into thin air, then you may feel, "Lord, I'm going mad" or something of the sort (unless the whole situation is such that you have reason to suspect that it was some clever trick). But what, the sceptic may press now, if such experiences were quite frequent? Would you be prepared to *dis*solve the connection between different sense experiences which form the hard core of our idea of a solid object, to *un*do what language has done—to part with the category of thing-hood? And would you then be living in a phenomenalist's paradise with color patches and the other paraphernalia of the sense-datum theory, in a disobjected desubstantialized world? To say in such circumstances, "Look, it's just tabling now" would be a joke (for even in the weakened verb forms "tabling," "chairing" an element of the thing-category lingers on). That is why the sceptic struggles to express himself in a language which is not fit for this purpose. He expresses himself misleadingly when he says that he doubts such-and-such *facts:* his doubts cut so deep that they affect the fabric of language itself. For what he doubts is already embodied in the very forms of speech, e.g. in what is condensed in the use of thing-words. The moment he tries to penetrate those deep-sunken layers, he undermines the language in which he ventilates his qualms—with the result that he seems to be talking nonsense. He is not. But in order to make his doubts fully expressible, language would first have to go into the melting-pot. (We can get a glimmering of what is needed from modern science where all the long-established categories—thinghood, causality, position —had to be revolutionized. This required nothing less than the construction of some new language, not the expression of new facts with the old one.)

If we look at the matter in this way the attitude of the sceptic is seen in a new light. He considers possibilities which lie far outside the domain of our current experience. If his doubts are taken seriously, they turn into observations which cast a new and searching light on the subsoil of language, showing what possibilities are open to our thought (though not to ordinary language), and what paths might have been pursued if the texture of our experience were different from what it is. These problems are not spurious: they make us aware of the vast background in which any current experiences are embedded, and to which language has adapted itself; thus they bring out the unmeasured sum of experience stored up in the use of our words and syntactical forms.

For another thing, a question may decide to go in for another career than dissolving: it may pass into science. . . . A whole chapter might be written on the fate of questions, their curious adventures and transformations—how they change into others and in the process remain, and yet do not remain, the same. The original question may split and multiply almost like a character in a dream play. . . . The question is the first groping step of the mind in its journeyings that lead towards new horizons. The genius of the philosopher shows itself nowhere more strikingly than in the new kind of question he brings into the world. What distinguishes him and gives him his place is the passion of questioning. That his questions are at times not so clear is perhaps of not so much moment as one makes of it. There is nothing like clear thinking to protect one from making discoveries. It is all very well to talk of clarity, but when it becomes an obsession it is liable to nip the living thought in the bud. This, I am afraid, is one of the deplorable results of Logical Positivism, not foreseen by its founders, but only too striking in some of its followers. Look at these people, gripped by a clarity neurosis, haunted by fear, tongue-tied, asking themselves continually, "Oh dear, now does this make perfectly good sense?" Imagine the pioneers of science, Kepler, Newton, the discoverers of non-Euclidean geometry, of field physics, the unconscious, matter waves or heaven knows what, imagine them asking themselves this question at every step—this would have been the surest means of sapping any creative power. No great discoverer has acted in accordance with the motto, "Everything that can be said can be said clearly." And some of the greatest discoveries have even emerged from a sort of primordial fog. (Something to be said for the fog. For my part, I've always suspected that clarity is the last refuge of those who have nothing to say.)

The great mind is the great questioner. An example in point is Kant's problem "How is geometry possible?" The way to its solution was only opened up through the rise of the "axiomatic method." . . . Through the rise of this technique it became apparent that the word "geometry," as understood by Kant, covers, in fact, two totally different sciences, mathematical and physical geometry. It was the failure to distinguish between them that produced Kant's perplexity. "So far as the laws of mathematics refer to reality, they are not certain; and so far as they are certain, they do not refer to reality" (Einstein). Kant's credit lies in having *seen* that there is a problem, not in having solved it.

But here a new problem presents itself: How do we know what will satisfy a given question? More generally: How does the answer fit the question? Questions of the current sort ("What is the right time?") show already by their form what sort of answer to expect. They are, so to speak, cheques with a blank to be filled; yet not always so: Augustine's question, "How is it possible to measure time?" or Kant's question, "How is geometry possible?" do not trace out the form of the answer. There is no *obvious* link between question and answer, any more than there is in the case of asking "What is a point?" When Hilbert's idea—that the axioms of geometry jointly provide the "implicit definition" of the basic terms—was first propounded it came totally unexpected; no one had ever thought of that before; on the contrary, many people had an uneasy feeling as if this were a way of evading the issue rather than an answer, amongst them no less a man than Frege. He thought the problem still unsolved.

Now is there anything one can do to make a man like Frege see that the axiomatic method provides the correct answer? Can it, for example, be *proved* to him? The point to which attention must now be drawn, though it should really be obvious, is that such a proof cannot be given, and it cannot because he, the asker, has first to be turned round to see the matter differently. What is required is a change of the entire way of thinking. Indeed, anyone who is puzzled by this problem and yet refuses to accept Hilbert's solution only betrays that he has got stuck in the groove hollowed out by the form in which the question is put. "A point is—" he begins and then stops. What is to be done to help him to get out of the groove or, better still, to make him shift for himself when he feels "cramped" in it, is a *discussion*, not a proof.

Frege behaves not so very unlike a man mystified by the question, "What is time?" We may suggest converting the latter into the question how the word "time" is being used (which would bring him down to earth). But aren't we cheating him? We seem to be holding out the answer to *one* question, but not to that one which he was asking. He may suspect that we are trying to fob him off with the second best we have in store, his original question still remaining an enigma. Similarly Frege: he considered it a scandal that the questions "What is a point?" "What is a number?" were still unanswered.

In either of these cases, the aim of a discussion, in the absence of a proof, can only be to change the asker's attitude. We may, for instance, scrutinize similar, or partially similar, cases, point out that the form of the answer is not always that of the question; by going patiently over such cases, the vast background of analogies against which the question is seen will slowly change. The turning up of a wide field of language loosens the position of certain standards which are so ingrained that we do not see them for what they are; and if we do this in an effective manner, a mind like Frege's will be released from the obsession of seeking strainingly for an answer to fit the mould. Arguments are used in such a discussion, not as proofs though but rather as means to make him see things he had not noticed before: e.g., to dispel wrong analogies, to stress similarities with other cases and in this way to bring about something like a shift of perspective. However, there is no way of proving him wrong or bullying him into mental acceptance of the proposal: when all is said and done the decision is his.

But here more is at stake than loosening a cramped position—it is a question of escaping the domination of linguistic forms. How often are we merely following the channels carved out by numberless repetition of the same modes of expression—as when we say, unsuspectingly, "Time flows" and are, when confronted (say) with Augustine's paradox, suddenly shocked out of complacency. Existing language, by offering us only certain stereotyped moulds of expression, creates habits of thought which it is almost impossible to break. Such a mould is, e.g. the actor-action scheme of the Indo-European languages. How deep their influence is can perhaps be surmised from Descartes' conclusion from thinking to the presence of an agent, an ego, different from the thinking, that does the thinking— a conclusion so natural and convincing to us because it is supported by the whole weight of language. Frege's obsession with the question "What is a number?" is another case. As we can speak of *"the* number five," five, Frege argued, must be the proper name of an entity, a sort of Platonic crystal, indicated by means of the definite article. (A Chinese pupil of mine once informed me that Frege's question is unaskable in Chinese, "five" being used there only as a numeral in contexts like "five friends," "five boats," etc.). . . . A philosopher, instead of preaching the righteousness of ordinary speech, should learn to be on his guard against the pitfalls ever present in its forms. To use a picture: just as a good swimmer must be able to swim up-stream, so the philosopher should master the unspeakably difficult art of thinking up-speech, against the current of clichés. . . .

The philosopher contemplates things through the prism of language and, misled (say) by some analogy, suddenly sees things in a new strange light. We can cope with these problems only by digging down to the soil from which they spring. What we do is to light up the mental background from which the question has detached itself; in a clearer perception of some of the crucial concepts the question transforms itself into another one. Not that it has been answered in the current sense. Rather we have removed the factors that prompted the question by a more profound and penetrating analysis. The essence of this process is that it leads the questioner on to some new aspect—and leads him with his spontaneous consent. He agrees to be thus led and therefore ends by abandoning his search. We cannot constrain anyone who is unwilling to follow the new direction of a question; we can only extend the field of vision of the asker, loosen his prejudices, guide his gaze in a new direction: but all this can be achieved only with his consent.

By our critical analysis we try to counteract the influence of the language field, or (what comes to the same) we may help the questioner to gain a deeper insight into the nature of what he is seeking first of all—make him see the build of the concepts and the moulds in which he expresses the question. What matters is more like changing his outlook than proving to him some theorem; or more like increasing his insight. Insight cannot be lodged in a theorem, and this is the deeper reason why the deductive method is doomed to fail: insight cannot be demonstrated by proof.

What it comes to in the end is that the asker of the question, in the course of the discussion, has to make a number of *decisions*. And this makes the philosophical procedure so unlike a logical one. He compares, for instance, the case before him with analogous ones and has to *judge* how far these analogies hold. That is, it is for him to decide how far he is willing to accept these analogies: he has not, like a slave, to follow blindly in their track.

Science is rich in questions of this type. They are not scientific questions properly and yet they exercise scientists, they are philosophic questions and yet they do not exercise philosophers.

What I have wanted to say in this section and have not said, or only half-said:

(1) Philosophy is not only criticism of language: so construed, its aim is too narrow. It is criticizing, dissolving and stepping over *all* prejudices, loosening all rigid and constricting moulds of thought, no

matter whether they have their origin in language or somewhere else.

(2) What is essential in philosophy is the breaking through to a *deeper insight*—which is something positive—not merely the dissipation of fog and the exposure of spurious problems.

(3) Insight cannot be lodged in a theorem, and it can therefore not be demonstrated.

(4) Philosophic arguments are, none of them, logically *compelling:* they really screen what actually happens—the quiet and patient undermining of categories over the whole field of thought.

(5) Their purpose is to open our eyes, to bring us to see things in a new way—from a wider standpoint unobstructed by misunderstandings.

(6) The essential difference between philosophy and logic is that logic *constrains* us while philosophy leaves us free: in a philosophic discussion we are led, step by step, to change our angle of vision, e.g. to pass from one way of putting a question to another, and this with our spontaneous agreement—a thing profoundly different from deducing theorems from a given set of premises. Misquoting Cantor one might say: the essence of philosophy lies in its freedom.

IV

There is a notion that philosophy is an exercise of the intellect and that philosophic questions can be settled by argument, and conclusively if one only knew how to set about it. What seems to me queer, however, is that I cannot find any really good hard argument; and more than that, the example just discussed must make it doubtful whether any compelling argument *can* be found. Out of this plight I incline to come to a new and somewhat shocking conclusion: that the thing cannot be done. No philosopher has ever proved anything. The whole claim is spurious. What I have to say is simply this. Philosophic arguments are not deductive; therefore they are not rigorous; and therefore they don't prove anything. Yet they have force.

Before going into the matter, I want to show, quite summarily first, how unplausible the view is that rigorous arguments are applied in philosophy. A first alarming sign can perhaps already be seen in the notorious fact that the ablest minds disagree, that what is indisputable to the one seems to have no force in the eyes of the other. In a clear system of thought such differences are impossible. That they exist in philosophy is weighty evidence that the arguments have none of the logical rigor they have in mathematics and the exact sciences.

Next, arguments, in the way they are thought of, must contain inferences, and inferences must start somewhere. Now where is the philosopher to look for his premises? To science? Then he will "do" science, not

philosophy. To statements of everyday life? To particular ones? Then
he will never be able to advance a single step beyond them. To general
statements? If so, a number of questions raise their ugly heads. By what
right does he pass from "some" to "all"? ("To Generalize is to be an
Idiot," W. Blake.) Can he be sure that his premises are stated with such
clarity and precision that not a ghost of a doubt can creep in? Can he be
sure that they contain meat, are not analytic, vacuous, definitions in
disguise and the like? Can he be sure that they are true? (How *can* he?)
And even supposing, what is not the case, that all these requirements
could be met, there is still another task looming before him when it
comes to developing the consequences: can he be sure how to operate
with the terms? (How *can* he?) I am not letting out a secret when I say
that the ordinary rules of logic often break down in natural speech—
a fact usually hushed up by logic books. Indeed, the words of common
language are so elastic that anyone can stretch their sense to fit his own
whims; and with this their "logic" is queered. . . .

This brings me to another point. Ordinary language simply has not
got the "hardness," the logical hardness, to cut axioms in it. It needs
something like a metallic substance to carve a deductive system out of
it such as Euclid's. But common speech? If you begin to draw inferences
it soon begins to go "soft" and fluffs up somewhere. You may just as
well carve cameos on a cheese *soufflé*. (My point is: language is plastic,
yielding to the will to express, even at the price of some obscurity. Indeed, how could it ever express anything that does not conform to the
cliché? If logicians had their way, language would become as clear and
transparent as glass, but also as brittle as glass: and what would be the
good of making an axe of glass that breaks the moment you use it?)
But language is not hard. And that is why it is dangerous in philosophy
to hunt for premises instead of just going over the ground, standing back
and saying: look. . . .

I have not raised any of these questions wantonly; they force themselves on everyone who tries to arrive at a clear and unbiased view of
the matter. Should these difficulties not have their origin in the nature of
philosophy itself?

v

I proceed now to consider philosophic arguments, especially those
which are regarded as constituting a decisive advance, to see whether
they give us any reason for modifying the view advocated here. There
are only a few classical cases. One of them is Hume's celebrated argument to show that the relation of cause and effect is intrinsically different
from that of ground and consequence. Now in what does this "proof"
consist? He *reminds* us of what we have always known: that, while it is
self-contradictory to assert the ground and deny the consequence, no

such contradiction arises in assuming that a certain event, the "cause," may be followed not by its usual effect but by some other event. If it is asked "Is this a proof?" what is one to say? It certainly is not the sort of proof to be found in a deductive system. Much the same applies to Berkeley's argument when he tells us that, try as he might, he cannot call up in his mind an abstract idea of a triangle, of just a triangle with no particular shape, any more than he can conceive the idea of a man without qualities. Is this a proof? He points out the obvious. (Only it wants a genius to see it.)

To take my own argument against logical fatalism, it is not strict. The decisive step consists in following a certain analogy with other cases. It is analogical, not logical. . . . No philosophic argument ends with a Q.E.D. However forceful, it never forces. There is no bullying in philosophy, neither with the stick of logic nor with the stick of language.

VI

In throwing such strong doubts on the power of arguments as used by philosophers I may seem to deny them any value whatever. But such is not my intention. Even if they are lacking in logical rigor this certainly has not prevented an original thinker from using them successfully, or from bringing out something not seen before or not seen so clearly. So in the case I have discussed: something *is* seen in that argument, something *is* made clear, though perhaps not quite in the sense intended by the arguer. If so, something very important has been left out from the picture.

Perhaps our objections have been doing injustice to philosophic arguments. They were, quite mistakenly as I hope to have shown, supposed to be proofs and refutations in a strict sense. But what the philosopher does is something else. *He builds up a case.* First, he makes you see all the weaknesses, disadvantages, shortcomings of a position; he brings to light inconsistencies in it or points out how unnatural some of the ideas underlying the whole theory are by pushing them to their farthest consequences; and this he does with the strongest weapons in his arsenal, reduction to absurdity and infinite regress. On the other hand, he offers you a new way of looking at things not exposed to those objections. In other words, he submits to you, like a barrister, all the facts of his case, and you are in the position of the judge. You look at them carefully, go into the details, weigh the pros and cons and arrive at a verdict. But in arriving at a verdict you are not following a deductive highway, any more than a judge in the High Court does. Coming to a decision, though a rational process, is very unlike drawing conclusions from given premises, just as it is very unlike doing sums. A judge has to judge, we say, implying that he has to use discernment in contrast to applying, machine-like, a set of mechanical rules. There are no computing machines for doing the judge's work nor could there be any—a trivial yet significant fact. When the judge reaches a decision this may be, and in fact often is, a rational result, yet not one obtained by deduction; it does not simply follow from such-and-such: what is required is insight, judgment. Now in arriving at a verdict, you are like a judge in this that you are not carrying out a number of formal logical steps: you have to use discernment, e.g. to descry the pivotal point. Considerations such as these make us see what is already apparent in the use of "rational," that this term has a wider range of application than what can be established deductively. To say that an argument can be rational and yet not deductive is not a sort of contradiction as it would inevitably be in the opposite case, namely, of saying that a deductive argument need not be rational.

This alters the whole picture. The point to be emphasized is that a philosopher may see an important truth and yet be unable to demonstrate it by formal proof. But the fact that his arguments are not logical does nothing to detract from their rationality. . . .

. . . Indeed, examples aptly arranged are often more convincing and, above all, of a more lasting effect than an argument which is anyhow spidery. Not that the "proofs" proffered are valueless: a *reductio ad absurdum* always points to a knot in thought, and so does an infinite regress. But they *point* only. The real strength lies in the examples. All the proofs, in a good book on philosophy, could be dispensed with, without its losing a whit of its convincingness. To seek, in philosophy, for rigorous proofs is to seek for the shadow of one's voice.

In order to forestall misinterpretations which will otherwise certainly arise I have to concede one point: arguments on a small scale, containing a few logical steps only, may be rigorous. The substance of my remarks is that the conception of a whole philosophical view—from Heraclitus to Nietzsche or Bradley—is never a matter of logical steps. A *Weltanschauung* like any of these or even a new approach like that of Wittgenstein is never "arrived at," in particular it is not deduced, and once found it can neither be proved nor refuted by strictly logical reasoning; though arguments may play a part in making them acceptable. But some authors have disdained even that.

The one remaining question to be asked is this: if the philosopher's views cannot be derived from any premises how has he ever arrived at them? How can he get to a place to which no road is leading? This leads to a new and deeper problem.

VII

To ask, "What is your aim in philosophy?" and to reply, "To show the fly the way out of the fly-bottle" [1] is—well, honor where it is due, I

1. I.e., to dissolve a problem by showing the mistake that has led to it.—*Editor.*

suppress what I was going to say; except perhaps this. There is something deeply exciting about philosophy, a fact not intelligible on such a negative account. It is not a matter of "clarifying thoughts" nor of "the correct use of language" nor of any other of these damned things. What is it? Philosophy is many things and there is no formula to cover them all. But if I were asked to express in one single word what is it most essential feature I would unhesitatingly say: vision. At the heart of any philosophy worth the name is vision and it is from there it springs and takes its visible shape. When I say "vision" I mean it: I do not want to romanticize. What is characteristic of philosophy is the piercing of that dead crust of tradition and convention, the breaking of those fetters which bind us to inherited preconceptions, so as to attain a new and broader way of looking at things. It has always been felt that philosophy should reveal to us what is hidden. (I am not quite insensitive to the dangers of such a view.) Yet from Plato to Moore and Wittgenstein every great philosopher was led by a sense of vision: without it no one could have given a new direction to human thought or opened windows into the not-yet-seen. Though he may be a good technician, he will not leave his marks on the history of ideas. What is decisive is a new way of seeing and, what goes with it, the will to transform the whole intellectual scene. This is the real thing and everything else is subservient to it.

Suppose that a man revolts against accepted opinion, that he feels "cramped" in its categories; a time may come when he believes, rightly or wrongly, that he has freed himself of these notions; when he has that sense of sudden growth in looking back at the prejudices which held him captive; or a time when he believes, rightly or wrongly, that he has reached a vantage point from which things can be seen to be arranged in clear and orderly patterns while difficulties of long standing dissolve as though by magic. If he is of a philosophic cast of mind he will argue this out with himself and then, perhaps, try to impart what has dawned on him to others. The arguments he will offer, the attacks he will make, the suggestions he will advance are all devised for one end: to win other people over to his own way of looking at things, to change the whole climate of opinion. Though to an outsider he appears to advance all sorts of arguments, this is not the decisive point. What is decisive is that he has seen things from a new angle of vision. Compared to that everything else is secondary. Arguments come only afterwards to lend support to what he has seen. "Big words, not every philosopher, etc.:" but where should one get one's bearings if not from the masters? And besides, once tradition has given way there is always ample scope for specialists to reduce some "pockets of resistance." Unpalatable though it may be, behind the arguments so well-planned, so neat and logical, something else is at work, a will to transform the entire way of thinking. In arguing for his view, the philosopher will, almost against his will, have to undermine current categories and clichés of

thinking by exposing the fallacies which underly the established views
he is attacking; and not only this, he may go so far as to question the
canons of satisfactoriness themselves. In this sense, philosophy is the re-
testing of the standards. In every philosopher lives something of the reformer. That is the reason why any advance in science when it touches the
standards is felt to be of philosophic significance, from Galileo to Einstein
and Heisenberg. . . .

Is there any truth in what I am saying? I shall not argue. Instead, let
me remind you of some observations which will be familiar to you. It is
notorious that a philosophy is not made, it grows. You don't choose a
puzzle, you are shocked into it. Whoever has pondered some time over
some dark problem in philosophy will have noticed that the solution, when
it comes, comes with a suddenness. It is not through working very hard
towards it that it is found. What happens is rather that he suddenly sees
things in a new light—as if a veil had been lifted that screened his view, or
as if the scales had fallen from his eyes, leaving him surprised at his own
stupidity not to have seen what was there quite plain before him all the
time. It is less like finding out something and more like maturing, out-
growing preconceived notions. . . .

The view advocated here is that at the living center of every philosophy is a vision and that it should be judged accordingly. The really
important questions to be discussed in the history of philosophy are not
whether Leibniz or Kant were consistent in arguing as they did but rather
what lies behind the systems they have built. And here I want to end with
a few words on metaphysics.

To say that metaphysics is nonsense *is* nonsense. It fails to acknowledge
the enormous part played at least in the past by those systems. Why this is
so, why they should have such a hold over the human mind I shall not
undertake here to discuss. Metaphysicians, like artists, are the antennae
of their time: they have a flair for feeling which way the spirit is moving.
(There is a Rilke poem about it.) There is something visionary about great
metaphysicians as if they had the power to see beyond the horizons of
their time. Take, for instance, Descartes' work. That it has given rise to
endless metaphysical quibbles is certainly a thing to hold against it. Yet if
we attend to the spirit rather than to the words I am greatly inclined to
say that there is a certain grandeur in it, a prophetic aspect of the compre-
hensibility of nature, a bold anticipation of what has been achieved in
science at a much later date. The true successors of Descartes were those
who translated the spirit of this philosophy into deeds, not Spinoza or
Malebranche but Newton and the mathematical description of nature. To
go on with some hairsplitting as to what substance is and how it should
be defined was to miss the message. It was a colossal mistake. A philosophy is there to be lived out. What goes into the word dies, what goes into
the work lives.

Plato

"Philosophy" Alfred North Whitehead says, "is only a series of footnotes to Plato." Certainly the themes we have been considering are all present in Plato—the interplay of mysticism and logic, the collision of tough- and tender-minded temperaments, the sense that the human mind is affected by the body in which it dwells and by the language it uses. In the *Symposium* Plato draws these themes together to present his view of philosophy's origin and significance. Philosophy, he says, is the most complete fulfillment of Eros, of love.

In his attention to Eros, as in so many other ways, Plato is peculiarly our contemporary. But he is different from us in at least one important respect. His thinking is marked by an attitude which, because it is essentially the reverse of an attitude familiar to a Judeo-Christian civilization, can be a cause of misunderstanding for those who read him today. Plato does not put "desire" in one category and "the good" in another. He is a pagan Greek, and takes it for granted that "the good," whatever it may mean, is a name for some scheme of properly organized human desires. In this sense, he believes that "the good" is what men naturally seek, and that human reason is the instrument that helps them to find their way. We do not find in him the idea, which St. Augustine expressed, that human flesh is a contamination, and that we can tell what is evil simply by looking at what men's desires push them to. Plato recognizes the meanness and ignorance of human passions, and there is a puritanical side to him which provides an intimation, as Nietzsche observes, of later Christian ideas. He puts sensuality low on the scale of human virtue, and believes that the highest levels of wisdom and happiness are attained by transcending the body. But as the *Symposium* shows both by its explicit argument and by the dramatic setting and story that surround this argument, Plato thinks that men attain the highest level of wisdom and happiness by mounting the steps of a ladder whose base is planted firmly in physical human nature.

Indeed, when Plato speaks of "good" or "virtuous" men, as he repeatedly does in the *Symposium* and in other dialogues, it is useful to bear in mind what the Greeks meant by such terms. They didn't hold a Sunday-school view of morality. Frederick Woodbridge, who was a colleague of John Dewey's at Columbia for many years, used to remark that the history of morals was told in the history of the word "virtue": it began, with the Greeks, by meaning strength in a man, and it had come,

among the Victorians, to mean weakness in a woman. The model of the
good or virtuous man whom the Greeks had in mind was the *kalos kagathos*.
He was a gentleman, gregarious by nature and active in public life. He
loved words and argument. He was sensitive to beauty, and should, the
Greeks thought, be physically attractive himself. There was a touch of
magnificence in his bearing, and a love of color. He was magnanimous
with others, liberal though not ostentatious with money, and indifferent to
hardship if it was forced upon him. But he was *not* meek or humble. He
sought to be fair and just in his dealings, and prudent and temperate in
his conduct, but he admired talent, strength, and accomplishment, and he
saw no virtue in poverty and no higher wisdom in simpleness of mind.
Most conspicuously missing from this calendar of virtues is one quality
which we rank high today—pity for weakness.

That the Greeks should have believed that men naturally desire to
be good, given this conception of virtue, is not strange. To be "good" or
"virtuous" meant to them simply to carry out the idea of what it was to be
a man. Such a fulfillment of human potentialities, it seemed to them, was
inevitably dazzling, beautiful, intrinsically attractive. Hence the identification in Plato's philosophy, as the *Symposium* shows, of goodness and beauty.
And hence, too, the absence in Greek philosophy of long disquisitions on
the kind of question so familiar to us: What is conscience? Why should I
listen to it? Why be moral? Plato and Aristotle thought of immorality as a
lack of strength—of what we call character—or as a lack of taste and knowledge, not as defeat by satanic impulses. "All men are pregnant," says Diotima to Socrates in the story he tells in the *Symposium*, "both in body and
in soul; and when they are of the right age, our nature desires to beget. But
it cannot beget in an ugly thing, only in a beautiful thing." All men—at any
rate, all well-born, well-favored, well-educated men, with the leisure to develop themselves—are pregnant with virtue and beauty, Plato suggests. And
when this pregnancy is aborted, something of intrinsic value is lost.

This is the context in which Plato's views in the *Symposium* are to be
understood. His discussion takes it for granted that man is an animal with
a certain form or structure, that he grows and fulfills himself by moving in
a certain direction, and that if this process is not curtailed he reaches with
proper cultivation, a state, like that of a tree in flower, in which all his
powers are best displayed. To arrive at this state is his end or purpose or
"good." It is the Idea that gives his life its significance. And for the best
and happiest men, the culminating state is that of the philosopher.

There are two other questions to which it is probably useful to give
our attention before we turn to the *Symposium*. The first is whether Plato
is an accurate reporter of Socrates' ideas, or uses Socrates simply to state
his own views. More and more, as Plato went on in the writing of his
dialogues, he presented through Socrates ideas which Socrates almost
certainly did not have. In the *Symposium* Plato faithfully captures, in all

probability, Socrates' style, his belief that we must clarify our basic ideas in order to know what we are talking about, and his underlying moral vision. But Plato adds a new dimension to Socrates' concern to find the right definitions for the terms we use; he develops a theory—the theory of Ideas—much more philosophically ambitious than any that Socrates, from the other evidence we have, appears to have envisaged. In a sense, it might be said that Plato presents Socrates fulfilled and perfected—Socrates as he, Plato, thinks Socrates would (or should) have thought if he had followed the logic of his position to the end. There are even those who think that Plato in fact greatly distorts Socrates' ideas, and turns a spokesman for democratic liberty and equality into a defender of artisocratic inequality and authoritarian government. But while considerable disagreement exists about just how profoundly Plato changes Socrates' ideas, it is generally accepted that Plato does go beyond Socrates, though he takes his point of departure from genuine facts about his teacher. Socrates is for Plato not only the man Socrates, but the model of the philosopher and the philosophical life, and he plays a dramatic as well as intellectual role in the dialogues. He does more than advocate, he *illustrates*, Plato's ideal of wisdom in action.

The second question concerns the place occupied in the dialogue by homosexual love. It is often said that the Greeks did not have the same taboos with regard to homosexual love that we have. This view is probably an oversimplification. In the Platonic dialogues, including the *Symposium*, many statements about homosexuality have a defensive ring, which suggests that antagonism to homosexuality did exist in Athens. In the major dialogue of Plato's old age, the *Laws*, Plato calls homosexuality unnatural. Nevertheless, it is clear that homosexual love in Plato's Athens, though it may not have been approved, did not have to be furtive or concealed, particularly when it was practiced by the privileged classes.

In part, the role of homosexuality in Athens can be explained by the position of women in this society. The collaboration between men and women was conceived to be sexual and familial, but not to include the wider spectrum of activities—such as politics, literature, and philosophy—which draw free citizens together and make possible noble attachments between them. Once again, one must be careful not to overgeneralize. The poet Sappho obviously found room in Greece to exercise her talents. The attention that Euripides gives to women in his tragedies, and the importance assigned to Diotima, the wise woman of Mantineia, in the *Symposium* itself, also indicate that the Athenians were not entirely successful in keeping woman in her place.

In general, however, the social position of women in Greece did mean that the possibility of having heterosexual relationships combining physical and intellectual satisfactions was slender. Women spent their time mainly in the home. Free citizens spent their time mainly out of doors, in talk, government, and public activities. The chances for many-sided companionship with women were thus limited. In contrast, as the *Symposium* suggests, homosexual love could be regarded as potentially superior because it united physical pleasure with intellectual and emotional satisfaction and mutual respect. Nevertheless, what Plato says about love is relevant to heterosexual love in its modern, more democratic form. If there is a problem in applying his ideas, it is probably the one to which George Bernard Shaw alludes in *Man and Superman:* Will women, who have a biological function to perform—who must keep the race going—be as compliant as the young men in Plato's dialogues, and let their lovers neglect them for philosophy?

The *Symposium* suggests, rather dramatically, that even young men may not be altogether compliant. Santayana once remarked that the secret of Aristotle's philosophy was that in it every ideal was treated as having a natural basis and everything natural was conceived as having an ideal fulfillment. Plato's philosophy too is an exploration of the relationship of the natural and the ideal, the material and the intellectual. But in Plato the relationship is one of contrasts, tensions, ironies. And his dramatic method is as important as his arguments in bringing out this relationship. The *Symposium* shows philosophy against the background of human passions, egoism, and talk for talk's sake; it shows philosophy at its heights of vision and disinterestedness, but also in its struggle against the gravitational pull of lechery, vanity, and political ambition. The idea of goodness, and the ideal of pure beauty, are discussed by a group of men of whom some are dissolute, others cynical, others wispily romantic. The dialogue is a prime example of Plato's method of presenting philosophical issues as they arise in the everyday work and play of his fellow citizens, some young and full of hope, others displaced and disillusioned, but all forced by circumstances—or by Socrates—to ask themselves why they think as they do, what the purpose of their lives is, and how they can get some control over the deadly drift of their society toward disaster.

Thus, the company that takes part in the banquet which constitutes the setting of the *Symposium* includes a poet, a playwright, a doctor with a theory, hangers-on, professional partygoers. Homosexuality is in the air. The banqueters have hangovers, and are trying to recover from their revelries of the night before, so they decide on this occasion to talk rather than drink, and to talk about love, each man taking his turn. But they don't carry through with their resolution. After Socrates has made his climactic speech, Alcibiades, the representative of all that is most brilliant in traditional Greece—handsome, charming, a natural leader, a gifted general and political man—enters, drunk and scabrous; the participants take to drink and all ends in riotous disorder.

Yet the memory of the party remains. And the memory makes it more than just another party; Plato tells the story of that night as though it has been passed on by word of mouth—he represents it as the account of a man named Apollodoros, who in turn heard it from Aristodemos, who was there—and the effect is to suggest that the memory is enduring and impersonal, that it has an eternal life of its own. For what has occurred transcends the drunkenness. A spark has been struck that illuminates a truth, and makes the party something other than a transitory event.

That truth is expressed by Socrates in the selection presented here, and I shall not summarize what he says. Before he delivers his speech, however, other speeches have been given, which contribute both to the argument of the *Symposium* and to its mounting drama. In the dialogue the first to speak is Phaidros, a conventional man of letters who delivers a conventional discourse in praise of love. Stereotyped though it is, it introduces material on which the subsequent discussion builds. Phaidros says that love is the oldest of the gods: it has no parents, it is the beginning of things. And he stresses the fact that love changes the behavior of those it touches: the lover is led to behave honorably because he wishes to appear admirable to his beloved, and because he is moved to self-sacrifice. Thus, two points emerge from his discourse. Love has no antecedent purpose, being itself the begetter of life, of purpose. And love is a socializing emotion, the drive in the individual that explains not only his living in society but his social view of himself.

After Phaidros, the next speaker is Pausanias. Pausanias is the lover of Agathon, the host of the party; much of his speech is a thinly veiled defense of homosexual love. He discusses the varying attitudes toward homosexuality existing in different places, and reflects on the inconsistencies of Athenian opinion with regard to this subject. But Pausanias' discourse also serves a larger purpose in the dialogue. It prepares the way for what Socrates is to say, because its central theme, though Pausanias is transparently disingenuous in developing it, is that there is a distinction between noble and ignoble forms of love.

When Pausanias has finished, it is Aristophanes' turn. But the great comic poet, whose play *The Clouds* is a lampoon of Socrates, is taken with hiccups, and gives his turn to Eryximachos, the doctor. Eryximachos is the kind of person who spoils a party: he is a pedant, a man with an axe to grind, a semieducated fool. He takes off, trying to show his learning, and comes close to suffocating every man in the room with boredom. Having started with Pausanias' distinction between higher and lower forms of love, Eryximachos moves on to his own specialty, medicine, and then to music, astronomy, and reading the stars. Every one of these fields, he argues, shows the same distinction between higher and lower love. He is like a doctrinaire Marxist or Freudian; in demonstrating how true his idea is, he beats it to a pulp. Yet he, too, carries the dialogue along. Though he caricatures the idea of love, he nevertheless manages to suggest that love is more than a relation between human beings, that it is the sign and vehicle of a larger cosmic force.

Aristophanes' speech, with which the selection I have made begins, is the perfect sequel to Eryximachos' pontifications. The comic poet finally has his hiccups under control, though it isn't plain whether he has been cured by Dr. Eryximachos' prescription or by Dr. Eryximachos' bromidic discourse. In any case, he launches into an earthy, mischievous account of the origins of love. In his speech we come upon the idea of the lover as a person looking for his other half. The function of Aristophanes' contribution is threefold: it offers a change of pace; it lets the air out of the rhetoric about love; and it opens up the theme, on which Socrates builds, that love is a reaction to incompleteness, that it is an emotion whose fulfillment gives a man the sense of coming home again, of finding himself, of rediscovering what he once knew or possessed but has strangely forgotten or lost.

Agathon, the host of the party, then delivers his speech. He is flushed with victory, having just won the prize for a tragedy performed at a dramatic festival at the Theatre of Dionysos. Agathon returns to the lofty tone of the first speakers, but he hits a different note: love is the youngest of the gods, and belongs to the young; and love is the most beautiful of the gods, and is always a virtue, never a vice. That it should have a "higher" and a "lower" form is incompatible with its nature. Agathon's speech presents a young man's romantic image of love. But in conjunction with the other speeches that have been delivered, it poses once more the paradoxes about love that Socrates, who will speak next, must face. Eros seems to be at once the oldest and the youngest of natural forces, the original source of human actions and yet also the emotion that each man rediscovers for himself. And it seems, too, to be a source both of licentiousness and foolishness and of nobility. It shows man at his most mortal—driven by an imperious animal drive—and yet it somehow lifts him to forms of consciousness that serve no immediate animal purpose. Socrates' speech, which is at the center of the selection we shall read, unravels these paradoxes.

But Socrates' speech, though it is the high point, philosophically, of the dialogue, is not its dramatic climax. This is the entrance of Alcibiades, who pulls the members of the company down to earth again. He turns their attention from abstractions about love and philosophy to a quite pointed and personal discussion of his love for Socrates. The first part of his speech is reproduced in the selection that follows. Alcibiades goes on to give a detailed account of Socrates' character, in which he recalls Socrates' courage in battle, his refusal to be drawn into homosexual activities, and his unflinching personal rectitude at all times.

Alcibiades was the key figure whom Socrates was subsequently alleged by his accusers to have corrupted. The *Symposium* is one of the dialogues in which Plato tries to set the record straight, and defend his teacher. His vindication of Socrates is a vindication of philosophy as well. But it is an earthy, concrete vindication, an account of philosophy's practical import as much as its intellectual achievements. The time of the banquet is 416 B.C., when Socrates is fifty-three, some seventeen years before his execution. Apollodoros' recital of what happened takes place about fifteen years after Socrates' death. The translation is by W. H. D. Rouse.

Symposium

. . . "Well, Eryximachos," said Aristophanes. "I intend to speak in a different way from you and Pausanias. For it seems to me that mankind have wholly failed to perceive the power of Love; if they had, they would have built to him their greatest sanctuaries and altars, and they would have made their greatest sacrifice to him; but now nothing of the sort is done, although it most assuredly ought to be done. For he is the most man-loving of gods, being the helper of man, and the healer of those whose healing would be the greatest happiness to the human race. Therefore I will try to introduce you to his power, and you shall teach the others.

"First you must learn about the nature of man and the history of it. Formerly the natural state of man was not what it is now, but quite different. For at first there were three sexes, not two as at present, male and female, but also a third having both together; the name remains with us, but the thing is gone. There was then a male-female sex and a name to match, sharing both male and female, but now nothing is left but the title [hermaphrodite] used in reproach. Next, the shape of man was quite round, back and ribs passing about it in a circle; and he had four arms and an equal number of legs, and two faces on a round neck, exactly alike; there was one head with these two opposite faces, and four ears, and two privy members, and the rest as you might imagine from this. They walked upright as now, in whichever direction they liked; and when they wanted to run fast, they rolled over and over on the ends of the eight limbs they had in those days, as our tumblers tumble now with their legs straight out. And why there were three sexes, and shaped like this, was because the male was at first born of the sun, and the female of the earth, and the common sex had something of the moon, which combines both male and female; their shape was round and their going was round because they were like their parents. They had terrible strength and force, and great were their ambitions; they attacked the gods, and what Homer said of

Otos and Ephialtes is said of them, that they tried to climb into heaven intending to make war upon the gods.[1]

"So Zeus and the other gods held council what they should do, and they were perplexed; for they really could not kill the tribe with thunderbolts and make them vanish like the giants—since then their honours and the sacrifices of mankind would vanish too—nor could they allow them to go on in this wild way. After a deal of worry Zeus had a happy thought. 'Look here,' he said, 'I think I have found a scheme; we can let men still exist but we can stop them from their violence by making them weaker. I will tell you what I'll do now,' says he, 'I will slice each of them down through the middle! Two improvements at once! They will be weaker, and they will be more useful to us because there will be more of them. They shall walk upright on two legs. And if they choose to go on with their wild doings, and will not keep quiet, I'll do it again!' says he, 'I'll slice 'em again through the middle! And they shall hop about on one leg! Like those boys that hop on the greasy wineskins at the fair!' says he; and then he sliced men through the middle, as you slice your serviceberries through the middle for pickle, or as you slice hard-boiled eggs with a hair. While he sliced each, he told Apollo to turn the face and half the neck towards the cut, to make the man see his own cut and be more orderly, and then he told him to heal the rest up. So Apollo turned the face, and gathered up the skin over what is now called the belly, like purses which you pull shut with a string; he made one little mouth, and fastened it at the middle of the belly, what they call the navel. Most of the wrinkles he smoothed out, and shaped the breasts, using a tool like the shoemaker's when he smooths wrinkles out of his leather on the last; but he left a few, those about the navel and the belly, to remind them of what happened. So when the original body was cut through, each half wanted the other, and hugged it; they threw their arms round each other desiring to grow together in the embrace, and died of starvation and general idleness because they would not do anything apart from each other. When one of the halves died and the other was left, the half which was left hunted for another and embraced it, whether he found the half of a whole woman (which we call woman now), or half of a whole man; and so they perished. But Zeus pitied them and found another scheme; he moved their privy parts in front, for these also were outside before, and they had begotten and brought forth not with each other but with the ground, like the cicadas. So he moved these parts also in front and made the generation come between them, by the male in the female; that in this embrace, if a man met a woman, they might beget and the race might continue, and if a man met a man, they might be satisfied by their union and rest, and might turn to work and care about the general business of

1. Otos and Ephialtes were the two giants who piled Mt. Pelion on Mt. Ossa in order to climb to heaven.—*Editor.*

life. So you see how ancient is the mutual love implanted in mankind, bringing together the parts of the original body, and trying to make one out of two, and to heal the natural structure of man.

"Then each of us is the tally [2] of a man; he is sliced like a flatfish, and two made of one. So each one seeks his other tally. Then all men who are a cutting of the old common sex which was called manwoman are fond of women, and adulterers generally come of that sex, and all women who are mad for men, and adulteresses. The women who are a cutting of the ancient women do not care much about men, but are more attracted to women, and strumpetesses also come from this sex. But those which are a cutting of the male pursue the male, and while they are boys, being slices of the male, they are fond of men, and enjoy lying with men and embracing them, and these are the best of boys and lads because they are naturally bravest. Some call them shameless, but that is false; no shamelessness makes them do this, but boldness and courage and a manly force, which welcome what is like them. Here is a great proof: when they grow up, such as these alone are men in public affairs. And when they become men, they fancy boys, and naturally do not trouble about marriage and getting a family, but that law and custom compels them; they find it enough themselves to live unmarried together. Such a person is always inclined to be a boy-lover or a beloved, as he always welcomes what is akin. So when one of these meets his own proper half, whether boy-lover or anyone else, then they are wonderfully overwhelmed by affection and intimacy and love, and one may say never wish to be apart for a moment. These are the ones who remain together all their lives, although they could not say what they expect to get from each other; for no one could suppose that this is sensual union, as if this could make anyone delight in another's company so seriously as all that. Plainly the soul of each wants something else— what, it cannot say, but it divines and riddles what it wants. And as they lie together suppose Hephaistos [3] were to stand beside them with his tools, and ask, 'What do you want from each other, men?' And if they were at a loss, suppose he should ask again, 'Is it only that you desire to be together as close as possible, and not to be apart from each other night or day? For if that is what you desire, I am ready to melt you and weld you together, so that you two may be made one, and as one you may live together as long as you live, and when you die you may die still one instead of two, and be yonder in the house of Hades together. Think if this is your passion, and if it will satisfy you to get this.' If that were offered, we know that not a single one would object, or be found to wish anything else; he would simply believe he had heard that which he had so long desired, to be united

2. Tallies, like half of a broken coin or bone kept by friends or parties to an agreement, or the split laths of the old English exchequer, or the cut parchments of an indenture.—*Translator.*

3. The god of fire.—*Translator.*

and melted together with his beloved, and to become one from two. For the reason is that this was our ancient natural shape, when we were one whole; and so the desire for the whole and the pursuit of it is named Love.

"Formerly, as I say, we were one, but now because of doing wrong we have been dispersed by the god, as the Arcadians were dispersed by the Lacedaimonians. There is fear then, if we are not decent towards the gods, that we may be sliced in half again, and we may go about like so many relief carvings of persons shown in half-view on tombstones, sawn right through the nose, like tally-dice cut in half. For these reasons we must exhort all men in everything to be god-fearing men, that we may escape this fate and attain our desire, since Love is our leader and captain. But let no man oppose Love—and whoever is the gods' enemy does oppose him. For when we are friends with this god and reconciled to him, we shall find and enjoy our very own beloved, which now few are able to do. And don't let Eryximachos chip in and make fun of my speech, and say that I mean Pausanias and Agathon; I should not be surprised if they are really of this class, and both males by nature, but indeed I speak in general of all men and women, that the way to make our race happy is to make love perfect, and each to get his very own beloved and go back to our original nature. If this is the best thing possible, the best thing to our hand must of course be to come as near it as possible, and that is to get a beloved who suits our mind. Then if we would praise the god who is the cause of this, we should rightly praise Love, who in the present gives us our chief blessing by bringing us home to our own, and for the future offers the greatest hopes; that if we duly worship the god, he will restore us to our ancient nature and heal us and make us blessed and happy.

"There is my speech about Love, Eryximachos, very different from yours. Then, as I begged you, do not make fun of it, but let us hear what each of the others will say, or rather, each of the two others; for only Agathon and Socrates are left."

"I will do as you ask," said Eryximachos, "for I did very much enjoy hearing that speech. And if I did not know that both Socrates and Agathon were experts in love matters, I should be afraid they might be puzzled what to say when such a world of things has been said already. But as it is, I don't fear at all."

Then Socrates said, "You played your part well yourself, Eryximochos; but if you were where I am now, or rather perhaps where I shall be, when Agathon has made his speech, you would be very much afraid, and like me now, you wouldn't know where you were."

"You want to put a spell on me, Socrates," said Agathon, "and make me shy through thinking that the audience has great expectations of a fine speech from me!"

Socrates answered, "I should have a very bad memory, Agathon, if

I thought you would be shy now before a few people like us, since I saw your courage and spirit when you mounted the platform along with the actors, and faced all that huge audience, ready to display your compositions without the smallest sign of confusion."

"What!" said Agathon, "my dear Socrates, you don't really think I am so full of the theatre that I don't know a few men with minds are more formidable to a man of sense than many without minds!"

"I should make a mistake, my dear Agathon," Socrates said, "if I imagined anything vulgar about you; I am quite sure that if you were in company with any you thought intelligent, you would rate them above the many. However, perhaps we are not intelligent—for we were there too, and we were among the many—but if you should meet with others who are, you would be ashamed of doing before them anything which you might think ugly. What do you say to that?"

"Quite true," said he.

"And before the many, would you not be ashamed if you thought you were doing something ugly?"

Then Phaidros put in a word, and said, "My dear friend Agathon, if you answer Socrates, he will not care what becomes of our business here! He won't care anything about anything, so long as he can have someone to converse with, especially someone beautiful. For myself, I like hearing Socrates arguing, but it is my duty to care about the praise of Love, and to exact from each one of you his speech. So just pay up to the god, both of you, and then you may argue."

"Quite right, Phaidros," said Agathon, "I am ready to speak; Socrates will be there another time, and often, to talk to. . . ."

When Agathon had spoken (Aristodemos told me), all applauded; the young man was thought to have spoken becomingly for himself and for the god. Then Socrates looked at Eryximachos, and said, "Now then, son of Acumenos, do you think there was no reason to fear in the fears I feared?[4] Was I not a prophet when I said, as I did just now, that Agathon would make a wonderful speech, and leave me with nothing to say?"

"Yes, to the first," said Eryximachos, "you were a prophet there, certainly, about the wonderful speech; but nothing to say? I don't think so!"

"Bless you," said Socrates, "and how have I anything to say, I or anyone else, when I have to speak after that beautiful speech, with everything in it? The first part was wonderful enough, but the end! The beauty of those words and phrases! It was quite overwhelming for any listener. The fact is, when I considered that I shall not be able to get anywhere near it, and I have nothing fine to say at all—I was so ashamed that I all but took to my heels and ran, but I had nowhere to go. The speech reminded

4. He puts in his own little drop of parody.—*Translator.*

me of Gorgias,[5] and I really felt quite as in Homer's story; [6] I was afraid that Agathon at the end of his speech might be going to produce the Gorgon's head of Gorgias—the terror in speech-making—directed against *my* speech, and turn me into stone with dumbness. And I understood then that I was a fool when I told you I would take my turn in singing the honours of Love, and admitted I was terribly clever in love affairs, whereas it seems I really had no idea how a eulogy ought to be made. For I was stupid enough to think that we ought to speak the truth about each person eulogised, and to make this the foundation, and from these truths to choose the most beautiful things and arrange them in the most elegant way; and I was quite proud to think how well I should speak, because I believed that I knew the truth. However, apparently this was not the right way to praise anything, but we should dedicate all that is greatest and most beautiful to the work, whether things are so or not; if they were false it did not matter. For it seems the task laid down was not for each of us to praise Love, but to seem to praise him. For this reason then, I think, you rake up every story, and dedicate it to Love, and say he is so-and-so and the cause of such-and-such, that he may seem to be most beautiful and best, of course to those who don't know—not to those who do, I suppose—and the laudation is excellent and imposing. But indeed I did not know how an encomium was made, and it was without this knowledge that I agreed to take my part in praising. Therefore the tongue promised, but not the mind, so good-bye to that. For I take it back now; I make no eulogy in this fashion: I could not do it. However, the truth, if you like: I have no objection to telling the truth, in my own fashion, not in rivalry with your speeches, or I should deserve to be laughed at. Then see whether you want a speech of that sort, Phaidros. Will you listen to the truth being told about Love, in any words and arrangement of phrases, such as we may hit on as we go?"

Phaidros and the others (continued Aristodemos) told him to go on just as he thought best. "Then, Phaidros," he said. "let me ask Agathon a few little things, that I may get his agreement before I speak."

"Oh, I don't mind," said Phaidros, "ask away." After that Socrates began something like this:

"Indeed, my dear Agathon, I thought you were quite right in the beginning of your speech, when you said that you must first show what Love was like, and afterwards come to his works. That beginning I admire very much. Now then, about Love: you described what he is magnificently well, and so on; but tell me this too—is Love such as to be a love of something, or of nothing? I don't mean to ask if he is a love of mother or

5. Gorgias, the celebrated Sophist, adopted an artificial, affected style. See Plato's *Meno.*—*Translator.*

6. *Odyssey* xi. 634. Odysseus, at the end of his visit to the Kingdom of the Dead, grew pale with fear that Persephone might out of Hades send upon him a Gorgonhead, and turn him into stone.—*Translator.*

father; for that would be a ridiculous question, whether Love is love for mother or father; I mean it in the sense that one might apply to 'father' for instance; is the father a father of something or not? You would say, I suppose, if you wanted to answer right, that the father is father of son or daughter. Is that correct?"

"Certainly," said Agathon.

"And the same with the mother?"

This was agreed.

"Another, please," said Socrates, "answer me one or two more, that you may better understand what I want. What if I were to ask: 'A brother now, in himself, is he brother of something?' "

He said yes.

"Of a brother or sister?"

He agreed.

"Then tell me," he said, "about Love. Is Love love of nothing or of something?"

"Certainly he is love of something."

"Now then," said Socrates, "keep this in your memory, what the object of Love is; [7] and say whether love desires the object of his love."

"Certainly," said Agathon.

"Is it when he *has* what he desires and loves that he desires and loves it, or when he has not?"

"Most likely, when he has not," said he.

"Just consider," said Socrates, "put 'necessary' for 'likely'; isn't it necessary that the desiring desires what it lacks, or else does not desire if it does not lack? I think positively myself, Agathon, that it is absolutely necessary; what do you think?"

"I think the same," said he.

"Good. Then would one being big want to be big, or being strong want to be strong?"

"Impossible, according to what we have agreed."

"For I suppose he would not be lacking in whichever of these he is?"

"True."

"For if being strong he wanted to be strong," said Socrates, "and being swift he wanted to be swift, and being healthy he wanted to be healthy— you might go on forever like this, and you might think that those who were so-and-so and had such-and-such did also desire what they had; but to avoid our being deceived I say this—if you understand me, Agathon, it is obvious that these *must* have at this present time all they have, whether they wish to or not—and can anyone desire that? And when one says, 'I am healthy and want to be healthy,' 'I am rich and want to be rich,' 'I desire what I have,' we should answer, 'You, my good man, being possessed of riches and health and strength, wish to go on being possessed of them

7. Agathon had just said it was beauty.—*Translator.*

in the future, since at present you have them whether you want it or not; and when you say, "I desire what I have," consider—you mean only that you want to have in the future what you have now.' Wouldn't he agree?"

Agathon said yes.

Then Socrates went on, "Therefore this love for these blessings to be preserved for him into the future, and to be always present for him—this is really loving that which is not yet available for him or possessed by him?"

"Certainly," he said.

"Then he, and every other who desires, desires what is not in his possession and not there, what he has not, and what he is not himself and what he lacks? Those are the sorts of things of which there is desire and love?"

"Certainly," he said.

"Come now," said Socrates, "let us run over again what has been agreed. Love is, first of all, of something; next, of those things which one lacks?"

"Yes," he said.

"This being granted, then, remember what things you said in your speech were the objects of Love. I will remind you, if you wish. I think you said something like this; the gods arranged their business through love of beautiful things, for there could not be a love for ugly things. Didn't you say something like that?"

"Yes, I did," said Agathon.

"And quite reasonably too, my friend," said Socrates; "and if this is so, would not Love be love of beauty, not of ugliness?"

He agreed.

"Well now, it has been agreed that he loves what he lacks and has not?"

"Yes," he said.

"Then Love lacks and has not beauty."

"That must be," said he.

"Very well: do you say that what lacks beauty and in no wise has beauty is beautiful?"

"Certainly not."

"Then if that is so, do you still agree that Love is beautiful?"

Agathon answered, "I fear, Socrates, I knew nothing of what I said!"

"Oh no," said he, "it was a fine speech, Agathon! But one little thing more: don't you think good things are also beautiful?"

"I do."

"Then if Love lacks beautiful things, and good things are beautiful, he should lack the good things too."

"Socrates," he said, "I really could not contradict you: let it be as you say."

"Contradict the truth, you should say, beloved Agathon," he replied; "you can't do that, but to contradict Socrates is easy enough.

"And now you shall have peace from me; but there is a speech about Love which I heard once from Diotima of Mantineia,[8] who was wise in this matter and in many others; by making the Athenians perform sacrifices before the plague she even managed to put off the disease for ten years. And she it was who taught me about love affairs. This speech, then, which she made I will try to narrate to you now, beginning with what is agreed between me and Agathon; I will tell it by myself, as well as I can. You will see that I must describe first, as you did, Agathon, who Love is and what like, and then his works. I think it easiest to do it as the lady did in examining me. I said to her very much what Agathon just now did to me, that Love was a great god, and was a love of beautiful things; and she convinced me by saying the same as I did to Agathon, that he is neither beautiful, according to my argument, nor good. Then I said, 'What do you mean, Diotima? Is Love then ugly and bad?' And she said, 'Hush, for shame! Do you think that what is not beautiful must necessarily be ugly?' 'Yes, I do.' 'And what is not wise, ignorant? Do you not perceive that there is something between wisdom and ignorance?' 'What is that?' 'To have right opinon without being able to give a reason,' she said, 'is neither to understand (for how could an unreasoned thing be understanding?) nor is it ignorance (for how can ignorance hit the truth?). Right opinion is no doubt something between knowledge and ignorance.' 'Quite true,' I said, 'Then do not try to compel what is not beautiful to be ugly, or what is not good to be bad. So also with Love. He is not good and not beautiful, as you admit yourself, but do not imagine for that reason any the more that he must be ugly and bad, but something between these two,' said she. 'Well, anyway,' I said, 'he is admitted by all to be a great god.' 'All who don't know,' she said, 'or all who know too?' 'All without exception.' At this she said, with a laugh, 'And how could he be admitted to be a great god, Socrates, by those who say he is not a god at all?' 'Who are these?' said I. 'You for one,' said she, 'and I for another.' And I asked, 'How can that be?' She said, 'Easily. Tell me, don't you say that all the gods are happy and beautiful? Or would you dare to say that any one of them is not happy and beautiful?' 'Indeed I would not,' said I. 'Then don't you call happy those possessed of good and beautiful things?' 'Certainly.' 'Yet you admitted that Love, because of a lack of good and beautiful things, actually desired those things which he lacked.' 'Yes, I admitted that.' 'Then how could he be a god who has no share in beautiful and good things?' 'He could not be a god, as it seems.' 'Don't you see then,' said she, 'that you yourself deny Love to be a god?'

"Then what could Love be?" I asked. 'A mortal?' 'Not at all.' 'What then?' I asked. 'Just as before, between mortal and immortal.' 'What is he then, Diotima?' 'A great spirit, Socrates; for all the spiritual is between

8. A well-known Greek city in the Peloponnesus. The names perhaps suggest "the prophetess Fearthelord of Prophetville."—*Translator.*

divine and mortal.' 'What power has it?' said I. 'To interpret and to ferry across to the gods things given by men, and to men things from the gods, from men petitions and sacrifices, from the gods commands and requitals in return; and being in the middle it completes them and binds all together into a whole. Through this intermediary moves all the art of divination, and the art of priests, and all concerned with sacrifice and mysteries and incantations, and all sorcery and witchcraft. For God mingles not with man, but through this comes all the communion and conversation of gods with men and men with gods, both awake and asleep; and he who is expert in this is a spiritual man, but the expert in something other than this, such as common arts or crafts, is a vulgar man. These spirits are many and of all sorts and kinds, and one of them is Love.'

" 'Who was his father,' said I, 'and who was his mother?' She answered, 'That is rather a long story, but still I will tell you. When Aphrodite was born, the gods held a feast, among them Plenty, the son of Neverataloss. When they had dined, Poverty came in begging, as might be expected with all that good cheer, and hung about the doors. Plenty then got drunk on the nectar—for there was no wine yet—and went into Zeus's park all heavy and fell asleep. So Poverty because of her penury made a plan to have a child from Plenty, and lay by his side and conceived Love. This is why Love has become follower and servant of Aphrodite, having been begotten at her birthday party, and at the same time he is by nature a lover busy with beauty because Aphrodite is beautiful. Then since Love is the son of Plenty and Poverty he gets his fortunes from them. First, he is always poor; and far from being tender and beautiful, as most people think, he is hard and rough and unshod and homeless, lying always on the ground without bedding, sleeping by the doors and in the streets in the open air, having his mother's nature, always dwelling with want. But from his father again he has designs upon beautiful and good things, being brave and go-ahead and high-strung, a mighty hunter, always weaving devices, and a successful coveter of wisdom, a philosopher all his days, a great wizard and sorcerer and sophist. He was born neither mortal nor immortal; but on the same day, sometimes he is blooming and alive, when he has plenty, sometimes he is dying; then again he gets new life through his father's nature; but what he procures in plenty always trickles away, so that Love is not in want nor in wealth, and again he is between wisdom and ignorance. The truth is this: no god seeks after wisdom or desires to become wise—for wise he is already; nor does anyone else seek after wisdom, if he is wise already. And again, the ignorant do not seek after wisdom nor desire to become wise; for this is the worst of ignorance, that one who is neither beautiful and good nor intelligent should think himself good enough, so he does not desire it, because he does not think he is lacking in what he does not think he needs.'

" 'Then who are the philosophers, Diotima,' said I, 'if those who seek after wisdom are neither the wise nor the ignorant?' 'That's clear enough even to a child,' she answered; 'they are those between these two, as Love is. You see, wisdom is one of the most beautiful things, and Love is a love for the beautiful, so Love must necessarily be a philosopher, and, being a philosopher, he must be between wise and ignorant. His birth is the cause of this, for he comes of a wise and resourceful father but of a mother resourceless and not wise. Well then, dear Socrates, this is the nature of the spirit; but it was no wonder you thought Love what you did think. You thought, if I may infer it from what you say, that Love was the beloved, not the lover. That was why, I think, Love seemed to you wholly beautiful; for the thing loved is in fact beautiful and dainty and perfect and blessed, but the loving thing has a different shape, such as I have described.'

"Then I said 'Very well, madam, what you say is right; but Love being such as you describe, of what use is he to mankind?' 'I will try to teach you that next, Socrates,' she said. 'Love then is like that and born like that, and he is love of beautiful things, as you said he is. But suppose someone should ask us: "Socrates and Diotima, what is meant by love of beautiful things?"—I will put it more clearly: "He that loves beautiful things loves what?" ' Then I answered, 'To get them.' 'Still,' she said, 'that answer needs another question, like this: "What will he get who gets the beautiful things?" ' I said I could not manage at all to answer that question offhand. 'Well,' said she, 'suppose one should change "beautiful" to "good" and ask that? See here, Socrates, I will say: "What does he love who loves good things?" ' 'To get them,' said I. 'And what will he get who gets the good things?' 'That's easier,' said I; 'I can answer that he will be happy.' 'Then,' said she, 'by getting good things the happy are happy, and there is no need to ask further, why he who wishes to be happy does wish that, but the answer seems to be finished.' 'Quite true,' said I. 'But do you think this wish and this love is common to all mankind,' Diotima said, 'and do you think that all men always wish to have the good things, or what do you say?' 'That's it,' said I, 'it's common to all.' 'Why then, Socrates,' said she, 'do we not say that all men are lovers, if they do in fact all love the same things and always, instead of saying that some are lovers and some are not?' 'That surprises me too,' I said. 'Don't let it surprise you,' she said. 'For we have taken one kind of love, and given it the name of the whole, love; and there are other cases in which we misapply other names.' 'For example?' said I. 'Here is one,' she said. 'You know that poetry is many kinds of making; [9] for when anything passes from not-being to being, the cause is always making, or poetry, so that in all the arts the process is making, and all the craftsmen in these are makers, or poets.' 'Quite true,' I said. 'But yet,' said she, 'they are not all called poets; they have other names, and one bit of this making has been taken,

9. The root meaning of "poetry" in Greek is "making."—*Editor.*

that concerning music and verse, and this is called by the name of the whole. For this only is called poetry, and those who have this bit of making are called poets.' 'That is true,' I said. 'So with love, then; in its general sense it is all the desire for good things and for happiness—Love most mighty and all-ensnaring; but those who turn to him by any other road, whether by way of money-making, or of a taste for sports or philosophy, are not said to be in love and are not called lovers, but only those who go after one kind and are earnest about that have the name of the whole, love, and are said to love and to be lovers.' 'I think you are right there,' said I. 'And there is a story,' said she, 'that people in love are those who are seeking for their other half, but my story tells that love is not for a half, nor indeed the whole, unless that happens to be something good, my friend; since men are willing to cut off their own hands and feet, if their own seem to them to be nasty. For really, I think, no one is pleased with his own thing, except one who calls the good thing his own and his property, and the bad thing another's; since there is nothing else men love but the good. Don't you think so?' 'Yes,' I said. 'Then,' said she, 'we may say simply that men love the good?' 'Yes,' I said. 'Shall we add,' she asked, 'that they love to have the good?' 'Yes, add that,' I said. 'Not only to have it, but always to have it?' 'Add that too.' 'Then to sum up,' she said, 'it is the love of having the good for oneself always.' 'Most true, indeed,' I said.

"She went on, 'Now if love is the love of having this always, what is the way men pursue it, and in what actions would their intense earnestness be expressed so as to be called love? What is this process? Can you tell me?' 'No,' said I, 'or else, Diotima, why should I, in admiration of your wisdom, have come to you as your pupil to find out these very matters?' 'Well then, I will tell you,' she said. 'It is a breeding in the beautiful, both of body and soul.' 'It needs divination,' I said, 'to tell what on earth you mean, and I don't understand.' 'Well,' she said, 'I will tell you clearer. All men are pregnant, Socrates, both in body and in soul; and when they are of the right age, our nature desires to beget. But it cannot beget in an ugly thing, only in a beautiful thing. And this business is divine, and this is something immortal in a mortal creature, breeding and birth. These can not be in what is discordant. But the ugly is discordant with everything divine, and the beautiful is concordant. Beauty therefore is Portioner and Lady of Labour at birth. Therefore when the pregnant comes near to a beautiful thing it becomes gracious, and being delighted it is poured out and begets and procreates; when it comes near to an ugly thing, it becomes gloomy and grieved and rolls itself up and is repelled and shrinks back and does not procreate, but holds back the conception and is in a bad way. Hence in the pregnant thing swelling full aready, there is great agitation about the beautiful thing because he that has it gains relief from great agony. Finally, Socrates, love is not for the beautiful, as you think.' 'Why

not?' 'It is for begetting and birth in the beautiful.' 'Oh, indeed?' said I.
'Yes indeed,' said she. 'Then why for begetting?' 'Because begetting is, for
the mortal, something everlasting and immortal. But one must desire immortality along with the good, according to what has been agreed, if love
is love of having the good for oneself always. It is necessary then from this
argument that love is for immortality also.'

"All this she taught me at different times whenever she came to speak
about love affairs; and once she asked, 'What do you think, Socrates, to be
the cause of this love and desire? You perceive that all animals get into a
dreadful state when they desire to procreate, indeed birds and beasts alike;
all are sick and in a condition of love, about mating first, and then how to
find food for their young, and they are ready to fight hard for them, the
weakest against the strongest, and to die for them, and to suffer the agonies
of starvation themselves in order to feed them, ready to do anything. One
might perhaps think that man,' she said, 'would do all this from reasoning;
but what about beasts? What is the cause of their enamoured state? Can
you tell me?' And I said again that I did not know; and she said, 'Then
how do you ever expect to become expert in love affairs, if you do not
understand that?' 'Why, Diotima, this is just why I have come to you, as
I said; I knew I needed a teacher. Pray tell me the cause of this, and all
the other love lore.'

" 'Well then,' she said, 'if you believe love is by nature love of that which
we often agreed on, don't be surprised. For on the same principle as before,
here mortal nature seeks always as far as it can be to be immortal; and this
is the only way it can, by birth, because it leaves something young in place
of the old. Consider that for a while each single living creature is said to
live and to be the same; for example, a man is said to be the same from boy-
hood to old age; he has, however, by no means the same things in himself,
yet he is called the same: he continually becomes new, though he loses parts
of himself, hair and flesh and bones and blood and all the body. Indeed,
not only body, even in soul, manners, opinions, desires, pleasures, pains,
fears, none of these remains the same, but some perish and others are
born. And far stranger still, this happens to knowledge too; not only do
some kinds of knowledge perish in us, not only are other kinds born,
and not even in our knowledge are we ever the same, but the same happens
even in each single kind of knowledge. For what is called study and
practice means that knowledge is passing out; forgetting is knowledge
leaving us, and study puts in new knowledge instead of that which is
passing away, and preserves our knowledge so that it seems to be the
same. In this way all the mortal is preserved, not by being wholly the
same always, like the divine, but because what grows old and goes leaves
behind something new like its past self. By this device, Socrates,' said she,
'mortality partakes of immortality, both in body and in all other respects;
but it cannot otherwise. Then do not be surprised that everything naturally

honours its own offspring; immortality is what all this earnestness and love pursues.'

"I heard this with admiration; and I said, 'Really, Diotima most wise! Is that really and truly so?' She answered as the complete Sophists do,[10] and said, 'You may be sure of that, Socrates. Just think, if you please, of men's ambition. You would be surprised at its unreasonableness if you didn't bear in mind what I have told you; observe what a terrible state they are in with love of becoming renowned, "and to lay up their fame for evermore" and for this how ready they are to run all risks even more than for their children, and to spend money and endure hardship to any extent, and to die for it. Do you think Alcestis would have died for Admetos, or Achilles would have died over Patroclos, or your Codros [11] would have died for the royalty of his sons, if they had not thought that "immortal memory of Virtue" would be theirs, which we still keep! Far from it,' she said; 'for eternal virtue and glorious fame like that all men do everything, I think, and the better they are, the more they do so; for the immortal is what they love. So those who are pregnant in body,' she said, 'turn rather to women and are enamoured in this way, and thus, by begetting children, secure for themselves, so they think, immortality and memory and happiness, "Providing all things for the time to come;" but those who are pregnant in soul—for there are some,' she said, 'who conceive in soul still more than in body, what is proper for the soul to conceive and bear; and what is proper? wisdom and virtue in general—to this class belong all creative poets, and those artists and craftsmen who are said to be inventive. But much the greatest widsom,' she said, 'and the most beautiful, is that which is concerned with the ordering of cities and homes, which we call temperance and justice. So again a man with divinity in him, whose soul from his youth is pregnant with these things, desires when he grows up to beget and procreate; and thereupon, I think, he seeks and goes about to find the beautiful thing in which he can beget; for in the ugly he never will. Being pregnant, then, he welcomes bodies which are beautiful rather than ugly, and if he finds a soul beautiful and generous and well-bred, he gladly welcomes the two body and soul together, and for a human being like that he has plenty of talks about virtue, and what the good man ought to be and to practise, and he tries to educate him. For by attaching himself to a person of beauty, I think, and keeping company with him, he begets and procreates what he has long been pregnant with; present and absent he remembers him, and with him fosters what is begotten, so that as a result these people maintain a much closer communion together and a firmer friendship than parents of children, because they have shared between them children more beautiful and more immortal. And everyone would be content to have such children born to him rather

10. That is, by making a speech.—*Editor.*
11. A legendary King of Athens.—*Editor.*

than human children; he would look to Homer and Hesiod and the other
good poets, and wish to rival them, who leave such offspring behind them,
which give their parents the same immortal fame and memory as they
have themselves; or if you like,' she said, 'think what children Lycurgos [12]
left in Lacedaimon, the saviours of Lacedaimon and, one may say, of
all Hellas. Honour came to Solon also, in your country, by the begetting
of his laws; and to many others in many countries and times, both
Hellenes and barbarians, who performed many beautiful works and begat
all kinds of virtue; in their names many sanctuaries have been made because they had such children, but never a one has been so honoured because of human children.

" 'These are some of the mysteries of Love, Socrates, in which perhaps even you may become an initiate; but as for the higher revelations,
which initiation leads to if one approaches in the right way, I do not
know if you could ever become an adept. At least I will instruct you,' she
said, 'and no pains will be lacking; you try to follow if you can. It is necessary,' she said, 'that one who approaches in the right way should begin
this business young, and approach beautiful bodies. First, if his leader leads
aright, he should love one body and there beget beautiful speech; then
he should take notice that the beauty in one body is akin to the beauty in
another body, and if we must pursue beauty in essence, it is great folly not
to believe that the beauty in all such bodies is one and the same. When
he has learnt this, he must become the lover of all beautiful bodies, and
relax the intense passion for one, thinking lightly of it and believing it to
be a small thing. Next he must believe beauty in souls to be more precious
than beauty in the body; so that if anyone is decent in soul, even if it has
little bloom, it should be enough for him to love and care for, and to
beget and seek such talks as will make young people better; that he
may moreover be compelled to contemplate the beauty in our pursuits and
customs, and to see that all beauty is of one and the same kin, and that
so he may believe that bodily beauty is a small thing. Next, he must be led
from practice to knowledge, that he may see again the beauty in different
kinds of knowledge, and, directing his gaze from now on towards
beauty as a whole, he may no longer dwell upon one, like a servant,
content with the beauty of one boy or one human being or one pursuit,
and so be slavish and petty; but he should turn to the great ocean of
beauty, and in contemplation of it give birth to many beautiful and magnificent speeches and thoughts in the abundance of philosophy, until being
strengthened and grown therein he may catch sight of some one knowledge,
the one science of this beauty now to be described. Try to attend,' she
said, 'as carefully as you can.

" 'Whoever shall be guided so far towards the mysteries of love, by
contemplating beautiful things rightly in due order, is approaching the last

12. The Spartan lawgiver.—*Translator.*

grade. Suddenly he will behold a beauty marvellous in its nature, that very Beauty, Socrates, for the sake of which all the earlier hardships had been borne: in the first place, everlasting, and never being born nor perishing, neither increasing nor diminishing; secondly, not beautiful here and ugly there, not beautiful now and ugly then, not beautiful in one direction and ugly in another direction, not beautiful in one place and ugly in another place. Again, this beauty will not show itself to him like a face or hands or any bodily thing at all, nor as a discourse or a science, nor indeed as residing in anything, as in a living creature or in earth or heaven or anything else, but being by itself with itself always in simplicity; while all the beautiful things elsewhere partake of this beauty in such manner, that when *they* are born and perish *it* becomes neither less nor more and nothing at all happens to it; so that when anyone by right boy-loving goes up from these beautiful things to that beauty, and begins to catch sight of it, he would almost touch the perfect secret. For let me tell you, the right way to approach the things of love, or to be led there by another, is this: beginning from these beautiful things, to mount for that beauty's sake ever upwards, as by a flight of steps, from one to two, and from two to all beautiful bodies, and from beautiful bodies to beautiful pursuits and practices, and from practices to beautiful learnings, so that from learnings he may come at last to that perfect learning which is the learning solely of that beauty itself, and may know at last that which is the perfection of beauty. There in life and there alone, my dear Socrates,' said the inspired woman, 'is life worth living for man, while he contemplates Beauty itself. If ever you see this, it will seem to you to be far above gold and raiment and beautiful boys and men, whose beauty you are now entranced to see and you and many others are ready, so long as they see their darlings and remain ever with them, if it could be possible, not to eat nor drink but only to gaze at them and to be with them. What indeed,' she said, 'should we think, if it were given to one of us to see beauty undefiled, pure unmixed, not adulterated with human flesh and colours and much other mortal rubbish, and if he could behold beauty in perfect simplicity? Do you think it a mean life for a man,' she said, 'to be looking thither and contemplating that and abiding with it? Do you not reflect,' said she, 'that there only it will be possible for him, when he sees the beautiful with the mind, which alone can see it, to give birth not to likenesses of virtue, since he touches no likeness, but to realities, since he touches reality; and when he has given birth to real virtue and brought it up, will it not be granted him to be the friend of God, and immortal if any man ever is?'

"This then, Phaidros and gentlemen, is what Diotima said, and I am quite convinced, and, being convinced, I try to persuade other people also to believe that to attain this possession one could not easily find a better helper for human nature than Love. And so I say that every man ought to honour Love, and I honour love matters myself, and I practise them particularly and encourage others; and now and always I sing the praises of Love's power and courage, as much as I am able. Then let this be my speech of eulogy to Love, if you please, Phaidros, or call it anything else you like."

When Socrates had done speaking, there was applause from the rest, and Aristophanes started to say something about Socrates' allusion to his own speech, when suddenly there came a knocking on the courtyard door and a great din as of some party of revellers, and they heard a girl-piper's notes. Then Agathon said to the staff, "Boys, go and see about that. If it is one of our friends, ask him in; if not, say we are not drinking now, we are just going to bed." In a few minutes they heard the voice of Alcibiades in the yard, very drunk and shouting loud, asking where Agathon was, and take him to Agathon. So he was brought in to them by the piping-girl, who with some others of his company supported him; he came to a stand at the door crowned with a thick wreath of ivy and violets and wearing a great lot of ribands on his head, and said, "Good evening, you fellows, will you have a very drunken man to drink with you, or shall we only put a garland on Agathon, which we came for, and then go? For I tell you this," he said, "I could not get at him yesterday, but here I come with the ribands on my head, that I may take them off my head and just twine them about the head of the cleverest and most beautiful of men, if I may say so. Will you laugh at me because I'm drunk? I tell you, even if you laugh, that this is true and I know it. Look here, tell me straight, do I come in on those terms or not? Will you drink with me or not?"

Then they all cheered and told him to come in and take his place, and Agathon gave him a formal invitation. So he came in leaning on those people, pulling off the ribands at the same time to put them on Agathon, and as he held them in front of his eyes, he did not see Socrates, but sat down beside Agathon, between Socrates and him, for Socrates made room for him. He sat down and embraced Agathon and crowned him. Then Agathon said, "Take off Alcibiades' shoes, you boys, and let him make a third on our couch."

"All right," said Alcibiades, "but who is fellow-drinker number three here?" At the same time he turned round and saw Socrates; when he saw him, he jumped up and cried, "What the deuce is this? Socrates here? You lay there again in wait for me, as you are always turning up all of a sudden where I never thought to see you! And now what have you come for? And again, why did you lie there, not by Aristophanes or some other funny man or would-be funny man, but you managed to get beside the handsomest of the company!"

Then Socrates said, "Agathon, won't you defend me? I find that this person's love has become quite a serious thing. From the time when I fell in love with him, I am no longer allowed to look at or talk with a hand-some person, not even one, or this jealous and envious creature treats me outrageously, and abuses me, and hardly keeps his hands off me. Then don't let him try it on now, but do reconcile us, or if he uses force, defend me, for I'm fairly terrified at his madness and passion."

"No," said Alcibiades, "there's no reconciliation between you and me! My word, I'll punish you for this by and by; but now, Agathon," he said, "give me some of the ribands, and let me wreath this fellow's wonderful head—there!—so he can't quarrel with me and say I wreathed you and didn't wreath the man who beats all the world at talking, not only the other day like you, but always!" While he spoke he took some of the ribands and wreathed Socrates, and then reclined himself.

When he was settled, he said, "I say, men, I think you are sober. That won't do, you must drink! We agreed on that. Then I choose as prince of the pots, to see that you drink enough, myself. Let 'em bring it in, Agathon, the biggest goblet you have! No, better than that! You, boy there; bring that cooler," said he, for he saw it would hold more than half a gallon; first he filled that and drank it off himself, then told the boy to fill for Socrates, saying, "For Socrates, men, my trick is nothing; he drinks as much as anyone tells him, and never gets drunk one bit the more."

So the boy filled for Socrates, and he drank; then Eryximachos said, "Well, Alcibiades, what do we do? Are we just to say nothing over the cup, and to sing nothing, but only to drink like thirsty men?"

Alcibiades answered, "Good evening to you, Eryximachos, best son of a best father you, and he was very sober too!"

"Same to you," said Eryximachos, "but what are we to do?"

"Whatever you say," he replied, "for we have to obey you. 'One medicine man is worth a host of laymen.' Command what you will."

"Then listen," said Eryximachos. "Before you came in, we decided that each one in turn from left to right should recite the most excellent speech he could as a eulogy in honour of Love. All the rest of us, then, have made their speeches; but since you have made none, and since you have drunk your bumper, you are the proper one to speak; and when you have spoken, lay your commands on Socrates, what you like, and let him do the same with the next man to the right and so with the rest."

"Good," said Alcibiades, "but look here, Eryximachos, I don't think it's fair to tell a drunken man to risk a speech before sober men! And at the same time, bless you my dear! do you really believe anything of what Socrates has just said? Don't you know that the truth is exactly the opposite of what he stated? For if *I* praise anybody in his presence, god or man other than himself, this man will not keep his two hands off *me*."

"Won't you shut up?" said Socrates.

"On my honour, you need not make any objection," said Alcibiades. "I would not praise a single other person in your presence!"

"Very well, do this if you like," said Eryximachos; "praise Socrates."

"What's that?" said Alcibiades. "Must I, Eryximachos? Am I to have at the man and punish him before your faces?"

"Hullo," said Socrates, "what's your notion? To praise me and raise a laugh, or what will you do?"

"I'll tell the truth! Will you let me?"

"Oh yes, let you tell the truth, I even command you to do that."

"Then I'll do it at once!" said Alcibiades. "Look here, this is what I want you to do. If I say anything that is not true, stop me in the middle, and say that I am lying; for I won't tell any lies if I can help it. But if I speak higgledy-piggledy trying to remember, don't be surprised, for it is not easy to set out all your absurdities nicely in order, for one in my state.

"I am to speak in praise of Socrates, gentlemen, and I will just try to do it by means of similes. Oh yes, he will think perhaps it is only for a bit of fun, but my simile will be for truth, not for fun. I say then, that he is exactly like a Silenos, the little figures which you see sitting in the statuaries' shops; as the craftsmen make them, they hold Panspipes or pipes, and they can be opened down the middle and folded back, and then they show inside them images of the gods. And I say further, he is like Marsyas [13] the Satyr. Well anyway, Socrates, your face is like them, I don't suppose you will deny that yourself! In everything else, too, you are like them, listen what comes next. You are a bully! Aren't you? If you don't admit that I will find witnesses. Well, aren't you a piper? Yes, a more wonderful performer than that Marsyas! For he used to bewitch men through instruments by the power of his mouth, and so also now does anyone who pipes his tunes; for those Olympos [14] piped, I say were from Marsyas who taught him; then it is his tunes, whether a good artist plays them or a common piping-girl, which alone enravish us and make plain those who feel the need of the gods and their mysteries, because the tunes are divine. The only difference between you is, that *you* do the very same without instruments, by bare words! We, at least, when we hear someone else making other speeches, even quite a good orator, nobody cares a jot, I might say; but when one hears you, or your words recited by another, even a very poor speaker, let a woman hear, or a man hear, or a boy hear, we are overwhelmed and enravished. I, indeed, my friends, if you would not have thought me completely drunk, would have taken a solemn oath before you, and described to you how this man's words have made me feel and still make me feel now. When I hear them my heart goes leaping worse than frantic revellers', and tears run from my eyes at the words of this man, and I see crowds of others in the same state. When I heard Pericles, and other good orators, I thought them fine speakers, but I felt nothing like that, and no confusion

13. In Greek mythology a celebrated player on the pipe.—*Translator.*
14. A Phrygian musician.—*Translator.*

in my soul or regret for my slavish condition; but this Marsyas here has brought me very often into such a condition that I thought the life I lead was not worth living. And that, Socrates, you will not say is untrue! And even now at this moment, I know in my conscience that if I would open my ears I could never hold out, but I should be in the same state. For he compels me to admit that I am very remiss, in going on neglecting my own self but attending to Athenian public business. So I force myself, and stop my ears, and off I go running as from the Sirens, or else I should sit down on the spot beside him till I become an old man. I feel towards this one man something which no one would ever think could be in me—to be ashamed before anybody; but I *am* ashamed before him and before no one else. For I know in my conscience that I cannot contradict him and say it is not my duty to do what he tells me, yet when I leave him, public applause is too much for me. So I show my heels and run from him, and, whenever I see him, I am ashamed of what I confessed to him. Often enough I should be glad to see him no longer among mankind; but if that should happen, I am sure I should be sorrier still, so I don't know what to do with the fellow.

"The pipings of this satyr have put many others into the same state as me; but let me tell you something else to show how like he is to my simile, and how wonderful his power is. I assure you that no one of you knows this man; but I will show you, since I have begun. You see, of course, that Socrates has a loving eye for beauty, he's always interested in such people and quite smitten with them, and again he is ignorant of everything and knows nothing; that is his pose. Isn't that Silenosity? Very much so! He wraps that round him like a cloak, like the outside of the carved Silenos figure; but inside, when he is opened—what do you think he is full of, gentlemen pot-fellows? Temperance! Let me say that he cares not a straw if one is a beauty, he despises that as no one would ever believe; and the same if one is rich, or has one of those mob distinctions which people think so grand. He thinks all those possessions are worthless and we are nothing, yes, I tell you! Pretending ignorance and making fun of his fellows all his life—that's how he goes on. But when he's in earnest, and opened out—I don't know if anyone has seen the images inside; but I saw them once, and I thought them divine and golden and all-beautiful and wonderful, so that one must in short do whatever Socrates commands. . . ."

When Alcibiades had ended his speech, there was much laughter at his frankness, because he seemed to be still in love with Socrates. But Socrates said, "You're sober, I think, Alcibiades, or you would never have wrapped all that smart mantle round you in trying to hide why you have said all this, and put your point in a postscript at the end; for your real aim in all you said was to make me and Agathon quarrel: you think I ought to be your lover and love no one else, and Agathon should be your beloved and loved by no one else. But I see through you; your satyric and silenic drama has been shown up. Now, my dearest Agathon, don't let him gain anything by it; only take care that no one shall make you and me quarrel."

Then Agathon said, "Upon my word, Socrates, that's the truth, I am sure. I notice how he reclined between me and you in order to keep us apart. Then he shall gain nothing by it, and I will come past you and recline there."

"Yes do," said Socrates, "recline here below me."

"Oh Zeus!" cried Alcibiades, "how the creature treats me! He thinks he must have the best of me everywhere! Well, if nothing else, you plague, let Agathon recline between us."

"Impossible!" said Socrates. "For you have sung my praises, and it is my duty to praise the next man to the right. Then if Agathon reclines below you—I don't suppose he is going to praise me again, before I have praised him as I should? Then let him alone, you rascal, and don't grudge my praise to the lad; for I want very much to sing his glory."

"Hooray, hooray!" cried Agathon, "I can't stay here, Alcibiades. I must and will change my place, and then Socrates will praise me!"

"Here we are again," said Alcibiades, "the usual thing; where Socrates is, there is no one else can get a share of the beauties! And now how easily he has invented a plausible reason why this one should be beside him!"

Then Agathon got up to go and lie down beside Socrates, but suddenly a great crowd of revellers came to the doors; seeing them open as someone was going out, they marched straight in and found places among the diners, and the whole place was in an uproar. No order was kept any longer and they were forced to drink a great deal of wine. Eryximachos and Phaidros and some others went out and departed (so Aristodemos told me), and he fell asleep himself, and slept soundly for a long time, as the nights were long then, and he woke up towards day when the cocks were already crowing. When he awoke he saw the others were either asleep or had gone, but Agathon and Aristophanes and Socrates were the only ones still awake, and they were drinking out of a large bowl from left to right. Socrates was arguing with them; Aristodemos told me he could not remember much of what was said, for he was not listening from the beginning and he was rather drowsy, but he told me the upshot of it was that Socrates was compelling them to admit that the same man ought to understand how to compose both comedy and tragedy, and that he who has skill as a tragic poet has skill for a comic poet. While they were being forced to this, and not following very well, they began to nod, and first Aristophanes fell asleep, and while day was dawning, Agathon too. Socrates made them comfortable, then got up and went away, and Aristodemos himself followed as usual. Socrates went to the Lyceum and had a wash, and spent the day as he generally did, and after spending the day so, in the evening went home to bed.

Afterword

It is so common to dwell on the disagreements among philosophers—philosophers do it themselves—that it is easy to overlook the fact that they sometimes agree. The philosophers we have read in this concluding section differ in language, style, the interests they bring to philosophy, the very definition they give of the subject. James tells us that philosophy is the activity of a biological creature trying to fulfill its needs; Russell thinks it ought to be the effort of a biological creature to escape its biology; Royce stresses the entanglement of the philosopher in a particular time and limited culture; Waismann is preoccupied by the mysterious phenomenon of human language, which shapes our thinking and which we ourselves have consciously shaped only in small measure; and Plato says all of these things and more: he sees philosophy as penetrated through and through by Eros and yet transforming Eros, as a product of human mortality which is also a kind of triumph over mortality. And yet, though each of these philosophers has his own point to make, they are all making one point in common: philosophy has a kind of paradox at its heart.

For each is saying that philosophy grows out of a subsoil that lies below the ordinary ranges of conscious thought; and each is saying that the difficulty and the glory of philosophy lies in the fact that it attempts to dig back into the very subsoil that gives it its life, to explore it, turn it over, and expose it to the sun. In Royce's metaphor, the task of philosophy is to play "cat and mouse" with our hidden preconceptions, to search for and try to catch what is "instinctive, inarticulate, and in part unconscious" in our thinking. Philosophy is the effort to catch the mouse—to seize and appraise, and thus to control, the aboriginal stuff out of which human reasoning springs.

And so we have before us what might be said to be the final problem of philosophy, the problem that gives the subject both its irony and its savor. When we take an overview of philosophy, we cannot help noticing how curious an enterprise it is. It is the attempt to use the tools of thought to evaluate the tools of thought. It isn't simply the effort to catch the mouse; it is the mouse's effort to catch himself. Can such an enterprise succeed? What, indeed, does the word "success" mean in relation to it? What is the significance of philosophy if it succeeds in doing what it sets out to do? And what is its significance even if it fails? When we set the finer points of argument aside, we find that these are the questions to which the philosophers we have just read address themselves. And not at all surprisingly, though they give their answers, they suggest, by their tone as well as by what they explicitly say, that the questions themselves are probably more interesting, and more valuable, than any answer they can give.

James, at first blush, seems to take the simplest and most unequivocal approach. Philosophy, in his view, is inescapably an expression of individual temperament. A man needs a philosophy that suits him as he needs a house or job that suits him. But why, then, do professional philosophers torture themselves trying to dream up arguments designed to persuade their fellows? Why aren't they satisfied to speak frankly in the first person, and to claim nothing more for their point of view than that it is theirs? In part, it can't be doubted, James thinks their behavior slightly comical: he believes it would be better, very often, if philosophers simply admitted that they were describing things as they saw them, and that they needed to see them in this way to make their personal adjustment to the world. One of the great services that James performs for philosophy is to remind philosophers of the mouse of egoism that scampers through their pages, dressed in the costume of objective truth. He restores a sense of proportion to the subject, and makes it harder—though, unhappily, he doesn't make it impossible—for philosophers to be stuffed shirts.

Yet even James doesn't stop at this point. Despite the value he attaches to the expression of individual temperament, he does not say that a philosopher can be satisfied if he satisfies only himself. For something more than sheer arrogance, as he recognizes, lies behind the philosopher's attempt to persuade others of the truth of his views. Up to a point, such an endeavor is a biological necessity, a social necessity, and a requirement for the health of philosophy itself. The discipline may begin in disagreement and end in disagreement, but though this is its fate, its purpose—the vital impulse that keeps it alive—is to achieve agreement insofar as this is possible.

Even ordinary unphilosophical men seek the agreement of others. To hold views about the nature of the world that do not square with the views of anyone else in any respect is to court madness, and probably to be mad. Individuals, for all the differences among them, share some common traits, move in a common world, and have certain experiences that are more or less similar. Their outlooks, if they are related at all to the world, must reflect these shared circumstances and not only the idiosyncrasies of individual perspective. And these imperatives bear even more heavily on the professional philosopher. He may speak for himself, but his entire effort is to speak for himself fully, judiciously, candidly, lucidly. And so, if he succeeds, even if he only half succeeds, he moves on to a terrain where he speaks for and to others. The account he gives to himself of the nature of things is an account which they, hopefully, may also give, at least in part. Thus his philosophy enters the public domain; whether he wills it or not, it is a candidate for the attention and allegiance of others. So it is that, as James says, "the finally victorious way of looking at things will be the most completely *impressive* way to the normal run of minds."

I wish James were more precise in spelling out just what he means by "the most completely *impressive* way to the normal run of minds." If he means "satisfying" or "comfortable," these are strange synonyms for "true." Men are frequently impressed, satisfied, made comfortable, by untruths and even by downright lies. And what is "the normal run of minds"? If we mean by "normal" the statistically average, then normal minds normally converge around the fashions and prejudices of the moment. The history of intellectual achievement is a history of the triumph of the abnormal over the normal.

Moreover, though James gives a somewhat contrary impression, philosophers do not differ from "normal" men in being more tender-minded or tough-minded than the latter. They differ, the evidence suggests, in being more sharply pulled internally between these two tendencies. The conflict between tender-mindedness and tough-mindedness is present *within* Berkeley's philosophy, and within Plato's, Spinoza's, Santayana's, Nietzsche's, Russell's and indeed, James's own. To impress the normal run of mind may thus mean simply to impress the normal, relatively untroubled mind—to fuzz the edges of issues, and to make them seem easier to resolve than they are. From this point of view, the philosophy that wins a final victory will be the philosophy of the bland.

Quite obviously, James would be far from accepting such a conclusion. His imprecision has permitted such an interpretation, sometimes by naïve and overly eager supporters, more often by overly eager opponents. But in his own view, I think, he is simply making the point that "proof" in philosophy is an odd affair. It contains elements of logical demonstration, but it also contains another ingredient, which we can describe only by turning to words like "taste," "imagination," or "good sense." It isn't just in drawing correct conclusions from his premises that a philosopher shines. It is in his choice of premises, and in the feeling he displays for the significant issues as he carries in his discussion. And in philosophy one test of such taste, imagination, or good sense is a man's capacity, no matter how original his ideas may be, to stay in touch with the mainstream of human experience.

This is a simple point, perhaps, but it is often neglected, and it is a point of capital importance. It makes philosophy subject to tests we apply to literature, law, or politics as well as to the tests of logic. In the end, when all his arguments have been presented, a philosopher still has to show that he knows what's up, and that he can distinguish the important from the unimportant. He makes his ultimate appeal to his readers' sense of the fundamental contours of human experience. And though he may give his own personal tone to this appeal, he speaks as a public not a private man. In determining Spinoza's special place in the history of philosophy, his geometrically marshaled arguments are of relatively minor importance. What counts is that he speaks in a tone induplicably his own, and yet seems to describe men's collective condition. In James's phrase, he impresses the normal mind—the normal mind understood as the sane and informed mind, balanced and equable in the face of shifting opinion. When James speaks of "the finally victorious way of looking at things," I think he has this kind of victory in view. Indeed, this "normal" mind, balanced and equable, is in part the product of philosophy, in part the result of its educational work in human society.

With respect to their views concerning the central task of philosophy, then, there is perhaps not as much difference between James and Russell as might appear. James, like Russell, believes that philosophy should be an effort to correct bias, not to express it. Nevertheless, Russell is undoubtedly more forthright in advocacy of the position that philosophy should seek the truth in a neutral spirit. He goes much further than James in his suspicion of instinct and intuition as instruments appropriate to philosophy, and shows, I believe successfully, that they are too blunt to be used for philosophy's careful purposes, and too imperious and uncontrolled to be allowed to dictate philosophy's answers. Russell recognizes, of course, that instinct, intuition, and personal predilection play a part in philosophy. But he takes this as a fact which, like death, has to be lived with and struggled against; he does not regard it as a fact to be applauded.

And yet, if James overemphasizes one side of the story a bit, Russell somewhat overemphasizes the other. He speaks of philosophy as a "science," and when he uses the term he apparently means much more than that philosophy should seek to eliminate wishful thinking from its conclusions. If philosophy "is to be a genuine study," he writes, "it must have a province of its own, and aim at results which the other sciences can neither prove nor disprove." The idea seems unnecessarily restrictive, and indeed, it is not plain what it would really leave philosophy to do. What is this special philosophical province, at once "scientific" and yet not like any other science? If we put the problems of logic aside, and if we exclude valuative questions as rigorously as Russell seems to propose, what results does philosophy achieve that do not belong to the realm of the empirical sciences? The question can be turned around: How shall we classify Russell's own argument in "Mysticism and Logic"? That it is philosophy is undeniable. But is it "science"? Or is it a value-laden argument on behalf of objectivity?

Philosophy, as Russell says, should seek to emulate the spirit of the sciences—to proceed by disciplined argument, appraise evidence carefully, and accept the facts for what they are even when one would like them to be different. In order for it to do this, however, it need not seek to insulate itself as completely as Russell seems to suggest in a value-free territory. It is possible, though difficult, to try to introduce a scientific spirit into the examination, and even the advocacy, of values. In his best works Russell's own example shows that a philosopher can espouse values without losing his capacity to consider them as though they were hypotheses to be approached in a critical frame of mind.

Indeed, Russell's essay glides over a fundamental problem. His argument that philosophy should be scientific depends on an implicit distinction between factual assertions, which belong to the realm of science, and value judgments, which are presumably subjective. But how to make this distinction explicitly, and whether it can be defended at all, are among the most debated issues in philosophy. In science, for example, when we speak of "the facts," we mean states of affairs whose existence and character have been ascertained as the result of inquiries that have been conducted in accordance with certain established norms. But the norms that define dependable inquiry are notoriously subject to change from one age to another, and when we look back at those that have prevailed in earlier times, even in the honored territory of science, the influence of the surrounding society's mores and needs is evident. Thus, human interests and predispositions, no matter how hard we may try to erase them, seem to be indelibly engraved in that picture of things which we choose to call "the facts." Russell gives considerable attention to these issues in a number of his works. In "Mysticism and Logic," however, he merely assumes the answer to them. To this extent, his argument in the essay is incomplete.

Nevertheless, incomplete though it is, the essay makes an invaluable point. It reaffirms an ideal—that every effort should be made to keep facts and wishes apart. This is an ideal which is now under concerted attack, not least in philosophy. But if it falls, it is difficult to see what will differentiate scientific and scholarly work from other kinds of intellectual labor. And if philosophy is not to be committed to this ideal, how will it be different, except in its pretentiousness, from the grossest forms of propaganda, special pleading, and intellectual gamesmanship? No one in this century has spoken more compellingly to this point than Russell, even though, no more than anyone else, was he able to live up perfectly to the principles it implies.

James stresses one side of the issue—the emotional aspects of philosophy, its role as an expression of human interests. Russell stresses the other side—the scientific aims of philosophy, its effort to be disinterested. Josiah Royce is what is known as a "philosophical idealist," and he does what comes naturally to thinkers who belong to this school of thought: he tries to bring the two sides together in a higher synthesis. In Royce's view, philosophy's task is to present a synoptic view of the world, in which the findings of the sciences lie down harmoniously with the intuitions of poets, the insights of religion, and the experiences of ordinary men. Philosophy does indeed express human feelings. But Royce is convinced that when it expresses them most accurately and completely, when it presents them in all their connections, it is no longer simply an expression of feeling. It is an account of the universe of which human emotions are a part.

It is a mistake to think of Royce as an eclectic. He regularly expresses his scorn for the idea that men can find the truth in philosophy simply by collecting different points of view and making a *bouillabaisse* of them. In his view, each insight, whether religious or scientific, each expression of a man's experience, whether poetic or prosaic, must be analyzed, sifted, and criticized. Its internal inconsistencies and confusions have to be sought out and expelled. If this is done, Royce is persuaded, the particular insight or idea under examination will turn out to have much more to it than we may at first have supposed. It will be seen to involve presuppositions, to contain implications, that connect it logically to other insights or ideas, including many that may seem superficially to be opposed. Accordingly, if we could really complete this process of analysis, we would come upon the whole truth about the world, and we would see that the world is a single, logical, harmonious whole. Thus, Royce thinks of philosophy as a quest for the Absolute. It is the gradual discovery of the higher logic, the World Spirit, which moves through every moment of thought and consciousness.

This is not the place to consider the merits of Royce's philosophy in any detail. Suffice it to say that it raises some troublesome questions. If we hold the view that reality consists of one organic whole, with no independent parts, the conclusion that necessarily follows is that if any one thing in the world were different from what it is, everything else would have to be different. A canary in Rio de Janeiro is somehow connected to an earthquake in western Turkey. This view strains credulity. But Royce doesn't labor the case for his philosophy in the chapter from his work that we have read, and we need not labor the case against it. Indeed, as he himself reminds us, it is easy to spend one's time refuting a philosopher and in the process miss his point. If we treat Royce's views metaphorically, as Santayana treats religion, we find that he has something instructive to say about the origins and functions of philosophy.

Philosophy is man's mind become articulate: it is his preconceptions become conscious, his instincts and aspirations spelled out in words and examined with regard to their place in a larger scheme of history. And because philosophers give articulate voice to human thoughts and purposes, they are also the critics of these thoughts and purposes. For to speak clearly, to say what one means coherently, is not simply to express one's thoughts; it is to reform them, to correct them. Philosophers, therefore, cannot be said to be simply describers of the world; still less are they merely the passive spokesmen for the opinions that reign in it. When they perform their distinctive task well, they change men's perceptions of the world in describing it, and shape human interests in stating them. They are the consciousness of man, reflecting back on itself, and thereby becoming more conscious.

Thus philosophy, Royce suggests, contributes to human progress even when it doesn't succeed in answering the specific questions it proposes. For progress, if it means anything, means the emergence of mind, of spirit. And mind and spirit—increased self-consciousness—are precisely what do emerge, and what remain as the ultimate deposit, from the philosophical enterprise of self-scrutiny.

Waismann, a very different man from Royce, is nevertheless not too far, in his own views, from this conception of the significance of philosophy. To be sure, Royce's emphasis is on the continuities in history and philosophy. Waismann, in contrast, has science at the center of his attention and in particular, the rapidly changing science of the present century. In consequence, he stresses the discontinuities in philosophy. For progress in science—and progress in philosophy, if we can speak of it there—is not simply a matter of the steady, linear accumulation of knowledge. Such progress often involves sudden changes of direction, the emergence of radically different gestalts, or complex visions, that destroy old categories and put problems in a new light. Einstein's contribution to physics is an example. Yet, despite Waismann's emphasis on the discontinuities that mark intellectual progress, he finds in philosophy essentially the same values that Royce does.

Like Royce, he values philosophy for the contribution it makes to *consciousness*, to self-awareness on the part of the thinker about the nature of his thinking; and, again like Royce, it is the questions that philosophy poses, not its answers, that he regards as of the greatest importance. To ask what philosophy contributes to human knowledge, and to imagine that the only way to deal with this question is to produce a stock of accepted proofs accumulated by philosophy, is to misconceive the issue. "The great mind is the great questioner." Philosophy's arguments and putative proofs are of value, indeed, mainly because they are ways of getting men to entertain new questions and thus take the blinkers from their minds.

Indeed, the value of Waismann's essay lies more in the emphasis he places on the role of philosophers as questioners, I think, than in his denial that they ever come up with proofs. In fact, he doesn't quite say that. He says that they never, except in matters of detail, come up with proofs of the kind we find in mathematics, proofs that have demonstrative certainty. But he agrees that it is possible for a philosopher to pile up arguments that have a cumulative rationality, and that it is right for us to be persuaded by such arguments. Though this is not "proof" in the strictest, mathematical sense of the term, it is "proof" in one of its ordinary, everyday meanings.

In Waismann's discussion of the problem, however, the fact that strict proofs are infrequent in philosophy is treated as a consequence, in the main, of the fluid language in which philosophers, like ordinary men, must present their arguments. I think there are other reasons as well, and perhaps simpler ones. An argument can persuade people and still not be a sound proof; it may still fail to meet impersonal standards of validity. And conversely, a proof can be valid and still not persuade; for persuasion is a matter of satisfying one's audience. People often resist a proof because they find its conclusions unfamiliar, uncomfortable, or threatening to their cherished beliefs. Such resistance frequently occurs in philosophy.

It would be surprising if it didn't. For philosophy involves the analysis of fundamental standards and ideals; it holds up to the light concepts and commitments, intellectual and emotional, which are so deeply engrained in the pattern of our personal and social lives that it is painful even to have to become conscious of them, much less to abandon them. Can it be expected that such an enterprise will produce results to which men will yield without a struggle? That philosophers do not persuade one another easily doesn't necessarily indicate that they never produce arguments with probative force. It may only indicate that philosophers, like other men, don't always accede to probative force.

Indeed, the fact that philosophy deals with emotionally saturated issues points to another aspect of the question of proof in philosophy. Much philosophical discussion turns, explicitly or implicitly, on differences about the values by which men should live. Can such discussions ever arrive at conclusions on which all men ought to agree? In one sense, yes; in another, no. A philosopher can examine a scheme of values, indicating the presuppositions on which it rests, exploring its internal consistency or inconsistency, and studying the conditions under which it can be put into practice and the consequences that flow from doing so. Other philosophers may hold different values from his, and yet it is possible for them to agree, after looking over the evidence, that he has correctly analyzed the scheme of values under examination: it does indeed have the presuppositions, the logic, the conditions and consequences which he has delineated. In this sense, they can share a common opinion with him.

Moreover, they may even agree that he has taught them something about their own values. For it often happens that when people study value schemes carefully, they discover that only certain of these schemes can be intellectually defended. Most of the rest turn out to be internally inconsistent or self-defeating, or too narrow in focus to provide adequate guidance in the varied circumstances of human life, or too remote from the facts to be put into practice successfully. The philosophical study of values sharpens and concentrates the spectrum of human choice, and can therefore produce a measure of convergence of opinion with regard to the values by which men should live. When various schemes of values are examined it often turns out, indeed, that the schemes that can be defended overlap at many points.

Accordingly, the philosophical discussion of values may frequently lead to conclusions on which men, guided by the evidence, may reasonably agree. And yet, in the end, some room for choice of course remains. No purely logical or factual argument can compel a man to choose one scheme of values rather than another; some appeal to his preferences is also necessary. Accordingly, in discussions of ethics, politics, education, and the like, we can hope for some convergence of opinion, but we cannot expect unanimity. The search for universal agreement with regard to questions about how men should live is inappropriate. Thus, when Waismann says that philosophy involves "decisions," not "proofs," he is right, but he pays insufficient attention to one reason why this is so—namely, that philosophy is a critique of human values.

Indeed, if we look at the whole broad range of questions that philosophers have considered, there is some imbalance in the view that philosophy is simply a handmaiden to the sciences, or a solver of linguistic puzzles. It has also been related to religion, politics, morals, education, the law, the arts. Plato isn't concerned only with eternal issues, and when he wrestles with an intellectual paradox he isn't interested in that paradox for its own sake alone. He wants to give advice to his contemporaries about the reorganization of their collective life. Similarly, a philosopher today who analyzes concepts like "welfare," "liberty," and "equality," is not engaged—or should not be engaged—in bringing to light the meaning of ideas that dwell in some timeless realm. Though he can lean on past discussion, though he must lean on it to avoid unwittingly repeating its errors, he is also concerned with the new applications of these ideas that have developed, and the new problems that have arisen around them, as a result of changing social conditions. Philosophy, conceived from this point of view, is an effort to sort out and clarify the choices that a society must make; and its work is never done, nor does it have an agenda of problems that is fixed and eternal. For new circumstances require new choices and new ideas.

Nor is it always easy, in philosophy, to separate what is a judgment of values from what isn't. Waismann, for example, adopts a more sympathetic point of view toward the questions put forward by extreme skeptics than Peirce does, and this is due in considerable measure to the fact that he takes a different approach to the concept of a "question." If we are trying to settle the disagreement between Peirce and Waismann, which approach shall we use? That depends, in part, on what we think the purpose of an inquiry into skepticism is; and when we decide on a purpose we are deciding about values. Thus, it often turns out that even when philosophers present themselves as neutral problem solvers, the issues they debate are actually disguised value disagreements.

Yet the debates are not therefore useless, provided the value disagreements can be brought to the surface. For to explore the implications of a value disagreement is to learn something objective about it; and even if, at the end, we only conclude that more than one set of values is legitimate, this is a positive accomplishment. Among its by-products are a lessening of fanaticism, a heightened understanding of alternatives, a more judicious approach to one's own point of view. Philosophy can thus bring vision and insight in relation not only to questions of language and science, but to the more immediately controversial issues in which men may find themselves involved.

However, although Waismann's approach highlights only one of philosophy's several functions, he doesn't propose a narrow view of the subject. On the contrary, he helps us to see that the subject belongs to the humanities. It is the expression of human astonishment at the human situation; it offers the human mind a way to swim upstream against its most inveterate habits, and thus keep itself free and capable of wonder.

But for a fully adequate perspective on philosophy's significance, it is probably best to return, in the end, to the man with whom systematic philosophy begins. Plato has the capacity of making objections to his views seem almost beside the point. Suggest that he has misstated an issue and he will produce, often from the very dialogue under examination, a passage that presents your very point, probably more effectively than you have. Accuse him of having too contemplative a conception of philosophy and he confronts you with the whole body of his dialogues, bursting with talk and the impatience of young men, and almost smelling of the wine they drink. Plato can meet many questions head on. But what he does even better is to disarm his questioner, and make him seem myopic and small-minded. He doesn't refute his critics, he overwhelms them.

Underneath its glittering surface, the *Symposium* is an account of the natural history of philosophy and, indeed, of human civilization. Man is an animal in the grip of Eros, of love, and love seeks the secure possession of what it loves. It is what reveals man as occupying an in-between state: he is neither wholly animal nor fully divine, for he is able to envisage the decay and death of what he loves even as he possesses it, and yet he is unable to live as the immortal gods live.

Thus, human civilization. Men form families, create institutions like property, government, and law, educate their young, and celebrate their ideals in religion and games, all in the effort to preserve beyond the span of their lives the things for which they care. And thus philosophy. It emerges because men make choices in organizing their lives, and need principles that can help them to make these choices. The role of philosophic reason is to lead the passions, which in their uncorrected state are disorderly and vagrant, toward objects more capable of stabilizing and satisfying them.

But philosophy also does something more than help men to make their choices in the light of clearer principles. Families, cities, laws, though they give the passions a wider and more secure field of action, are nevertheless all vulnerable. They, too, change and die. And so the final step for philosophy is to detach itself from the material world, to become alienated from it by choice, and to dwell among Ideas whose perfection is such that place and time make no difference to them and mortality cannot touch them. Eros is not eliminated in the life of pure reason; but it is sublimated, transformed, and finally rendered triumphant.

Is all this hocus-pocus? What does Plato have in mind when he speaks of seeing absolute Ideas in nothing but their luminous essence? In the first place, he is referring to the objects on which purely conceptual thinking concentrates. We draw a series of round figures on paper and call them "circles." But none of them is in fact a circle, not perfectly so; each departs in some way, small or large, from the idea of a circle: its perimeter is not equidistant at all points from its center. Yet only in terms of the idea of a circle, which these drawings approximate, can we describe them intelligibly or perform various sorts of mental operations on them. Thus, we can speak consequentially about the deformed circles we see with our eyes only because we see, in our mind's eye, the idea of what a circle is.

This, in part, is what Plato has in mind when he puts forward his theory of Ideas. The realm of Ideas is the precondition for logical thought: what exists is literally unthinkable without it. Yet to speak of Plato's Ideas as purely logical or intellectual necessities is to fail to grasp the special status and value he assigns to them. They are primary not only in thought, but in reality. They are what is substantial; the world we see, compared to them, is insubstantial. The good man has carried through to its fulfillment the Idea of a man; the good society embodies the essential principle and purpose on which a social order thrives. And the man and the society that fall short are only half there, half-realized; looking at them and imagining that they are real is like looking at the world through a broken mirror and believing that what we see is the sum and substance of things.

What Plato has done, in effect, is to give us the world as it appears to an artist: the world is important for the ideal forms it suggests. When he speaks of the contemplation of Ideas, he has in mind the kind of experience we have in the presence of a work of art like a classic Greek statue. In the statue, the perfection that a physical human body merely intimates is caught and immobilized; and though we recognize the physical passion in us that makes us find this frozen figure beautiful, that passion is now experienced with the pain and longing removed. It is not destroyed, but it is transmuted; its fierceness and restlessness are gone. We look on an object free from the poisons that our strivings and seekings inject into the objects of the ordinary world. This finished thing, this distilled essence of our observations and desires, cannot disappoint us, for it cannot be changed, or grow worse, or be improved. It is what it is. And so it is preferable to the unfinished, ill-defined, precarious things that make up what we ordinarily call "the real world."

Yet it is difficult to think of our ordinary, precarious, poisoned world as unreal. We know what Nietzsche thought of Plato's ideas, and of the conception of philosophy that goes with them. He regarded them as the products of an act of self-delusion, excuses for escaping the grit and danger of struggle and effort. Is Plato not aware of the resistance that his conception of "reality" generates? He is perfectly aware of it. In many of his dialogues, and particularly in one called *Parmenides*, Plato himself raises severe objections to his theory of Ideas. If there is a perfect Idea of everything, the old philosopher, Parmenides, asks the young Socrates, must there not also be perfect Ideas of mud and dirt? What is good or beautiful about these? And if every individual thing differs from every other, must there not be, in the heavenly realm, an Idea of every individual thing? Will that realm, then, not be as crowded, disorderly, and unintelligible as the world of our ordinary experience? The young Socrates has no good answers to any of these questions.

The *Symposium* itself contains Plato's ironical comment on the theory of Ideas. Repeatedly, it puts Ideas into juxtaposition with the physical things that are supposed to be only their dim copies, and the physical things dominate the Ideas. Pausanias, praising love and talking piously about its higher and lower forms, is making a case all along for his own licentiousness. Eryximachos, speculating on the cosmic significance of love, turns the idea into a parody of itself, and suggests the comic element, the pretentiousness, in all such cosmic speculations, including those by Socrates that come shortly after. And when Socrates has finished praising the Idea of Beauty, Alcibiades, the most beautiful man in Athens, enters and takes over the party. Beauty in the flesh, vain, drunk, and lecherous, shouts down Beauty in the abstract.

Does Plato think that Ideas can be separated from the material conditions in which they take shape for us? Does he think that philosophers can transcend their mortal condition, and understand the world as gods might understand it? He does not quite answer these questions; he retains an ambiguous reserve toward them. He means his theory of Ideas to be taken seriously, but he recognizes that it expresses an aspiration, that it portrays a world in which philosophers would like to believe and in which they would wish to live, and not a world whose existence he has managed to demonstrate beyond reasonable doubt. Nor is he quite sure that philosophers should be permitted to live in this world, if it exists. In the *Republic* he says that in the Perfect State they will be ordered back to earth so that they can perform their duties as the teachers and rulers of men: they are citizens, and cannot be exempted from the obligation to be useful to their fellows.

Plato offers, in short, a two-sided view of philosophy. The subject is born out of the tensions between the practical and the ideal, between the limitations under which we must live and the perfections to which we aspire. And philosophy's function is precisely to give men this two-sided view of their affairs, to bring them into touch with the concerns of civilized humanity and yet to show them how not to be engulfed by these concerns. A man who has been influenced by philosophy will recognize that he is bound to his countrymen, and that his task is to bring clarity and honesty to the criticism of the principles by which they and he live. But he will realize, too, that these principles, even after they have been criticized and corrected, are not final and complete. Behind them are other principles, of which they are only the intimations. And so, though he will be attached to the visible society around him, he will also be detached from it. He will recognize that there is another country—the country constituted by principles in their perfection, by Truth, Beauty, and Goodness in their essence—to which he also owes his loyalty. A man can want to perform useful work in the world, and he can also want to retreat from it. Philosophy gives him a chance to do both.

Thus does Plato explain why philosophers have been nuisances to their fellows—dialecticians, critics, skeptics—and yet bearers of the images that move men. Socrates, for Plato, personifies philosophy. And it is Alcibiades, the most worldly of men, who in the *Symposium* sings his ironical praises: Socrates is a bully, Alcibiades says, a pied piper, a seducer who comes promising gifts and then remains not as the lover but as the critic in whose presence one is ashamed to be what one is: "Often enough I should be glad to see him no longer among mankind; but if that should happen, I am sure I should be sorrier still, so I don't know what to do with the fellow. . . . Pretending ignorance and making fun of his fellows all his life—that's how he goes on. But when he's in earnest, and opened out—I don't know if anyone has seen the images inside; but I saw them once, and I thought them divine and golden and all-beautiful and wonderful, so that one must in short do whatever Socrates commands."

The *Symposium* does more than offer a comment on the defeat of philosophy by the foolish facts of existence; it offers a comment as well on the kind of triumph that philosophy can win. Socrates, though he is blinded by a beauty that lies beyond the world, is a firm friend, a good citizen, a brave man. And he alone remains sober at the banquet and keeps his dignity. He isn't priggish; he is, in fact, the life of the party. But he is able to go about his business the next day with his powers not diminished but replenished. In its very detachment, philosophic reason seems to have a practical effect. The vision of what really counts, beyond the drinking and shouting, may not keep men from drinking and shouting. But it gives the one who has that vision a second home, and because he has that home he lives more easily with his fellows and with himself.